Penguin Books
The Sceptical Feminist

Janet Radcliffe Richards was born in Yorkshire in 1944, the eldest daughter of a schoolteacher and a Unitarian minister. She was educated at the Henrietta Barnett School, a girls' grammar school in north London, and afterwards took degrees in philosophy at the universities of Keele, Calgary and Oxford. Since 1979 she has been Lecturer in Philosophy at the Open University. Since the writing of this book her original interests in metaphysics and philosophy of science have extended to ethics and social philosophy, and in general to the application of philosophy to practical issues. Her main work at the moment is on wider problems of discrimination and disadvantaged groups, but she is also increasingly involved with problems of medical ethics; she is now a member of the ethics committee of the Royal College of General Practitioners, after several years on the ethics committee of the Royal College of Physicians. If she ever takes up guerilla warfare her first targets will be factory farmers and the designers of replacement windows.

The Sceptical Feminist

A PHILOSOPHICAL ENQUIRY

Janet Radcliffe Richards

PENGUIN BOOKS

For
Nancy Radcliffe Richards
and Dudley Richards

PENGUIN BOOKS

Published by the Penguin Group
Penguin Books Ltd, 27 Wrights Lane, London W8 5TZ, England
Penguin Books USA Inc., 375 Hudson Street, New York, New York 10014, USA
Penguin Books Australia Ltd, Ringwood, Victoria, Australia
Penguin Books Canada Ltd, 10 Alcorn Avenue, Toronto, Ontario, Canada M4V 3B2
Penguin Books (NZ) Ltd, 182–190 Wairau Road, Auckland 10, New Zealand

Penguin Books Ltd, Registered Offices: Harmondsworth, Middlesex, England

First published by Routledge and Kegan Paul 1980
Published in Pelican Books 1982
Reprinted in Penguin Books 1991
Reprinted with a new introduction and two new appendices 1994
10 9 8 7 6 5 4 3 2 1

Printed in England by Clays Ltd, St Ives plc
Set in 10/11½pt Linotronic Garamond

A considering man may very well question the truth of those very suppositions which chymists as well as peripateticks, without proving, take for granted; and upon which depends the validity of the inferences they draw from their experiments . . . which though a chymist perhaps will not, yet I do, look upon as the most important, as well as difficult, part of my task.

Robert Boyle
The Sceptical Chymist 1661

Contents

Acknowledgements

One of the many ways in which this book departs from much recent feminist tradition is that it cannot be said to derive from a group of women which was its inspiration and the origin of most of its ideas. I am afraid that it was men who instigated it, and the work has been very largely solitary. However, there are several people to whom I owe a great deal.

The principal of these is Ted Honderich, without whom the book would never have been thought of, started or finished; who read the first and last of the many drafts, prevented near disaster at a couple of points by drawing my attention to important parts of the philosophical literature, and was the cause of my sharpening several arguments.

I am also very grateful to Neil Sanders for endless support and encouragement throughout its writing.

Several friends have read and commented on various parts of the manuscript at various stages. Carol Lee has given particularly valuable help, and has also supplied me with very useful anecdotes and quotations. Many thanks are owed to her, as well as to Yvonne Reynolds and my sister, Judith Richards.

Various people have been very helpful in discussion, but most valuable of all have been the members of my 1978–9 Philosophy and Feminism class at the City University, London: Tany Paterson Alexander, Bobby Baker, Diana Cook, Isobel Cox, Betzy Dinesen, Kate Flannery, Bernadette Wrenn Hill and Kay Symons. The evenings spent with this group have been splendid. Apart from improving the book a good deal they have brought it away from the pages and into reality by showing what a group of women can be like; a thing which most people have as yet had no chance to see, and as unlike the popular caricatures of groups of housewives or groups of feminists as can be imagined. If these are the women of the future, the future cannot come too soon.

Introduction to the Second Edition

It is an uncomfortable business, this returning to the writings of one's youth (well, early middle age) with a view to their reissuing. There may be some authors whose habitual bedtime reading is their own books, but I suspect that most of us, having eventually had the manuscript wrenched away with forceps and not enough chloroform by a publisher whose patience has reached its limits, consign our personal copy of the finished product to some corner where it will gradually disappear under assorted clutter and render the probability of accidental encounter as remote as possible. So when, after fourteen years in which reprintings have gone ahead without any intrusion into the author's oblivion, the publisher suddenly reappears saying that it is time for a new edition, and making it clear that she has ways of making you cooperate, there is obviously a rather gruesome time ahead.

It was inevitable that the book would, by this time, be displaying (what estate agents would call) a wealth of period features. All kinds of things had changed since the late seventies, when it was being written. Feminism and feminist theory had moved on in an unflagging stream of new books, articles and journals, and new issues had come to the forefront of public debate while others had receded. The position of women and the public perception of feminism had also changed. Many once-controversial campaigns had now been won, and women had, like other disadvantaged groups, increasingly found themselves protected by ideas of affirmative action and the politically correct.

On the other hand, whether such changes really make a

book out of date, as opposed to just giving it the charm supposed to go with period features, depends not on whether new issues have arisen, but on whether the old ones have really retreated. And it seems to me that whatever changes there have been in the position of women and the arguments about it, nearly all the issues dealt with in this book are still around in one form or another.

It is important that the book was never meant as a description either of the situation of women, or of public opinion, or of feminism. Its purpose was to try to work out what, if anything, women had reason to complain about, not by an empirical study of what their situation actually was, but by trying to sort out the criteria for judging whether any situation gave grounds for complaint, and by assessing the arguments used by defenders and opponents of the status quo. This kind of enquiry is relatively independent of the details of current politics. Particular topics may rise and fall in feminist and public consciousness, but the fundamental problems are only a little younger than the hills. Some do appear here in forms that bear about them the distinct marks of their time: Chapter 3, for instance, was motivated by the idea of Women's Liberation, which now seems to have passed from sight, and Chapter 7 by the popular idea that feminists went around burning bras to prove they were not sex objects. But the underlying problems, of freedom and conditioning and of women's sexual pleasing of men, are as pressing as they ever were.

Much the same goes for the way in which the topics are discussed. The obvious way to set about the analysis of the issues was to take up ideas and arguments that were in the political air, particularly when they seemed mistaken in any way. Some of these are less frequently heard now, and feminist arguments, in particular, often have a quite different sound. The old feminist resistance to ethics and rationality discussed in Chapter 1, for instance, has now largely been superseded by claims about the need to appeal to new, feminist, standards of these things rather than to abandon them altogether. New arguments like these obviously need to be discussed in their own right (and something is said about this in the second of the new essays in the Appendix), but what matters most for the continuing relevance of this book is whether the old ones are still doing the rounds, and I think it is true to say that they all are. For one thing, a change of rhetoric need not always imply a change of substance; and if, for instance, instead of repudiating rationality anyone tries appealing to new standards of rationality according to which contradiction does not matter (see p. 401), the arguments presented here against irrationality apply exactly as before. But how often that happens can be left open. As long as all the discussions are understood as being about the merits of particular arguments whenever they do occur, and not as implying any claims about how often this is, I hope it will be found that they are all still relevant to the current debates.

Of course if the book were being written now it would be different in all sorts of ways. It would address different arguments, and include different topics. No contemporary book about feminism could possibly treat lesbianism in the passing way this one does, for instance, nor omit such issues as pornography, harassment, and the vast expansion of feminism into the academic disciplines. What matters most for now, however, are not the omissions (which will be remedied some other time), but the persistence of the original problems; and I think that, in spite of all the changes, most of them still remain. There is still deep-rooted injustice to women, whose extent is widely underestimated, and the feminist cause still suffers because the real nature and strength of its case is frequently misunderstood. As long as this remains true, I hope the book can still, anachronisms and all, serve much of its original purpose.

2

When the original editor did eventually manage to get the manuscript into his hands his publicist's eye was instantly riveted by its potential for controversy, and he hoped with glee that half the audience would say it was brilliant and the other half that it was the worst feminist book they had ever read. This, I need hardly say, was not my view of the matter; unmixed delight would have seemed a much better idea. But what happened was – let us say – closer to his ideal than mine. The book did meet with some approval, but it also ran into fierce opposition from a good many established feminists. And this should really not have been surprising. A book that starts by describing itself as a battle on two fronts is hardly inviting cries of joy in unison, and an author who announces direct disagreement with what large numbers of people are saying is not entitled to be astonished if they disagree back rather than instantly wilting under the power of the argument.

Still, although the book does contain a good deal of controversial material, with which many feminists, in particular, really do disagree, what does seem worth commenting on – because of some seriously puzzling questions it raises – it is the extent to which criticisms have been based on straightforward misunderstandings. I know it is always tiresome when authors complain that they have been misunderstood, and I have no intention of grinding through the details, but it would not be an exaggeration to say that *most* of the criticisms, particularly from the feminist direction, have been addressed to positions I do not hold. Some of them have been quite extreme: one well known feminist, for instance, challenged me in a public debate to justify my opposition to reverse discrimination, when Chapter 4 contains what seems to me a pretty strong defence of it. Others have been, to a greater or lesser degree, more understandable. But they have all, obviously, been disturbing, and naturally raise the question of what could have been done to avoid them: how much was my fault, how much the readers', and how much just the nature of things.

One thing that would probably have helped is a difference of style. I called the book an enquiry, as indeed it was (about which more in a moment); but on returning after all these years I can see that this is not what it looks like. It looks like the work of a brisk and confident outsider striding into the fray to take the existing protagonists by the scruff of the neck, and this is bound to be irritating (to say the least) to people who have been battling away for some time. It is not really judicious, if you have an eye to making friends and influencing people, to march on with an announcement of battle, even if on two fronts, and even if against ideas rather than people; nor is it a good idea to launch directly, in the first chapter, into a set of criticisms of one side. I suspect that some of the strongest misperceptions arose from some readers' taking a rapid dislike to the book's author, and interpreting everything else in the light of what they thought somebody like that would say.

A difference of approach might therefore have lessened the extent of feminist misunderstanding. On the other hand it might only have increased the problem in the other direction. There have been misunderstandings from the conservative side as well, which seem to arise partly from comparable presumptions about what a feminist – even a sceptical one – could be expected to think, and presumably there would have been more of these if the disagreements with familiar feminist ideas had been less forthright. So it is not entirely clear that another policy would have fared better on the whole.

And anyway, this is obviously not the whole problem. It is clear that the sources of misunderstanding go much deeper than this, and at deeper levels present more radical problems. Most are occupational hazards of applied philosophy. People unfamiliar with the subject (as with many other subjects) are likely to mistranslate what they hear into more familiar terms, and arguments intended to disrupt a particular conceptual scheme may be mistaken for (objectionable) claims within it, or analyses of conceptual problems interpreted as empirical generalizations, or criticisms of arguments taken to imply repudiation of their political conclusions. And, at the very simplest level, problems frequently arise from a failure to recognize how carefully arguments of this kind have to be read and thought about. If a book of this kind is skimmed, it is bound to be misunderstood.

No doubt some of these problems could have been anticipated and prevented; certainly I can see that in many places the arguments given here, even when technically correct, are nothing like full enough. On the other hand, in areas of conceptual difficulty and strong feelings there does seem to be an inherently limited relationship between what an author puts into an analysis and what the reader gets out. It is impossible to block all misunderstandings, no matter how much effort is made, because even if everyone could be persuaded to spend enough time and care on reading (and why should they, unless they are already convinced it would be worthwhile?), no one could begin to anticipate all the possible directions from which different people might come. And anyway, any attempt to do this beyond a certain point would have costs of its own. The more time that is spent in trying to anticipate and block some people's misunderstandings, the more everyone else's attention is likely to wander. Even more fundamentally, the more time that is spent on persuasion, the less there is for the business of trying to work out what people ought to be persuaded of. This problem seems to have no satisfactory solution.

Unlike my publisher, I rather wish I had managed to make the book less controversial, and I certainly wish I had managed to make the arguments clearer to people who think they disagree with them. On the other hand, my hope must be, in compensation, that perhaps even unsympathetic feminists may recognize some virtue in an approach of this kind. Probably because the book presents the arguments by which I myself arrived at feminist conclusions in the first place, it does seem to have changed the minds of some people who initially thought of themselves as opposed to feminism. If it had been less direct it would probably have been less readable; if it had been less obviously critical of some conspicuous parts of feminism it would have been less effective in persuading some of the uncommitted that it was possible to be a strong, radical feminist of a rather unfamiliar kind. Even my critics may, perhaps, at least think that a useful first step, and recognize that we are, in the most important sense, on the same side.

3

This book really was the enquiry of its subtitle. Writing it was not a matter of trying to defend an existing set of conclusions, but of trying to work out what to think about a set of puzzling problems and frequently being surprised by where the arguments led. It was not even my idea. The suggestion came out of nowhere from the publisher, through the recommendation, apparently, of someone else whose identity no one has ever been able to establish. In fact since I was at the time working on metaphysics and philosophy of science, and had never thought systematically about feminism or even moral and political philosophy, I have always rather suspected a mistake of identity somewhere along the line. Whatever the cause, however, the effect was that metaphysics was for the time being abandoned, and an investigation of this unfamiliar territory begun.

It soon became clear that the metaphysics would have a long wait. Not only did feminist issues turn out to be more serious than I had previously thought; they were also much more complex. Every problem solved raised a dozen more, and every gleam of light revealed more cobwebby corners. The book eventually came out when it did not because the end was in sight, but because the publisher was obviously not going to wait much longer. This is just as well, since if I had waited to finish I should be waiting still; but progress (I hope) went on, and it was tempting, with a new edition in prospect, to start playing around with the text to improve all the things that could be much better done.

It quickly became clear, however, that this would not be a good idea. In particular, the most important developments in my attempts to sort out the subject were not matters of detail. Most of them lay in fundamental areas of theory (which is not surprising, since these are the most difficult), and to incorporate them properly would have meant restructuring the whole thing. That would not have been a new edition, but another book. The best solution, therefore, seemed to be to deal with the fundamental issues by adding two more recent articles at the end of the book, while leaving the original text pretty well intact. A few very small changes have been made, correcting local errors of fact or making slight alterations of tone, but since they affect neither the argument nor the pagination they are not worth commenting on.

The two appended articles have complementary purposes. The first in a way looks back to the book, presenting a clearer version of its central thesis than I could pin down at the time. The second, in contrast, moves beyond the position reached there, showing by implication what I now take to have been the main shortcoming of theory in the book, and giving some indication of my current position. They are also complementary in matching the two directions of the original argument (the battle on two fronts), the first concentrating on mistakes in traditional conservative arguments, and the second on a problem in current feminist theory. And they are both about dichotomies: the first about one that should not have existed – the division of the sexes into their traditional separate spheres – and the second about a distinction that I think needs to be made, but seems not to be, between different kinds of idea prevalent in present-day feminism.

These were both written as self-standing articles, rather than as supplements to the book. As they have implications for the content of the book, however, something needs to be said about how they fit.

The first article, *Traditional Spheres and Traditionalist Logic*, collects and extends various arguments which were separated in the book, but which really belong together. It makes direct use of material from Chapter 5, which, although I did not realize it at the time, contains the most important points of theory, and links it, more firmly than happens in the book, with the arguments about discrimination in Chapter 4. It presents what now seems to me the essence of the feminist case, and the main arguments supporting it.

The second article, *The Great Gulf of Feminism*, deals with problems on which I am still working (as its unpolished state may suggest), and represents both a significant advance on the arguments of the book and a change of mind about some parts of it. Most affected are Chapters 3 and 4. In Chapter 3 liberalism is presented and defended as a foundation for feminism, but, as this article shows, I now think that the two issues are quite distinct, and that the feminist case should be made without any appeal to liberal ideals. Much the same applies to Chapter 4, where it is argued that the two parts of Rawls's difference principle can be coalesced. Although this is probably true for the specific circumstances considered there, the general question of how much social equality there should be is quite unrelated to the feminist issue of equal treatment.

The main effect of all this, from the point of view of the book, is that the essential feminist case can be made even to people who disagree with the arguments about freedom presented in Chapter 3, or who (like some of my philosophical critics) think the book would have been better without any mention of Rawls. How much difference it makes to arguments elsewhere in the book depends on the position of the reader. For anyone who takes a Rawlsian or liberal kind of line, everything goes through pretty much as it is (the discussion of discrimination and reverse discrimination, for instance; and, probably, the arguments about marriage and the family in Chapter 9). For anyone who does not, the conclusions reached in the book need to be adapted in the light of the article, in ways that I hope will not be too difficult to work out.

Even with this additional material the enquiry is nowhere near at an end, and various hints in the articles may indicate the kind of work to be tackled next. This, however, is not something that can be embarked on in supplementary essays or odd notes. It will just have to wait for the next book. In the meantime, I hope that this one, with all its short-comings, can still help to clarify the central problems for anyone who is puzzled by them, and demonstrate to the doubtful how much feminist work remains to be done.

Introduction to the First Edition

This book is a battle on two fronts. On the one hand, it takes strong issue with the many people who think that there is no justification for the existence of a feminist movement: the ones who think that women's demand for equality with men was misguided in the first place, or that they have now got it, or that women are better off than men. On the other hand, it is equally against a good deal of common feminist dogma and practice. For all the strength of the fundamental feminist case, feminists often weaken it by missing the strongest arguments in its support, or allowing themselves to get entangled in nonessential issues, or insisting on making integral to the feminist cause ideas which are either irrelevant, probably false, or actually against the interests of feminists and often everybody else as well. If the arguments which are to be presented here succeed in their intention, feminism will emerge from the enquiry as necessarily radical, but with firmer foundations, less vulnerability to attack, and at the same time more general acceptability than it has at present.

Having said that, however, I must explain immediately what I mean by 'feminism'. The word seems to have no precise and generally recognized meaning, but it has picked up a good many connotations of late, and an unexplained statement of support for feminism may therefore easily be misunderstood, and taken to imply commitment to more than is intended. In saying that feminism has a strong fundamental case, what I mean is that there are excellent reasons for thinking that *women suffer from systematic social injustice because of their sex*. Throughout the book I shall be taking that proposition as constituting the essence of feminism, and counting anyone who accepts it as a feminist.

This seems to me by far the best definition of 'feminism' to adopt. However, even though it is a very convenient one, and even though there is no clear and well entrenched rival definition to conflict with it, it does miss a good many commonly accepted connotations of the word. Something should therefore be said in explanation and justification of it, to avoid misunderstandings in future.

The most obvious way in which current usage is ignored when feminism is defined as an opposition to the sex-based injustices from which women suffer is in its seeming to count *far too many* people among feminists. Most people, whether they are feminists or not, do not regard as feminists people with just *any* kind of belief that women are badly treated by society. Feminism has come to be associated with particular theories about what kind of thing is wrong and whose fault it is, how it came about and what should be done to put matters right. It is extremely difficult to pin down with any exactness the kind of ideological commitment which is needed for someone to count as a feminist (which is not surprising, since feminists are by no means a homogeneous mass), but most people probably think that a general outline is clear. Feminists are, at the very least, supposed to have committed themselves to such things as participation in consciousness-raising groups and non-hierarchical organization, to the forswearing of femininity of appearance and demeanour, and to belief in the oppressiveness of families, the inherent equality of the sexes (or the superiority of the female) and the enslavement of women as the root of all oppression. In view of these deeply entrenched ideas of what feminism consists in, is it reasonable to start a book on feminism with a definition which leaves them out?

I think it is reasonable. Admittedly when a definition alters generally accepted usage there are bound to be dangers of misunderstanding, but there is a very good reason for taking the risk, and trying to get the more general definition widely adopted. It is this. Although people do usually seem to think of feminists as being committed to particular ideologies and activities, rather than to a very general belief that society is unjust to women, what is also undoubtedly true is that feminism is regarded by nearly everyone as *the* movement which represents the interests of women. This idea is perhaps even more deeply entrenched than the other, but it is a very serious matter for feminism that it should be thought of in both these ways at once. This is because of what seems to be an ineradicable human tendency to *take sides*. While it would be ideal if everyone could just assess each controversial problem on its own merits as it arose, what actually happens is that people usually start by deciding whose side they are on, and from then onwards tend to see everything that is said or done in the light of that alliance. The effects of this on the struggle for sexual justice have been very serious. The conflation of the idea of *feminism as a particular ideology* with that of *feminism as a concern with women's problems* means that people who do not like what they see of the ideology (perhaps because they are keen on family life, or can't imagine a world without hierarchies, or just don't like unfeminine women) may *also* tend to brush aside, explain away, sneer at or simply ignore all suggestions that women are seriously badly treated. Resistance to the feminist *movement* easily turns into a resistance to seeing that women have any problems at all.

Since there is no doubt that feminism is commonly thought of as having a monopoly on the representation of women's interests, therefore, and since all feminists, however firm their ideological commitments, must want as many people as possible to be willing to listen to arguments about the position of women rather than reacting with hostility whenever the subject of feminism comes up, it is in the interests of everyone who cares about justice to have as many people as possible thinking of themselves as feminists. That is the main reason why the wider definition is needed.

There is also another reason. If feminists themselves think of feminism as the movement which defends women's interests and *also* as being ideologically committed in particular directions, the effect will be to fossilize current feminist views. Any feminist who has the idea that giving up her current views is equivalent to giving up feminism may be very unwilling to look at her ideas critically and abandon them if they are implausible. But however committed any feminist may be to her ideology she must allow that there is a difference between maintaining the ideology and accepting more generally that women are unjustly treated, and since human fallibility means that she *may* turn out to be wrong about the first, it seems better that feminism should be thought of as the wider of the two. The broad definition of feminism allows feminism to survive the failure of any particular set of theories about the position of women, and to adopt it is therefore to make it much easier to take a flexible attitude to particular feminist theories.

It is therefore not simply idiosyncratic to define feminism as a movement for the elimination of sex-based injustice; it is important to the movement itself, even in its most ideologically committed parts, to accept such a definition. It will therefore be adopted here without any further justification. However, it will be worthwhile to point out, before leaving the subject, two other respects in which this definition forces a departure from the usual connotations of 'feminism'.

In the first place, then, feminism tends to be thought of as *a movement of women*, and certainly many feminists absolutely reject the idea of allowing men into the movement. However, men can (at least in theory) be as strongly opposed to the injustices from which women suffer as women can, and therefore they have to be allowed by this definition to count as feminists. There is nothing wrong with that, however. Men's being admitted to feminism does not entail that they ought to be allowed to participate in all feminist activities, and women who think that men have for far too long been telling them what they are really like and what they really want are quite entitled to insist on doing some investigating on their own, without men standing on the sidelines making helpful suggestions all the time. Admittedly, men claiming to be feminists have to be viewed with a certain amount of caution, since many have already discovered (sometimes without realizing it) that pretensions to feminism are new and valuable weapons in the cause of male supremacy ('I was a feminist before you were born; you can't accuse *me* of not standing up for your interests' and so on). However, their needing to have an eye kept on them is no reason for keeping them out altogether. They can be valuable political allies, as we know from the experience of the early feminists who could have made no progress at all without the help of men, and some men are quite as capable of useful logical thinking and scientific investigation as women. And anyway, if women try to keep them out they risk having what should be a struggle for justice turn into an old-fashioned battle of the sexes. Perhaps it should be added, however, that because of all too familiar problems about the English language, feminists will generally, although misleadingly, be referred to as if they were female.[1]

The other unexpected result of defining feminism as a movement opposed to the systematic social injustices suffered by women because of their sex is that feminism turns out to be not only not a movement *of* women, but not a movement *for* women either. It obviously cannot be one which supports the interests of all women under all circumstances, because there must be many situations where, even now, women treat men unjustly, and a movement concerned with *justice* cannot automatically take the side of any woman against any man. However, more subtly, feminism should not even regard itself as a movement *to support women who suffer from injustice*. This is because many injustices suffered by individual women have nothing to do with their sex, and could equally well be suffered by men. If, for instance, there are men and women in slavery, it is not the business of feminists to start freeing the women. Feminism is not concerned with *a group of people it wants to benefit*, but with *a type of injustice it wants to eliminate*. The distinction is important, even though on the whole the elimination of that injustice will benefit more women than men. Once again, this consequence of the new definition does no harm: on the contrary, it is far more reasonable to ask people to support a movement against injustice than a movement for women.

That is all that needs to be said about the nature of feminism, but it is probably also worthwhile to say something about the nature of the enquiry which is going to be pursued. In what follows, the subjects to be covered, the ways they are dealt with, and the conclusions which are reached may often be unexpected; perhaps equally unexpected by feminists and their opponents. To the extent that this is so, it is at least partly because the study is mainly a *philosophical* one. Feminism on the whole is still relatively little concerned with philosophy. It tends to be preoccupied with debates about what might broadly be called factual matters: the history of women's oppression, differential treatment of girls and boys, the effect expectation has on performance, economics and power, women's role in children's books, male sexual fantasy, anthropological studies of women, political methods, and so on. Disagreements are of a kind to be decided by further empirical evidence. Philosophical questions, in contrast with these questions about matters of fact, can be classified roughly as those whose solution has nothing to do with empirical matters, but depends on reasoning: on techniques like finding contradictions, showing what follows from what, exposing ambiguities, working out presuppositions, clarifying confusions and so on. These techniques are rather neglected in feminism, but they are extremely important: they are needed to deal with the most fundamental issues, and they can generate very powerful arguments. However, since discussions of The Nature and Value of Philosophy are always exceedingly boring and usually unenlightening, I shall say no more about the matter, but leave it to the arguments themselves to explain, and I hope justify, the approach.

One final note. The structure of the argument has made it necessary to work from general to particular: from arguments which are relevant to many areas of enquiry to ones which deal with specifically feminist issues, such as femininity, sex objects and birth control. The earlier chapters are, therefore, perhaps less obviously of direct relevance to feminism than are the later ones, and they are also rather harder going. There are no rules to prevent anyone who wants to get straight into the thick of familiar questions from starting with the later chapters, but I hope that anyone who does so will come back to the earlier ones later. This is partly because the later ones cannot possibly be properly understood without the arguments of the earlier ones, but also because feminism often suffers from staying too close to women, and not looking enough at the general principles which have to be worked out and then applied to women's problems. The early chapters are not only relevant, but essential.

I

The Fruits of Unreason

1 · THE UNDERMINED FOUNDATIONS

Some time ago, as the recent wave of feminism was rising to its full intensity, a group called the New York Radical Women put out a statement of principles, beginning like this:[1]

We take the woman's side in everything. We ask not if something is 'reformist,' 'radical,' 'revolutionary,' or 'moral.' We ask: is it good for women or bad for women?

At about the same time, and apparently not a thousand miles away, was produced another document, the *Redstockings Manifesto*, which contains a similar statement:[2]

In fighting for our liberation we will always take the side of women against their oppressors. We will not ask what is 'revolutionary' or 'reformist,' only what is good for women.

Now these are both formal statements of principle, presumably deliberated over and agreed on by the members of the groups concerned, and therefore the sort of document to which an outsider might reasonably turn for an indication of what was going on in feminism. Nevertheless, the thought that anyone might do this should be horrifying to any feminist who regards the movement as dedicated to achieving justice for women. This is because, taken as they stand, these statements imply that in their determination to advance the cause of women, the feminists who formulated them are prepared to throw all constraints of morality to the winds; that right or wrong, fair or unfair, they will pursue anything whatever which is to the benefit of women.

The basis of this accusation is not only the explicit statement that questions about what is moral are not to be raised. As well as that there is the resolution always to be on the side of women, with no apparent concern about whether the side of women in any particular case happens also to be the side of justice. And to reinforce the case still further, there is the fact that both documents state that the only questions to be asked are about what is, or is not, good for women. It is true that 'good' can be used to mean 'morally good', but it is quite impossible to interpret it that way in this context; to say that something is good *for* a group means only that it is to the group's advantage. Apparently, therefore, moral considerations have no weight at all with these two feminist groups.

This conclusion cannot be avoided by arguing that since women have been badly treated throughout history there is now a balance to be restored, and women will have to be given far more than equal shares with men if justice is to be done. That is no doubt true, but it does not affect the point. If women need more than men in order to achieve sexual justice, the principles of justice will themselves determine how much more they need. There is no point at which it is reasonable to forget about the principles and concentrate only on the advantage of the oppressed group. However badly it has been treated, it is always possible that if it thought of nothing but its own interests it might eventually get too much, and begin to treat its former oppressor unjustly.

Nevertheless, someone might reply, even though that may well be true as a matter of theory, it is quite irrelevant to practice. In day to day activities, where we have to make decisions in far too great a hurry to allow for elaborate computations of justice, we have to be guided by rules of thumb. And since it is most unlikely in practice that women could ever achieve more than was their due, we are justified in taking the advantage of women as our general guide to action.

That is a stronger argument, but it still does not work. Even if sexual oppression is the worst type of oppression (a question to be left open for the time being), and even if the most oppressed people in the world are women (which is probably true), sexual oppression is still not the only form of oppression, and women are not the only oppressed people. Many men are far more oppressed than many women, and any feminist who was determined to support women in all situations would certainly encounter some where her support of women against men would increase the level of injustice in the world. Even though we may often have to make very rough guesses about the fairest thing to do, and even though in doing so we may often justifiably favour women against men, we cannot make a general rule that we should always do so. Or at least, if such a rule is justified, it needs far more elaborate defence than it has ever been given, and the onus is on any feminist who thinks it ought to be defended to provide reasons.

No feminist whose concern for women stems from a concern for justice in general can ever legitimately allow her only interest to be the advantage of women. Does this mean, then, that the New York Radical Women, the Redstockings and others like them have to be regarded as pursuing a different sort of feminism, one whose motivation is not moral? That is certainly what the evidence so far seems to suggest, but the trouble with that conclusion is that it seems completely at odds with the tone of the rest of the two statements from which the quotations are taken; the parts not quoted here. They are full of anger about suffering and abuse, disregarded feelings and unfair privileges, and convey the fiercest possible moral indignation. Even in the passages quoted above, chosen for their explicit non-moral stance, there is some indication of this where the Redstockings write of the oppressors of women. 'Oppression' is not a morally neutral word. To claim that women are oppressed by men is not simply to say that men are in a position of advantage or power over women, but to imply that that power is unjustly held. But if all this is true, it looks as though it is after all a wish to see justice which motivates these feminists.

In other words, there is a contradiction. On the one hand there is the description of what is wrong with the position of women, written in terms of moral censure; on the other there is the statement of intended action, which seems to admit of no moral constraint at all. How can we explain this?

We could of course just conclude that some feminists, like many other people, were out for all they could get for their group, but also like other people found it convenient to give a moral gloss to their selfish intentions, and cast their intended victims in the role of villains. But although there may have been something of this in the background of the two feminist statements, it seems far more likely that what happened was something like this. These feminist groups really did start by wanting to achieve a just society, and having decided what a society of that sort would be like, looked at the position of women and saw that it was exceedingly unfair.[3] The more they looked, the worse the situation turned out to be: much of what was wrong had been hidden or taken for granted, and far more would be needed to put things right than even well-intentioned people dreamed of. This led to a good deal of justifiable indignation. But where passions are high it is easy to lose a sense of proportion, and the feelings generated their own momentum and went too far. The perception that women were ill-treated came to fill the whole field of vision, until it seemed that nothing women could achieve could be more than they were in justice entitled to.

This conclusion, however, does not follow from the original ideas of a just society, and worse still, *it is actually in conflict with them.* No matter how oppressed women have been, to fight with nothing in view but the good of women is to fight for *an unjust society*, the opposite of the intention which generated the fervour in the first place.

Perhaps that artificially chronological account obscures

the real criticism. The complaint being made is not that these feminists started out with one intention but somewhere during the course of their activity changed their minds, and started pursuing something else. People often change their minds during times of political activity, and a group of women who started out by worrying about injustice and women's oppression (as opposed to their simply not having everything their own way) might well decide after a while that morality did not amount to much and might as well be forgotten. That could be objected to, of course, but the objection would not be the *logical* one which is being made now. The point about these groups is that they have apparently *not* abandoned their original concern for justice. What they seem to have done is allow their perception of the extent of women's oppression to extend itself until the elimination of women's suffering has become the *criterion* for justice. But this cannot be done. No matter how great the suffering of an oppressed group, and no matter how much it will have to be given before justice is done, its advantage can never be *the same thing* as justice. To identify the two is to allow for the possibility of the oppressed group's being given too much, and to set out on a path which leads to injustice, *injustice according to the very principles by which it was established that women were oppressed in the first place*.[4] The heavenly city is being built with stones stolen from its own foundations.

It is no doubt true that since the original principles have never wholly been lost sight of, these feminist groups would probably not, when it came to the point, support any flagrant injustice to men. But it seems equally certain that in borderline cases, where there might be injustice but it was not obvious, a group whose principle of action was to support women would probably not look too hard to see whether men might be being treated unfairly. No group whose concern is for justice can reasonably be complacent about carelessly formulated principles which might lead away from fairness while appearing to support it.

2 · THE EXTENT OF THE MISTAKE

If we take it that the proper aim of feminism should be to establish a society in which there is sexual justice, it is obviously important that feminists should take care not to fall into moral confusion, and accidentally start on a course which could itself lead to injustice. However, important as that is, pointing it out was not the real purpose of the argument of the previous section. Its real importance was to illustrate a certain sort of mistake, which is just as serious for any feminist with no particular interest in morality as it is in the context of justice. Whatever your aims, it must go against your interests to act according to a hastily formulated maxim which is actually in conflict with those aims, and may lead by a different route to the position which you were trying to escape.

Here is another example of the same mistake, this time having nothing at all to do with morality. A feminist of my acquaintance said that the members of her group would not be interested in going to an evening class working on a non-polemical analysis of feminist issues. She said that they would have no interest in hearing evidence which might try to show that traditional ideas about women were right after all. People had for ages been producing spurious arguments to prove all kinds of absurdity about women, and there was no point whatever in listening to any more such nonsense.

Since evenings are scarce, nobody can be blamed for deciding there are better things to do than go to unappealing evening classes. However, if the remarks are taken to show attitudes to evidence, rather than timetables, they are serious. If feminists now have a better idea of what women are like than people used to have, that is only because some people eventually got round to looking at evidence about the nature of women, instead of being blinkered by prejudice and seeing only what happened to support what they wanted to believe. But now, it seems, some feminists may be falling into precisely the same mistake. Having used new evidence to revise the old ideas about women, and to put forward theories of their own which they find more attractive, they elevate them to too great a height, and presume them true. Having done that, they use their new theories to dismiss any further incoming evidence which conflicts with them.

But this way of going about things once again cuts the ground from under feminist feet. The whole point of challenging the traditional view of women was to prevent their being forced into uncongenial positions in society by people's wrong ideas about them. If feminists at any point start to presume their current theories in sociology, psychology or anything else can be taken as certainly true, when in fact there is always an overwhelming probability that the truth has not yet been reached, they are only heading for the same unhappy state of things by a different route. If we really want to make society as well suited to people's natures as possible, we cannot afford to ignore any evidence; not even when it is produced by the opposition.[5]

The mistake is of just the same structure as the one described in the previous section. There, feminists were in search of justice; here, they want to understand the nature of women, to make an attack on the superstitions which are used to justify forcing them into uncongenial social situations. There, the perception that women were unjustly treated slipped into the idea that the well-being of women was the criterion for justice; here, the recognition that the original theories were wrong has slipped into the conviction that the new ones are right. In both cases the hastily reached conclusion has outgrown its roots and taken on an independent existence, *and has become a tool for undermining the very principles which were used to support the conclusion in the first place*. An attack on injustice has turned unnoticed into a device for perpetrating injustice; a determination to find out the truth about women has become an obstacle in the way of the truth's being found.

These are not just isolated examples. It seems to be a common phenomenon in feminism (though of course not only in feminism) for enthusiasm to result in an idea's getting dangerously out of hand and working against its supporters. Another illustration of this is the idea some feminists have of trying to get away from what is *male*, on the grounds that what is male is oppressive to the female, or, more generally, just bad. Now of course feminists are on strong ground when they argue that much of what is and has been accepted by male-dominated societies is bad. However, it is disastrous to go from there to the idea that what we ought to be doing is setting out to eliminate all that is male and encourage all that is female, because, quite obviously, unless *everything* male is bad, eliminating the male is going to mean eliminating much that is good as well.

Nevertheless, some feminists do seem to slip into the idea that maleness can be used as a criterion for badness. One of the most striking recent examples of this is an argument against cloning as a method of sexless reproduction. Some feminists suggested women might try reproduction by cloning as a way of getting rid of the male even in what seemed to be his one essential function, but others have raised an objection. To do this, they say, would be to make use of *male science*, and if women are tempted to do that they will escape one form of male domination only to put themselves under another.[6] This is a catastrophic direction for feminist argument to take. I have nothing whatever to say in defence of cloning as a means of reproduction, since the present method seems a good deal better, but this *reason* for its rejection is disastrous. If feminists are going to construct their brave new world for women on the principle of using only material untouched by male hands, they will have to abandon just about everything, all the good along with the bad. Once again, no matter how black they may think the male soul, and no matter how much they may think that the male is inimical to the female, they cannot use maleness as the criterion for badness: the conclusion that men left so much to be desired could have been reached only by having an *independent* criterion by which to assess their moral worth in the first place. To lose sight of that independent criterion is to risk, in their determination to root out whatever is male, returning to a bad state of things by a different way.[7]

Another example of the mistake is often connected with the idea of conditioning. Feminists quite rightly want women free, choosing for themselves what happens to them, but realize that as a result of the thoroughness of men's control over women, some women are not in a position to be able to choose effectively even when they seem entirely unconstrained. This may account for women's resistance to some feminist ideas. From there, however, it is all too easy to slide into the convenient idea that *whenever* women make choices which feminists think they ought not to make they must be conditioned, so giving feminists an excuse to discount those opinions. But if that happens there is obviously a risk of forcing women again, even though in a different direction from before, because the *nature* of someone's choice is not enough to show that it comes from conditioning. The attempt to free women turns into a different way of coercing them. (This is discussed more fully in Chapter 3.)

The examples go on and on. Feminists object legitimately to the tyranny of sexual roles, and complain if men and women are expected by virtue of their sex alone to do different sorts of work. But if, like some feminists, we go to the extent of presuming that we have not got rid of the tyranny until men and women are doing the same sorts of work, we risk a different problem: that of forcing them to do the same things even though they may possibly have inclinations (on average) to do different things. Or we complain about sexism, meaning that people count sex as relevant in contexts where it is not, and then slip into accusations of sexism whenever anyone has the temerity to suggest that there are *any* differences between the sexes. To do that is to say that sex should not count under circumstances where it *is* relevant, and that is a kind of sexism (making a special case of sex) in itself. Sometimes this self-defeating elevation of feminist insights into the standards by which everything else is to be tested even becomes quite formal. Irene Peslikis (one of the Redstockings) has a list of 'Resistances to Consciousness',[8] ideas which might beguile feminists into questioning prevailing ideology and are therefore to be rejected outright, apparently even when it looks as though there may be good evidence for believing them. Current doctrine is presented as the standard by which to assess the truth or acceptability of everything else, and is itself thereby made unquestionable.

When feminist theory is presented in that sort of way there is a special danger, because it conveys the impression that anyone who is against the dogma is against feminism. But to question these mistakes, even from outside the movement, is not to be against feminism. *Whatever* feminists want, whether it is justice, equality, freedom, happiness, female supremacy or the total elimination of men, they will not reach it by leaping to hasty conclusions and accepting as articles of faith principles which will undermine their real intentions. The fact that something is born of feminist effort, and comes out of the movement, is not enough to show that it is good for feminism.

3 · THE PURSUIT OF UNREASON

No doubt it could be argued that the last thing any feminist ought to be doing is drawing public attention to widespread carelessness about reasoning in the feminist movement, as has just been done. It plays straight into the hands of the enemy. Of course feminists are incapable of reasoning, men are likely to say; women have never been able to reason. They are always full of emotion and apt to be carried away by strength of feeling, which is why all this pursuit of equality is nonsense in the first place. Whenever feminists try to deny their inferiority to men, they confirm it with every word they say.

We are actually forced to no such view of inherent feminine inadequacy in reasoning, in spite of the serious mistakes sometimes made by feminists. Apart from the fact that most men are none too marvellous when it comes to reasoning either, there is on the feminist side the very powerful argument that even if women are less good at reasoning than men that is hardly surprising, since men have always taken very good care that women should never have the opportunity to learn. That does not prove that when given the chance they will be competent, of course, but it certainly shows that men are not entitled to make many presumptions about women's potential on the basis of their present performance. A feminist should be quite happy to accept that women at present are likely (on average) to be less adept at argument than men, and one of the reasons for working through mistakes in reasoning is to get women better at it, and make their position less open to masculine attack.

This is a perfectly adequate reply to any anti-feminist accusation of women's irrationality, and therefore there is no need to be unduly cautious about presenting mistakes in feminist reasoning to the public view. However, there is a more serious problem in this area. If male chauvinism were all we had to cope with, things would not be too difficult. The trouble is that the traditional feminist who thinks that women are bound to have been held back by educational deprivation meets her most serious opponent not in men, but in *a new breed of anti-rational feminist, which unexpectedly embraces the enemy position*. Of course (this new feminist apparently thinks) women are less rational and more dependent on feeling than men. This has nothing to do with education. Women really are so by nature, and much the better for it. Rationality, like other things male, is something we are better without.

It is actually very difficult to prove that feminists hold these views. *Arguments* against *reason* do not start off on the firmest of ground, and they could hardly deceive even their proponents unless they were kept in a permanently slippery state, shifting from one meaning of 'rational' or 'logical' to another as the occasion demanded. They hardly ever get written down, therefore: to the extent that they can be seen directly they tend to live a precarious oral existence in the form of multiply ambiguous slogans such as 'logic isn't everything', 'people are more important than logic' and the like. More often their existence can only be inferred from other things which are said. But there is undoubtedly evidence that feminism has some tendency to get stuck in the quagmire of unreason from time to time, or at least to get dangerously close to its brink. Because of that the whole issue of rationality is an important matter in feminism. However, in case anyone should regard the whole accusation as totally implausible, and the attack as directed against nothing but straw women, some evidence for the claim must be produced.

There is, for example, Germaine Greer, one of the most attractive of recent feminist writers, and anything but straw. She writes[9] with the utmost cheerfulness that her own arguments 'have all the faults of an insufficient regard for logic and none of its strengths' (already implying that there are strengths in a disregard for logic) and goes on to say that in argument between women and their menfolk

The rules of logical discourse are no more relevant than the Marquess of Queensberry's are to a pub brawl. Female hardhead-edness rejects the misguided masculine notion that men are rational animals. Male logic can only deal with simple issues: women . . . are more aware of complexity.

It is true that this statement, especially when seen in its full context, is susceptible of a dozen interpretations at least, and I can imagine that it might well seem unfair to interpret it as an attack on logic. But *no* single interpretation seems to cover all the paragraph says, and anyway, as was pointed out a moment ago, clear and unambiguous statements opposing logic are likely to be rare. Imprecise statements, like this one, thrive on their elusive state; they can be defended according to one interpretation and then applied using another, and any feminist going along with what is said in this one would probably quite happily accept on weekdays that it was acceptable or even commendable to show a contempt for logic, even if she was careful to say on her philosophical Sundays that the argument was not actually against *logic*, but something else. Whatever Germaine Greer intended in detail, there is no doubt that she conveys the impression that logic is a rather unimportant thing which you can take or leave, like a set of rules for boxing, but which on the whole is better left. (Notice also that it is supposed to be *male*.)

Then there is Sheila Rowbotham, quoting approvingly from Norman Mailer's *The White Negro*:[10]

The real argument which the mystic must always advance is the very intensity of his private vision . . . no rational argument . . . and certainly no sceptical reductions can explain away what has become for him the reality more real than the reality of closely reasoned logic.

To this she adds 'This was the only place I could find an explicit statement of what I felt to be "real".' This too could mean more than one thing. If it were only an insistence that no reasoned arguments could prove that people's feelings did not exist, or were not strong, or did not matter, she would be quite right. However, in approving of a contrast's being drawn between vision and logic she is going further than that: she is regarding the two as *rival means of finding things out*, and must mean that the intensity of feeling is a guide to reality which no argument can vitiate. But that certainly is a defence of irrationality, since it means that no arguments must be allowed to count against anything which is believed passionately enough.

Those are examples of more or less explicit justifications of unreason, but in many more places the same thing is implicit. For instance, to take an unwritten case, one feminist who had been joining in an analysis of some feminist arguments said afterwards that her group would be interested in the conclusions the lecturer had reached, 'but they would only see it as her way of expressing her experience as a woman'. But if an analysis of an argument, a discussion of contradiction and consistency, can be seen as nothing more than an expression of personal experience, there is no room at all for reasoning. According to that view of things a demonstration that an argument is inconsistent, or that a conclusion is ill-supported by the evidence, is no different in kind from a feeling of resentment at a man's patronizing treatment, or guilt about not living up to the image of the ideal woman. Anyone disagreeing with the argument need not find reasons. She need only say 'that is your experience; mine is different', and since all experience is equal, there is an end of the discussion. There is nothing more to be said.

Another example of an implied defence of irrationality comes in Irene Peslikis's 'Resistances to Consciousness', which have already been mentioned.[11] Among them she lists as objectionable: 'Thinking that some women are smart and some women are dumb. This prevents those women who think they're smart and those women who think they're dumb from talking to each other and uniting against a common oppressor.' But if we are not allowed to regard some people as cleverer than others, it should have the consequence that we give equal weight to what they say, and regard all of them as equal in all discussion (which is of course the intention). Is that possible? If we notice that some women say what is obviously well judged and consistent, and that others make unsupported or contradictory assertions, how can we help noticing that there are differences in ability? It could be done only by starting out with the maxim that everything which was said must be of equal value, and nothing more was to be said for the well-judged than the absurd; or rather, that descriptions like that were not applicable. That is the most thoroughgoing anti-rationalism.

By way of a final example, here is another quotation from Sheila Rowbotham, this time in a different book, on the history of feminist revolution.[12]

What I write is simply a contribution to a permanent communication, which comes from me personally but only exists because of other women. An individual woman who appears as the spokeswoman for the freedom of all women is a pathetic and isolated creature. . . . No woman can stand alone and demand liberation *for* others because by doing so she takes away from other women the capacity to organize and speak for themselves. Also she presents no threat. An individual 'emancipated' woman is an amusing incongruity, a titillating commodity, easily consumed.

But what is wrong with a woman's becoming aware of some injustice in the position of women, and (if it is within her skill) doing what she can to remove it? Why should her being alone vitiate her efforts? What about the woman who perceives on her own (which is perfectly possible) an inconsistency in male attitudes, and demands its removal, for the sake of other women? What about the researcher in psychology, who sees that a common mistake is being made and demands its recognition, for the sake of other women? What makes these people pathetic? The value of such isolated contributions can be seen as contemptible only as a result of some view which insists that nothing is of value without the support of other women (whether or not they understand what is being said) and that without that support anything is worthless. But if an argument, or piece of evidence, or defence of women, can be assessed only according to whether it is generally accepted by other feminists and not in its own right, there is once more nothing to be reasoned about. Mass support becomes the standard by which to assess everything.

Examples such as these could be multiplied indefinitely, but there are enough here to make the point. There is no doubt at all that there is in much of feminism an anti-rational element. Even feminists who may be sceptical of my interpretation of the intentions behind the explicit anti-logic statements (the first two quoted) must find the sentiments of the last three illustrations familiar, because the ideas of the primacy of experience, the equality of sisters, and solidarity given by the group (some feminists insist that nothing be *presented* by individuals, only by groups) are immediately recognizable as characterizing much of recent feminism. Perhaps it was not immediately obvious that such views, or at least their common interpretations, were actually anti-rational. I hope it is now clear that they are.

one who disagrees with this interpretation of what
on in the examples, however, let me say two things.
rst is that even if other consistent interpretations of
feminist statements are possible (which I doubt), that
es not prove that these other interpretations were intended by their authors. I have no doubt at all that the
quotations were meant, or at least are often approvingly
interpreted, in the way which has been described. And in
the second place, even if no one, when pressed, will admit
to holding these anti-rational beliefs, and insist they really
meant something else even if they did not say it clearly, the
argument is still worth putting forward because what it
makes clear beyond question is that this area is full of
confusions. Making clear the possible interpretations of
confusions is the beginning of sorting them out. Even if this
analysis did nothing more than prevent confusion, it would
be worthwhile.

4 · WHAT RATIONALITY IS

It cannot be denied that adopting an anti-rational stance has
its uses; it can be turned into an all-purpose escape route
from tricky corners. Whenever a feminist's conclusions are
challenged by a man (or by an unliberated woman who has
been conditioned into thinking the same way) she can say
that the challenge is based on male reasoning, and refuse to
argue any further. Nevertheless, in spite of these advantages
of unreason, feminists should be cautious. Before so cheerfully consigning rationality to men feminists should be clear
about precisely what it is, and make sure that it really is
something women do not want for themselves.

There is much talking at cross purposes about the whole
subject. The nature of logic, for instance, is very widely
misunderstood, a matter for which men can be held to have
a good deal of responsibility in view of their habit of using
'illogical' as an all-purpose abuse of women. A letter to a
women's magazine a few years ago was about a man's having

said that women were illogical because they drove cars without knowing how they worked. (The woman who wrote the letter had apparently replied that in that case men must be illogical too, since they ate meals without knowing how they were cooked – showing that she was in fact perfectly competent at logic, however deficient as a motor-mechanic.)

Logic covers a much smaller area than many people think. At root it is about *consistency*. It is not just an arbitrary set of rules which might have been otherwise and which could be done without, like the Marquess of Queensberry's, or like the various rules and conventions which keep women in their traditionally subservient place. It is a set of rules presupposed by the existence of language; not just some particular language, but any language. The most fundamental rule is that of non-contradiction. Essentially, whatever is meant when something is said, whether the words are used with their usual meanings or not, if the statement is to mean anything at all it must *exclude* some possibilities. In other words, to say for instance that something is red all over, in the standard use of those words, is to imply at the same time that it is *not* all kinds of other things, such as green or blue or spotted or striped. If, therefore, you say that something is red and blue all over at the same time, really meaning that and not something silly like constantly changing colour or being of a red and blue pattern, you have *failed to say anything at all* about the way things are since to be red is, among other things, to be not-blue.

Similarly, to say 'if it's red all over, it can't be blue', making an inference from redness to non-blueness, is to rely on the same rule; to assert both would be to say nothing because if one can truly be asserted, the other cannot. And that is what is wrong with being illogical. Being illogical is not having strong feelings, or mixed feelings, or changing your mind, or being unable to express things and prove things, or anything of the sort. It is maintaining that incompatible propositions are both true, and in doing so maintaining *nothing*, since to make an illogical statement is to make no statement at all. But since this is so, and since the purpose of language is to convey information, to use language at all is to rely on logic.

Feminists therefore cannot disregard logic. It is also quite clear (looking at the matter less fundamentally) that they do not even try to, since they are always accusing men of inconsistency of one sort or another. A feminist who thinks there is nothing wrong with inconsistency is in no position to complain if men expect women to carry heavy loads when those loads consist of children or shopping or washing, but say that they can't lift (the same) heavy loads when it is convenient to have rules excluding women from well-paid work. What is happening is that these men have committed themselves to *nothing at all* about what women can do, since they have implied that they both can and cannot lift loads of a certain weight. They invent the conflicting facts as they go along, to suit their convenience. Of course feminists complain, and they complain on grounds of logic.

That is why feminists must be logical. But logic is only part of rationality, though people sometimes use 'logical' very loosely to mean generally rational, and often when women are accused of being illogical what is really intended is that they are irrational in relying too much on intuition. Instead of looking carefully at the available evidence before settling on a belief, which is supposed to be the rational thing to do, they are said to leap to unfounded conclusions. Men, conversely, are supposed to be much more careful about looking at the evidence for what they believe. And at this point the feminist who is sceptical about the value of reason may feel she is on much stronger ground. After all, she may say, for centuries men have been assembling facts and presenting what passed for proofs of this or that, and because we were brainwashed into thinking that male reason must be everything men said it was, we believed the lot. Now we are beginning to see that most of what they claimed was false. So much for male rationality, the feminist may well say. We should have done a good deal better to rely on female intuition all along.

We can forget for the moment the question of whether reason really is male and intuition really female, since that is a highly moot point and totally irrelevant here. We need only assess the comparative value of the two. The real issue seems to be of a contrast between reaching a conclusion 'by reason' (that is, by collecting evidence and basing the conclusion on it) and 'by intuition' (where the conclusion is reached by a leap of the imagination, and the person who has come to the conclusion cannot say how it was reached). Actually this contrast is misleading: the two are not totally different ways of doing something, but ends of a spectrum. Whenever evidence is collected there is always some guesswork involved in arriving at the conclusion, and on the other hand even when people cannot say much about how they reached their conclusions they can usually give some small indication. Still, it is certainly possible to discuss the merits of tending towards one end of the range rather than the other.

Feminists argue that intuitions are often right. They cannot possibly say that they are always right, of course. For one thing, they take the strongest exception to some of the intuitions which men have about women, and for another thing people's intuitions conflict: they cannot all be right. What must be intended, therefore, is something like this. Intuitions are often correct, and men are wrong if they think they can dismiss an idea of a woman's just because she can't give a clear account of how she reached it; similarly, men often give evidence for their conclusions but get them wrong nevertheless, so we have no reason to think that reason is better than intuition.

That is all right as far as it goes. Whether conclusions are reached by intuition or by reasoning, some of those conclusions are going to be right and some wrong; neither method is a certain way to truth. However, how do we know that some are right and some are wrong, and which are which? Obviously *because of the evidence*, which shows that sometimes (or even often) conclusions reached by intuition are valuable, and perhaps even that it is safer to rely on a particular woman's intuitions than her husband's 'reasoning'. But it is no good trying to use arguments of this sort as a defence of irrationality, because to the extent that intuition can be defended, *that defence stems from reason*. It is by reasoning that we show that intuitions cannot always be dismissed.

The point is that rationality does not dictate how ideas should be arrived at, but only that the extent to which they are believed should be proportional to the evidence. Irrational people are not the ones who reach ideas without much explicit evidence, but those who refuse to look for and consider evidence which would count for or against them. That is *prejudice*, a thing to which feminists must certainly be opposed. Men's prejudices about women are not the ideas they have which women do not like, nor the ones which happen to be false; they are the ones which are kept to irrationally, in spite of the evidence. If feminists defend irrationality they are in no position to complain if men resist all evidence and go on believing until the end of time that women are inherently weak, unreasonable and given to fits of the vapours. For that matter, they could not even complain if men took it into their heads to believe that women had black and yellow stripes and laid eggs. It is only through insisting that the evidence should be looked at carefully that women are able to attack the prejudices of men. Feminists cannot possibly support irrationality in any form.

5 · WHAT RATIONALITY IS NOT

Perhaps this conclusion should be reinforced in another way. Some speculation is called for here, but it does seem likely that part of the inclination some people (not only feminists) have to be suspicious of reason stems from confusing it with other things which are certainly to be rejected, and which look a little like reason from a distance though they are actually quite different things. If such things are clearly distinguished from reason, reason is less likely to be resisted.

The first of these confusions seems to consist in identifying reason with the *use* men often make of skill in reasoning. 'Men in general', wrote Mary Wollstonecraft,[13] 'employ their reason to justify their inherited prejudices against women, rather than to understand them and to root them out'; a thing which most women are well aware of, even though they may rarely attack their menfolk with such accusations. And as Simone de Beauvoir said[14]

[Women] are unable to state their views and draw conclusions, for lack of intellectual technique. That is why their husbands, even though of comparatively mediocre ability, will easily dominate them and prove themselves to be in the right even when in the wrong. In masculine hands logic is often a form of violence, a sly kind of tyranny.

Germaine Greer also makes a similar point in the section from which the earlier quotations were taken[15]: 'in most situations logic is simply rationalization of an infra-logical aim. Women know . . . that arguments with their men-folk are disguised real-politik.' In other words, women feel that men often use reason as an instrument of the oppression of women. It can be a device to make the weaker argument appear to defeat the stronger.

It is certainly true that skill in argument may be used to give the appearance of proof where there is none, and it is also true that women have often been men's victims in this way. However, the fact that something may be put to a bad use does not show that it is bad in itself. If we object to skill in reasoning on the grounds that it may be misused, we might just as well try to abolish medicine on the grounds that someone who understands it knows how to poison people as well as how to cure them. Reason is not the same thing as men's often questionable use of reasoning. The way to cope with men's treachery is not to outlaw the use of their weapons (especially since women cannot do without these themselves) but to become expert enough in their use to prevent further harm from being done. Women should be so adept in argument that they can see what is happening if men seem to have proved that black is white, instead of being driven into a baffled and furious silence.

The second feminist objection to reason seems to stem from an idea that it is in conflict with invention and imagination. Consider, for instance, Germaine Greer's statement that male logic could deal only with simple issues,[16] implying that anyone determined to be logical must be confined to a limited and inadequate view of things. In a rather similar-sounding vein Robin Morgan in the introduction to *Sisterhood is Powerful*[17] (an anthology already referred to several times in this chapter) comments on the 'blessedly uneven' quality of the collection, taking pride in its including everything from 'well documented, statistically solid pieces' to 'intensely personal experiences', with no trace of 'a kind of linear, tight, dry, boring male super-consistency which we are beginning to reject'. However, in saying that a valuable juxtaposition of all kinds of heterogeneous material is opposed to *consistency* she seems to suggest that anyone committed to logic would reject her collection. It is not surprising if a feminist who reaches this position thinks logic is something better ignored.

Now of course someone who insists on doing nothing but manipulating the information which is already there and drawing consequences from it is not going to come by much in the way of new ideas. Nor is anyone who will not venture an inch beyond the evidence which has been collected, and refuses to experiment or guess or try things out. However, there is absolutely nothing which can *rationally* be said in defence of either of these dreary attitudes. People who say that irrationality is always to be avoided are not trying to claim that reason on its own can do everything. In fact modern philosophy of science takes the view that the most striking advances in science have not been made in any predictable way by people working within a set routine, but by sudden flashes of insight and imagination which presented new and fruitful ways of looking at the world.

Feminism has much to do in the way of producing such new ideas, since a good deal of opposition to feminism comes from failure to understand what alternatives to the present state of things are possible. *Reason itself shows the importance of imagination and inspiration*, because it shows the limits of what can be achieved by reason on its own.

Finally, in addition to the idea that if men use reason for bad ends reason must be bad and the idea that reason is opposed to imagination, there is another which is very commonly held: the belief that reason is a cold and impersonal thing, opposed to all feeling and therefore to the most important things in life. 'I believe in love, and love isn't rational', one man said recently (just to show that it is not only women or feminists who are given to this sort of approach). And there is the passage from *The White Negro*, already quoted,[18] which insists that feelings should be accepted as real despite any rational attempts to explain them away. The feminist complaint seems to be rooted in the idea that men's general technique in coping with those of women's feelings for which they have little sympathy is first to prove they are irrational, and then proceed to disregard them. It is hardly surprising if women think that their feelings deserve more attention than that, and become suspicious of reason in the process.

Of course it is right to insist that feelings should never be disregarded, and no argument of any sort can possibly show that feelings do not matter, let alone that they do not really exist. However, philosophical and other reasoned arguments are not (or at least should not be) directed against the existence or importance of strong feelings. They challenge only the claim that strong feelings can be taken on their own *as a guide to truth*. The philosopher does not question the intensity of the mystic's experience, only what the mystic sometimes takes that experience to prove. Reason does not usually cast doubt on the strength of the lover's feeling, only (perhaps) whether the strength of the feeling can be taken to show that the beloved is all that the lover believes, or much about how long the love will continue. Strength of feeling cannot possibly be taken as a guide to the truth of what is believed, because people may have equally strong beliefs which conflict with each other. Caring about feelings is a very different matter from taking feelings as a guide to truth, and it is only taking them as a guide to truth which is irrational.

Furthermore, caring about people's feelings actually *demands* that one should reject the irrational position of taking feelings as a guide to truth. If a feminist really cares about women's misery, she must be prepared if necessary to disregard entirely these women's (and even her own) strong intuitions about how these feelings came about and how they can best be removed, since these intuitions may be entirely mistaken. Much of the scope for the study of psychology lies in the fact that it is common for people to know very well that they are miserable but be quite wrong about what should be done to put things right. Finding the best way involves great care in objective collecting and assessing of evidence, and to be careless about this is to be careless about the feelings which are supposed to be so important. Feminists are set on a course for disaster if they say (as the New York Radical Women do elsewhere in their statement of principles[19]) 'We regard our feelings as our most important source of political understanding.' Feelings may well be the reason for a decision that action is necessary, but they are on their own the source of no understanding whatever, and the consequences of thinking that they are can be disastrous.

Perhaps the explanation for some women's having been led to think that reason disregards feelings is one of the contexts in which accusations of unreason tend to be made. When men and statistics 'prove' that something is best (like having motorways through the middle of towns) they are inclined to say that anyone who objects is just being unreasonable. Actually people are often unreasonable about things like that: they may not realize that there is a connection between things like motorways, which they do not want, and the high standard of living (by some measurements) which they do want. But not all the opposition stems from such unreason. Some of it comes from *preferring* to be without lorries thundering through communities, even at the expense of not having fridges and televisions and food as cheaply as would otherwise be possible. The question may not be one of reason versus unreason, but of one set of preferences versus another. If women's preferences have often differed from men's, and men have mistaken this difference for an inability to understand things and have therefore accused women of being unreasonable, it is not surprising that some women have come to the conclusion that there is much to be said for being unreasonable. That, however, is not the proper moral to draw. What needs recognizing is that a man's claim to reasonableness is not a sufficient condition for the truth of that claim. That is a fact which no feminist should have any difficulty in accepting.

6 · THE LEGACY OF OPPRESSION

We are now in a position to bring the wheel full circle and end the analysis where it began, by showing how the elements of irrationality in feminism, which lead feminists to adopt principles which are in conflict with their most fundamental convictions and which tend to undermine what they are really trying to achieve, *stem themselves from the same mistake*. Feminist irrationality itself arises out of trying to push good early insights further than they will go, and once entrenched tends to work against what feminists really want. I want to conclude by showing how this comes about: how good and valuable feminist ideas lead to unreason and so to their own destruction.

Basic to much recent feminist practice has been the idea of *sisterhood*, which embodies a resistance to 'male' ideas of hierarchy. It involves a determination among members of the women's movement to work together as equals, without leaders, sharing each other's experiences and sharing all kinds of work (rather than leaving the unskilled work to some women and reserving the intellectual and public parts of things for the best-educated). Central to the method has been the idea of the *consciousness-raising group*, where women get together away from men, and work to express and analyze their experiences and feelings, and of course to support each other.

Without claiming to speak for anyone but myself, let me suggest some of the virtues of these ideas.

First, there is much to be said for the determination to do a good deal of the work of feminism with other women and away from men. Women may well refuse to play the game of arguing with men, because, as Simone de Beauvoir says, they know the dice are loaded.[20] This is not only (as some liberally-minded men are most complacently happy to concede) because women are relatively uneducated in argument, and do better to practise on their own at the beginners' end of the pool before taking on anything as advanced as men. It is also because some men are so arrogantly convinced that women can have nothing of value to say that they hardly bother to listen or presume from the start that they must be wrong, and there is a limit to the point of trying to argue with a stone wall. And in addition to that, far oftener than is generally supposed by men, it can be quite simply *dangerous* for a woman to assert herself with a man, because men still commonly hold so many sorts of power. If the best you can possibly get is a Pyrrhic victory and the worst a total disaster, it is better to avoid the encounter altogether until your position is stronger. If there is to be any hope of winning in the long run, much of the early work of feminism must be done among women.

Second, there is the importance feminists lay on the expression of feelings. That too is absolutely right, because most of us (men included) spend a good deal of our efforts in a perpetual conspiracy against ourselves by trying assiduously to appear as social convention demands we should. The consequence is that when those conventions are of a sort to make most people unhappy we have no way of finding out, because no one will admit to being what established convention regards as a failure. Obviously it is necessary to feminism to find out what women really do feel, and the consciousness-raising environment makes this much easier than it would be outside. Furthermore, the stress on the equal importance of everyone's feelings is crucial. It is a most important insight of feminism to realize that the least articulate women are very likely to be the most oppressed, and that no matter how long it takes, their feelings must be understood. Difficulty in self-expression must not be taken to indicate that a woman has nothing worth saying, and some groups go in for quite formal devices to make sure that the least fluent and coherent women are not pushed to the side by the confident and well-educated ones. To allow that to happen would be to allow just what is complained about in men's treatment of women.

And finally, there is the simple matter of support. A good many of the battles which women have to fight are on a very small scale, concerned with home or work rather than large scale political issues. Women are very often in exceedingly weak positions, but it does make things easier if there is something to fall back on, and other people in similar positions are the ones who understand best what sort of support is needed.

There is nothing but good in any of this, as far as it goes. There is no mistake in the stress feminists place on the importance of sisterhood and personal experience. The only error comes when these perceptions are taken further than they will go, and allowed to slip into the various shapes of unreason which have already been discussed in this chapter. There is nothing wrong with women's retreating from men to find an atmosphere where they can better understand their own problems, but there is a great deal wrong if this good principle turns into a feeling that everything male ought to be rejected, and results in a suspicion of logic or science. Feminists can get nowhere without logic and science. It is right to say that people's feelings are of overriding importance, but it is disastrous to go too far and think that strong feelings are therefore the best guide to truth, because that makes it impossible to find the best ways to make people happy and protect them from suffering. It is right to regard all women's experiences as important, and perhaps even to say that the most important experiences are those of the most oppressed and least articulate women. But to go to the extreme of saying that every woman's opinion about what should be done or how things should be explained is equally valuable is to hold the whole movement back; the women who do have special skills have to lose them in the communal voice, and if the least effective women are as much in public as the others the cause is done no good. Much the same happens if the idea of support and solidarity goes too far. Women need support from each other, but if this is taken to imply that nothing can be done without the support of the group, one woman with a clearer perception of some problem than the rest may be tied down and rendered ineffective by them.

Cracks are beginning to appear in the ice; recognized feminists are questioning the established doctrines. Juliet Mitchell and Ann Oakley, for instance, have written of the ideas of sisterhood and personal experience that 'They are useful as starting points, but after that they act as distractions from another equally essential enterprise', and they criticize 'a move towards rigidity and inflexibility within the women's movement which results from a premature codification of personal insights as political rules'.[21] But not everyone has reached that point yet, and since the old ideas are moving only slowly the fullest battery of arguments is needed to hasten them on their way.

Here is one final addition to the arguments presented so far. Feminists are rightly very anxious that the domination of men over women should not slip past their notice in some disguised form; it is that impulse which accounts to a large extent for the suspicion of male logic and male science. But consider this description by Simone de Beauvoir of women in their traditional state, reduced by men to shadows of their potential selves:[22]

Not accepting logical principles and moral imperatives about the laws of nature, woman lacks the sense of the to her the world seems a confused conglomeration of specia. This explains why she believes more readily in the tittle-tattle neighbour than in a scientific explanation. No doubt she respects the printed book, but she respectfully skims the pages of type without getting at the meaning; on the contrary, the anecdote told by some unknown in a queue or drawing-room at once takes on an overwhelming authority. Within her sphere all is magic; outside, all is mystery. She is unfamiliar with the criterion of plausibility; only immediate experience carries conviction – her own experience, or that of others if stated emphatically enough.

Could there be a more apt description of the new feminist in her consciousness-raising group? Apart from respecting the printed book, consciousness-raising woman is the direct spiritual descendant of her oppressed grandmother, and the intuitions on which she bases her approach are equally the direct result of her constriction by men. The stress feminists lay on the differences between women together in captivity and women coming out together into freedom as sisters has perhaps blinded some of the strugglers to the overwhelming similarity in other respects. The fact is that if women accept that they have been deprived of the opportunity for full development and are therefore less than they should be, they cannot at the same time be full of confidence about the accuracy of their own intuitions. It is essential that *in addition to* their concern for individuals and their experiences feminists must learn the logic and science which have been the traditional preserve of men. To resist them is to cling to the very deprivation of which women complain, and try to move into liberation loaded with the heaviest chains of their oppression.

2

The Proper Place of Nature

I · FOUNDATIONS FOR UTOPIA

The aim of feminism is to transform the present state of
things, which leaves a good deal to be desired, into something which is as it should be for women. Any feminist who
wants to set about her work systematically, therefore,
should start with as clear a vision as possible of what such an
ideal world would look like.

The trouble with some planners of utopias, however, is
that in their endeavours to describe the best of all possible
worlds they forget that plans for anything have to take
account of the situation in which they are to be used. Very
often the designs produced are of a sort which would have
been excellent if we had been omnipotent and creating a new
world out of nowhere, but are not in the least suitable for
us, situated as we are, entirely dependent on the materials to
hand and our own skills in manipulating them.

The unsuitable sorts of plan are the ones which go in for
describing in detail both the institutions and so on which are
thought ideal, *and* the harmony, altruism, happiness and
freedom which the idealist foresees as the consequences of
these institutions; the sort of plan which states, for instance,
'The ideal for which we are aiming is a world where everyone is happy and fulfilled, everyone is economically equal,
central government organizes all industry, education and
welfare, men and women do the same kinds of work, and
children are born artificially and reared by the community.'
And the reason why plans of this sort are not suitable for
our purposes is that they may describe states of affairs which
are, for all we know, *impossible* to achieve by working with

the materials which are available. For instance, the nature of people may be such that it is false that they are happiest when working communally. However many possibilities for change there are in the present world, even if they are infinite, there must still be infinitely more imaginable states of affairs which could not possibly be brought by natural means out of this one (rather as the series of prime numbers is infinite, but does not contain all numbers). If the utopia we are supposed to be aiming for happens to be one of the impossible ones, we shall be wasting our time.

Perhaps someone will object to this. Surely, it may be said, we should be aiming for the best state of things we can possibly imagine? Even if what we envisage does happen to be impossible, we shall do better by aiming for an ideal which is unattainable than by setting our sights lower from the start. However this argument, as it stands, is wrong. Even though we should of course aim as high as we can, that still does not justify planning an ideal which takes no account of practical possibilities. If you plan your ideal house without taking into account the nature of the materials you have to deal with, without allowing for the fact that bricks cannot be supported by thin glass or foundations laid in quicksands, the result is not a splendid house whose only drawback is that it falls rather short of the impossible ideal; it is a total disaster. In the same way, any architect of a feminist utopia who makes her plans on the basis of the way she would have liked the world and the people in it to be, rather than on the basis of what they actually are, is almost certain to produce something far less good than if she had accepted the limitations of her materials from the start. Certainly we can always aim to change any particular thing we do not like, but in a system where everything is causally enmeshed with everything else, we have to allow for the fact that any such change involves changes in other things, and those may not be ones we want.

The moral of this for feminist (and other) idealists has nothing to do with settling for low standards. It concerns only the *form* plans should take. The most important thing is that our ideals should not commit us to any details about the kinds of social arrangements which will be found in the ideal society. They should involve only *general principles which provide criteria for deciding when one society is better than another*: principles like, for example, 'the ideal society is one where there is the maximum total happiness', or 'everyone should be economically and socially equal, irrespective of total happiness', or 'the most important thing is to maximize human achievement'. Having found acceptable principles which take that kind of form, we shall always be in a position to decide between different possible kinds of society, and know whether or not things are improving.

The advantage of working along these lines is that our ideals are cast in such a form as to allow for our ignorance of matters of fact. As our knowledge progresses, and we decide certain states of affairs are possible or impossible, we can use the guiding principles to adjust our political ideals. Of course we often have to act as though our present beliefs about matters of fact are true; that all will be well if we have universally available crèches, or make men and women as much alike as possible, or get rid of capitalism, or whatever, but the important thing is not to get transfixed by theories such as these, or elevate them to the status of dogma. All beliefs about matters of fact, apart from those which really are established beyond all reasonable doubt, should be held endlessly open to revision. That way we have the best possible chance of finding out when our presumptions are wrong, and altering our political course towards the ideal accordingly.

Of course, however careful we are there is not the slightest guarantee that we ever shall reach the best possible state of the world, and if by any chance we did we should not know that we had and should almost certainly spoil it all by trying to do better. Nevertheless, finding out as much as possible about the nature of the world as it is is the only thing which can give us any reasonable hope of success. All feminists should therefore be committed to an unending, unprejudiced investigation of the nature of the world as it actually is.

2 · THE RAW MATERIAL

The matter of finding out about the natures of things is of importance for everyone, but particularly so for feminists. This is because there are large areas of controversy where alleged matters of fact are always being held up in opposition to feminist arguments, and where feminists have the best possible reasons to argue that the traditional beliefs about these facts are wrong. Of these the most significant concerns *the nature of women*, and in particular the extent to which women differ, or do not differ, from men. Alleged differences between men and women have always been used to justify the traditional position of women in society, and feminists have always argued that popular beliefs about these differences are unfounded.

There are various reasons for suspecting that tradition is likely to be wrong. One obvious one is that most of the pronouncements about the natures of women and men have been made by men, most of whom can hardly count as disinterested observers. All dominant groups have strong motives for inventing unfounded theories about the people over whom they have the ascendancy, because in that way it is possible to carry on any degree of oppression in the disguise of perfect moral rectitude. Baden-Powell, for instance, justified his withholding anaesthetics from Africans by asserting that they were less sensitive to pain than Europeans; comfortable beliefs about the dull sensitivities of the lower classes allowed middle-class Victorians to remain complacent about the atrocious home and working conditions the inferior group had to suffer, and many people now believe what they please about the feelings of animals to keep their consciences unruffled whenever the facts of vivisection or factory farming are forced on their attention. In the same way, it is so much in the interests of men to believe that women like nothing better than devoting their lives to the care of men and their offspring, and that anyway women would be quite incompetent to take on the kinds of activity men have chosen to monopolize, that feminists are entirely justified in being generally suspicious of male theories about the nature of women.

However, that is not the only reason for thinking that traditional ideas about the natures of men and women are likely to be wrong; there is another, even more fundamental, one. It is that even to the extent that common beliefs about the differences between the sexes are objectively based, and not just the product of male wishful thinking, they are still usually based only on differences between men and women as they *appear*. Men are *seen* to be interested in politics or business while women tend to talk about homes and men and babies; men are *seen* to have mechanical or business abilities while women are baffled when confronted with the engine of a car and don't know what to make of bank statements, and so on. But even to the extent that propositions such as these stem from impartial observation (which is true of by no means all of them) they are still not enough to show that women and men really are different by nature. You cannot tell the nature of anything just by looking in a casual and unsystematic way at how it appears, because whenever something is observed it is in some environment or other, and *the total phenomenon results not only from the nature of the thing under observation, but also from the environment it is in*. From the epistemological point of view the nature of anything is an abstraction; something which can never be seen directly, but can be inferred, if enough care is taken, by allowing for the influence of the environment in the total phenomenon. If, therefore, two things appear different, they may not be different in nature at all: they may simply be in different environments. And this, of course, is what most feminists claim about many of the alleged differences in nature between men and women.

Of course the opposition resists the argument. Allowing for the effects of the environment, it thinks, is something we do as a matter of course. If we find one child speaking English and another speaking French we need no philosopher to point out that the difference has nothing to do with their inherent natures. However, although in many cases we certainly do allow for the influence of environmental differences on people's growth and behaviour, in order to do that we must both be aware of those differences and understand their significance, and the feminist argument is that there are all kinds of systematic differences in the environments of men and women which are so subtle, or so universally taken for granted, that they have gone completely unnoticed or are underestimated. It is only relatively recently, for instance, that we have noticed that boy and girl children are differently treated almost from birth, or understood how radically people's performances are influenced by what is expected of them.

Because of the importance and subtlety of these systematic differences in environment, people may easily be mistaken about the nature of women and men in two different ways. They may be wrong both about *the nature of adult women and men as they actually are*, and about *the potential of male and female children*. If, for instance, we find that in general adult women are less good at concentrating on some task than adult men are, we do not have to insist that there must be some inherent difference between the sexes to account for it. We can speculate, as Simone de Beauvoir does,[1] that 'it is not a matter of mental weakness, of an inability to concentrate, but rather of division between interests difficult to reconcile'. The traditional demands made of women, which are now so familiar that we hardly notice them, make a great deal of difference to how well they can concentrate on other things, and it is not at all unreasonable to think that if men were in the same position they would probably find just the same difficulty. And to the extent that adult women *really are* different in nature from adult men, rather than just appearing different because of the different environment in which they now find themselves, this does not necessarily come from an innate difference in the natures of males and females. If, as seems likely, women in general really are more patient than men, so that they would act more patiently even in precisely identical situations, we could again follow Simone de Beauvoir,[2] and wonder whether this difference came from women's being brought up relatively powerless, and therefore having little choice but to resign themselves to whatever they did not like. Perhaps with the same background men would have been the same. There is certainly good reason to think so.

This must not be misunderstood. When we say that women's lack of concentration, or their patience, is environmentally produced, we are not saying that women by nature are *really* singleminded or impatient, and that the present environment has not shown them as they really are. It is not that we are now seeing women *as they are not*, and that if we could get them into a different environment we should see them as they really were. The point is that *no* single environment can show the nature of anything, because to know the nature of anything (a woman, a lump of iron, x-rays, mosquitoes or black holes) is to know its *potential*; that if it is in one environment it will appear or behave in one way; that if it is in another, it may be different. The reason we do not know about the nature of women, and of course men, is not that we have seen them in the *wrong* environments, but that we have not seen them in enough different ones. You know something about the nature of iron if you know that it looks grey, feels heavy and is cold to the touch, but you know far more if you know that *if* it is left in a damp place it will rust, *if* it is stroked with a magnet it will become a magnet itself, *if* it is heated enough it will melt, and so on. In the same way, seeing women and men as they are now shows us something about their natures, but in order to have a better understanding we should have to know how they would respond in different situations, and in particular, how each sex would respond in the other's environment.

This is a thing which cannot be found out just by guesswork. Some men are inclined to think, for instance, that if women had the capacity for genius mere differences in environment would not have been enough to account for their having manifested so little in the course of history; their inferiority must therefore be inherent. But this is not reasonable. It is impossible to say in advance how anything will respond to a totally new situation. Anyone who had always lived in the tropics, and known water only as a clear liquid which evaporated when heated, could not possibly have guessed without experience that it would become solid when it got cold enough. Men who think that women have little potential may be similarly mistaken. The only thing we can do when we want to find out the nature of anything is systematically see how it reacts in different environments. This can be done either by deliberately varying the environment and seeing what happens (which is the principle of scientific experiment), or, where this is impossible (as was the case with astronomy until recently), watching for natural variations in the environment and noting their effects on the object being studied. The reason why it is important for feminists to study history and anthropology is that knowing how women acted in different times and under different circumstances gives us a greater understanding of their natures than seeing them only here and now.

This is a kind of work which must be carried forward with care and perseverance if we are to find out about the raw material we have to work with in planning our ideal society. And in the meantime we can certainly argue strenuously that traditional ideas about women and their differences from men are founded on totally inadequate evidence, and ought to be regarded with systematic scepticism.

3 · VESTED INTERESTS

Recent discoveries of the extent and significance of systematic differences in environment between men and women are indeed enough to prove that most of the evidence people thought they had about the natures of men and women is totally inadequate to support the usual conclusions. However, it is important to realize that that is *all* they do. We may know that traditional views are almost certainly wrong, but it does not follow that we know which views are right.

When we find that environmental differences between two things are probably enough to account for their appearing to be different from each other, it certainly follows that they *may* be intrinsically alike in nature, but not that they certainly *are*. For instance, the difference in social expectations of the behaviour of men and women is enough to account for the fact that women show emotion far more readily than men do; even if they were precisely the same by nature this would account for different behaviour. It does not, however, prove that they *are* the same by nature. Perhaps women really are by nature more inclined to show emotion, *as well* as being socially encouraged to do so. Or again, the fact that women have, during most of history, been forced by their biology (and men) to spend nearly all their time in the care of small children is a perfectly sufficient condition of their having made relatively little impact on the history of the world; if men had had to do the same they would not have had time for other things either. However, it does not follow that men and women have the same inherent capacities. Perhaps women are inherently different; perhaps nature made them less interested in other things to ensure that they would be sufficiently inclined to care for their children.

Of course our ignorance is lessening. In several areas we have made a great deal of progress, and have certainly shown that women are capable of acquiring skills traditionally thought beyond them, as soon as they are given the opportunity. In the most complicated areas, however, dealing with innate desires, temperament and so on, it is very difficult to find out how different men and women are. In the first place, social customs are so deeply entrenched that there are relatively few natural variations in environment we can watch, and manipulating society for the purpose of experiment is difficult. We still do not often have the chance to see men and women in each other's situations. Even where superficial movement in this direction does occur, where, for instance, men and women take on kinds of work commonly associated with the other sex, there is a limit to what such experiments can show, because of more subtle things which are much harder to change: attitudes, expectations, conventions and all the rest. And as well as all this there is the problem that since we know already that many significant differences in environment went unnoticed for a very long time, we are bound to suspect that there may be ones which we are missing still. Although our knowledge has progressed a good deal, the fact remains that our ignorance is still vast.

Furthermore, it is perhaps worth pointing out, this position of ignorance is in principle as bad from the point of view of knowing about the nature of one's own sex as knowing about the nature of the other. Women are hardly in a better position than men to know about the nature of women. Of course they have more opportunities for study, and have fewer (or perhaps different) prejudices to contend with, but the theoretical problem is still the same. A person's nature is not something that person can find out just through introspection. To know your own nature, as to know the nature of anything else, is to know how you would react in different situations, and, as has been said already, much of the scope for the study of psychology lies in the fact that people can be mistaken about how they will react to new situations, and which elements of the situations they are in at present are producing which of their present reactions.

For now, therefore, and presumably for a long time to come, we have to accept that our state is one of considerable ignorance. Knowledge of ignorance is itself a kind of knowledge, however, and anyone who is trying to gain an understanding of people in order to see how to arrange society for their benefit does better to work on the basis of that than on the basis of outright error.

This being so, we now have to account for what must be regarded as a puzzling phenomenon. It is that in spite of the undoubted extent of our ignorance, there are many feminists who speak about the natures of men and women as though much of the truth about them were already known; and in spite of the fact of the importance of knowledge for planning the ideal society, many of them actually seem to resist the evidence which might assist towards that knowledge. There must be very few feminists, for instance, who would even admit to considering the *possibility* that women might on the whole be less capable of works of genius than men: for most feminists, the inherent equality of the sexes in all such matters is part of the official doctrine. Many feminists seem to assert with absolute confidence (depending on the kind of feminist) that children do not need their mothers, or that women's sex drive is inherently equal to men's, or that the pain of childbirth stems from adverse social attitudes, or that women are inherently better rulers than men, apparently quite unshaken by the lack of any really hard evidence about such matters. Some feminists, like the one referred to in the last chapter,[3] are so committed to their beliefs that they are unwilling even to look at evidence which might tend to dislodge them. And no doubt there are still feminists who actually resist accepting evidence which forces itself on their attention, as the early feminists Angelina Grimke and her husband Theodore Weld seem to have done:[4]

Angelina had a history of gynaecological trouble, which Weld referred to as the 'accidents' which weakened her . . . this phrasing may have been an evasion, for 'accidents' could be viewed as providential, while gynaecological disorder would have to be admitted as a sex-linked source of trouble that might complicate their ideology.

(This is a particularly interesting illustration because it long predates any feminist impulse towards deliberate irrationality.)

If the elimination of prejudice is of such importance for the founding of utopia, why should feminists act like this? Why should they sometimes seem to have *vested interests* in believing some things rather than others, even though in doing so they risk believing what is false?

One possibility is the motive attributed earlier to men who had vested interests in believing certain things about the nature of women. It has always been politically useful to men to argue that women are by nature suited to the position in which men have kept them, and feminists could presumably have similar political motives for persuading people to believe various things which might not be true. If, for instance, feminists wanted women to have power irrespective of how well they would use it, then it would certainly be in their interests to insist that women were well suited to hold power. If they wanted to make sure that women had the careers they wanted, no matter what effect that had on anyone else, it would be to their advantage to argue that children came to no harm through being left in crèches all day, whether they did or not.

However, even though that might account for some feminist carelessness about evidence, it is not something which should be gone in for by a movement which is supposed to be concerned about justice. Feminists do not want to do the kind of thing they have always criticized men for doing. And furthermore even if they did want to disregard justice, or even if they could occasionally argue that justice demanded their having other people deceived or confused about what the truth was, there could still be no possible advantage in being wrong or confused themselves. If feminists' woman-advancing projects are going to bring about economic collapse or generations of deprived children that is certainly a thing it is important to know about, even if they decide not to care. And above all, feminists can have no conceivable reason for hiding truths about women from themselves. If, for instance, they pretend to themselves that gynaecological disorders do not exist, the only consequence will be that they make no provision for putting them right, and perhaps force women who do in fact suffer from them to pretend they do not, or feel guilty about letting the side down.

No doubt there are dozens of psychological explanations of why people should be determined to believe certain things about themselves. Wishful thinking is certainly a large factor. Most of us would rather think that the fault for our failures lay in our stars and circumstances rather than in ourselves. There is also the fact that people seem on the whole to dislike intellectual disruption, and have a strong attachment to beliefs to which they have professed commitment, or on the basis of which they have been working. Such matters as these no doubt come into the explanation. There does, however, seem to be one aspect of the feminist form of fact-evasion which is especially worth commenting on. It is that many feminists seem to think that the feminist case *depends* on the facts about the natures of men and women. As one feminist said recently, 'if we aren't saying that men and women are inherently equal, what *are* we saying?' And since the idea that the whole existence of feminism depends on what is true about men and women is so widespread, not only among feminists but also among their opponents (who maintain the opposing 'facts' with equal passion and usually even less justification) more should be said about the matter.

4 · THE ISSUE OF THE NATURAL

Of course if feminism really did depend on beliefs about matters of fact, and those turned out to be mistaken, we should simply have to accept that feminism should be abandoned. We must certainly take that attitude to any specific feminist demand whose justification does depend on the truth of particular propositions. If, for instance, feminists demand that equal numbers of men and women should occupy important positions because they believe the sexes to be inherently equally competent to hold them, and it turns out later that they are not equal, then that demand must be dropped. If it turns out that children would come to harm in crèches, the demand for crèches must go. And if it is argued that some selection process must be unfair because it gives privileges to more men than women, and it then turns out that by purely objective criteria more men than women should have been chosen, the accusations of unfairness must be dropped.

However, although so much is certainly true, what appears to be equally certain is that many people do seriously overestimate the extent to which feminism depends on the facts about the natures of men and women, and that this is why passions run so high when the facts come under consideration. Feminism, as it happens, by no means stands or falls according to whether women are inferior to men, or equal to them, or superior to them, in any or all respects.

In the first place, the strongest of the feminist arguments about justice for women have *nothing whatever* to do with the extent to which men and women are alike or different by nature. They concern the *socially contrived* differences of *situation* of the sexes, which have put women in an artificially worse position than men, and which have nothing to do with which sex is better off by nature. Feminists often lose a great many points to their opponents by letting themselves get embroiled in debates about whether women or men are superior by nature, because there are many contexts in which we could even *concede* the opposition's highly dubious assertions about the nature of women and still win the feminist point. This is most important. People who try to challenge the very existence of feminism by talk of maternal instincts or inherent male dominance are either deliberately fogging the issue or just confused. In neither case ought they to be allowed to get away with it.

However, there is no need to elaborate arguments along that line here, since they will be dealt with fully later on. The important matter for the rest of this chapter is another way in which people commonly overestimate the force of matters of fact in feminism. It comes of their thinking that finding out the natures of things tells us far more than it actually does about the course society ought to pursue. Facts about the nature of men and women do not on their own make it clear what the institutions governing their relationship and social position ought to be.

Suppose, for instance, that women are at a serious disadvantage to men because the female flesh is heir to more ills than the male. That, certainly, is a thing which ought to be known by anyone going in for utopia design. But why should it follow that because of this weakness (if they have it) women are unfit to hold power? We could equally well draw precisely the opposite conclusion, and say that we must not allow this natural weakness to put women at a disadvantage or deprive the world of the benefit of their abilities, and must therefore put great effort into gynaecological medicine. And suppose that men are naturally dominant because of the miraculous testosterone of which we hear so much these days.[5] Why should feminists be reluctant to admit it, or anti-feminists to think that it clinches their case? Even if men are naturally inclined to dominance it does not follow that they ought to be allowed to run everything. Their being naturally dominant might be an excellent reason for imposing special restrictions to keep their nature under control. We do not think that the men whose nature inclines them to rape ought to be given free rein to go around raping, so why should the naturally dominant be allowed to go around dominating? One of the functions of society is to protect its weaker members.

The reason why it is important to know about what people are like when trying to achieve the best possible society is only that we need a clear view of the material there is to work with. Knowing about the material does *not* determine what ought to be done with it. What we decide to try to do depends on our values, and facts and values are separate things. Or, as many philosophers have put it for a long time, 'ought' cannot be derived from 'is': statements of value cannot be deduced from statements of fact. Achieving the ideal society depends on the *separate* activities of working out values and experimenting to find out facts.

All this reinforces the original conclusion that feminists should not think that they have a vested interest in discovering the facts to be one way rather than another. However, the idea that once you know the nature of something you know what ought to happen to it, and that if it is the nature of women to bear children they ought to bear children, or if men are by nature inclined to aggression they ought to be given full scope to be aggressive, is so deeply ingrained that something more should be said about it. In order to get the matter clear it is necessary to cut through a particularly thorny bit of undergrowth which has, since the dawning of ideas of women's emancipation, been lying in wait to entangle the forces of both sides in its coils. It is the issue of what is or is not *natural*, a matter which must be put in order before anything else is attempted.

Roughly, the position is this. The traditional view of the nature of women, and the idea which has been constantly used in arguments to resist feminists, is that women ought to be in the position which society has ordained for them because *it is their nature* to fit that position. Women are *by nature*, it is said, inclined to the bearing and care of children, and to live in a relatively confined sphere, in need of the protection of men, and so on. And since this is so, to alter the present social arrangements, which allow for all this, would be to go *against nature*, and in doing so invite disaster.

Of course feminists have never accepted that, and they very early found themselves in a position to produce strong counter arguments. As they began to have some understanding of the extent to which the so-called nature of woman was environmentally produced they replied that it was not by *nature* that women were so different from men, but by contrivance. Women are not by nature petty, vain, or domesticated: if they are like that now it is because men have made them so. 'What is now called the nature of women', Mill wrote,[6] 'is an eminently artificial thing – the result of forced repression in some directions, unnatural stimulation in others.' The fact that men think this hothouse product is of nature's doing rather than their own is only because it is what they are used to. So Kate Millett[7] says of Ruskin and his defence in terms of nature of his separate spheres for men and women, that he has 'deliberately confused the customary with the natural', and as Mill said in another passage from 'The Subjection of Women',[8] 'So true

is it that unnatural generally means only uncustomary . . .
The subjection of women to men being a universal custom,
any departure from it quite naturally appears unnatural.'

The opposition, however, refuses to be persuaded, and
these arguments are countered (when they are countered
with anything more than stout denial) by allegations that
there are of course natural differences between men and
women, even though there may be a few socially induced
ones as well. They cannot all be environmentally produced.
Maternal instinct, it is argued, cannot possibly be socially
acquired: it is a natural characteristic, and one which fits
women for a different social position from men. Recent
discoveries about hormones have reinforced this line of
attack. Even though very few things in this area are by any
means established beyond doubt, conservatives have been
very eager to add such evidence as they think there is (with,
of course, a little amplification here and there) to their
armoury.

Debates along these lines, which must in one form or
another be familiar to nearly everyone, seem when reduced
to their essentials to take this form. Everything has (the
underlying agreement between the opposing camps seems
to be) a true nature; a form which nature intended that it
should have, but away from which it can be forced by alien
influences. Second, everything *ought* to be as nature intended because, as Mill said (in another essay, 'On Nature',
which will be referred to a good deal in the next few pages[9]),
'That any mode of thinking, feeling or acting is "according
to nature" is usually accepted as a strong argument for its
goodness.' About those matters the two sides appear to be
in agreement. What they disagree about is *what is* natural
for anything, and it is to settle this matter that all the
arguments about instincts, hormones and socially acquired
characteristics make their appearance.

Once the issue is reduced to its essentials in this way,
furthermore, it becomes obvious that arguments which use
the idea of the natural are even commoner than might at first
sight appear, because they are identical in intention with all

the talk of distortion, deformation and artificiality which so commonly occurs in feminist contexts. In all these cases, as in the case of explicit arguments about what is natural, it is implied that women are being made into something which, in some sense, it is not their real nature to be, and that this new form is bad. The examples of this are endless. Juliet Mitchell, for instance, says that women's liberation 'assumes the distortion of everybody's life and potential today' under capitalism.[10] Shulamith Firestone argues that all forms of the biological family have caused 'specific psychosexual distortions in the human personality'.[11] Germaine Greer says 'In order to approximate those shapes and attitudes which are considered normal and desirable, both sexes deform themselves.'[12] And John Stuart Mill writes 'no other class of dependants have had their character so entirely distorted from its natural proportions by their relation with their masters'.[13]

All this is, of course, an extremely brief sketch of a complicated position. However, it is deliberately so. Although it would in theory be possible to discuss the problem of the natural by considering all the contexts in which it arises in feminism, analyzing each one of them individually, that will not be attempted here. For reasons which will soon be evident, that way madness lies. Instead it will be much better to head straight for the centre of the problem of the natural in its own right, and return to the context of feminism later.

5 · AN ANALYSIS OF THE NATURAL

It has been said that the two sides in feminist disputes about the natural seem to agree that there is indeed a natural state for women to be in, and that the natural state, whatever it is, is good. Both sides think that the real thing is better than the travesty which (from the feminist point of view) men have made of women, or (from the traditional point of view) feminists are now trying to produce. Since, then, the area of disagreement is about what *is* natural, perhaps we should begin by trying to decide what it means to say that something is in its natural state.

The best way to begin is probably to look at the kinds of argument people produce when they are trying to prove that something is *not* in its natural state. Something of this has been suggested already. Usually what people seem to do is point to the existence of *environmental influences* of one sort or another, which are supposed to have been the cause of the brainwashing, conditioning, or other distortion in question. Feminists, for instance, often try to seek out the male influences in the present-day female character, obviously with the idea in mind that to get the real female the alien male influence must be eliminated. Outside feminism people very often insist that an opinion or taste is not really yours if it is possible to point to other people who influenced you in some way. 'You only think that because your parents do', they say, or 'you have been indoctrinated by trendy school teachers', seeming to imply that the real you would not have thought such things, and that your appearing to think them is the effect of some outside thing which has nothing to do with what you really are at all. All of which suggests that for a thing to be its real self its characteristics and desires must stem entirely from its own nature, without outside influence. (This, presumably, accounts for wanting to find out the *nature* of something to assist in arguments about what is *natural* for it.)

However, as soon as this is said the absurdity is obvious. If 'natural for' or 'according to the nature of' something means 'that which stems from its nature alone, without outside influence', it follows that nothing can possibly be in a natural state. Everything is always in some environment or other, and influenced by other things all the time. What everything is *must* be a product of its own inherent nature and the environment it finds itself in. So the criterion for 'natural' cannot possibly be 'uninfluenced'. Anyway, even if *per impossibile* we could imagine something entirely out of the reach of any other influence, it would still not provide an account of a natural state which would suit the requirements of people who want to argue about what is natural for things, because if this were what it meant for something to be natural, the natural could hardly count as good. If your pursuit of natural woman, for instance, led you to try to suspend her in empty space away from all influences, she would just die.

It follows, therefore, that no sense can be made of recommending what is natural if by that is meant what stems only from the nature of the thing in question, with no influence from anywhere else. Therefore, presumably (since it is always influences of one kind or another which are blamed for distortions) it must only be *some* influences, and not others, which produce what is unnatural. Some environments must be all right. We must, therefore, try to find a definition of 'natural' which allows for this, and at the same time makes it clear why the natural is to be recommended.

The issue of what is natural and why it should be counted as good is one which has often been discussed by philosophers, three particularly well known discussions being those of Hume, Mill and Moore.[14] All three of these writers come to the same two main conclusions. The first is that 'natural' can mean a good many different things. The second is that according to *none* of these possible meanings can the natural be taken as any guide at all for distinguishing good from bad. If these accounts are compressed and their essence extracted, what appears is something like this.

In the first place, 'natural' can mean everything that happens in the natural world, everything that is not miraculous or brought about by the supernatural. However, if that is taken to be the meaning of 'natural', the recommendation to act naturally is quite useless, because it is impossible to do anything else. Besides, even if we were not part of the natural world and had it in our power to act either naturally or supernaturally, why should it be considered good to act naturally? The natural world contains quite as much evil as good. It cannot be used as a way of distinguishing the two.

The second common interpretation takes the natural to

be that which is opposed to the human, that which 'takes place without the agency, or without the voluntary and intentional agency of man'.[15] But as a criterion for deciding between one line of activity and another, that is as useless as the first. The first included all actions; this one seems to exclude them all. It is obviously self-defeating to recommend that anyone should *follow an instruction* to act without conscious intention, since consciousness is needed to follow instructions. If this account of acting naturally is to be of any use at all, therefore, it must be interpreted less stringently, and taken to mean something like 'act so as to alter the natural world as little as possible', 'act only by impulse and instinct, without reasoning', or 'act so as to make minimum use of specifically human abilities, concentrating only on the minimum necessary for the sustenance of life'. However, although it would be possible to follow any of these instructions there is apparently once again not the slightest reason why anyone should. To quote Mill again, 'the very aim and object of action is to alter and improve nature',[16] and 'All praise of civilization, or art, or contrivance is so much dispraise of nature. . .'[17] Could anyone seriously mean to argue that all specifically human activity was bad, and everything else better? It is an absurd view. At the very least, it is quite obviously not one which is held by anyone who recommends that women should do or be what is natural. It would rule out equally all household crafts and child care on the one hand, and all following of culture and careers on the other. It cannot be that.

What else is left? 'Follow nature' might, as Mill suggested, be taken by some people to mean simply 'take note of nature, observe it'. But that is equally good advice whether you are planning to do good or to do evil. Or it might mean 'copy nature', but that is no use either. Again as Mill said, 'In sober truth, nearly all the things which men are hanged or imprisoned for doing to one another are nature's everyday performances.'[18] Nor is it any good to take 'natural' with another of its common meanings, 'normal' or 'usual'; that cannot distinguish good from bad since, as Hume said,[19] according to that criterion 'perhaps virtue will be found the most unnatural'. We seem forced to conclude, therefore, that in no readily understandable sense of the word 'natural' does there seem to lie any reason at all for acting according to nature rather than against it.

Why then should anyone ever have imagined there was anything at all to be said for acting naturally? The answer to the question must be very complicated, involving as it must the history of mankind's intricate relationship with the universe and understanding of it, but one or two suggestions can be made.

To do this the question of what is to count as natural must be approached from what might be called the other end. We have so far been considering definitions of 'natural' which make it more or less clear *how* to act naturally, but according to which any consistent attempt to do so would be absurd. Perhaps the recommendation to act according to nature can be better understood by forgetting these definitions for the moment, and thinking instead in terms of the *consequences* of acting according to nature: seeing natural behaviour as that which brings about a certain result.

An account of one deeply entrenched set of attitudes to nature which would explain a recommendation to act according to nature is given by Passmore.[20] Mankind has, during most of its existence, tended to regard nature (where nature is seen as that which is 'human neither in itself nor in its origins') as in many ways like human beings, with desires and intentions of its own, and capable of being influenced by argument and entreaty in the way that people are. This view of nature is one which has been officially rejected for two thousand years, but[21]

the ordinary countryman was harder to convince that natural processes cannot have intentions. . . . As late as the nineteenth century German foresters thought it only prudent to explain to a tree they were about to fell exactly why it had to be cut down. In Ibsen's *Wild Duck*, Old Ekdal is convinced that the forest will 'seek revenge' for having been too ruthlessly thinned; in Buchner's *Woyzeck* a countryman explains the drowning of a man in a river by telling his companion the river had been seeking a victim for a long time past.

When such an attitude as this prevails there is no doubt at all why it is bad to act against nature: to do so is to offend the natural world, and therefore invite revenge. Passmore thinks that even though consciously held views of this sort vanished a long time ago they still exert an influence, and that in recent ecological literature ideas of nature's having its revenge for people's misdeeds has more to it than just metaphor. It does certainly seem to be true that when people talk about upsetting the balance of nature they are not referring to just any changes made to the natural world, but only to those which will have unwelcome consequences.

A second reason why people think that they should act according to nature seems to stem from what Popper called 'a stage at which both natural and normative regularities are experienced as expressions of, and as dependent upon, the decisions of man-like gods or demons'.[22] This view is characteristic of Christianity as well as primitive religions. The idea is more or less that mankind, along with all the rest of creation, was designed for a certain purpose in the scheme of things; the laws which control the actions of inanimate things and those which govern the proper behaviour of people are the same in kind, with the only difference that the ones supposed to bind people can be ignored because of their ability to choose what to do. They cannot, however, be ignored with impunity. Religion always takes the view that transgressors will be brought to book. This again makes it clear why one should act according to nature: to do so is to fulfil the purpose for which one was designed, and to act against it is ~ risk bringing down the wrath of God. As Betty Friedan pointed out,[23] the nineteenth-century people who called those women wanting equality with men 'unnatural monsters' thought that the subservience of women was God-given, and that to want anything else would bring down punishment in the form of the destruction of the home. This is a sort of view which certainly still remains. It appears in such ideas as that if God had meant us to fly he would have given us wings. As Mill said,[24]

the charge of presumptuously attempting to defeat the designs of Providence still retains enough of its original force to be thrown in as a makeweight along with other objections when there is a desire to find fault with any new exertion of human forethought and contrivance.

Some trace of it even remains among people who certainly do not accept it literally; something suspiciously like it seems to underlie a feminist version of the wings and flying theme which appeared in a letter to the BBC: 'If women had been meant to wear bras, they would have been born with them.'

Finally there is a third idea, perhaps closer to modern feeling than either of the previous two, though less well rooted in tradition. It is connected with the Aristotelian theory that everything has a specific nature which it strives to fulfil; that as long as the essential parts of its nature are unfulfilled the individual has an active tendency to fulfil them, and the more it succeeds in doing that, the more perfect an individual of that sort it is. Putting it that way shows the connection of the Aristotelian view with some current ideas, but as it is most misleading as an account of Aristotle on nature (much too large a subject to embark on here), it is perhaps best to see the current view as one in its own right. It is roughly that what is natural for something is that which is in accord with its nature in the sense of being conducive to its well-being, encouraging it to flourish. There is no doubt that this is what is in the minds of many feminists when they talk about the present state of society as one which is not natural for women: it is inconsistent with the nature of women in the sense that it leaves them unhappy and unfulfilled, and opposes deeply rooted characteristics which cannot be opposed without damage. And once again, if this is what is meant by 'natural', it is clear why the natural is a thing to be recommended. Making people happy and fulfilled needs no complicated justification.

We have then, as a result of this investigation, a clear idea of why the natural is thought to be good. To do what is natural according to any of these three interpretations is to bring about something which is recognizably good and desirable. And here we come to the crux of the whole problem of the natural. According to the definitions of the natural given at the beginning of this section, those of Hume, Mill and Moore, once you had chosen which definition of the many to go by it was more or less clear *how* to act naturally: you might act normally, or unthinkingly, or like an animal, or whatever. What was not at all clear was *why* you should do anything of the sort. According to the three accounts of nature which have just been given, on the other hand, it is not in the least difficult to understand *why* one should act in accordance with nature, but we have the opposite problem. It is not at all obvious *how* to do what is according to nature, and therefore good. We can tell only by trial and error what is going to upset the balance of nature, or bring down the wrath of God, or make people frustrated and unhappy. The only way to discover what is unnatural is to act unnaturally and discover that catastrophe follows. But then it is of course too late, at least for that occasion.[25] In other words, the two kinds of account of what is natural *cannot be brought together*.

This conclusion is not just accidentally true of the accounts of the natural which have been illustrated here: it is generally true. There is no way of making the two ends meet. We can, if we want to, give an account of the natural which makes it clear how to act naturally; we can call natural whatever is least thought about, or least interfered with by people, or something like that. But in that case the natural course of action cannot be guaranteed, or even thought likely, to produce the good things we want. On the other hand if we define the natural in terms of its good consequences, so that the natural state of things is the one in which people are happy, or the environment remains in decent order, or some such thing, it is very far from obvious what to do to achieve it. But it is there that the whole lure of arguing with the natural lies: *it looks like a short cut.* As long as the definitions can by carelessness or calculated sleight of hand be kept sufficiently vague, it can be made to appear that there is some definite way in which we can achieve all the good things we want, without having to go through all the complications of trial and error to find out how to produce them.

Of course there is no such short cut, but people will persist in believing that there is. Consider, for instance, all the recent propaganda in favour of the naturalness of breast feeding. To say that this is natural in the most obvious sense is to say, more or less, that it is what is done by apes and primitive people; what we would be doing if we had not invented bottles and milk substitutes. But the subtle implication of this is that breast feeding is bound to be best for both mother and baby. Now of course there is no doubt at all that it usually is the best thing for both, at least in the present state of technology: there is everything to be said for breast feeding whenever possible. The important question here, however, is whether it is good *because* it is in this sense natural: whether its being natural is enough to show that it is good.

The answer is, of course, that it is nothing like enough, as can be shown very easily. In the first place, if we thought the natural (primitive) was always good, we ought to reject all advances of science as dangerous, which of course we do not. People who approve of breast feeding 'because it is natural', for instance, hardly ever fail to make full use of modern hygiene and medicine: it would not occur to most of them to follow apes and Stone Age women when it came to treating the baby's illnesses, which they should do, if they really thought the natural was always best. Then again, although breast feeding is usually best, it is not always so. The mother may not have enough milk, or may suffer from mastitis, and nature's way in situations like that is just to let the baby die, or leave the mother in pain. For them the natural is far from best. (The only reason breast feeding is usually good is that nature has had a long period of natural selection in which to develop breast milk by trial and error. The errors were the babies who died. Would they have been best off with the natural, if anything else had been available? Nature's aims, in so far as it can be said to have any, have to do with reproduction, not the prevention of suffering.) And finally, although breast milk may generally be best now, there is not the slightest reason to presume that it always will be, let alone that it *must* be. Science makes advances all the time, and it is quite possible that one day we may find an artificial way of feeding which results in bonnier, bouncier babies than any mother's milk could produce. It is not inconceivable. And then mothers' milk, the natural thing, would no longer be best.

Anyone who wants to argue that breast feeding is best *because* it is natural must argue that the natural is always (or at least usually) best, and that cannot be done. Even people who claim that they think nature can do no wrong refute themselves by implication every hour of every day. If we know that breast milk is usually best, it is by ordinary, laborious investigation, comparing the natural thing with all the alternatives (by all means making use of arguments about natural selection where appropriate). *We know it is good because we have found it to be so, not because it is natural.* Anyone who thinks we know it by a direct inference from 'natural' to 'good' is in great danger of keeping mistakenly to the natural in other contexts, where investigation would show beyond any doubt that it was not best at all.[26]

Another rather similar example of mistaken arguing from the natural came from a women's group called the Essex Road Health Group, talking on a BBC broadcast. They were arguing that the menopause should not be treated hormonally because, as they said, the menopause was natural and 'happened to all women', and 'nature never does anything without a reason'.

Now of course the menopause is natural in several rather obvious senses of the word: it does, as the group said, happen to all women; it is inevitable, it is not a product of society, and so on. However, the women concerned seemed to think that that on its own was enough to show that the menopause *could not of itself have any bad consequences*, so that any there were must come from elsewhere. They thought that the discomfort of the menopause must, since the menopause was natural, come from the social situation of women.

However, there is no reason whatever to presume any such thing. Even if evolution had good reason for producing the menopause (a matter about which there are many theories) we have no reason to presume that it would necessarily have got rid of menopausal discomfort. However miserable it may have been for individuals there is no reason *a priori* to presume that biological fitness would have been enhanced by the elimination of the discomfort; the least of evolution's concerns must be the sufferings of animals past their reproductive years. Of course it *might* be possible to show that menopausal discomfort was socially induced, but that would need a proof of its own. There is no justification whatever for presuming that because the menopause is natural in the sense of being primitive, inevitable, or whatever, it is also in accord with the nature of women *in the very different sense* of being congenial to them. The consequence of a blind faith that menopausal discomfort must be socially induced might be to condemn generations of women to unnecessary misery while endless experiments were made with social circumstances, all to no avail because the symptoms had absolutely nothing to do with society. This sort of arguing from the natural is an unmitigated menace. If the people who use the arguments come to the right conclusions, it is entirely by accident and for the wrong reasons.[27]

And finally, another line of the same sort, commonly issuing from the anti-feminist camp, is the argument that it is *natural* for women to have children, and therefore if we encourage them to concentrate their attention elsewhere they will only be unhappy and frustrated. The mistake is the same. When we say it is natural for women to have children all we mean is that primitive women do and that we do unless we take care to keep men at bay or put ourselves on the pill. However, that has nothing whatever to do with the question of whether being without children will leave us frustrated through the dissatisfaction of some deeply rooted instinct. As a matter of fact I can see no reason to presume that women must have an instinct to have children. Presumably our evolution would not have got far without our having both a sex drive and an instinct to look after the children once they arrived, but since it was so long before people discovered that there was any connection between sex and children it is hard to see what an instinct *to have children* could have been. But, once again, even if we could prove that women had an instinct to have children which would leave them frustrated if left unfulfilled, the proof would have to be a separate one. It cannot be made in a simple transition from one sense of 'natural' ('what would happen in a jungle') to another ('what makes women satisfied').

These are decisive examples, but once the issue is made clear a whole wasteland of half-formulated ideas of the same sort comes into view, showing that even when the confusion has no clearly definable consequences it is often nevertheless there, lurking in the background to leap out when it gets the chance. There are hints throughout feminism in tones of voice and turns of phrase. Read any account, for instance, of the (supposed) early existence of matriarchies, primitive communal child care, or the (again supposed) use of ornament in early society only for ceremonial purposes and not for attracting men, and see whether it is possible to resist the view that the feminists who are recommending these sorts of thing are implicitly backing their recommendations with the suggestion that these things are natural in the sense of being early or primitive. Or conversely, watch for the subtle tones of disapproval whenever the suggestion appears that some characteristic or convention or social structure is a product of society, and not the sort of thing you would find among apes. It is often hard to pin down, because as usual there are generally other things which might be meant, but there is no doubt about the pervasiveness of the idea. It is therefore most important to make the position clear. As long as the natural and its associated confusions remain in the air, feminists may mistakenly pursue what is in some sense natural, but is not in the least natural in the sense of being congenial to the nature of women, and likely to make them happiest.

6 · ESCAPING THE TRAP

This is not a complete philosophical account of the natural, but that does not matter for our purposes because what it does do is provide an adequate formula for dealing with the natural whenever it rears its head in argument. It always appears as a powerful weapon, but as long as we understand why it has that appearance it is not difficult to deal with. Let us review the situation.

In the first place, the meaning of 'natural' is variable, and the situation is probably much worse than Hume, Mill and Moore suggested when they said that the word had many meanings, and so was multiply ambiguous. It seems far more likely that the way to analyse the concept is along the lines first outlined by J. L. Austin in his discussion of 'real', [28] and later extended by Roland Hall to include a good many other words, which he called 'excluders'. [29] Very roughly, 'natural' seems to work something like this. It has a general meaning of 'without intervention', 'without inter-ference', 'without influence' or some such thing, but it does not mean without *any* influence – totally uninfluenced. Whenever the word is used it implies the absence of *some particular* influence or range of influences, and what that influence is *is determined entirely by the intentions of the speaker in a particular context*. This means that what is to count as natural or unnatural is entirely context dependent, and therefore that the list of meanings of the word 'unnatur-al' is as long as the list of things which might be considered interferences in some context or other. In other words, it is endless. It is far worse than a simple matter of ambiguity or even multiple ambiguity, where there is a finite list of meanings which could be dealt with in turn. This is why it would have been hopeless to tackle the problem of the natural by considering all the contexts in which it appeared in feminism: there is no limit to them. On the other hand, of course, this is one of the reasons why the natural can be made so much use of as an argument against the unwary; there is nothing whatever which cannot be counted as natural or unnatural in some context or other, and the ingenious manipulator of the idea can therefore prove anything at all to be unnatural, at will. If you are clever or muddleheaded enough you can even juggle with several meanings at once, and contrive to show that what your opponents want is unnatural while claiming the things you approve of are natural, even though they may, in fact, be unnatural according to precisely the same criterion.

The second thing which makes the natural such an invaluable tool of argument, apart from its infinite versatility, is the fact that the good connotations of 'natural' are so deeply entrenched that once anything has been said to be natural there is usually no need to produce a separate argument for its being good. That is taken for granted. If someone says 'natural' the audience just presumes 'good'. If they disagree with what is being said they are more likely to argue about whether the thing in question is really natural than about whether something agreed to be natural is in fact good. (At the beginning of the discussion of the natural in this chapter I suggested that this was what feminists often did.)

For these two reasons the idea of the natural is one of the most useful means ever devised for establishing moral points, and can be used by the skilful against the uncautious in almost any context to establish anything at all. As Kate Millet said, 'The natural is all too often a convenient gadget which can be directed at random to justify class, absolutism or any other system',[30] which is, as Mill said, 'ready to break out whenever . . . the native promptings of the mind have nothing to oppose them but reason'.[31]

None of this is meant to imply that whenever people talk about what is natural they are necessarily confused, let alone practising calculated deception. It is not even meant to suggest that the idea of the natural ought to be removed forthwith from our conceptual system, as nothing more than a trap. However, there are morals to be drawn. The main one is that whenever a feminist finds that someone attacks her ideas with the accusation that whatever she is recommending is unnatural, the last thing she should do is carry on the debate in those terms and say that it is not she but her opponent who is wanting what is unnatural. Talk about the natural can *always* be translated into propositions which are unambiguous and discussable. When people claim that they want something because it is natural we can ignore that issue altogether and concentrate on the manageable questions of what they want to achieve (it may not be something we want at all) and why they think that the method they propose will lead to it. Those are clear areas for debate, and to keep to them avoids the possibility of having a good line of argument thrown awry by someone else's treachery or confusion.

7 · DIVERGENCE

There is one final aspect of the morass of ideas about the natural which deserves comment. It concerns the debate about whether men and women should be brought up to be the same or different in nature, and whether they should do the same or different kinds of work.

At the basis of all the confused ideas people have about the natural is the view that there is for each individual a proper line of growth and position in the world which should not be interfered with, and that to know the nature of something is to know what that proper line of growth is. Traditionally it was thought that men and women were different by nature, from which it was inferred that they ought to be brought up to be different: if we tried to interfere in this natural arrangement we should bring down all kinds of disasters on ourselves.

Feminists, having found out that men and women were not nearly so different from each other at birth as people had always supposed, hastened to reverse the traditional conclusion. Men and women were much the same by nature after all, so they should, therefore, be brought up to be much the same. However, we shall never rout the enemy completely if we attack only the conclusions and leave the premises unscathed, and if feminists take this kind of line they are doing exactly the same as the traditionalists. Even though the two camps reach different conclusions, both are making the fundamental mistake of thinking that if you know the nature of something (what it is like) you *ipso facto* know what is natural for it (what it ought to be like, how it should develop).

This is false. As was said earlier, to know what women are like (or what anything else is like) is to know only about *potential*. It is to know such things as that *if* you prick them, they will bleed, *if* you poison them, they will die, or *if* you wrong them, they will be revenged. It is not to know that any of these things should or should not be done to them. If we know that men and women are different at birth that does not show that they should be kept different; if they are more or less the same that is not enough to show that they should be kept the same. Why should we not increase or decrease the differences? If women are born weaker than men, why should we leave them that way or make them still weaker? Why should we not try to make them as strong as men, or perhaps even make them stronger by deliberately weakening men? Facts and values, once again, are separate things.

However, we can take the matter further than that. Throughout this discussion we have taken certain values for granted: we have accepted without question that it is good to avoid the wrath of the gods and the revenge of inanimate nature, and to make people happy and fulfilled. But even *given* these value judgments, it *still* does not follow that knowledge of people's natures is enough to determine uniquely how they should develop and what kind of society they should live in. *It is a mistake to think that there can be only one route to the best possible state of affairs*, or that there is a single best state of affairs at all, even once you have settled what your values are. Why should there be? It is perfectly possible in principle that if, for instance, a woman has several talents which cannot all be developed, she might be made equally happy by the development of any one of them, or indeed by being kept in a sheltered environment where she had no thought of using any talents at all. Knowledge of her nature and a desire to make her happy may not in themselves be enough to determine which direction she should be encouraged to take. For this reason, whether men and women are born the same, or slightly different, or very different, we have the choice in any case of trying to make them more different, or less different, or of keeping the differences more or less the same. Furthermore, whichever of these general policies we decide to adopt, there are still endless choices about the forms those samenesses and differences might take. In principle any number of them may be compatible with the greatest happiness for men and women, or with maximizing whatever else we regard as most desirable.

Of course it is impossible to prove that there really do exist totally different possible states of things which are all equally good according to whatever set of values we adopt. However, whether or not it is true that there are, all we need for practical purposes is the lesser point that even if there is only one ideal state of things, we cannot possibly know *that* there is or *what* it is. And it is certainly not a thing to be gathered by studying how alike men and women intrinsically are, because even if they are born more or less alike, the greatest happiness for both might, for all we know, come of their being made radically different from each other.

There are several conclusions to be drawn from all this. The first is that it is necessary to throw out the idea, which has plagued our culture for far too long, that the road to salvation is clear for all to see, and that anyone who does not must be blind or pernicious. No feminist is entitled to presume that someone who does not go along with a particular political programme is against women; feminism may legitimately take many different forms. You do not have to be a traditional sexist to think that there is something to be said for different sexual conventions, or be determined to oppress women if you do not much take to the idea of test-tube babies. If feminism is a movement to find justice for women it is not equivalent to, for instance, a wish to eliminate or even minimize sexual differences, even though that might be one way to go about it. To forget that is to invite bitterness and contention, and to see enemies where there are none.

The second point is related to that one. There is a tendency for political controversy to run along two lines; for disputes to be either about matters of moral principles, or about matters of fact. The usual form of political debate is to try to show that your opponent is either steeped in moral turpitude or ignorant about the facts (or, of course, preferably both). However, these are not the only areas in which scope for disagreement lies. Even if we had our moral principles completely worked out and agreed on, and even if we knew everything there was to know about the state of the world, we might *still* disagree about what to do, because our preferences were different from each other's. Preferences do come into questions of political programmes, and since they may decide questions where all other matters are equal there is nothing intrinsically bad about being concerned with them. We must be able to defend preferences without feeling the need to argue that what we prefer is better in some *other* way (better principled or more true to the facts) than what other people prefer. For that reason I shall not hesitate to defend my own preferences in some parts of this book.

The main conclusions of the chapter are these. We need to know about the nature of the world we are dealing with, to as great an extent as possible, in order to proceed with our programme of change with any hope of success. Nevertheless, the knowledge we have of the natures of things *in no way dictates* what use should be made of the raw material. It does not dictate our values, and even within a set of values there may be enormous scope for different routes to be taken. There may actually be several possible states of the world which are equally good. Even if there are not, however, we cannot know that there are not. The choice in theory is bewildering.

It is likely to remain so, and probably we shall never be able to do much better than set out on promising-looking paths and hope for the best. However, we can narrow the choice a little by going further into a discussion of moral principles. So far it has been presupposed that it is important to care about people's happiness. That seems beyond question, but now the very different and more difficult ideas of freedom and justice must be assessed, and looked at from the point of view of feminism.

3

Enquiries for Liberators

I · THE ULTIMATELY WORTHWHILE

The principal complaint of feminists, reduced to its barest essence, is that men have contrived by various means to get for themselves an inordinately high share of the good things of life, leaving women with a corresponding disproportion of the bad. This means that one of the most important tasks confronting feminists is to work out principles of how the good and bad things in the world should be distributed among the people in it, and so make it clear how much women ought to have. However, there is a limit to the value of establishing what it is for things to be shared out fairly if it is not clear which things are and which are not worth having, and before going on to the question of distributive justice it is necessary to decide which things are good and bad in themselves. It is not possible to maximize the good and share it out fairly without first deciding what things are to count as good.

There are some things about whose goodness or badness there can be no doubt. No reasonable person, for instance, can regard suffering, frustration and distress as anything but intrinsically bad, to be avoided except when they have to be endured as a means to good. One thing all feminists must want is to lessen women's unhappiness. However, there are other things whose value is nothing like so clear, and one of the most important of these is freedom, or liberty.[1] People differ in the value they give it, and this has far-reaching repercussions for their politics.

Freedom is a central issue in feminism, since even in those parts of the movement which do not actually call themselves

'Women's Liberation' it is generally agreed that freedom for women is one of the things which must be achieved. That, however, is probably as far as the consensus goes. The area is full of confusions and talk at cross purposes. This chapter is intended to sort out the central questions and provide some answers.

2 · KINDS OF FREEDOM

The first thing to do is to point out that there is one part of the ordinary English use of the word 'free' which is a very clear distraction from the main issue, and a good deal of confusion will be avoided if it is removed from the path at the outset. This concerns the distinction between being free (*simpliciter*), and being free *from* something.

Whenever something calling itself a liberation movement appears on the political scene, as happens not infrequently, it is natural to presume that it is trying to get for the people it wants to liberate an increase in something rather like a possession: they are to be given more liberty rather as they might be given more money, or more health care, or more holidays. However, this is not necessarily so, and we have to move cautiously. To liberate people is usually to free them *from* something or other, and in order to say with perfect linguistic propriety that you want to free people from something, nothing more is necessary than your intending to get rid of something which you take to be bad for them. It does not matter whether they agree with you about the badness of the thing you want to remove. Feminists may talk of liberating women from wifehood, even though a woman so liberated against her will might put the matter very differently and say that she had been *deprived* of the possibility of being supported by a husband. In principle you could claim to liberate people from absolutely anything as long as you disapproved of whatever it was, and any reforming movement can with only the slightest ingenuity formulate its aims so as to present itself as a liberation movement. If we had no more than the name to go by, we could not tell whether something calling itself Women's Liberation was trying to free women from the power of men, or conventional stereotypes, or political responsibility, or the lure of the unfeminine, or even the blandishments of the feminist movement. Unexplained, it could be anything whatever.

What is quite certain is that there is no necessary connection whatever between a movement's wanting to free people *from* something and its being concerned to give them an increase in some commodity which could legitimately be described as freedom. It is *possible* for the two intentions to be combined: if you free people from something which restricts their freedom, such as a tyrannical government, you certainly increase their freedom in doing so. However, there are all kinds of cases where you might want to free people *from* something without wanting to increase their freedom (*simpliciter*) at all. A liberation movement might even have the aim of the monkeys in Thurber's fable, who came to liberate the bears from freedom and the dangers of choice.[2] If you think that freedom is a bad or dangerous thing, you can quite properly aim to free people from it. Whenever a liberation movement appears on the horizon, therefore, supporters of freedom should look closely before getting carried away with the idea of liberty and joining in.

The discussion of liberty in this chapter is not concerned with the matter of freeing people *from* various evils, because whether liberation from something is good depends on the logically prior question of whether the thing they are to be liberated from is really bad. The problem here is to define, and consider the value of, freedom as a possession.

3 · FREEDOM AS A POSSESSION

Obviously the first thing to do is to establish what freedom in this sense of the word actually is. However, there is some danger in putting it that way, since it gives the impression that there already is something determinate whose nature is waiting to be discovered by the careful enquirer. This is not the right way to look at it at all. 'Free' is a word which often has a precise meaning to be discovered *in particular contexts*, but take it out of context, give it a capital letter and try to establish what Freedom in general is, and the matter is quite different. In fact the connotations of 'free' seem to vary so much from one context to another, to the extent even of conflicting with each other, that it is probably quite hopeless to try to find any general meaning of the word which will not be obviously inadequate or even wrong in some ordinary contexts. This is no doubt why over the years philosophers have produced so many different accounts of the nature of freedom.

If the language actually contains no determinate answer to the question of what 'freedom', independently of particular contexts, really means, then the question of *what freedom really is* is one which has no answer. Nevertheless the idea of freedom in general, as a kind of thing which people can gain or lose, is very commonly used. Furthermore, 'freedom' is like 'natural' in having such good connotations that people are only too delighted to take advantage of any confusion to juggle with half a dozen meanings of the word at once in order to confuse their opponents and win political points. The only thing to do, therefore, is to be determined to keep whatever definition is being used clear at all times, never presuming that it must be clear because everybody knows what freedom is.

There are various possible acceptable definitions of freedom, all reflecting various aspects of the context-dependent use of 'free' (and all ignoring some of them). It is necessary here to fix on what seems to be the best of them, defend it, and then decide on the value of freedom *as explained in that particular way*, bearing in mind that if a different explanation is taken, the assessment of the value of freedom may have to change.

The best account seems to be this. Roughly speaking, freedom can be explained by saying that *people are free to the extent that they are in control of their own destinies, and not controlled by other people or other alien forces.* This definition, it should be stressed, makes freedom not a thing which you either have or have not, but something of which you have more or less. Feminists think that men have too much, at the expense of women, who have correspondingly little.

Anyone who regards this as a satisfactory account of freedom, or at least is prepared to accept it as the one which is to be used from now on in this book, can leave the rest of this section and go straight on to the next. However, there are people who do not find this definition acceptable, and for such people something had better be said in defence of this definition before going any further.

The reason for some people's objection to explaining freedom as the ability to control one's own destiny is that it seems to draw no distinction between freedom and power, and to our ordinary way of thinking, as the philosopher Thomas Hobbes pointed out, there is a considerable difference between the two. Our inability to do various things we should like to do may come from lack of freedom, but equally it may not. A bird in a cage is not free to fly, but in our case the inability to fly has nothing to do with an absence of *freedom*. No one is stopping us from flying, it is just that we can't do it.

If the way feminists use the word 'freedom' does not take account of this, it means the feminist position is open to attack. For instance, it is a common feminist complaint that women are not (or at least have not been through most of history) free to control their own reproduction, partly because there has never been enough research into contraception, and partly because even when contraceptives have been in existence they have often been expensive or difficult to get. Someone like Hobbes, however, would presumably argue that it was quite misleading to say that because of these things women were not *free* to control their reproduction. Even if women are justified in asking for more contraceptives, he would be likely to say, feminists are cheating in describing their demand as a demand for freedom. They are not asking for the removal of a constraint which prevents their doing what they otherwise could have done, but assistance to make them capable of doing what they otherwise could not do. And as Isaiah Berlin said, 'Everything is what it is: liberty is liberty, not equality or fairness or justice or culture. . . Nothing is gained by a confusion of terms.'[3] That is quite right, of course, and if we want to talk about freedom in contexts like this one, where it seems more natural to talk about ability or power, we must justify doing so.

In general when people complain about limitations on freedom the complaints arise, as has been suggested already, within particular contexts. The complaint is that other people[4] are coming between them and *what they otherwise could have done*. Now what anyone 'otherwise could have done' is clearly a thing which is heavily context dependent, because what you can do at any time depends not only on your own intrinsic abilities, but also on the situation you are in. Whether you are able to go by bicycle from A to B, for instance, depends not only on your ability to ride a bicycle, but also on whether there is a working one available and what the terrain is like. Someone who comes and punctures your tyres as you are setting off to B normally interferes with your freedom, because *but for* that interference you could have done it. But if the bicycle had its chain missing, or there were an unbridged river between A and B, having your tyres punctured would not interfere with your freedom to cycle there because you could not have done it anyway. Whether a particular interference does restrict your freedom to do something depends on whether you could have done whatever it was *but for that interference*. Complaints of infringements of freedom, occurring as they usually do within specific contexts, always refer to what could otherwise have been done *within that context*.

However, things are very much more difficult when we try to find a *general*, *context-free* meaning for the word 'free'; a meaning which allows us to say without any reference to a particular context how free someone is. When

people say things about freedom in general they usually try
to keep the idea that interference with freedom is a positive
thing; an active intervention in what otherwise would have
been the case. But it should be obvious from the previous
paragraph that explaining freedom in general in such a way
as this just cannot get off the ground, because there is no
way of saying in general, out of context, what people could
or could not have done but for a particular interference.
Once again, what people can do depends not only on their
intrinsic abilities but also on environment, and even intrinsic
ability depends òn earlier, formative environment. But if we
have no general standard for what someone can do uninter-
fered with, there is no general criterion either for what is to
count as interference. If we are to have a *general* account of
what it is to increase or lessen freedom, the criterion of
active interference, which does well enough in particular
contexts, is one which has to go.

However, this is not too serious as long as it is clear. We
cannot expect to carry all the connotations of a context-
dependent word over into a context-free use. And anyway,
another problem about trying to keep the idea that you
infringe someone's freedom only when you actively hinder
and not when you fail to help is that it takes no account of
another thing which is certainly an important ingredient in
the concept of freedom: the idea that *your freedom is
diminished when other people's desires come between you
and your desires*. The effects other people can have on your
desires are not limited to direct prohibitions and forcible
interventions, but extend to the whole man-made environment in which we live. If when we complain of lack of
freedom we are objecting to the fact that someone else's will
is getting between us and our desires, we are not trying to
say that people are preventing us from doing what we could
have done in a state of nature. We can say that our freedom
is curtailed if the social background, against which we are
working, is arranged to their benefit rather than ours. To
quote Berlin again:[5]

It is argued, very plausibly, that if a man is too poor to afford something on which there is no legal ban – a loaf of bread, a journey round the world, recourse to the law courts – he is as little free to have it as he would be if it were forbidden him by law. . . It is . . . because I believe that my inability to get a given thing is due to the fact that other human beings have made arrangements whereby I am, whereas others are not, prevented from having enough money with which to pay for it, that I think myself a victim of coercion or slavery.

If we are going to have a general idea of freedom as a state in which other people's desires do not interfere with our own, it has to take account of the fact that we could have had things more to our liking if other people had made different social arrangements. To the extent that these arrangements have been made to the advantage of one group rather than another the second's freedom is curtailed, because its members can do less of what they want to do than they could have done if things had been different. In the case of contraceptives, for instance, we can argue that although in a sense women were free to get contraceptives as long as there were no laws preventing their manufacture or distribution, men as effectively prevented women's getting them by making sure that science was entirely in the control of men as they would have done by making laws. If laws which make contraceptives inaccessible can be said to restrict women's freedom to get them, it would be silly to argue that general social arrangements whose consequences were the same did not restrict in the same way.

The conclusion of this is that the only reasonable way to talk about freedom in general in a social context is this: *your freedom is restricted by society to the extent that different social arrangements might have made it possible to do more of what you wanted.* If society could have made it possible for you to do something but has not, it has to that extent restricted your freedom. This means that *within a social context freedom and power are virtually the same*; the only powers whose lack does not count as a lack of freedom are those which could not have been given by any possible social arrangement.

This has one consequence which must go severely against many people's intuitions about freedom. It is that for you to have the greatest possible freedom it would be necessary for everyone else in the world to become your servant, and totally subordinate their desires to yours: according to this account of freedom as long as you are prevented from doing anything by other people's wishes for themselves, their desires are interfering with what you want to do. Many people, having it fixed in their minds that freedom is a good thing, think that it is a thing which everyone ought to have, and, since no one ought to have unlimited power, the ability to fulfil desires to that extent should not count as freedom. This is the point being made by the people who distinguish between liberty and licence. Licence is, to put it very roughly, too much of what liberty is the right amount of.

That is a fair enough objection, in a way. There is no doubt that the connotations of 'freedom' tend to be good, while those of 'power' are morally neutral or even bad. The account of freedom I have given goes against these intuitions, and we would keep closer to them if we said that freedom was the amount of power to which we were morally entitled. However, as I said at the outset, there seems to be no general account of freedom which does not conflict with some intuitions, and this one also goes against some: For instance, most people would say that to take an axe away from someone who was about to run amok was curtailing liberty even though it was the right thing to do, and we all talk about depriving criminals of their liberty when they are sent to prison, even when we approve of the punishment.

Since, therefore, there seems to be no context-free account of freedom which fits intuitions in all contexts, I propose to keep to the one which I have outlined. It has the very great advantage of allowing us to separate the questions of how much freedom we have and how much we ought to have, which are run together by the account of freedom as the right amount of power. However, the other one could have been taken. The important thing is to be clear about the definition, and not confuse arguments by slipping from one to the other.

4 · A DEFENCE OF LIBERTY

Here, then, is an acceptable account of freedom as a possession: you are free to the extent that other people's desires do not come between you and your own. Another, apparently rival, account will appear later in the chapter, but for now we shall concentrate on this one. If this is freedom, what is its value?

One obvious and common defence of freedom is that it is a means to happiness. People who approve of freedom say that it leads to happiness because we are made unhappy if we know that other people control what we do, or because we know better than anyone else what we want and will be made happiest by being left to decide for ourselves, or because freedom leads to strength and self-reliance which in turn lead to happiness. Other people are doubtful about these arguments, and say that, on the contrary, too much freedom makes people unhappy. People do not really know what is best for them, it is argued, so they may be happier if other people make the decisions. Midge Decter, for instance, in her arguments against Women's Liberation, says that what is making women dissatisfied is not a lack of freedom but a surfeit of it.[6]

All these arguments are of course important, but here they are beside the point. Here the issue is not whether freedom is an effective means to some *other* end like happiness, but whether it is good *as an end in itself*. Can we argue that freedom is good irrespective of whether it leads to happiness or anything else we value? And if so, how valuable is it in comparison with these other things?

In some sense there can be very little argument on subjects like this one, because with questions of ultimate values there does not seem to be any common ground for discussion between people who disagree. If people really, in the last analysis, value different things, there is nothing more to be said. However it is possible to do something not unlike arguing. It does seem possible to make it clear by illustration that a great many people, whether they realize it or not, do in fact value freedom as an end in itself, and that many value it even more than happiness.

It is probably true in some broad sense to say that everyone seeks happiness and avoids pain (taking both those words in the most general possible sense, where happiness is any pleasing, enjoyable state, and pain is any state which is inherently unpleasant). However, most people have different attitudes to the desirability of happiness from those they have to the undesirability of pain. People wish to avoid *all* pain, except where it is seen as a necessary means to an important end. Pain is always regarded as bad in itself, and looked at on its own is always to be avoided. However, the same is not true of happiness. People want it, certainly, but they do not all want happiness no matter what form it takes, in the way that they wish to avoid all unnecessary pain. Many people want to achieve happiness only through certain routes to which they are committed, and would rather fall short of it while pursuing it in a way they wanted than attain a sort they did not want. This is something people can test for themselves by a few thought experiments.

Suppose, for instance, you were an outstandingly gifted but miserably neurotic artist or musician, and someone offered you a drug which would make you happy, but would result in your losing all your ability. There are already drugs along these lines, but we are to think of one so entirely effective that once having taken it the patient would not even regret having lost the desire or ability to compose or paint. Suppose also that you had complete faith in its efficacy, and in the intentions of the person who offered it. Would you take it? Some people would no doubt be very happy to, but there must be many who in such a situation would rather remain unhappy than achieve happiness at the cost of losing a skill they valued far more than any prospect of happiness.

Suppose, again, you lived in a country with a political régime you disliked intensely, with no way of escaping and not much hope of making things more to your liking. Suppose also that the government had a programme of 're-education' which you believed would be completely effective, and which would make you entirely happy with the political situation afterwards. Would you be willing to undergo this programme? Many people would certainly not. They would rather remain unhappy than be so radically changed. Or suppose that you were very dissatisfied with your life as it was. Would you welcome the opportunity (to take a classic example) to become a satisfied pig? Again, probably not.

Of course these thought experiments are all rather artificial. They presuppose impossibilities, and anyway are not specific enough: whether we should be willing to become satisfied pigs would probably depend a good deal on the degree of our unhappiness as human beings. Nevertheless, the arguments are useful because they do suggest that to many people there are things which are more important than happiness.

So far, of course, this does not prove that anyone prefers *freedom* to happiness because the discussion has only been about which of two things we should take if we were in a position to choose, and as long as there is a question of choice some freedom is built into the example. All this shows is that there are occasions where people would choose to cling to what might be called their identities, rather than lose them for the sake of happiness. No doubt they would like happiness as well, but given the necessity of choice, happiness might well be abandoned first. However, it is possible to look at the question of freedom by considering similar cases which involve other people.

Why is it, for instance, that so many people object to Soviet dissidents' being put in psychiatric hospitals? Of course there are several reasons. We may not think the 'treatment' will work, and we may not like the system the patients' minds are being changed to fit. However, even supposing we did approve of the political system, and supposing we did believe that after treatment the dissidents would fit happily into Russian society and regard their former activities and attitudes as absurd, would we then approve of the practice? Probably not. We might be happy for people to be offered such treatment if they wanted it, but still think that they should be allowed to choose for themselves whether they would rather be altered and made happy, or remain unhappy but still themselves. And if we think that it is more important to give people this choice than to force happiness on them, it means we are in favour of freedom, and regard it as more important than happiness.

There are many other examples of this sort of attitude. For instance, most of us would be shocked by this advertisement described by Sheila Rowbotham:[7] 'There was a picture of a young mother with a pram in front of a big block of flats and the heading "She can't change her environment but you can change her mood with Serenid-D" .' There are all kinds of reasons for being upset about putting people on happiness drugs, including being afraid of side effects and long-term consequences. Nevertheless, part of the objection is to the idea of making women happy *without fulfilling their desires*. If we were concerned only with happiness for people we should not worry about putting them on effective happiness drugs. If happiness is all that matters there is nothing intrinsically wrong with brainwashing, or forcible medication, or giving people sedatives and tranquillizers instead of coping with their emotional problems. Most of us do care about allowing people to determine the course of their own lives, rather than having other people make them happy in ways they do not want. Since there can hardly be a feminist in existence who would regard it as an acceptable solution to women's problems that someone should invent some kind of medication or special process of re-education which would make women happy in their present lot, but had to be administered against their wills, we must think that most feminists value freedom more than happiness for women. The firm feminist rejection of male paternalism comes not only through the recognition that men's apparent concern for women's well-being is by some curious coincidence remarkably well adapted to the interests of men. Even if men's dominance were wholly good for women, we should still reject its being forced on them. As Kant said, 'paternalism is the worst despotism imaginable'. And as Mill said, 'the only purpose for which power can be rightfully exercised over any member of a civilized community, against his will, is to prevent harm to others. His own good, either physical or moral, is not a sufficient warrant.'[8]

There is probably no way of arguing with any feminist who disagrees with all this, as doubtless some must. However, the principle of freedom will be taken as fundamental to feminism throughout this book, and where it produces statements with which feminists disagree, at least it will be obvious where the disagreement stems from. Freedom is being taken as a fundamental good in its own right, and a thing of which we should, therefore, all have as much as possible. How much each individual should have when the claims of other people are taken into consideration is a question of distributive justice, the subject of the next chapter.

5 · INNER FREEDOM

Two main propositions have been argued for in the previous two sections. One is that we are free to the extent that we can do as we like (which means that we are not properly described as free or not-free, only as more or less free). The other is that freedom, understood in this way, is good in itself. We should all have as much of it as possible, and if our freedom is to be curtailed it is to be for the sake only of other people, not ourselves.

However, we now have to look at the question of whether

feminists do indeed think that freedom is a good thing, and want it for women. If freedom is the ability to fulful one's desires, and if feminists do want it for women, they should surely be trying to make the world as much as possible as women would like it to be. However, it is a most conspicuous fact about some feminists that they seem to include among their aims things which not only *men* find objectionable, but which women do too. There are all kinds of things which women seem to want and have no wish to change, and yet which many feminists apparently want to abolish. Traditional marriage and division of labour seem to be happily chosen by many women; many enjoy making themselves attractive to men, and giving men certain kinds of service in return for being protected by them. Many would rather look after a home and family than do anything else. And many, with the appearance of total freedom, choose to enter beauty competitions (which are watched as willingly by millions more women), or to become striptease artists, 'hostesses' of various sorts, and prostitutes.

Of course, you can argue here that some of these apparently free choices are not very free at all, because choosing the best of a bad lot does not give women what they really want. They probably would not choose to become housewives or prostitutes if better things were readily available to them. There is much truth in that, no doubt, but it does not provide the slightest reason for taking away the best there is and leaving these women with something which must, in their eyes, be still worse. The true liberator can always be recognized by her wanting to *increase* the options open to the people who are to be liberated, and there is never any justification for taking a choice away from a group you want to liberate unless it is demonstrable beyond all reasonable doubt that removing it will bring other, more important, options into existence. To give women freedom we must give them more choice, and then if they really do not want the things they are choosing now, like homes and families, those things will just die out without our having to push them.

Of course there are many feminists who do want to increase the options open to women. Consider, for instance, the programme for the picketing of a Miss America Pageant, which stated 'There will be . . . Lobbying Visits to the contestants urging our sisters to reject the Pageant Farce and join us . . . we do not plan heavy disruptive tactics. . ."[9] That was genuinely liberating. The women entering the competition might not have thought of other routes to success, or they might not have realized that there were groups of people where different things were valued. However that is, or at least seems (it is not always easy to know how literally things are to be taken) a very different matter from the demonstrations at the Miss World competition in London where feminist protestors would apparently have liked to disrupt the whole proceedings. To prevent women from doing what they have chosen to do is not to be concerned with their freedom. Nevertheless, that does seem to be the aim of some feminists.

But that is not the end of the matter. This kind of feminist need not accept yet the accusation that she is not really offering women freedom. In general, when the liberators of women or anyone else take the view that they know better than the beneficiaries of their efforts what should be done for them, they will argue that these people are *conditioned*, and therefore not in a state of mind to be able to choose freely no matter how many alternatives are open to them. *That* is why the liberators sometimes have to make choices on their behalf.

This kind of view certainly has intuitive plausibility about it. However, it does present many problems, and in particular the immediate one of seeming to call for (at least) a modification of the account of freedom so far given. It has been argued so far that an individual's freedom is a function mainly of how many choices there are available. If we are to accept, however, that it may sometimes be acceptable to *restrict* such choices in the name of freedom, on the grounds that the person to be liberated is conditioned and therefore unable to choose, a new element seems to have entered into the idea of liberty. It seems that to be free it is not enough to have a wide range of options open. As well as, or perhaps even instead of, having such options, the free individual must be in a certain state of mind. Freedom must be at least in part an internal thing.

There certainly is no doubt that some such view is widespread in feminism. Perhaps the most striking indication of it is the use of the word 'liberated' when applied to women. To the outsider as well as to the feminist a liberated woman is not one who is free to choose among a great many options, but one who makes *certain kinds of choice*; she is not a woman with a tolerant and helpful husband who encourages her to achieve all her ambitions, but one who would not stand any nonsense from her husband if he tried any.

Now there is indeed a long philosophical tradition of saying that true freedom does not consist in being in an environment which permits you to do as you please, but consists (at least partly, depending on the theory) in being in a particular state of mind. Theories like these still do keep to the basic idea of freedom as the satisfaction of desire, but it is differently interpreted and analyzed. There are innumerable variants on the theme, but we need consider only two, and without too much detail.

The first, and more extreme, is the idea that freedom is contained *entirely* within the mind of the free person, with outside circumstances irrelevant. According to this view you are truly free when your desires have been so adjusted that you desire nothing you cannot get. According to the Stoic idea, for instance, if the slave reaches total tranquillity of mind while the master is in the grips of unrealized desire, the slave is the freer of the two. And in Christianity, the reason for saying that perfect freedom is to be found in the service of God is that once the Christian has achieved a state of mind in which nothing is desired but to do the will of God, that desire need never be unfulfilled: the will of God can be done in any circumstances whatever. This extreme idea of freedom is not much found in feminism, although there are traces of it. The woman who determines that she will no longer care about things which previously obsessed her, like the approval of men, may be looking for freedom in this way. If she ceases to care about what men think she can act to please herself rather than men, and so lessen the extent of her unfulfilled desire.

The second, more moderate, view of internal freedom is one more commonly found in feminism. This idea is that being in the right state of mind is not enough on its own to make you free: to be free you *also* need the kind of freedom we have been discussing in this chapter, which involves being able to do as you like. However, that is not enough on its own, and a necessary condition of your choosing freely is that you should be in the right state of mind before deciding among the options which are open to you. There are all kinds of variants on this idea, but common to them all is something like the view that each individual has a *true self* which should be doing the choosing, but that its activities are obstructed by various contaminants which have got into the person in some way, and which prevent real choice as effectively as obstructions in the environment do. Plato, for instance, thought that there were parts of the soul, and that the lower parts were always trying to pull the highest part from its chosen path. A common idea in religion is that the uncontaminated soul would choose what was good, but that evil powers may take possession of it and force evil choices. More recently, there is the psychoanalytic idea that you cannot be truly free without getting rid of the neuroses which come between yourself and your real desires. Of course, an idea along these lines is very common in feminism. The domination of men has been so complete that the male has entered women's souls, making them choose on behalf of men and against their own interests. That they think themselves free is beside the point: all that shows is how well the work of conditioning has been done.

Now it is quite clear that however difficult all this may be to work out in detail, there is something in it. It is also true that (risky as it may sound) it is *sometimes* reasonable to override people's immediate wishes in the cause of their greater freedom, even when the earlier definition of freedom is taken and we say that people are free to the extent that they can do as they like. For instance, if a friend wanted to achieve something which was very important to her, and we knew beyond any doubt that she was setting about it the wrong way but could not persuade her to change, we might override her immediate wishes because we wanted her to get something which we knew she wanted more. Or again, since freedom is not simply a matter of how many immediate choices there are, but also of *scope* of choice, we might override some trivial choice to make sure that there was a greater range of choices later on. This is always being done in the case of children. Parents are not (necessarily) working against their children's freedom if, for instance, they do not let the children decide which schools they should go to. If a school is so much better than another that it will allow the children far more important choices later on in life, it is in the interests of the children's freedom that they should not be allowed to choose now.

Nevertheless, it is obvious that if we are going to take this sort of line, we have to take *great care*. If women's wishes are to be ignored in the name of their freedom, on the grounds that they are conditioned, it is essential to know exactly what is meant by conditioning, why it is supposed to impair freedom, to what extent it is legitimate to ignore what people want if they are conditioned, and how to distinguish women who are conditioned from the ones who are not. If we do not take care, we run the risk of planning a scheme in which the only freedom women get is the freedom to do what their liberators want them to do.

That is a tempting line anyway. As an early feminist Margaret Rhondda said, 'the passion to decide to look after your fellowmen, to do good to them in your way, is far more common than the desire to put into everyone's hand the power to look after themselves'.[10] The danger becomes intensified a thousand times when you can do this but still be able to convince yourself that you are offering freedom because the whole issue has been obscured under more or less indiscriminate accusations of conditioning. If the idea of conditioning is to be used to enhance freedom, and not as a general device by which a liberation movement can do as it likes in the name of freedom, it must be pinned down more precisely.

6 · CONDITIONING AND THE REAL WOMAN

There is one point which must be made quite clear before going any further. The conditioning which was referred to in the previous section is supposed to be a sort of thing which is *actually a constraint* on a woman; something which comes between herself and her true desires. Now the word 'conditioning' is one which is extremely commonly used in feminism, in all kinds of circumstances, and what must on no account be presumed is that *whenever* the word is used the so-called conditioned desires, attitudes and responses are things which actually do prevent the real woman from fulfilling her real desires.

In feminist contexts the usual ground for making an accusation of conditioning is to point to the social root of the habit of mind in question (which is, of course, always one which is disapproved of). Women want to make themselves beautiful only because society has made them want to; they think that their mission in life is to be mothers because everyone has been drumming it into them since the age of two; they lack ambition because they have been brought up from birth to think that the female is the natural servant of the male and on no account to compete with him. This may all be true. However, to establish that a woman is conditioned in *that* sense of the word is nothing like enough to show that she is conditioned in the very different sense of having something in her personality which gets between herself and the fulfilment of her real desires, and therefore that these environmentally produced characteristics limit her freedom.

The reason why conditioning in the sense of 'coming

from a (disapproved of) social influence' cannot be the same as conditioning in the sense of 'getting in the way of the true woman's desires' is obvious from the discussion of the nature of woman in the last chapter. You cannot distinguish between the woman as she now is and what is supposed to be the 'true' woman by pointing to the way society has shaped her. It is absolutely inevitable that the adult woman should be as she is partly as a result of social influence, and it is a thing we cannot possibly object to unless we are to suggest that people should be sent to grow up among wolves (and anyway there are social pressures even among wolves). We cannot say of social pressures *in general* that they turn the woman into something which is not her true self; on the contrary, they cannot be anything other than a contribution to what she actually is.

Of course we may not *like* the way women are at present, and if we do not we can argue that their upbringing ought to be changed. Very obviously, for instance, feminists are bound to disapprove of any upbringing which is so much at odds with women's intrinsic natures that they are bound to be unhappy. They can also reasonably object to women's being brought up to depend on men in the achievement of what they want, because that is unreliable and their success in life should be more firmly based. They can disapprove of women's being encouraged to see their main aim in life as relationships with men, and all their ambitions directed towards pleasing men in one way or another, because it is undignified and they want women to be dignified. They can say that women ought not to be brought up to confine their interests and activities to domestic matters and concentrate their energies on trivia, because they would prefer them to be well-educated, ambitious and serious-minded. Since there is no neutral way to bring children up (they must be surrounded by influences of one kind or another) we have a good deal of choice about how adults eventually turn out. We certainly could make women other than they are now, and it is not surprising that feminists would like to see a good many changes.

On the other hand, none of this provides any reason at all for saying that women as they are now, with the desires they have now, are not *free*. We may think it a good thing that women should be brought up to be happy, dignified, independent, serious and useful, but, once again, everything is what it is. Happiness is happiness, dignity is dignity, independence is independence: none of these things is freedom. Even though there may be some difficulty about finding a definitive account of freedom there are limits to what we can reasonably decide to adopt, and it really would be travesty of the language (as well as potentially treacherous) to say that people were not free just because we did not like the way they were, or that in making them into something we liked better we should be giving them freedom. We may argue with perfect justice that women are as they are because of social influences, but that is not enough to show that the choices they are making are not their own real choices. And if by 'conditioned' we want to mean 'not in a state to make free choices' we must mean something more than 'influenced by social pressures we disapprove of'.

Of course we can still, if we want to, say that 'conditioned' does just refer to socially induced characteristics in women, rather than aspects of a woman's character which somehow do get in the way of her real desires. However, this is dangerous. The word has now such deeply entrenched connotations of interference with freedom that if we take a definition which does not include those connotations we open the floodgates to mistakes and double dealing. I shall therefore take it that 'conditioning' is properly used only when it does refer to a real restriction on freedom. The problem is, now that we have decided that a woman brought up one way is no less her real self than a woman brought up any other way, to work out what form conditioning might take.

7 · FREEDOM AND CONDITIONING

Since we are trying to distinguish the social pressures which condition a woman from the ones which simply form her character, one obvious starting point is the fact that from the point of view of each individual there is a great difference between different kinds of social pressure. Whereas some are congenial and easily conformed to, others are not: some social pressures push people towards doing things for which they have an intrinsic dislike.

Nevertheless, people often go along even with these, because doing so is less unpleasant than suffering the social consequences of resistance. So a woman who has no natural interest in beauty may make herself as beautiful as she can; or one who is not interested in children may do her best to absorb herself in the concerns of a family; or a woman by nature apt to explore jungles may become a secretary, because that is the feminine thing to do and that way she will get social approval. None of this shows conditioning. The environment is constricting, but nevertheless a woman who makes the best choice among the limited set available to her is behaving perfectly rationally and choosing in her own interest, and as long as she is doing that the only restrictions on her freedom are external, not internal.

However, what happens to these women who go along with uncongenial social pressures when liberators appear on the scene, and suggest to them that the world would be a better place if women did not spend so much time on their appearance, or that children are not necessarily the ideal object of every woman's devotion? Or what happens if they find themselves in a situation where the uncongenial social pressures are beginning to lessen, and following their natural inclinations would bring down less social censure?

If they thoroughly understand the situation in which they have grown up there may be no difficulty. They may instantly join in the campaign to change the things which are alien to their natures, or at least take advantage of any

changes which come about. But this may well not happen.
Usually when children are subjected to pressures in growing
up they do not think separately about what they would like
to do and what adult pressures and encouragements compel
them to do; they just get into habits of doing what produces
the least unacceptable consequences. The result is that when
the situation changes, or when there is some prospect of its
changing, they may not rush to embrace the new but cling
to the habits they have grown up with. Probably they do
not understand that their present preferences came about by
the forcible suppression of their natural (that is, inherent)
inclinations, but even if they do they may well have difficulty in ridding themselves of the habits they have gathered.
These habits may then come between the adults and their
real desires.

A simple analogy can be drawn from an entirely different
context. When you learn to drive you rapidly pick up the
skills of braking and steering, and your responses to various
situations become so automatic that you can usually do the
right thing without thinking. But you may well learn these
habits without knowing much about how braking and steering work, and the result is that the first time you skid you
react in the way you always have reacted when the car moves
too fast in the wrong direction, by braking as hard as
possible and hauling the steering wheel round. The consequences are exactly the opposite of what you want. In order
to avoid the situation in future you have to do two things.
The first is to understand the theory, so that you know
under what conditions the usual methods will and will not
work, and the second is to free yourself of your habitual
actions.

As a motorist you have very definite desires (to move in
particular directions), but you yourself may interfere with
their fulfilment through ignorance, or bad habits, or both.
Much the same may happen with women. Their failure to
understand the situation they are in, and the persistence of
deeply entrenched habits, may get in the way of what they
want to do. And where this happens we can say that a

woman's state of mind is obstructing her desires, *without having to resort to dubious theories about hidden desires in the core of her imaginary real self.*

Failure to understand the nature of the world and the structure of possibilities within it acts against women in all kinds of ways. For instance, many women (if not all) are by nature as inclined as men to seek fame and fortune, but the traditional restricted upbringing of a woman means that in most cases there is only a limited number of forms in which she is capable of casting this ambition: she may think as a matter of course that success for a woman must take the form of being pursued by men, envied by women and renowned for beauty. But if that is the only way in which she can imagine making an impact on the world she is likely to have condemned herself to failure before even setting out. Few women succeed in being renowned for beauty, and anyway beauty does not last. Or she may have more specific ambitions, and look for political power, but may automatically presume that political success for a woman must take the form of being the wife of a politician, and in that case her potential for success is restricted from the start by the casting of her ambitions in a form which sets a low upper limit on possible success. If women squeeze their desires into a conventionally feminine mould they are likely to be doomed to failure from the first. But even if they succeed in escaping the trap of a narrow view of possibilities, femininity may still get in the way. A woman who has the clearest possible plans for a career, and has the capacity to succeed in it, may still fail because of habits of mind which interfere: perhaps she cannot avoid feeling that she ought to take care with her dress, or feeling guilty if she lets her husband do his fair share of the housework, however clearly she may understand the unreasonableness of such feelings. Her ingrained habits of mind prevent the fulfilment of her strongest desires.

This analysis seems to provide a very good account of what it is to be conditioned, and there is no difficulty at all about seeing it as an internal lack of freedom: something about the woman which prevents her from doing as she really wants. One aspect of conditioning is *ignorance*; probably the greatest curtailer of freedom there is, because if someone does not know or fully grasp that the world contains certain possibilities, as far as that person is concerned they might just as well not exist. The other aspect is the inability to change unwelcome aspects of oneself, which is as much a restriction on the fulfilment of desire as the inability to change anything in the outside world. If you want to be more beautiful, or run faster, or be stronger, or be able to charm people, but cannot do whatever it is, you are as curtailed in your desires as you would be through not having money, or influence, or a car, or tools for a trade.

The upshot of all this is that feminists are indeed right in thinking that lack of freedom can be internal: a woman may be in a state where her own mind prevents her from achieving what she really wants (a matter which must not be confused with her mind preventing what she would have wanted if she had been someone else). However, although the comparisons drawn in the last paragraph between internal and external restrictions on freedom do show that freedom can be limited by aspects of the mind, what they also show at the same time is that there is no intrinsic difference between external and internal lack of freedom: they are essentially the same sort of thing. Internal lack of freedom does not consist in being in a special state of mind or having a particular set of desires, only in having within oneself (rather than in surrounding circumstances) the things which prevent fulfilment of desire. This means that, in fact, there is no problem about reconciling the concept of internal freedom with the first account of freedom given in this chapter. The only acceptable interpretation of 'internal freedom' (the only account of it which does not involve calling something quite different by the name of freedom, or presuming that the real woman is something uninfluenced by society) is one which makes it essentially a matter of being unimpeded in one's desires by one's own ignorance and habits. This is important. Once it is clear people will be less

likely to be confused by the vague way in which 'conditioned' is often used, or lured into thinking that if women
have socially induced desires which the liberators disapprove of, they are necessarily not free.

8 · THE ATTACK ON CONDITIONING

When women are really conditioned, their preconceptions
and immediate desires do get in the way of what, in some
perfectly obvious way, they really want. If they are conditioned, therefore, it does seem that other people may be
justified in overriding their immediate desires in order to
produce not what the liberators think they should want, but
what they actually do want.

However, there is an obvious danger in taking this attitude, because the only case in which it would be reasonable
to override a woman's wishes in the name of her freedom
would be where it was absolutely certain that she was
conditioned, and equally certain what she really wanted and
how it could be brought about. And the simple fact of the
matter is that it is virtually impossible even to approach
certainty in cases like this, let alone reach it. It is very hard
to tell when, and to what extent, people are conditioned.

The main reason why this must be so is probably obvious
from what has gone before. The point is that it is quite
impossible to tell conditioned women from unconditioned
ones[11] by their preferences. The pressures on women to be
beautiful and maternal and domestic and deferential to men
have no doubt left in many women habits of mind which
will prevent their ever achieving what they really want to
achieve, but we are not entitled to presume that the pressures
which produced these mental blocks in some women did the
same for all. For the women to whom these pressures were
congenial, as they must have been for some, the desires
produced became their own most basic desires, and not
obstacles to the fulfilment of others. If a woman is interested
mainly in dress or nursery design it is no doubt true to say

that it can be attributed to her background to some extent: if she had been brought up differently she would have had different interests. However, these may be genuinely hers, and ideally suited to her nature. The 'conditioned' responses may be genuinely her own. It is therefore impossible to tell whether or not a woman is conditioned just by knowing about her likes and dislikes, or about her formative influences.

What that means is that the only attack which can be safely mounted against conditioning must be directed to its source. It is too dangerous to try to 'free' women who are regarded as conditioned by forcing them to do what the prevailing feminist ideology presumes they must want, because with that method there is always the danger of ignoring women's real wishes. They may not be conditioned at all. The only thing to do is start from the beginning and try, even at this late stage, to remove the cause of the trouble, and give conditioned women a chance to become unconditioned in a way which runs no risk of damaging those who are not, because it still leaves women to make their own choices.

There are two stages to this process, corresponding to the two aspects of conditioning. The first is to increase understanding of how the present state of things came about and how it works, so that women who have been doing what does not suit them can understand why, and at the same time what alternatives are possible. The second is to make help available to women who decide as a result of this that they do want to change their habits.

There are all kinds of ways in which advances could be made on these two fronts. The key to the first is *diversity*. Women must be exposed to all kinds of new influences and information (in addition to the old, of course, not instead of them) to make them fully aware of the possibilities the world contains. Some people, no doubt, will try to turn the freedom argument against this procedure by saying that if people have new alternatives thrust before them they are *forced to choose*, and that in itself is an infringement of liberty because people ought to have the freedom not to choose if that is what they would prefer. However, that argument cannot possibly work. This is because it is true as a matter of *logic* that people cannot be the ultimate determiners of their own degree of freedom. Whatever anyone chooses to do, that choice comes from among alternatives which already exist, and those alternatives were not themselves chosen. Since, therefore, the ultimate degree of freedom is always out of the hands of the individual we are right to insist that the choice given should always be as great as possible. We cannot, in the name of liberty for women, force them to do anything against their wills or bring about states of society they do not like, but we are bound to give them more knowledge of possibilities.

The second part of the attack on conditioning is to reinforce this for women who do decide that they would like to change their lives by giving them every help in overcoming unwelcome habits of mind: help ranging from the support of other women who understand the position to full-scale psychotherapy. As long as this was directed to bringing about what women themselves wanted, and not to persuading them into something they did not want, it would be genuinely liberating.

Still, however energetically we pursued such a programme, we should have to be hopelessly optimistic to think that we should actually eliminate all existing conditioning as a result of it, and perhaps this seems to justify the wish of some feminists to make a firm attack on the symptoms of conditioning, rather than going in this gentle way for its cause. However much we may want freedom for women, they could argue, even the freedom to stay conditioned, can we allow them this freedom if the price of it is to trap other women in the same bonds? Can we allow a conditioned mother to bring up her daughter in the same way? Surely for the sake of the daughters we ought to be willing to run the risk of attacking directly what we believe to be the mothers' conditioned desires, even though we may run some risk of going against their real wishes? Surely we should work directly against bad influences, and deliberately get rid of (for instance) beauty competitions, sexist literature in schools, and anything else we think objectionable, whatever the conditioned mothers may think of the matter?

However, even though conditioned mothers will certainly tend to bring up conditioned daughters, and although we certainly cannot allow that, this conclusion is not the proper one to draw. The way to prevent the daughters from becoming conditioned is not to keep them out of the range of influence of the things which are believed to have conditioned their mothers, because it was not *being in the range of those influences* which did the harm, but *being out of the range of others*. If we bring the daughters up on a diet of so-called non-sexist literature (much of what is around at present is actually *female* sexist) to think that there should be no sex roles, that does not free them from conditioning: it only brings them up with a different sort. If to get feminist approval a little girl is forced to sneer at the idea of beauty competitions, she is as much coerced as her mother was by parents who expected her to look pleased when she was given dolls and pretty party frocks. Once again, whether or not a girl is conditioned cannot be judged by which slogans she grows up chanting, because in theory she could be conditioned into chanting any.

The solution to the problem, as always with questions of freedom, is once again diversity. We can perhaps summarize the claims of conditioned mothers and those of daughters who are to be rescued from conditioning by proposing a solution to the widely debated problem of how free a parent should be to determine a child's education. We can put it this way. Within practicable limits, the parent should be allowed to say that the child *must* learn certain things, and have lessons from people of particular political, moral or religious views. On the other hand, no parent should have the right to *prevent* the child's learning anything (going to scripture classes in the wrong religion or having sex education) or being exposed to other people's views. The education authorities should have a positive duty to diversify influences, since in that way the parents' wishes are respected but the child's freedom is not impaired. That should be what feminists want. As Germaine Greer said of a similar problem, 'censorship is the weapon of the opposition, not ours'.[12]

9 · CONCLUDING NOTE

This chapter has been about the nature of freedom, its importance, and how to achieve it. What it has not dealt with in much detail is the relationship between freedom and other valuable things, such as the absence of suffering.

This is a complicated question, but in conclusion let me give a quick outline of the position I think acceptable. That is that freedom is the most important thing, and from their own points of view all people should be given as much freedom as possible. It is only when they are not in a position to choose, and we do not know what they would have chosen if they had been, that the questions of happiness and suffering arise separately. As long as they can choose they should decide their own priorities, restricted only by considerations of other people's freedom. But when we have to decide for someone else, we should make the decision on the basis of minimizing suffering. That is controversial, since many people would say that we ought rather to concentrate on maximizing happiness.[13] I hope, however, the difference between the two will not be important for too many of the discussions which are to follow, and during the rest of this book it will be presumed that our first consideration for any individual should be to maximize freedom, and our second to minimize suffering.

4

Sexual Justice

I · TWO KINDS OF INJUSTICE

Once the good things in life have been identified, the next problem is to determine how they should be shared out. This is the problem of justice, or fairness,[1] and if feminism is a movement devoted to the elimination of sex-linked injustice this is the most central question for feminists. This chapter is an attempt to say what fairness is, give some indication of how to recognize it, and in conclusion provide a justification of some of the practices known as reverse, or positive, discrimination.

The first point to be made on the subject of fairness is similar to one which was made at the beginning of the last chapter. There the analysis of freedom began by identifying one kind of freedom, freedom *from* something, which was not relevant to the main discussion, and the same thing must be done in the case of fairness. There are two kinds of fairness and unfairness, and they have to be distinguished. Only one of them is important here, and if the other is allowed to become entangled with it the whole problem becomes intractable.

The distinction which has to be made is a wider version of one which is familiar in jurisprudence, where a difference is recognized between what are often known as *formal* and *substantial* justice. Formal justice consists in applying laws consistently and impartially, whatever those laws happen to be, while substantial justice consists in having just laws. Of course, when feminists complain about injustice to women they are not thinking only of laws: they are concerned with the whole structure of society. But for the moment we can forget the wider question and look at the distinction between formal and substantial justice in the context of law.

Obviously the best state of affairs for any society is one where there are both kinds of justice at once; where there are just laws and they are justly applied. But suppose that there is injustice of one sort or the other. What difference does it make whether that injustice is formal or substantial?

First consider formal injustice. Obviously whether the laws are just or not, nobody likes to be on the losing side of a case of formal injustice. When you live in a society you make your plans by taking into consideration what the rules of the society are (even if you do not like them), and if, after you have arranged your life in accordance with the rules, somebody chooses not to apply those rules, your plans are thwarted. You are bound to regard that as a bad thing: if you had known how people had been going to act you would have made your plans differently. In fact to treat people with formal injustice is much the same thing as curtailing their freedom, because to do it is to lessen the control they have over their own destinies. From the point of view of the losing individual, formal injustice, seen in itself, is a bad thing.

However, it does not follow from this that formal injustice should never be allowed to happen. Suppose that there is in a society a system of laws which are substantially unjust. Where this happens, and these unfair laws are consistently and impartially applied (that is, where there is formal justice) it must follow that people are going to be treated unjustly. It must, therefore, also follow that where the laws are unjust it must be *substantially* just to disregard them in certain ways, and so perpetrate formal injustice. For instance, at the time when children were always legally the property of the husband, a judge who gave their custody to a responsible and ill-treated wife would have been treating the husband with formal injustice (he would have been breaking the law to benefit the wife), but we should certainly say that he had acted with substantial justice. The fact is that formal injustice sometimes is and sometimes is not substantially unjust, precisely as freeing people *from* something sometimes does and sometimes does not increase the amount of freedom they have. The principles of substantial justice determine whether any act of formal injustice is just or not.[2]

Roughly speaking, the matter can be put like this. The principles of *substantial* justice are the principles which determine who should have what; how things should be shared out. It can never be right, therefore, for someone to be treated with substantial injustice, because that would mean being given a wrong share of the good and bad in life. However, *formal* injustice is one bad thing among other bad things, and to suffer it is like suffering a curtailment of freedom. It is, therefore, like curtailment of freedom, a thing whose distribution is to be determined by principles of substantial justice.

As has been said already, feminist interest in justice goes far beyond laws and their application, but a similar distinction between two kinds of justice still has to be drawn. Feminists claim that there is substantial injustice in society not only in the form of laws which work against women and give men more than their fair share of the good things of life, but also in the form of institutions, conventions and attitudes which have the same effect. However, within this framework, as within a just framework, actions may be *formally* just or unjust. The formally just ones are those which keep to the expectations engendered by the social framework; the formally unjust ones are those which do not. Formal injustice in this extended sense occurs not only when laws are broken or misapplied, but also when any form of lying or cheating takes place, or when the rules and structures of society are changed, without due notice or compensation, to the disadvantage of people who have made their plans according to the old ones. When this happens and people claim that they are being treated unfairly, they are quite justified in their complaint: they are indeed being treated unfairly. However, it does not follow that they are being treated with *substantial* unfairness, which is what matters. Whatever principles of substantial justice anyone holds, it must be allowed that in a situation of unjust rules and institutions it is sometimes just to flout or change these institutions, in spite of the fact that people's reasonably founded expectations will be thwarted. It can never be just to keep rigidly to formal justice when the background is one of substantial injustice.

This is all of the greatest importance for feminism. Of course, if laws and so on work unfairly against women, and as well as that those unjust laws are misapplied to the further disadvantage of women, the unfairness is compounded; the formal unfairness of misapplying the law is doubly unfair. But in the other direction the same is not necessarily true. *If* the laws and institutions work unfairly against women, and *if* in changing them and improving things we have to do what is formally unfair to men, such as disappointing them of the privileges they have (unfairly) grown up to expect, we are not necessarily being substantially unfair to them. Formal unfairness may be the only means to substantial fairness.

This chapter is concerned only with questions of substantial justice; questions of who should get what. The purpose of this introduction has been to prevent its being confused with formal justice as the discussion goes on.

2 · TWO PRINCIPLES OF JUSTICE

The problem of justice is now defined, and the most convenient way to set about its solution seems to be to put forward some plausible-looking principles (in the hope that they look as plausible to everyone else as they do to me), defend them, and show what follows from them.

The first of these principles is that *the most important purpose of society is to improve the well-being of sentient things, which should all be as well off as possible*. I say 'sentient things' here because it does not seem proper to start an analysis of sex discrimination with a statement of species discrimination, but from now on I shall abbreviate and say 'people'. Well-being, of course, is a thing about whose nature people are likely to disagree. As was pointed out in the last chapter, some people may think happiness is the most important thing, others may think (as I do) that freedom is, and there are other possibilities too. However, whatever the good is thought to be, the first principle of justice suggested here is that everyone should have as much of it as possible: the good is a thing to be maximized.

The second (and last) principle is about distribution. Principles of justice seem to be necessarily connected with the idea of equality in one form or another, and the most acceptable version seems to me to be that *everyone's well-being is to be considered equally; when social structures are planned no individual or group is to be given more consideration than any other.*

I hope these two principles seem intuitively acceptable. However, their consequences need to be explained and also defended, because it may not be obvious at first sight that they do *not* entail that a sexually just society must be one of equality of well-being, on average, between men and women. A just society might take that form, according to these principles, but it need not; and since that must sound appalling to many feminists more must be said.

The first thing to point out is that any feminist who thinks that justice must entail equality of well-being between men and women cannot stop there. Sexual justice is, after all, only part of justice in general. If, therefore, justice involved equality on average between men and women, why should the members of all other groups not be entitled to equality on average as well? Why should there not be equality of well-being between the clever and the slow, the fit and the disabled, the strong and the weak, and, for that matter, the fair and the dark, the short and the tall, and all the rest? To pick on sexual equality as somehow *a priori* more important to establish than the others would itself involve a sort of sex discrimination: regarding sex as relevant in a context where it was not. However, the necessary consequence of accepting that *all* groups, no matter what they are, should be equal on average, is in fact that *all people should be equal*. Any feminist who is committed to equality on average of well-being between men and women is in fact committed to the *absolute equality* of well-being of all people.

Perhaps that looks all right; certainly many people would accept it. However, it is not at all clear that absolute equality would be a good thing. Imagine, for instance, a perfectly just mariner being blown in one direction past a series of the philosophically indispensable desert islands, and finding on reaching B's island that B was appreciably better off than A, whose island had been passed earlier. Would it be just to burn a field or two of B's crops to make B equal to A? Presumably most of us would be horrified at the idea. However, if we are it means that we are against equality for its own sake, and at the same time in favour of the two principles stated earlier. As they stipulate, neither individual is being taken into consideration more than the other (the same principle would have been followed if A's situation and B's had been reversed), and everyone is to be as well off as possible.

Still, the advocate of absolute equality of well-being might say, that example misses the point. Equality of well-being between totally isolated individuals or groups does not matter. The basis of the principle of absolute equality is that it is usually possible for people to share what they have, and where that is possible it should be done. In the last analysis all abilities, strengths, and advantages of situation are accidental; no one deserves more than anyone else, and things should be shared out until everyone is equally well off.

That sounds more plausible, and would probably be acceptable if the amount of good to be shared out were fixed as well as finite. However, it is not. How much there is to share depends on how much is produced, and that in turn depends heavily on social arrangements. It is entirely possible that if you insisted on absolute equality you might make everyone worse off than the *worst off* might have been in a carefully planned system of inequality. For instance, it is often argued that if taxation were relaxed so that some people were allowed to become very rich, they would work with so much enthusiasm that the worst off group would actually be better off as a result of their increased efforts than *anyone* would be under a system of equalizing taxation. That is much disputed, of course, but it could possibly be true, and its possibility illustrates the general point. And surely *if* something like this were true, it would be better to have an inequality which allowed *everyone, including* the worst off, to be better off than they would be under a system of total equality?

It will, of course, be immediately apparent to anyone who knows John Rawls's *A Theory of Justice* that the position being defended here is very like the first part of his *difference principle*, which states that social and economic inequalities are to be arranged so that they may reasonably be expected to be to everyone's advantage.[3] The account given here differs in some points of detail from Rawls's, but most of them are not significant for the purpose of the argument.[4]

This way of looking at justice is opposed to the view that it should consist in total equality, but it does follow from the two intuitively acceptable principles stated earlier. It considers everyone equally: which group is to be worst off is determined not by tradition or prejudice, but by the social arrangements which make the worst off group, whatever that is, as well off as possible. The level of well-being for the worst off group is the criterion for deciding which among several possible states of society is the fairest. The difference principle does not commit one in advance to any particular degree of actual inequality or equality; it would entail total equality only if that were the state of things which made the worst off as well off as possible. It also gives a clear account of why some people should have more than others even though in the last analysis no one deserves more than anyone else: it is because in that way everyone is better off than would otherwise be the case. And it gives an account of what it is for one group to be well off at the expense of another: that happens whenever one group is better off than another, *and* the less well off group's position could be improved by a different social arrangement which would leave neither group as badly off as the present position of the lower group.

The difference principle or something like it, therefore, does seem to provide a much better criterion of social justice than any principle based on an attempt to make everyone's well-being equal.

3 · SEXUAL JUSTICE

That discussion has been rather abstract, but it is a necessary prelude to considering the specific problems of women because we cannot say what is just for women without having some idea of what we should count as just in general. Some people are, of course, bound to disagree with what has been argued for, but from now on I shall take it to be established. The criterion for justice is not equality of well-being, but something like the difference principle; a just society is one in which the least well off group is as well off as possible. Now the principle must be applied to specific problems of sexual justice.

Rawls did in fact state the consequence of his difference principle for the position of men and women. He said that the inequality would be justified if women were better off under the present arrangement than they would be under one of greater equality,[5] and it does seem to be one indication of the intuitive acceptability of this criterion of justice that men have for centuries been justifying the subjugation of women on exactly this principle. Women are much better off under the firm control of men, it is said, than they could possibly be if left to their own devices. And anyway, if women were let out of the home there would be a general collapse of civilization, and women as well as men would be consumed in the holocaust. It should perhaps be pointed out that Rawls's way of putting the matter is highly tendentious, since it carries the implication that if there is to be sexual inequality for the sake of justice that inequality is bound to leave women underneath, a thing which there is not the slightest reason to presume. It might be better for everyone if women were better off than men, for all we know. The criterion should really be something like 'the present situation is unjust if we could improve the position of women without making men worse off than women are now'.

However, that is a detail. The real point is that justice according to this definition *does not entail equality on average between men and women*. (This is because it does not entail equality at all, but anyone who does still think that justice should entail equality of well-being should remember that even then it could not stop at equality on average between men and women, but would have to involve the absolute equality of everybody.) And of course this presents an extremely serious problem for feminists. If women's average inferiority to men on the scale of well-being does not prove that women are unjustly treated, how *can* we prove it? Can it possibly be proved? The difference principle may provide an intuitively acceptable definition of what a just state of things is, but is it of any use if it cannot give a clear guide to whether a particular state of things is just or not without our knowing in detail all the possibilities the world contains, and whether it would indeed make everyone worse off to make many alterations in the present state of society?

It is of course a serious drawback of the criterion, but not of a sort to mean that the principle ought therefore to be abandoned. There would not be the slightest point in accepting instead a quite different principle (like a principle of absolute equality) just because it left no doubt about when the specified state had been reached. If justice is what we want, we cannot abandon it for something else simply on the grounds that it would be easier to tell when we had reached that something else. There is unfortunately no alternative to struggling to find some determinate practical consequences of this highly abstract criterion of justice, so that we can identify as many symptoms of injustice as possible.

Within the context of feminism we can start to pin down parts of the question more precisely by making use of the fact that feminist complaints about society's injustice to women seem to fall into two main sets.

The first kind of complaint is that women have, traditionally, been systematically excluded from nearly all interesting and influential activity and most kinds of education, and have been left in a narrowly circumscribed sphere of children, domesticity, and occupations ancillary to men's. Their having been in this sphere has not (as some people are inclined to claim) just been an accident, arising from women's having had to spend so much time bearing and looking after children. There have been deliberate rules to exclude them from other activities. Of course this situation is now considerably better than it used to be, at least in most parts of the world, but it is still common for women to be passed over in favour of inherently less competent men, which is just a less extreme case of being excluded altogether. From now on both these practices will be referred to as *selection discrimination* against women.

The second feminist complaint is that even if all such practices were eliminated overnight (as the Sex Discrimination Act specified that they should be), the system would still be unfair to women because the basic social structures within which the competition with men takes place are still designed to favour men rather than women. In particular it is very difficult for women to compete in the male world because there is not much provision for combining important outside work with the bearing and rearing of children. However as well as that (it is said) women are at a disadvantage because of people's prejudices, habits and expectations, and according to some feminists women even suffer from having to live in a male-designed environment which is alien to the female temperament. Even if there were equal opportunity, in the sense of women's not suffering selection discrimination, they would still not have a fair chance in competition with men.

Both these claims, and especially the second, are controversial. However, let us suppose for the moment that they are true, because *even if they are* they are not enough to prove injustice to women according to the difference principle. This is because all feminists will have done if they establish these points is show that women are at a *disadvantage* to men, and that, as has been explained, is not enough to prove that women are unfairly treated. Inequality does not prove unfairness according to the difference principle. This means that feminists have to prove not only that these states of affairs are as they say they are (that women are discriminated against in competition with men, and that the competition is also rigged from the start to be harder for women) but *also* that these things are unjust.

This must now be set about. And since we have two problems (to show both that the accusations are true in fact, and also that if they are true there is injustice), it seems that the best place to start is with the issue of selection discrimination. This is because it is obviously extremely difficult to prove the truth of the vague proposition that the structure of society really does work against women, but relatively easy to prove the truth or falsity of an accusation of selection discrimination. It is an allegation about specific practices, whose existence (and the identity of whose perpetrators) is relatively easy to establish, and therefore if we can prove selection discrimination is always unfair we shall have a sharp point of attack. What I want to do now, therefore, is try to prove that according to the difference principle, selection discrimination is always unfair.

4 · SELECTION DISCRIMINATION

The question to be settled is this. Can we prove quite generally that it is always unfair to choose a man rather than a woman for something they would both like to do, when the woman could do it better than the man?

It is very important to get this question properly focused. We are considering at the moment only the rejection of women who are *actually* more suitable for the position in question than the competing men. If women are rejected because of poor education, that may show discrimination against them at an earlier point, but not at this one. If they are unsuitable because they will work badly with a prejudiced work force, or because someone is wanted who will not be away to have children, that may show unfairness in the structure of society, but does not involve the rejection of *actually suitable women* at this point. The selectors cannot be accused of selection discrimination as long as they choose the best candidate for the purpose in question. *Discrimination on grounds of sex is counting sex as relevant in contexts where it is not*, and leads to the rejection of *suitable* women. It is not discrimination on grounds of sex to reject women who are not suitable, even if their unsuitability is *caused* by their being women. When that happens it is their unsuitability, and not their sex, which has caused their rejection. The question at issue now is specifically whether discrimination against women who really are suitable for a position could ever be defended according to the principles of social justice which have been outlined here.

There is, of course, one perfectly obvious selection rule, applicable in any situation where people are competing for something they want. It is 'choose the candidate most suited to the position'. The question we are dealing with, therefore, is that of what possible reason there could be for adding to this eminently sensible rule, either openly or surreptitiously, the proviso 'but no women', or 'but make it harder for women'. There are various justifications around.

One which can be dismissed straight away is the suggestion which appears from time to time that the whole situation stems from kindness on the part of men, who want to protect women from all the hard things of life. It has already been argued that paternalism is not to be tolerated. Even if men did really think they were doing what was good for women in spite of themselves (which puts rather a strain on one's credulity) it would still not be justified. And while many women may still be perfectly willing to be grateful for any male chivalry which offers to take from them any chore they find burdensome, they can hardly be expected to respond with the same appreciation when men use their stranglehold on the running of everything to prevent women's doing the things they *want* to do. Feminists will believe men's good intentions when they make offers, not rules which they assure everyone are purely in women's interest.

However, although the kindness-to-women argument does appear, it is not the usual justification for discriminatory practices. By far the commonest argument takes the line that women are to be excluded because they are not equal to the task in question. They cannot be dockers or bus drivers because they are not strong enough,[6] they cannot go into the professions or business because they are not clever enough, or can't concentrate, or are prone to hysteria, or will leave to have children or follow their husbands. The usual feminist response to this line is an indignant denial of the whole thing: either the accusations are false, or if women are in some ways inferior to men it is because men have deprived women of proper education. There is of course much truth in this. However, this is one clear case in which feminists would do better to forget about factual arguments for a while and concentrate on the logic. This reasoning is absolutely absurd for two reasons (both, incidentally, clearly pointed out by Mill[7]).

In the first place, nearly all the differences claimed to exist between men and women are differences of *average*. No one with the slightest claim to sense could argue that *all* men were stronger or more intellectual or more forceful than *all* women. But the fact (when it is one) that the average woman cannot do something or other which the average man can do provides not a shred of justification for a rule or practice which also excludes all the exceptional ones who can do it, or demands that the women should perform better than the men to be admitted. You might as well try to argue that if black men were stronger on average than white ones, white men should not be allowed to lift heavy loads, or if Yorkshire people were cleverer than Lancashire ones, no one from Lancashire should be allowed to go to university. Average differences between men and women would account for different success rates in various activities, but they could not possibly account for selection policies which differentiated between them.

Second, even if there were cases where it looked as though all women actually might be worse at something than all men, that *still* would not account for a rule specifically excluding them or saying they should do better than men to be admitted, because, as Mill said, 'What women by nature cannot do, it is quite superfluous to forbid them from doing. What they can do, but not so well as the men who are their competitors, competition suffices to exclude them from . . .'.[8] If men really think, for instance, that a certain level of strength is needed for driving buses, why not just say what that level is and test all applicants for strength? If they really think that all women will fail, why *add* 'but no women'? If the presumption were true no women would get in anyway. It is ridiculous to say that a rule specifically excluding women is needed *because* the work calls for a certain level of strength which women are presumed never to reach. If this is an example of the wonders of male logic, perhaps it is hardly surprising if women feel that they cannot aspire to it.

Some people try to escape this conclusion by saying that if women are inferior to men on average in certain respects it is a waste of time to look at women applicants, because there is so little likelihood of their succeeding. Certainly if such average differences did exist it would account for advising people who were making selections not to spend too much time interviewing women: it is not possible to interview everyone, and some principles of simplification have to be followed. But still, that would not in the least account for general rules excluding all women, which would apply even to the ones who happened to be so strikingly good at their work that they could not be overlooked, and the ones who produced good evidence that they did not suffer from the usual defects of their sex. Maxims for the guidance of selectors, giving some indication of where to look for what is wanted, are quite different from the lists of characteristics needed for the job. If most women are unsuitable for something, it is understandable that a selector should miss by accident some of the ones who are suitable. It is quite different, and not acceptable, to refuse to consider any women, even the ones whose excellence cannot be missed.

In fact there is no escape from the obvious conclusion, which is this. If a general rule is made saying what characteristics are needed for a certain position, and to the list of these characteristics is added the proviso 'but exclude women' or 'make it harder for women', it is *not* added because it is thought that all or most women do not reach the required standards. You do not make additional rules to prevent what would not happen anyway under the existing ones. *The only conceivable reason for a rule or practice excluding women is its perpetrators' thinking that without such a rule women would have to be let in*: that on grounds of strict suitability women, or more women, would have to be admitted. And since the rule against women cannot be justified by saying that women are not generally suitable, it must follow that they are being kept out on other grounds, unspecified.

Since they are unspecified, and since it appears to be necessary to hide them under specious arguments about women's unsuitability, it must be presumed that the real reasons are not of a sort people want exposed to the light of day. It is not, however, difficult to work out what they must be. What, for instance, must be happening if an employer passes over a competent woman in favour of a less competent man? It means that the job will be less well done, and therefore (to put it schematically) that he will be losing money by appointing the man. Why should he do that? He is actually willing to *pay* for something or other, and it is hard to see what it could possibly be other than the simple cause of male supremacy. In other words, individual women are apparently *suffering in the cause of male supremacy*, and individual men are gaining in the same cause. What could possibly be more unfair than that?

However, perhaps it will be said that that conclusion has been reached far too quickly. To give the opposition a fuller opportunity, therefore, let us consider a much more ingenious defence of selection discrimination.

We can start with the fact that when we select someone for any purpose we are rarely looking for a single characteristic, because the position to be filled is always in some way complex. For instance, in looking for a doctor most of us do not want someone who just happens to be skilled in medical science. We also want someone who is kind and considerate and good at explaining things, and who treats patients with respect. Most of us would not be at all sorry if medical schools took such things more into consideration when planning their intake. We certainly do not think that they would be discriminating against nasty, inept or uncommunicative people in making this requirement, even though of course it would make life more difficult for nasty people who wanted to study medicine. All we should be doing would be making a fair selection for our requirements.

Now a sufficiently ingenious plotter against the well-being of women might argue in a similar way, as follows. He could say that when he kept women out of various positions, or allowed in only a few women, this was not because he had anything against women or wanted to advance the position of men; it was just that he, too, had a complex purpose. He thought it important for the good of all that there should be a lot of children, brought up at home by their mothers (just as it would be good for society as a whole to have kind and communicative doctors). When he made his selection for doctors, lawyers, miners or anything else, therefore, he had this complex purpose in mind. He did not choose women for the work, even though they could undoubtedly do it, because in that way they would be encouraged to leave home, and the results would be detrimental to the whole of society.

Forget for the moment that we may consider it bad to want to have more children, or unnecessary that children should be brought up at home. If we can show that the argument does not work even while accepting the opposition's dubious premises the victory will be twice itself. For now let us accept the legitimacy of the aim, and see whether the accusation that women are unfairly treated in being excluded from various activities can be escaped by these means.

To find this out, consider what method would be adopted by someone who wanted to increase the population, but was also motivated by the principle that everyone's well-being was to be maximized; that all people were to be given as much of what they wanted as possible. We are assuming that a higher population is for the benefit of everyone, but still the required children have to be produced by individual women, and women differ considerably in their interest in children. Some want them very much, and others not at all. A benevolent social planner would obviously like the children to be provided as far as possible by women who actually wanted to care for children, because in that way society would be getting what it wanted by means of individuals' getting more of what *they* wanted; obviously an ideal arrangement.

The first thing to do, therefore, is concentrate on the women who want children more than anything else, and make sure by means of marriage bureaux (if we are keeping marriage), fertility clinics, family allowances and domestic help that every woman who wants children can have as many as she likes. If after that there are still not enough children, we go on to women who like the idea of having children but are not willing to sacrifice other things like careers for them, and we find that by means of flexible working arrangements, part-time work, special arrangements to preserve increments and status during periods of absence, and so on, we can make it possible for these women to have both of the things they want (children and career). We make them happier than they would have been with only one, and at the same time produce the children which are wanted for the good of everyone. If even this does not produce enough children we move on to the women who have no special interest in children but who could easily be persuaded to have them, and make having children a thing which brings with it positive rewards, such as a higher income or social prestige. And once more we make everyone happy: the state gets the children it wants through giving individual women what they want. This is the method which must always be adopted by the ideal social planner. Maximizing the good means as far as possible producing the public good *through* what is good for individuals.

That is the socially just way of going about things, but it could hardly present a greater contrast with the method described before, where the supposed social good is achieved by closing other opportunities to women. It is true that in both situations society gets the children it wants, but there the similarities end. Social effort in this case is put not into allowing women who positively want children to have as many of them as possible, but into systematically closing other options until child-rearing becomes the most attractive one left, even for women who do not like the idea at all. And it is important to point out that *society as a whole loses by this method: the coercion of women into child care is carried out at cost to society as well as to individual women*. In the first place, if women are excluded from work other than child rearing, that work is less well done; women would not be specifically excluded unless it were thought that without that exclusion they would have to be admitted, as was argued before. There is what might be called a lower social product: less is produced for the good of all. Second, one may presume that women forced into child rearing will do it far less happily, and less well, than women who do it willingly, so both mothers and children will suffer. That is another social loss. And finally, the greatest loss of all comes with the women who despite all the restrictions still decide to work outside the home because of poverty, or because they will not choose home and family at any price. Because all the attractive things have been closed to force women into their homes there is now nothing left for them but boring and underpaid work, which they take on to their own extreme dissatisfaction and the benefit of absolutely nobody. They work, but are excluded from work which would have allowed them to contribute fully to society. Both individuals *and* society suffer. That is a total loss.

The situation is therefore this. If society wants more children there are two possible sets of procedures it can adopt. One encourages women to have children by removing obstacles and offering rewards; the other attempts to coerce them into having children by taking away all acceptable options. In the coercing situation there is a smaller social product than in the persuading one (that is, there is a lower total of well-being in the society), because some of the most competent people are excluded from what they would otherwise have done well for the benefit of all. And in addition to that, they themselves are made unhappy in the process.

Why then should anyone want such a situation? Why should men (who presumably must have made the original arrangements) settle for a lower total level of satisfaction than might be achieved? Whether they are aware of the answer or not, it is clear what it must be. The men must at some level of consciousness think that they themselves get more as a result of the coercion arrangement than they would by the other one. But if men get more when the total well-being is small than they would if the total were larger, women lose on two counts: *they get an unfairly small share of an unfairly small whole*. That is grossly unfair. Men are being kept in their position of advantage by the extreme general disadvantage of women, and individual women themselves lose additionally in the process. Women therefore do not do better, or anything like as well, as they would in a situation where they were in fair competition with men.

It should be noted, incidentally, that this conclusion cannot be escaped by arguing that the cost of producing children by the supposedly just method would be too high, and that society would suffer as a result of that. If the cost of inducing women to stay at home and have children is too high for society to bear, it means that women are demanding high rewards for doing the work, and that in turn implies that they cannot want to do it very much. If women do not want to have children without high rewards, and society as a whole is not willing to pay the necessary price, on what grounds can it be said that large numbers of children are for the benefit of everyone, or that society in general wants them? It looks as though the only way to come to this conclusion is by not counting women as part of society as a whole.

The conclusion of all this is that in a just society the way to make individuals produce what is for the general good is not to exclude some people from parts of the competition in order to force them to do something else. That way other work is less well done, and individuals are made unhappy in the process. The way to proceed is to make the work to be done attractive to the people we want to do it, that way getting the work done well and increasing the satisfaction of individuals in the process.

The conclusion is a pleasingly neat one from the point of view of selection discrimination. It is that it is never fair to eliminate a group from an area of activity (or to make admission harder for them than for other groups) on grounds which are unconnected with the purpose for which the selection if being made. *It is always unfair to practise selection discrimination against women* or against any other group.[9]

The really important part of this conclusion is that it still stands *whether or not the underlying structures, within which the selection is being made, are themselves just*. This is most important, because as has already been said it would be humanly impossible to recognize a state of justice once it had been reached: we should always go on trying to get something better. We may not know when we have the best possible organization from the point of view of social justice, but as long as we are *aiming* to produce what is of the greatest benefit to everyone, we must be wrong in eliminating any group from the competition, since that will not only lower the well-being of the members of that group but also lessen what is produced for the satisfaction of others.

It is interesting to note, incidentally, that this conclusion is much like the second part of Rawls's difference principle, which states that there is to be fair competition for the most desirable positions in society.[10] It shows that the second part of the principle is deducible from the first, and not a separate thing.

5 · THE PROBLEM OF REVERSE DISCRIMINATION

We have, then, established that discrimination against women, treating their sex as a reason for putting them at a disadvantage in competitions where sex is not relevant, is always substantially unfair.

Clear and neat as that conclusion is, however, and useful in allowing us to pin down demonstrable injustice and charge individual culprits instead of having to rail in general about the unfair structures of society (for which it is hard to blame anyone in particular), it does raise problems for feminists in the context of the issue of reverse discrimination. The usual form recommended for reverse discrimination is that women of a lower calibre than men should be chosen for certain work in preference to them. It is a thing which many feminists think ought to happen, but the last section seemed to show that this would be absolutely unfair; that reverse discrimination would be open to exactly the same conclusive objections as ordinary discrimination.

More specifically, the argument seems to show that several explicit provisions of the Sex Discrimination Act must be unfair. For instance, the Act states that when appointments are made to various positions there are certain things

which are not to be allowed to count against women applicants, the most striking of which, perhaps, is that they are
not to be rejected on the grounds that they will meet a
prejudiced public and work force. There is no doubt that
when people are prejudiced against women a man would
often do the required work better; if the public have no
confidence in a female door-to-door seller of insurance or
encyclopaedias a man will sell more. To insist that this sort
of thing should not be allowed to count against women is
actually to say that women should be appointed even when
they are less good than men. In other words, it provides for
a certain amount of positive discrimination.

It will not do to say in a vague way that sometimes it must
be all right to discriminate in favour of women. The argument of the last section showed that *whenever* considerations of sex entered into selections for whose purpose sex
was not relevant that was unfair, and the whole point is to
try to achieve fairness. We cannot simply assert that unfairness sometimes has to be tolerated. Of course it has already
been argued that sometimes *formal* unfairness has to be
tolerated in the interests of substantial fairness, but since the
necessity of selecting the best candidate is *part of the account
of what it is to be substantially fair* there is nothing higher
which can override it. You cannot say that some substantial
unfairness must be tolerated in the interests of greater
substantial fairness, in the way that some bad must be
tolerated to achieve a great deal of good, because fairness is
not a thing to be shared out; it is a principle according to
which other things are shared out. Anyone who is treated
with substantial unfairness gets the wrong amount of good
and bad.

If positive discrimination is to be justified, something
much stronger is needed. Some of the usual defences of it
which appear should be assessed.

Probably the commonest defence is the argument that
since women have been badly treated in the past, what they
should now be given is *compensation* for what they have
missed. Compensation is a method of making up for past

deprivation. It is not (to avoid confusion later on) a way of putting things right for the future, or improving matters generally; it is a means to give women the level of satisfaction they ought to have had anyway, by giving them enough now to fill the gap left by their previous deprivation. It is the sort of thing which would happen if an employer were to make up for employees' having been underpaid in the past by giving them all their back pay, with an allowance for interest and inflation, and perhaps damages.

If women have indeed been treated unfairly in the past, it does seem proper that they should be given compensation now. If men have had more than their fair share, they should give some of their ill-gotten gains to women, since they got them at women's expense in the first place. However, the question now is not of whether women should be compensated, but of whether the way to go about that is by means of positive discrimination. And there seems little doubt that it is not a proper means of compensation, for several reasons.

In the first place, you cannot actually compensate women in general for their past suffering by changing the rules now and allowing some women to achieve advantages for which they are not really qualified. Even if that would do as a compensation for the women chosen, it would be no compensation whatever for the others. It might perhaps improve things for the future, but that is not compensation. It would do nothing for the women who had been passed over earlier, and their unhappiness might even be increased by seeing other women being given advantages far beyond anything they had ever had. Reverse discrimination fails as a means of compensating women for their sufferings, both because you cannot compensate a group by giving benefits to some of its members (people need compensating individually or collectively, not by some method of representation), and anyway, the women who are individually compensated by discrimination are usually already the most privileged among women. Reverse discrimination is no compensation for women in general.

Perhaps then the idea is to compensate some individuals, rather than the whole group, for their past injustice. That looks more promising. However it still does not work as a justification of a general policy of reverse discrimination in favour of women. If the concern is really with underprivilege and its redress, why should it matter whether the person being helped is a woman rather than a man? Why should one discriminate generally in favour of women, when it might involve benefiting an already well off woman at the expense of a badly off man? If compensation is all that is at issue, why not have the rule that the worst off (of either sex) are to be compensated? To say that women's grievances should be redressed in preference to men's is to be unfair to men: it gives women the privilege of having their lack of privilege take precedence over men's lack of privilege, and when this is looked at from the point of view of deprived individuals there seems to be nothing to be said for it at all. Many men are less privileged than many women. The fact that women are on average less well off than men might justify someone's deciding to take particular care when assessing women candidates for anything, because there was a higher probability that they would need compensating than men would, but it would not justify a general rule.

Suppose, then, we argued that reverse discrimination should not be specifically in favour of women, but in favour of any underprivileged person. (That would still in practice tend to favour women, but would escape the charge that the practice was systematically unfair to men.) Even then it would not be justified.

This can be illustrated rather schematically. Suppose a benevolent man who runs a business is sympathetic to the problems of women, and is willing to do without some of his profit to benefit them. He has two positions to fill, one responsible and interesting, and one rather dull. In competition for them are a well qualified man and a less well qualified woman. He has two options: to give the better job to the woman or to give it to the man. Suppose first he gives it to the woman. She then has a high degree of satisfaction (we are to suppose that she is not so hopelessly incompetent as to be unhappy, only less good than the man would have been). Her inefficiency loses money for the firm, but the employer does not mind that because he is willing to make sacrifices to benefit women. The man, on the other hand, has a low degree of satisfaction in the lesser job. Suppose, however, that the employer takes the other option, and appoints the man to the better job. The man then has a high degree of satisfaction, and the firm makes the usual profit. The employer is willing to forgo this in the interests of the woman, as before, and so gives her a high salary for her work in the lesser job. She therefore has also a high degree of satisfaction, though of course of a different sort. There seems, therefore, to be no doubt about which arrangement the employer should make. He should not make an arrangement which would benefit the woman only, if he could make one which would benefit the man as well.

Of course that example is very artificial, and no doubt objections could be brought against it in its present form, but it does illustrate a general point. To have a general policy of appointing women to positions for which they are not well qualified is not the best way to compensate them for past injustice. We should do much better to allow the best qualified people to do the work, because if work is worth doing it is in the interests of all that it should be done well. If we make such arrangements it will mean that we have a greater social product with which to compensate women, and others, for their past injustices, and that is what we should do. Compensation should come not in the form of unmerited advancement, but in the form of other primary social goods (to use Rawls's term[11]).

The general conclusion of all these arguments is that although no doubt some compensation is due to women for their unjust treatment, the idea of compensation does not justify reverse discrimination in their favour.

Still, the defenders of reverse discrimination have no reason to retreat yet. All this talk of compensation, they can argue, is beside the point. If we are going to be fussy about the precise meaning of 'compensation', then let us concede that compensation is not what justifies reverse discrimination. What we want to achieve is not compensation but *an improvement of the position of women until society is fair to them*, and as a matter of fact probably the best way to achieve this is to appoint to positions of importance women who are rather less good at the work than the men who are in competition with them. As long as they are not such hopeless failures as to confirm everyone's ideas that women are not capable of any serious work, their holding those positions will be enough to make other women set their sights higher, and make people in general more used to seeing women in former male preserves and expecting more of them. High expectations make an important contribution to high performance. That is quite a different point from the compensation argument, though the two are very often confused. Furthermore it escapes all the objections to which the other is open, including, most importantly, the general argument that is is always unfair to select people for work on the basis of anything other than their suitability for it.

The point is this. If our present society is unfair to women, it is obviously fair that it should be changed; it is fair that we should set in motion social programmes to turn society into one which is better for women. We also think that when things are fairer to women society as a whole will benefit, because it will no longer waste their skills. Admittedly women now may not have the skills they should have had, and since it is probably too late for the women of this generation to acquire them we should perhaps think of compensating them for their disadvantage by other means, rather than giving them positions of responsibility. But that would be to take a short term view. We have to plan not only for the people who are alive now, but for the world our great-granddaughters will have to contend with. It would be unfair to them to let things go on as they are now, and unfair to their contemporaries to have potential skill wasted. Our social aims, therefore, become more complicated. We have to maintain our concern with high standards in the various professions, but we have also to think of the need to advance women. We want good doctors, certainly, but at the same time we want to encourage people to think of women as doctors. *If, as a matter of fact*, we think that the best way to achieve this is to have a good many successful women doctors, we may consider making rules which allow a woman to become a doctor with slightly lower medical qualifications than a man. *But this does not offend against the principle that there should be no discrimination in selection procedures, because we are still concerned to choose the best people for the job which needs doing.* It is just that the nature of the work to be done has changed, so that different people become suitable for it. We now want, for example, good doctors who *also* advance the position of women. As long as lowering the medical qualifications for women was causally relevant to the end to be achieved, it would be justified.

This way of looking at the matter does seem to remove the *prima facie* objections to reverse discrimination. Or perhaps a better way of putting it would be to say that reverse discrimination is not well named, because discrimination on grounds of sex involves counting sex as relevant in contexts where it is not, and the argument being put forward now is that in some unexpected contexts it *may* be relevant. In these contexts what appears to be discrimination in favour of women is not discrimination at all.

6 · THE ATTAINING OF SOCIAL JUSTICE

This no doubt looks like nothing more than a philosophical sleight of hand, since what it does is turn what looked like unfair selection for one purpose into fair selection for another. And since that needed only a formal transposition, it looks as though anyone could make such a move, and that a man who wanted to discriminate against women could make the same twist, and say that his selection was quite fair, but for another purpose.

However, that is not really the case. The argument does not justify *any* such move, and *any* practice of reverse discrimination. All it does is remove an objection which seemed to suggest that what is generally called reverse discrimination should be out of the question for anyone concerned with fairness. What it has done is to move the question to another place. Anyone who wants to justify any particular practice of reverse discrimination must now show two things: first, that the state of affairs to be brought about by the practice is a just one, and second, that the methods to be used are likely to be the right ones to bring it about. And as it happens, feminists are in a strong position to argue that the demand for reverse discrimination can adequately meet both of these challenges.

In the first place, even though the definition of justice according to the difference principle makes it hard to tell when a state of affairs is *actually just* (as just as possible), it is still not difficult to provide strong presumptive evidence that the present state of things must be *unjust* to women (that there must be other possible states of society which would be more just). This is because the two feminist complaints mentioned before (that there was selection discrimination against women, and that the underlying structures would still be unfair to them even if there were not) are connected. If a group is kept out of something for long enough, it is overwhelmingly likely that activities of that sort will develop in a way unsuited to the excluded group. We know for certain that women have been kept out of many kinds of work, and this means that the work is quite likely to be unsuited to them. The most obvious example of this is the incompatibility of most work with the bearing and rearing of children; I am firmly convinced that if women had been fully involved in the running of society from the start they would have *found* a way of arranging work and children to fit each other. Men have had no such motivation, and we can see the results. However, there are other consequences of women's exclusion. It has obviously affected public prejudices, making it hard for women to succeed even when they are intrinsically as capable as men, and women's own expectations of themselves, which make them withdraw from the competition even before it begins. The fact that there has been selection discrimination is enough to show that the underlying structures are *likely* to be unfair to women. (That is, to recapitulate, it is likely that the arrangement of things could be much improved for women without making men worse off than women are now.)

And this argument, of course, is not available to any man who wants to say that when he appears to discriminate against women, he is in fact making a fair selection for a different purpose. It has already been shown what unfairness is involved when a man tries to argue that in eliminating women from various activities he is in fact making a fair selection for his overall social purpose of having professionally competent people, but also children brought up by their mothers at home. However, the point can be put more generally than that. If you want to admit the members of one sex to various things on the basis of lower qualifications than those accepted for the members of the other, the only general social policy which could explain it would be a wish to *advance* the members of one sex at the expense of the other. To justify that it would be necessary to show that the sex to be advanced was at an unfair disadvantage already. Women can show that they are almost certainly worse off than they should be, and therefore in justice should be advanced. Men can show no such thing. There is no evidence that men are underperforming. No selection discrimination against women, therefore, can be justified on the grounds that it is a fair selection to bring about a state of justice for men. No doubt it brings about something some men consider desirable, but it is not a state of justice.

The second justification needed for any programme of reverse discrimination, apart from the argument that the present situation is unjust and needs changing, is that the methods to be adopted are in fact likely to make the changes needed. Most of the evidence needed for that is empirical, about how expectation affects performance, how habit forms and overcomes prejudice, and so on. However, the argument already used does go some way towards a justification of taking women into employment when they are less suitable than men (according to traditional criteria). If it is the case, as seems likely, that the past exclusion of women has made the situation uncongenial to them, and has made people unused to having women in significant places, then it seems that the best way to change things is simply to make sure that there are large numbers of women in these places. This will mean that they are in a position to change things, if they want to, and make the environment more congenial to them. It will also make people more used to women, and allow us to find out whether women can indeed do the things which they claim that they would be able to do perfectly easily if only men would stop throwing obstructions in their way.

7 · TRANSITION

Reverse discrimination as it has been described would be transitional. Sexual justice entails taking sex into consideration only when it is directly relevant to the matter in hand, and in the long run it will not be relevant to take sex into account when selecting miners or lawyers; nothing will come into consideration but ability for mining or the law. For the time being, however, we must regard sex as relevant to selections such as these, because we have to deal with the entrenched effects of its having been irrelevantly considered in the past. That is the only way to achieve a framework of sexual justice, even though there may be much dispute about details of method.

But still, some people argue, what about the period of transition? Is that itself not likely to be unfair to many people, and in particular to men?

If such a transitional period could be shown to be unfair that would be very serious. As has been stated several times already, injustice is not a thing to be tolerated on the grounds that it will lead to greater justice, because justice is itself a principle for deciding who should get what, rather than one of the things to be distributed. To disregard the claims of the people in the transition period is to flout one of the most basic principles of justice: that everyone's interests are to be considered equally. The claims of people now cannot be *sacrificed* to the claims of people in the future, any more than the interests of some people at any one time may be sacrificed to increase the well-being of others. We are not trying necessarily to increase the total satisfaction over time, but to make sure that what there is is shared justly among the people of all times, just as among the people at any one time. [12]

Anyway, the idea of a transition to a period of justice is a very risky one to entertain at all. Transitions are not separate from the rest of life. To think that they were we should have to believe that we could certainly reach utopia, that we should recognize it when we got there, and that nothing would happen to change it once it existed. But none of these is true. We *hope* that our techniques of reverse discrimination will lead to a situation of greater fairness, but we cannot be sure that they will, and so cannot be sure that 'temporary' unfairness would be justified. Or even if we did achieve something fairer, we would go on looking for something fairer still, and immediately set out in transition for something else. And even if we could recognize a totally just state of things once it existed, we should still have to allow for changes which were not of our devising; if people's desires changed, or there were natural disasters or gradual changes of environment, we should have to start again. Change is constant; we cannot plan for some kind of static society. If justice does not matter in transitions, it does not matter at all.

The upshot, therefore, is that we must make the transition periods, on the way to justice for women, *just in themselves*. At each stage we should try to increase justice. The idea of making things better for the future affects the way in which we try to do this, of course; that is why we actually go in for reverse discrimination, rather than achieving a present state of justice simply by giving women other primary social goods. It does not affect, or should not affect, our determination to make next year as socially just as we can contrive.

There are some obvious things to be taken care of, therefore. For instance, if we are to appoint women to positions which they are less capable (by present criteria) of assuming than are various men, we are likely to lower the total social product for a while (though probably to a much lesser extent than people with vested interests on the other side like to think). That in itself is all right: the principles of justice do not demand the greatest *total* satisfaction. We should make sure, however, that the worst off do not become worse off as a result, since that would itself be unjust. Once again, no one in this generation is to suffer for the benefit of people who may already be better off, or for the benefit of future generations.[13]

But still, it may be asked, what about the individuals who are not among the worst off, but are still being treated unfairly? Certainly men as a group ought to concede some of their unfair advantage to women as a group, but surely it is still unfair that *individual* men (and probably some women too) should have to make large sacrifices, rather than that the expense should be spread out evenly between men? What about employers who are made to employ women who will do the work less well than men would have done, like the ones at present who are not allowed to take public suspicion of women into consideration? They will lose a good deal of their profit, and therefore are effectively being forced to put some of their effort into improving the position of women, and only some into doing what they themselves want to do. This is the sort of thing Robert Nozick, in his *Anarchy, State and Utopia*, would count as forced labour.[14] And what about individual men, who are asked to sacrifice so large a thing as their careers in the interests of an underprivileged group? This was alleged to be unfair by Lord Justice Scarman.[15] He did also say that the unfairness nevertheless had to be tolerated for a while, but according to what has been argued so far that is not acceptable: if it really is unfair, it should not be tolerated.

However, feminists can produce arguments which allow for reverse discrimination in spite of these objections. In the first place, of course, a good deal of the unfairness which is complained about in contexts like these is *formal* unfairness. People suffer as a result of having their formally legitimate expectations thwarted by changes in the law and social structures. If women are to be favoured, men with expectations founded on what was the case before reverse discrimination started will be disappointed in them; employers who made their plans under previous legislation will find that they are disadvantaged by the unforeseen change. However, although these things are unquestionably bad for the people concerned (feminists are wrong if they regard them as unimportant), we cannot rule them out as a matter of course. It was shown at the beginning of this chapter that in the name of substantial justice some formal injustice would have to be tolerated; it is a bad thing among other bad things, whose fair distribution is to be decided according to principles of distributive justice. We cannot disregard complaints of this sort of unfairness where they are justified, but we must not confuse them with justified allegations of substantial unfairness, and see them as insuperable.

The second point is that not everything that looks at first sight like substantial injustice really is that. In many cases where reverse discrimination would meet with accusations of substantial unfairness, grounds for the accusation would come from taking the present (unfair) state of things as a norm against which to assess the change. For instance, a man who is apparently 'deprived of his career' as a result of positive discrimination in favour of women is not necessarily deprived of anything he was justly entitled to at all. A fair scheme of positive discrimination would not allow women to reverse the previous situation and make sure that masses of women were appointed to everything they could think of in preference to overwhelmingly better qualified men; it would aim to give these positions only to some (probably not even all) of the women who would have had them anyway, in fair competition with the men, if the women had had the same advantages as men in the past. But the only men excluded on this sort of principle would be the ones who, as far as we could tell, would not have succeeded anyway if the situation had been fair. Therefore their not succeeding cannot be considered unfair. It looks unfair to them only because they expected what was in fact *more* than their fair share.

Much the same applies in the case of a good deal of employment. The employer who is suddenly forced to pay much higher wages to his female employees does not deserve much sympathy, because he has already made a great deal of money out of the exploitation of women; if he is now in a worse position than people who always employed men, or paid women properly, that is only because they had fewer unfair benefits before.

But even after these two mistaken sorts of objection have been dealt with, reverse discrimination does still allow scope for substantial injustice. It is most unlikely that any scheme we can devise will bring about, immediately, exactly the distribution of good and bad required by principles of distributive justice, and it does seem that in many cases where there is formal unfairness there is likely to be substantial unfairness as well. This seems likely, for instance, in the case of employers who have not benefited particularly from the unfairness to women in the past, but will certainly suffer from the change (ones like the employer of door-to-door salesmen whose sales may go down when he has to take on women as well). It also seems true of the man whose career prospects suddenly disappear when the rules change. He is likely to be worse off than he would have been if the situation had been fair from the start, because even though his expectations were unfairly high he still suffers more from their being unfulfilled than if he had never had them in the first place: if he had known in advance what would happen, he could have made different plans.

This must all be taken into account, but not allowed to

stop the process of trying to achieve a fair society for women. Earlier it was argued that although badly treated women should be compensated for their position, that compensation should not take the form of giving them work they were not the most competent people to perform; instead they should be compensated with other primary social goods. Just the same is true in these cases. Our aim is to appoint people to fulfil a particular function (here, advancing the cause of women among other things), and if in doing this we perpetrate injustice we should not change our policies and allow the appointment of people who are not the best for the work (that is, the men who would have been best according to the old criteria). Instead we should think of other forms of compensation. This distinction between *compensating* with primary social goods and *changing society* by different criteria for employment (positive discrimination) is a most important one.

Anyway, the conclusion is clear. Transitional injustice is not to be tolerated, but accusations of injustice must not be allowed to prevent reverse discrimination where that is the best route to a state of justice. If it brings about injustice, the victims must be compensated in *other* ways.

8 · CONCLUDING NOTE

It may be objected to what has been said on the subject of justice that it gives too little practical guidance; that all the detailed questions of what policies should be adopted have been left open. That is true. To settle those, information about matters of fact must be added to the kind of theory which has been described here. However what is certainly true is that this kind of investigation must come first. *It is impossible to attempt to settle the practical questions before settling the theoretical ones of what things* count *as justice and injustice.*

The important conclusions are these. First, there is a distinction to be drawn between formal and substantial justice, and some things may therefore be unfair, formally unfair, and still to be tolerated, or indeed insisted on. Substantial injustice, on the other hand, can never be tolerated in the name of justice, since justice is the criterion for the fair distribution of good things, not another good thing to be shared. Second, if something like Rawls's difference principle is accepted as a criterion for justice, justice is not actual equality, which means that it is difficult to tell for certain whether a state of justice has been reached or not. It certainly cannot be inferred from the fact of one group's being better off than another. Third, selection discrimination on grounds of sex (or on grounds of anything else irrelevant to the purpose of selection) is always unfair under any circumstances (which is actually quite helpful for practice). Fourth, in spite of that we can justify some reverse discrimination as long as it is clear that what is being defended is choosing the best candidates for *another purpose than usual*, that of bringing about social justice. And finally, transitional injustice is not to be accepted, because transitions are not separate from the rest of life.

The Feminist and the Feminine

I · THE PROBLEM

Reason, nature, freedom and justice, the subjects of the four chapters in the first part of this book, are all very general ones. They are relevant to all political and moral discussion, although they have of course been considered in terms of feminism and feminist problems. The following chapters work the other way round. Their subjects are specifically feminist ones, though a good deal of what arises in the course of their discussion has consequences for other issues.

The issue of femininity is a suitable one to start with, because of the fierce passions it has aroused on both sides ever since the first stirrings of women's emancipation. The fear that an emancipated woman must necessarily be an unfeminine one has always been the basis of one of the opposition's main objections to feminism, and feminists have never (or at least not recently) made the slightest attempt to allay those fears, since most of them think that the creation of a feminine character is one of the most deeply-rooted and sinister parts of women's oppression, and that until women are free of femininity they will never be free at all.

However, for all this strength of feeling, the subject of the controversy manages to be surprisingly elusive. When actually faced with the question of what femininity consists in, most people find it very difficult to say. Lists are produced of candidate characteristics like gentleness, patience, introversion, domesticity, dependence and so on, but there are invariably puzzles and disagreements (what about vanity, curiosity, inconstancy and the like?), and even when any kind of conclusion does seem to be in sight there is always the problem of anomalous women who do not fit the description and yet for some reason still seem to be feminine. If it is feminine to be illogical, dependent and hysterical, why are countless women strong, rational and calm without apparently losing any femininity at all? How could Lucy Stone (an early American feminist) arouse public outrage by being unfeminine enough to speak in public, making most unfeminine political suggestions, and yet be found by one surprised member of her audience 'a prototype of womanly grace'?[1] Femininity is very hard to pin down, and that makes it difficult to see precisely what everyone is fighting for or against, and why.

As long as the discussion is pursued by concentrating on lists of supposedly feminine characteristics, the confusion is bound to remain (for reasons which will appear soon). It is better to start by taking a step backwards, and asking instead the more fundamental question of what lists of such characteristics are supposed to be lists *of*; what it is which determines which ones should be counted as feminine, rather than as masculine or neutral. This will make the subject more manageable, and at the same time make sure that femininity's (supposed) correlate, masculinity, is adequately dealt with as well.

In the first place, then, femininity and masculinity are obviously not the same as maleness and femaleness; it would be quite inappropriate to describe the fundamental distinguishing characteristics of the sexes as masculine and feminine. We must, therefore, be concerned with attributes which are in some way supposed to *accompany* these fundamental sexual ones, and the question is of what kind of accompaniment is at issue.

The most obvious answer to this question, and the one most often given, is that masculine characteristics are those usually occurring in males but not females, while feminine ones, on the other hand, are those more commonly found in females than in males. Characteristics so described are usually, in this context, taken to refer to *inherent* ones, innate in the sexes, and that in itself leads to a good deal of dispute, because feminists quite rightly argue that most of these supposedly inherent attributes are in fact socially induced. Still, there is no reason to presume that there cannot be *any* inherent feminine and masculine characteristics, if by this is meant non-sexual differences which tend to accompany the sexual ones. On the contrary, it is overwhelmingly likely that there are some. One reason for thinking this is that the various physical characteristics which people have are not neatly separated off from each other (or, of course, separated off from mental ones), and the whole person results from a combination of all the constituent parts. It is therefore likely that the combination of specifically sexual characteristics with others which may be equally distributed between the sexes may produce non-sexual characteristics more commonly found in one sex than the other. Another reason for thinking that there must be some general differences is that the reproductive difference between the sexes is likely to have resulted in natural selection's favouring different things in each of them. The reproductively successful males (at least in the pre-social days when presumably there was a sexual free-for-all) must have been the ones who succeeded in impregnating most females, while the impulse to mate must have been relatively unimportant in the female (since she would in general produce the same number of offspring whether she mated every day or twice a year), and the most successful females would have been the ones who selected the best mates and cared most conscientiously for their offspring. This would presumably lead to a strong sexual drive in males, and a strong desire to care for their offspring in females. Anyway, if for either of the reasons suggested, or indeed for any others, there are non-sexual characteristics and tendencies which generally divide strongly along sex lines, they can appropriately be called feminine and masculine.

Even though it seems likely that there are such masculine and feminine characteristics, however, there is fortunately no need to get involved in a discussion of how many there are, what they are or what effect they have, since it is quite clear that *this* kind of characteristic cannot possibly be the kind at issue in the great debate about women and femininity. It is obvious as soon as it is thought about, because what is remarkable about the masculinity and femininity which are at the centre of the debate is that they are the subjects of great *anxiety*. There is great *fear* that women might cease to be feminine and men masculine, and whether or not there are any inherent general differences between the sexes such differences cannot reasonably be a matter for any *concern*; at least in the past and present state of technology, there has been absolutely nothing that could have been done about them. The characteristics about which everyone seems to be so worried are obviously very far from inherent and unalterable, and femininity, in particular, must have been thought extremely vulnerable, if we are to judge by the lengths to which it was thought necessary to go to preserve it. In the name of femininity of mind and activity women were for a long time given totally separate kinds of education from men, kept out of all professional and public work, and even denied the vote. Even now most of this has changed there is still considerable anxiety, and women are exhorted not to become unfeminine now that they have the same opportunities as men, or told that it is all right for them to compete in the male world as long as they do not lose their femininity. This desirable characteristic is obviously thought a very fragile thing, since so much trouble is gone to on its behalf.

All the fuss about femininity (and to a lesser degree about masculinity) is obviously not about inherent differences between the sexes. It must therefore, very differently, be about what it is thought that the sexes *ought* to be like, and about what measures need to be taken to achieve whatever that is. That makes it clear, incidentally, why it is confusing to try to approach the subject of femininity and masculinity by compiling lists of characteristics, because, quite apart from disagreements people may have about what should go on the lists, there are two quite different lists at issue. One is about the supposed inherent differences between men and women (the subject of much controversy, because feminists think that most of the differences which are not entirely imaginary are socially brought about), and it is on *this* list of feminine characteristics that so many bad ones (curiosity, weakness, vanity, inability to concentrate and so on) traditionally appear, to provide a justification for the social position of women. The other list of feminine characteristics and occupations, on the other hand, is of what is thought *proper* for women as opposed to men, and lists the feminine virtues (patience, devotion and the like). It is for the achievement of this second set of feminine characteristics that separate areas of activity for women were designed, not for the achievement of feminine characteristics which could not have been otherwise.

Most feminists, with the exception of a few very radical ones who regard nature as part of the great conspiracy against women,[2] have no worries about any inherent tendencies to differences between the sexes (though they may be justifiably indignant about what these are often alleged to be). The feminist concern about femininity is not about such inherent characteristics. It is rather the fact that *men and women are under different social pressures*, encouraged to do different kinds of work, behave differently, and *develop* different characteristics, which is important. The object of this chapter is to look into this matter, and work out to what extent, if at all, it is possible to justify pressures which push men and women in the different directions of masculinity and femininity.

2 · MAKING THE DIVIDE

When any defender of the status quo for men and women is asked why society has different expectations of the two sexes and pushes them in different directions, the answer is nearly always the same. It is because the sexes are *indeed different*, and therefore no well-judging society could possibly regard it as proper to have the same expectations of them, regard the same activities as suitable for them, and so on. In the words of the arch-sexist Ruskin (who will provide a useful illustration of the type), quoted by Kate Millett,[3]

Each has what the other has not; each completes the other. They are in nothing alike, and the happiness and perfection of both depends on each asking and receiving what the other only can give.

Sentiments such as these are always expressed in such a way as to make the whole arrangement sound very nice and considerate; a sensitive division of labour for the good of all, with each individual being encouraged to contribute what it is suitable for him or her to give. But of course what immediately strikes the feminist about all this is that in spite of the sugary gloss of 'equal but different' which Ruskin and his like think proper to give their account of separate characters and areas of activity for men and women, it always seems to turn out that women differ from men in being *less* strong, *less* rational, *less* creative and less everything else worthwhile than men, and that these supposed deficiencies have traditionally been the excuse for excluding women from everything which men have been inclined to keep to themselves. Through all the euphemism there still comes the view of Aristotle, who attempted no such tactful suggestion of equality in difference when he said that a female was female in virtue of a certain lack of qualities, and Thomas Aquinas, who thought the female was a defective male.

It is not surprising that feminists have rushed to repudiate these unflattering allegations, meeting them with outright denial, or arguments that to the extent that they are true it is all men's fault for having systematically reduced women to such a state. However, although there is little doubt about the justice of the feminist case in such arguments, and in the not unnatural suspicion that it is not the interests of *women* which dictate the nature of the feminine role, concentration on this aspect of things deflects attention from what is really the main issue (as it did in the case of questions about discrimination, which are in several respects very similar). It makes the mistake of concentrating attention on the question of *what* we should expect of women rather than men, leaving untouched the logically prior question of *why we should put separate pressures on the two sexes at all*. It is logically prior, of course, because if we have no justification for the existence of separate pressures in the first place, the question of what those pressures should be does not even arise.

Now the Ruskin-type answer to the question of why we expect certain activities and characteristics of women and others of men does generally purport to cope with this aspect of the question as well as the other. In saying *that* men and women are different, as well as *how* they differ, it seems to give a justification of *having* different expectations of the sexes, at the same time as justifying *what* those expectations should be by reference to the differentiating characteristics of the sexes. For, if men and women are different, is that not a sufficient explanation of why they should be encouraged to do different things?

However, this does not work. Ruskin's descriptions of what men and women are like fall into a familiar ambiguity, already commented on in the last chapter. Suppose, for the moment, that what he says about the kinds of difference there are between men and women is true; then in what *sense* is it true? Does he mean that *all* women and *all* men have these masculine and feminine characteristics, and no member of either sex has the characteristics of the other? Certainly the implication is that this is the case, since it is implied that the sexual division of labour is a thing which suits everyone. However, it could not possibly be true. Even the most hardened of male supremacists, and even with women's educational disadvantages to assist his prejudices, could hardly assert that *all* women were inferior in all important respects to *all* men. But then, even supposing the ideas about the *nature* of the sexual differences to be justified, the Ruskin position becomes much weaker. At best, the division of labour is one which suits only most people, and has the effect of coercing the ones who are unusual for their sex into what does not suit them at all.

Perhaps it sounds as though there is nothing wrong with an arrangement which has this consequence. After all, in innumerable social situations it is necessary to make arrangements which suit the majority, and accept with regret that it would have been better for the minority if things had been different. The laws of a country, for instance, are (ideally) made to suit *most* of the people in it, and the others just have to go along with them; that is the whole idea of democracy. And, to take a more everyday example, a teacher planning end-of-term entertainments at a school may decide that one class should do an opera, because most of its members can sing, while another should do a play, because most of its members are good at acting, even though that leaves out the singers in the acting form and the non-singers in the opera form. It is hard on the minority, but it is necessary to do what is best for most of the group. If, therefore, the majority of women is suited to a particular kind of position and activity, surely it is reasonable to insist that all women should go along with it?

It might indeed be possible to find a justification of forcing all women to go along with what is alleged to suit most. However, any such argument would need another step. This is because, as a matter of logic, before you can justify a group's activities by reference to its general characteristics, you *first* need a justification for its acting as a single group at all, rather than (say) joining with a larger group, splitting into smaller ones, or having everyone act as individuals. Although we might agree that *if* women and men are to have separate sorts of social pressure put on their sexes the nature of those pressures should be determined by what suits most members of the group, that does not account for why the groups are to be treated as wholes, separate from each other, in the first place.

Of course such a justification might be available. For instance, the teacher of the earlier example might be asked by resentful pupils why the two classes should not combine, using the actors and singers of both classes to produce two separate performances using the abilities of all, leaving no one out, and she might have a perfectly good answer to the effect that although that would be an excellent thing if it could be arranged, difficulties of the school timetable made it impossible to arrange rehearsals in which the two groups could share. That may make things perfectly all right. After that reason for the separation in the first place, the decision about what each should do, to suit the majority, is justified. However, to take the other side of the logical point just mentioned, the justification of their *being* treated as separate groups cannot make any reference to their average characteristics, because of course their average characteristics cannot even be found until they have been divided into groups on some other basis. If the average determines *what* the groups shall do, *that* they shall act as groups can be justified by reference only to what makes them into two separate groups in the first place; to the universal differences between them.

This is why the Ruskin-type justification of separate spheres cannot work in the first instance. No justification which depended on average differences could do it, and Ruskin's appears to have any plausibility only because of the equivocal nature of generalizations about men and women, which are usually based (when they are based on anything at all) on *average* or *general* differences, but carry the impression that they refer to *universal* ones. Only universal differences could do the necessary work, and therefore if the existence of separate social pressures is to be justified at all it must refer only to these differences; to what each sex really has which the other has not, not in most instances only, but in all.

No doubt it is obvious what these are; there are only two of any social and cultural importance. The more important is difference and reciprocity in reproductive function: females bear and nurse the young of the species; males engender them in females. The other is their difference of role in sexual activity as an end in itself.

However, although so much is obvious, it is worthwhile to press the matter a little further. So far we have made the sexes indeed sound equal in their differences, but it should perhaps be pointed out, since we are working against a background of widespread presumptions of female inferiority, that a good deal of *female generosity* is needed to count the situation as anything like one of equality. The sexes are indeed equal and different in their sexual need of each other: in ordinary sexual relationships both are equally necessary. The same is true of their different functions in conception: sperm and ovum are equally necessary. *However, only the female has the ability to carry, give birth to, and nurse the child* once it is conceived, and this is an ability corresponding to which men have nothing at all. One of the principal differences between the sexes, in other words, is *women's possessing an ability which men have not*, and it would be closer to the truth to say that *men* were *men* in virtue of a lack of qualities, rather than that women were women on that account. (This is explicitly recognized by some cultures: the Zulus, for instance, apparently allow old women to break the taboo which prohibits women's approaching the army, on the grounds that 'they have become men'.[4])

If that sounds like female chauvinism, it must at least be recognized as an appropriate reply to the male chauvinism of Aristotle, Aquinas and the like, who contrived by some feat of their highly sophisticated reasoning processes to overlook woman's rather striking extra ability, and see her whole *essence* as a series of inadequacies and absences, while at the same time transforming man's inability to bear children into a special aptitude for everything else. However, there is more behind the point than simple one-up-womanship. Because their sex has been for so long a disadvantage, women need to be reminded of the fact that their extra ability (like any other ability) is in fact a great *advantage*, and has not looked like one in the past only because there has been very little choice about whether it should be used or not. Furthermore, as will become clear, it is important for the enquiry which we are now conducting.

However, we can for the moment leave those byways and return to the main argument. The really essential point is the one Kate Millett made in reply to Ruskin: that (as long as only universal differences are considered) 'the sexes are inherently in everything alike, save reproductive systems, secondary sexual characteristics, orgasmic capacity, and genetic and morphological structure'.[5] It is therefore only in these characteristics, which define the difference between men and women, that we must look to find any reason for society's imposing different pressures on the two sexes.

3 · KINDS OF PRESSURE

We are considering the general question of whether it is legitimate that men and women *as such* should be pushed in different directions by social pressures. To deal with that question adequately it is necessary to look at some of the different kinds of way in which society shapes individuals.

First, it is important to eliminate one possible source of confusion in the discussion, by pointing out a kind of influence which has considerable effect on the course of people's lives, but which cannot really be counted as a social pressure. It concerns people's *beliefs* about themselves and others. Opportunities open and close for all individuals according to what other people believe about their suitability as friends, confidants or employees, and even people's own choices among the opportunities open to them are much influenced by their own beliefs about themselves. Often people resist their strong desires to do something or other because they have reason to doubt (possibly as a result of other people's advice or the current state of psychological theory) whether it will make them happy.

It is quite inevitable that people's lives should be affected by their own and other people's beliefs in this way. Furthermore, and directly to the point of this discussion, it is equally inevitable that beliefs about individuals should be considerably influenced by beliefs about any clearly defined groups of which those individuals are members. This has nothing to do with prejudice. It is quite impossible for each individual, in all circumstances, to be assessed simply *as* an individual. It is always necessary to use general knowledge in the judgment of any particular situation, and one relevant piece of evidence in the assessment of any individual is bound to be what is generally true of other members of the group. This will of course tend to push any unusual members of a clearly recognizable group in the direction of the majority of the group. It is no surprise, therefore, if such influences should tend to make men and women move in the same direction as others of their sex.

It is certainly relevant for feminists to point out that in many cases where this kind of phenomenon occurs the wish is mother to the belief; much of what is believed about women stems from what is wanted of women. That is almost certainly true, and will be mentioned again later on. However, even if we could completely eliminate the double-think which goes on when women and men are advised to do different things, or selected for different functions, the general phenomenon would still exist.

When Ruskin-type apologists of femininity and masculinity produce their suggestions that society demands no more of men and women than what is suited to them, and asks of each individual what it most suits each to give, the impression given is that the social influences on men and women are all of the kind just described. It is implied that all society is doing is gently advising its members about what is to their own advantage, and selecting them for different situations on the basis of impartial assessments of their abilities. And if the pressures on men and women were indeed nothing more than these we could accept both that society was benevolent in its intention (even though mistaken about facts) and furthermore that individual men and women might be pushed more in the direction of others of their sex than was actually ideal for them as individuals. However, such influences are very far from being the only ones. We have not yet come to the real social pressures, and these are a very different matter, because they work on individuals without any consideration of what is suited to *them*: true social pressures work to make individuals suited to the wishes of *other* people. They are the pressures which are of importance in this discussion, and if we can find any of *these* which distinguish between men and women we can discount entirely any suggestion that they are placed on the two sexes for their own good.

There is a tendency, whenever people talk of social pressures, for them to be regarded as resulting from more or less deliberate social plans to produce a certain kind of society. This can be seen among both people who defend these pressures and those who attack them. Whenever a defender of the status quo feels it necessary to produce a defence of the kinds of social pressures there are (such as ones which make different demands of men and women), that defence very commonly takes the form of pointing out the beneficial consequences for everyone which result from that pressure, as if all social pressures came about as a result of the workings of some benevolent social planner who made sure that they were designed solely to bring the best out of everyone. People who disapprove of social pressures also tend to talk in much the same way, seeing them as a mechanism by which a powerful entity squeezes individuals out of their individuality and distorts them into standard social products which can easily be coped with. Whether they are approved of or not, social pressures tend to be seen as being of this more or less deliberate sort.

Now of course whenever society has such designs for people, good or bad, it will certainly exert pressures to make them conform. However, it does not follow that all social pressures have this kind of source, and probably the commonest of all are of a kind which might be called *indirect*. These have nothing to do with any general plan for society (even a subconscious one), but arise accidentally out of the various individual desires which people have. One way of putting it is to say that these indirect pressures exist not because anyone is determined to force you into a particular mould, but because you yourself want particular sorts of success, and to achieve them it is necessary to take account of other people's desires, and go along with what they approve.

This can be illustrated quite easily. Imagine, for instance, that you are a young man living in a community where most of the young women are devoted tennis players. It is easy to imagine that in such a place some young men might start taking up tennis as well because it provided a good means of access to the women, and that once some men had begun others who wanted to be in the running for the women would have to do it too. Here is a clear case of social pressure. You and others like you may not have much interest in tennis, but you are more or less forced to take it up in order to achieve what you want. However, no one is trying to coerce you into it. There is no plot by the Sports Council in the background. It is just that if you want to do well in the competition you must adopt the means.

Or imagine you are already an accomplished violin player. You may want to play in an orchestra, and if you do, you may well have to develop *additional* characteristics to please the people who select orchestra players. The more competition there is for the positions, the harder you will have to work at your ability to co-operate with other musicians, and your willingness to put up with temperamental conductors and irregular hours, or whatever. You are under pressure, but once again there is no background wish in society to have musicians conform to a particular pattern. Which pattern you conform to depends in the first place on what you want to do with your skills, and secondly on all kinds of accidents like the nature of the people who are making the decisions, and how strong the competition is.

The situation then is this. In order to enter a particular competition, you have to have certain minimum characteristics; to be a suitor to a woman you have to be male, and to be a possible orchestra player you have to be a musician. If a large number of people with the minimum characteristics want the same thing as you do they will all be trying to outdo each other in developing the other desirable characteristics. There is then social pressure on the members of the group. But that pressure is not on them *as* members of the group. It is not that society has decreed that all young men must play tennis or that all musicians must learn to put up with late hours, and that any who will not must be made to suffer. The pressure is on them *as people who are competing for a particular prize*, for which their group-membership gives the minimum requirements. If the pressures *appear* to be on all young men, or all musicians, that is only because they are nearly all in the same race. The pressure is in fact directed towards *the end they are seeking*, rather than the group as such.

This has considerable relevance for the question of whether there ought to be different social pressures on men and women; whether they should be pushed in different directions by society. The members of each sex want each other, in the first instance, for 'what the other only can give'; characteristics specifically concerned with being of the opposite sex. Obviously, however, people will want not just *anybody* of the opposite sex, but someone with as many additional desirable characteristics as possible. Of course people will have different ideas about what is desirable in a sexual partner to some extent, but there are still bound to be some people who are more sought after than others. This immediately introduces an element of competition (and therefore of social pressure), since to get the most desirable of the opposite sex you must make yourself as sexually desirable as possible.

Now as long as women and men want the same additional characteristics in each other, the pressures on both sexes will be the same. *If* however women want slightly different characteristics of men than men want of women, the pressures on the two sexes will be different. Women will try to conform to the ideal of the men they want, and men to the ideal of the women they want, in order to get for themselves the widest possible choice of mates. If we call the characteristics which women have to acquire for success with men feminine ones and the ones men have to acquire to attract women masculine ones, we have an account of how a society may develop social pressures towards masculinity and femininity without bringing anything sinister into the account. It is not that society in such a case thinks something *good* in one sex and not the other; it is just that for success people have to go along with what other people want. That is absolutely inevitable in any society, and could disappear only if people ceased to have any preferences at all.

Naturally any feminist who thinks that there are no inherent differences between men and women, and that there should be no cultural ones, will dismiss all this as irrelevant even if she accepts the principle of the argument: if men and women do not differ in what they want of each other unless they have been corrupted by society, the pressures on the two sexes should be the same. That, however, is a matter which need not be settled here. The important thing is to have given an account of a kind of social pressure which does not involve any kind of plot to make individuals conform to a pattern, but which certainly can result in different pressures on different groups, and could result in different pressures on men and women.

We have, therefore, succeeded in justifying in principle yet another set of social forces which might push men and women in different directions. However, it should be stressed in passing, for the benefit of people who defend femininity on general principles of benevolence, that this set of pressures has nothing in the least to do with plans for a carefully balanced society in which people do what suits them best. It all stems from accidental and selfish desires. The pressures on people are pressures to make them do what pleases other people, not what suits themselves. And the separate pressures on women and men, far from having anything to do with making each individual conform to the sexual average, push them in the direction of the sex's socially desired extremes.

4 · DIRECT SOCIAL PRESSURES

However, even though accounts have now been given of two sets of influences which *might* legitimately differentiate between men and women (one a set of genuine pressures, the other not), they were not intended to provide a complete explanation of the pressures which do *as a matter of fact* push men and women in different directions. Indeed they were partly intended to do precisely the opposite, and provide a contrast with the main kinds of pressure which do actually work to separate the sexes. Most of these are not like the innocuous indirect ones described in the previous section, but are what may be described as *direct*.

Direct social pressures can be explained by comparing them with indirect ones. The mark of what I have called an indirect social pressure is that individuals go along with it only if they are interested in achieving something or other; other people do not care whether they try to acquire the characteristics in question or not. Generally, if you are a musician, no one cares whether you want to go into an orchestra or not. A good education will provide you with the techniques to compete if you want to, but will not push you in one direction or the other. Direct social pressures, in contrast to this, arise *when people have a positive desire to make you into one thing rather than another*, quite irrespective of what your own desires are. A society, or individuals in it, may want you to be Christian, law abiding, adventurous, studious, deferential, warlike, honest, respectful of elders, or anything else. If instead of just ignoring you when you do not go along with these ideals people actually try to change you to make you conform, the pressures are direct ones.

It does not matter whether society is aware of having these ideals or not. Very often people put pressure on other people to make them conform without having the least idea that they are doing it. Nor does it matter how strong the pressure is. It may range from gentle persuasion to severe punishment or actual force, depending on the importance of what is wanted and the character of the people who are exerting the pressure. Throughout all these variations of awareness of intent and method of persuasion the principle is the same. Direct social pressures occur when people have a positive desire to have you behave in one way rather than another, and they are different from indirect pressures, where it is your own desire to compete (rather than other people's to have you conform) which makes you go along with them.

The difference between direct and indirect social pressures, in other words, has to do with the *direction* of the pressures; whether that direction is the same as or different from the direction of the desire. Suppose, for instance, A wants something from B. A may exert pressure on B to provide what is wanted, in which case B is under direct pressure from A: both the desire and the pressure originate from A and are directed to B. On the other hand, A may try to please B until B is willing to provide what is wanted in return, in which case (since A is having to go along with B's desires to get what A wants) desire and pressure work in opposite directions, and the pressure is indirect. To illustrate this (since As and Bs are not easy to follow) we can take an example from the last chapter. If a society wants children, and sets about getting them by means of closing other options to women, women are under direct pressure from society. If, on the other hand, society does as it should and offers women inducements to have children, society is under indirect pressure from women; indirect, because the reason for the existence of the pressure is not the women's desires, but society's own.

That example is not meant to suggest that direct social pressures should never exist. In spite of some people's woolly convictions that you ought always to be yourself (whatever that means), and that if anyone else makes positive demands of you, your natural rights are being infringed, it does seem out of the question that any society should fail to contain direct social pressures. In the first place, many are inevitable: people will always use whatever influence they have to make other people conform to their desires, and although we may increase social justice it must be impossible to prevent people's having unequal power. Second, many direct pressures seem positively desirable, since society would go to pieces unless it positively tried to prevent people from doing certain kinds of harm. The question of the extent to which such direct pressures are acceptable, however, is obviously an exceedingly difficult one, and it is just as well that for the purposes of this enquiry it can be ignored altogether. The only question which needs to be settled here is whether it is legitimate for such direct social pressures as do exist to differentiate between men and women.

There is no doubt that there has always been such a differentiation. It is not very long since it was absolutely clear, because the most extreme form of social pressure, removal of opportunity to do anything else, kept men and women firmly out of each other's spheres: education, rules about who could do what work and even the legal system itself placed men and women in different situations, and there was nothing whatever that most individuals could do about it. Where society cannot actually prevent what it thinks undesirable its next line of direct pressure is punishment (of varying degrees), and once again there is no doubt that the incurring of penalties traditionally depended not simply on the action done, but on the sex of the agent. For instance, prostitution, adultery and loose sexual behaviour were fiercely penalized in women, but not men. The most extreme cases of this differentiation have now gone, but very substantial parts of it still remain. Even the law and educational systems do not treat men and women identically, but of greater continuing importance is the fact that what is *approved* of in society is not independent of considerations of sex. Expressions of disapproval vary considerably in strength and may be very subtle, but where we feel disapproval there can be little doubt that somehow or other we show it, and there is equally little doubt that approval and disapproval is sex-connected. How many people, even among the most enlightened, would be *perfectly unmoved* by the sexes of the people involved when reacting to playing with dolls, dressing prettily, swearing, making open sexual advances, wolf-whistling, riding pillion on a motor bike driven by someone of the other sex, mending the car for someone of the other sex who had broken down, answering the front door in an apron, and innumerable other things? As long as social approval and disapproval are connected with sex, the direct social pressures on men and women are different. The question is, is it acceptable that they should be different?

Consider precisely what is involved. Society, or at least most of it, has *different wishes* for the two sexes, and puts different pressures on them. In the strongest form, the social pressure involves outright prevention; making it impossible for one sex to do what the other can do. There is little of that now, admittedly. The weaker forms of pressure involve making opportunity more difficult to come by for one sex than the other, or by punishing one (usually by means of clear social disapproval) for what would be approved or regarded with equanimity in the other. When these practices differentiate the sexes, what is possible or easy for one sex is made impossible or difficult for the other. But that, surely, is *precisely what was ruled out absolutely by the arguments about justice in the last chapter*.

There is no illusion here. The issues of femininity and discrimination may look very different, but that is at least partly because the matter of femininity is a complicated one, as we have seen. If we consider only the aspect of the subject of femininity which concerns direct social pressures – the conscious or unconscious, fierce or mild, desire that men should go one way and women another – the two subjects are identical. If the principles of justice worked out in the last chapter are to be accepted, differential direct social pressures are inherently objectionable, in just the same way as discrimination is. And that is the conclusion of this part of the investigation. Although some social forces and influences may reasonably distinguish between the sexes, direct social pressures which do so cannot be justified.

5 · THE NATURE OF FEMININITY

That, however, is far from the end of the matter, because so far all that has been shown is that there is a social injustice which affects both men and women, and may therefore seem to provide no special justification for *feminist* complaint. It is very often said by opponents of feminism that there are just as many difficulties for men as for women. Indeed many men insist that the division leaves women a great deal better off than men, and claim to wish that things were as easy for them. It is therefore necessary to go further, and not be satisfied simply with noting the *existence* of the different social pressures on the two grcups. It is important to understand the *nature* of those pressures, and in doing so try to define what the requirements of femininity and masculinity are; what is thought proper for women but not for men, and the other way round.

To do this it is once again useful to start by looking at the past, which very often provides a convenient magnifying glass for the present: present conventions and attitudes can often be better understood by looking at the more clearly defined social arrangements out of which they developed. It is also useful to look at the matter of origins for the sake of being prepared for debate with traditionalists, who would have feminists believe that the relative positions of men and women result from a combination of nature and benevolent social planning. What then were the original arrangements for the position of each sex, before recent reforms modified them?

The facts are stark, but beyond any question. All social arrangements, institutions and customs which defined the relative position of the sexes were designed *to ensure that women should be in the power and service of men*.

This no doubt sounds like pure feminist rant, but it is not.

It is proved by many quite incontrovertible facts about the *formal devices* which for most of history were employed by men to make sure that women were kept in their power, and involves no recourse to extravagant assertions about the general moral turpitude of men. There were all kinds of laws about the legal control of husbands over wives and fathers over daughters, and obstacles in the way of women's controlling property. There were rules keeping women from nearly every kind of pursuit which might have given them status or independence (reinforced by their being kept out of any education which might have suited them to such activities), so forcing them to depend for support on men. There were appalling sanctions on 'fallen women', which kept women bound to a particular man. There were laws which made it pretty well impossible for women to escape from the power of tyrannical husbands, since they would have to sacrifice everything, including their children, in the process. And to ratify it all, women were kept totally out of the making of law, so that until some men were willing to champion their cause there was no hope of their doing anything to change any of it.

To see the position of women in this way is to see clearly what femininity traditionally was. Feminine characteristics were the ones needed for making a success of the position into which women were forced, and roughly, therefore, to be feminine was to be pleasing to men. The whole essence of femininity is, or at least traditionally was, the limiting of all endeavour and activity to a confined end. Ideal femininity has never consisted in weakness and incompetence (contrary to much popular opinion, which seems to confuse descriptive and prescriptive femininity at this point as at many others); no man ever wanted a total loss of a woman. The idea was only to direct all abilities to being useful to men and their offspring, using a great deal of skill (the more the better) but always carefully directing it so that it presented no threat to men's position. It was unfeminine of women to want to study at universities or have the vote because in doing so they were showing that they had ideas about stepping beyond their allotted sphere: higher education and political power were not among the requirements for being a devoted wife and mother, and to seek them was to want to compete with men and become independent of them, rather than to remain in service to them.

All this makes it clear beyond a doubt that there was never anything in the nature of an *equal* division of function between men and women. There is nothing in the least comparable about masculinity. It is quite misleading to think of femininity and masculinity as similar sorts of thing; equal degrees of adaptation to different situations. Men have rarely been in situations where they have had to go out of their way to please women, except briefly during courtship. In fact masculinity has traditionally been no different from general success in whatever is valued by society, and virtually the only way any reference to women comes into the concept of masculinity is in the demand that no man should be subordinate or inferior to a woman. (The least masculine man is the one who is henpecked.) This all explains why, as Pauline Marks wrote, 'femininity had to be achieved, cultivated and preserved, while masculinity could be left to look after itself.'⁶

There is therefore no equality in the demands made of the sexes, and there is certainly no attempt to please women in their formation; only men. The situation was certainly not arranged by a benevolent Ruskinian social planner. Why then did it come about?

Most people probably think that humans go in for sexual pairing because it is natural for us in the way that it is natural for wolves and swans, and it is commonly argued that men have control of women because the strong must protect the weak. However, this sort of explanation will not do at all. Presumably women must in some sense tend to be weaker than men, or men could never have reduced them to such a state of subjection in the first place, but the suggestion that a weak group can be protected by being abandoned to the total control of a stronger one involves as remarkable a piece of twisted reasoning as can ever have been devised. If women are weak and need protection, it should have been the men who were controlled. A similar argument shows that the pairing arrangement cannot be one into which both sexes enter automatically as a result of some deeply-rooted instinct. If women had acquiesced willingly, there would have been no need for a colossal superstructure of law and convention to keep them in their place. The existence of rules to keep women in the power of men shows that men must have wanted of women something which women could not be trusted to provide of their own accord.

What can that have been? It cannot have been anything general like domestic service, because that would account only for the strong of both sexes making slaves of the weaker of either sex (which of course also happens), and not specifically for men's taking over women. The reason must have been (once again) to do with the universal differences between the sexes: with sexual capacity or childbearing. It is unlikely to have been the first, since a group so supremely confident of its own strength as men appear to be could have relied on getting women's sexual co-operation by rape, so their motivation must have been the other one. The non-bearers of children wanted to control the bearers of children. And the only possible explanation of that, as far as I can see, must have been their wanting to define a breeding territory from which other men were excluded, and which would guarantee at once both their having offspring and their being able to identify them as their own. Women can by nature be confident about both these matters; men cannot at all, as long as women are on the loose. Anyway, whatever the precise details, any explanation which is to fit the indisputable facts must involve men's wanting something which women had and they themselves had not, and which women could not be relied on to provide unconstrained.

The whole subject of the history of men's attitudes to women's childbearing, and the repercussions which many social scientists think are still discernible, is a fascinating one. Some think that in men's attitudes to women there are still traces of primaeval fear, reaching from the time when men did not know they had any part in procreation, and thought women magical.[7] Many psychologists think that much of the male impulse to exclude women from male activities results from a deep jealousy of the female's extra ability, and a wish to establish comparable territory for themselves,[8] a theory which is reinforced by anthropological discoveries of male initiation ceremonies which are clear imitations of childbirth.[9] It also seems at least arguable that many established customs which are usually explained in terms of the strong protecting the weak (men fighting in wars and women and children being rescued first from sinking ships) are really rooted in the fact that since from the point of view of reproduction most men are superfluous (from that point of view we could do perfectly well with a hundredth of the ones we have) they are *dispensable*, and could be more readily spared by a group than its women could be. However, interesting as all that is, and potentially useful for explaining many of the details of social arrangements concerning men and women, it is an area to be studied by other disciplines, and not particularly important here. The important point for this argument is that it can be established, *without* any reference to controversial theories, that men went to a good deal of trouble to get women into their power, and the only possible explanation of the original motive is women's ability to bear children. Nothing else seems to fit the indisputable facts.

We have, then, an account of the nature and origins of the feminine ideal. It would of course be silly to suggest that nothing has since changed. The principle of pairing to have children is far too deeply rooted for men now to have any conscious fears that unless women are controlled they will be deprived of families (though it will be interesting to see what happens if many women do take to rearing children on their own), and all the conventions confining women to the service of men have lessened considerably or disappeared altogether. Nevertheless, although the *reason* for special feminine activity has been forgotten, and the *extent* of the separate demands made of women lessened, *to the extent that there do still remain different conventions for proper male and female activity and behaviour, nearly all are of the traditional kind.*

This is unmistakable. For instance, *to the extent* that boys and girls are given different educations, what distinguishes the girls' is that it is home-directed, with needlework, cooking, 'home economics' and so on. The 'commercial' courses which are the exception still prepare them for what is nearly always service to a man outside the home. (Consider also the significance of girls' having been encouraged to take arts rather than science subjects.) Then, away from school, it is a rare home in which the man will not presume as a matter of course that the woman will take the responsibility for domestic matters (even if he occasionally 'does the washing up for Mary', making it clear that the act is supererogatory because it is really Mary's job) and be available when he wants her, even though she may work outside the home as well. Again, *to the extent* that different behaviour is approved for men and women it always involves women's not putting themselves forward, not henpecking, being loyal, going along with what the man suggests and so on. Women's magazines still dispense advice about how to be a highly competent assistant or partner to a man without making him feel threatened: how to cover up for your boss when he makes mistakes; how to get what you want for the family by letting your husband think he thought of it. At a more sophisticated level, manuals of sexual success instruct experienced women in the art of leading men sexually while giving the impression that it is the men who are taking the initiative. And, in addition to all this, hardly anybody gives a thought to the highly significant universal presumption that a woman and her children should take the man's surname. The special demands of women have lessened in their scope, but their nature is the same as it ever was.

This is not to deny that there are advantages in the female role. Because it is acceptable for women to depend on men, the threshold of respectability is set much lower for women than for men. Probably the reason why most vagrants are men is that women at the same level of social incompetence are usually caught in the net of a man's protection and kept in the fold. But this is small consolation to the women near the top of the social ladder who are prevented from going any higher by the same nets. And anyway, even though men can point to this advantage which women undoubtedly have, and no doubt others too, feminists have a total reply in saying that if these differential sex-based conventions were ended, all these enviable advantages would be open to men as well. The argument about which sex is better off does not arise (once again) unless it is already accepted that they are to have different things.

On the whole men seem to be in no hurry to embrace the opportunity to end these sex distinctions, and it is obvious why. Whatever the few drawbacks of power it is on the whole a good thing to have, and it is excellent that there should be a class of people on hand among whom one can generally be found to be acquiescent, available, and a general provider of personal comforts. No wonder, feminists may well say, men are so anxious that women should not lose their femininity.

6 · PLANNING THE ESCAPE

The argument at this stage is bound to leave some people in a state of dissatisfaction. There must be some who accept that women should not be kept in a state of contrived inferiority to men, but still feel that such inferiority cannot be a *necessary* concomitant of femininity, and that there must be something good about femininity in spite of all that has been said. There is something in this, and I hope the point will have been dealt with adequately by the end of the chapter. However, for now let us continue with the line of the argument, and start by recapitulating what has gone so far.

First, then, it has been argued that there probably are inherent masculine and feminine characteristics, characteristics which occur more commonly in one sex than the other, but that these should not cause anxiety to feminists. Feminist concern arises when women are pushed by society in different directions from men. However, some of the influences which make men and women tend in different directions from each other are quite innocuous. It is a fact of life that we must to some extent assess individuals (including ourselves) on the basis of what we know or believe about others who resemble them in striking ways, and therefore we may with the best will in the world encourage all women to do what suits most. Indirect social pressures, too, are an inescapable fact of life, and they could also quite acceptably differentiate between men and women – or at least between men and women who were interested in relationships with the other sex, which is nearly all. So far, at least in theory, there is nothing for feminists to object to.

However, by far the strongest forces which differentiate the sexes are none of these things, but what have been called *direct social pressures*, and they are quite a different matter. Although direct social pressures as such are bound to exist, when they differentiate between different groups they are inherently objectionable because they infringe the principles of justice established earlier: they prevent people's having equal opportunity to succeed in all areas of activity. The pressures of this kind which differentiate men and women are also, as it happens, additionally objectionable in giving nothing like equal roles to women and men: traditional femininity of activity and demeanour keeps women subservient to men. Though the traditions have weakened they have not disappeared. There are still different direct pressures on the sexes, and women's relative position is of the same *kind* as it ever was, although the *degree* has lessened.

What, then, should feminist policy be? In the light of what has been said, it seems clear: the aim should be to eliminate all direct social pressures which differentiate the sexes. Educational and professional opportunity should be absolutely equal, so that achievement is determined entirely by ability, and not by matters' being made easier for one sex than the other. Law should not make sex relevant in contexts where it is not. And disapproval of behaviour, whether its expression is mild or severe, should depend only on the nature of the behaviour in question, and not at all on the sex of the person whose behaviour it is.

An important corollary of this is that if it came about, men and women would have equal institutional power: social organization would not bring about asymmetrical dependence of the sexes on each other. It should be pointed out, however, that institutional and actual equality of dependence are not the same thing, and it might still turn out that one sex was by nature more dependent on the other than the other on it, and would therefore be under heavier indirect pressures even though the direct ones were identical. And (to risk a little more female chauvinism) although it is now generally believed that women have a stronger natural dependence on men than the other way round, it is far more likely that any such tendencies have been produced by women's institutionalized dependence, and that in fact precisely the opposite is true. If the evolutionary arguments presented earlier are right, and men's sexual drive is on the whole greater than women's, men will have a greater need of women in that respect than women of men; and it is certain that men are dependent on the co-operation of women for the identification of their offspring, while women have no such dependence on men. And to reinforce this by a familiar argument, it seems most unlikely that so much effort would have been put into making women artificially dependent on men if they had been naturally so. However, all that is beside the point here. The important point is that *institutions* should be arranged to make sure that neither sex as such is dependent on the other.

This policy certainly seems the one to pursue, given the nature of what is wrong. However, it is unfortunately almost certain that it would not be enough to put matters right, for several reasons.

First, the total elimination of differential direct pressures is probably impossible. For one thing, the directness of a social pressure has nothing to do with its obviousness, and although we might deal relatively easily with the most obvious kinds of discrimination, the subtlest ways in which people express disapproval and influence behaviour are probably quite invisible to us, and therefore impossible to attack. Another serious problem is that however effectively we implement a social policy for not treating the sexes differently, individuals are always going to have a certain amount of power over other individuals (obvious examples are parents over children, groups over members who are not in a position to escape to other groups), and therefore as long as significant numbers of *individuals* want the sexes different from each other, the pressures will continue to exist.

Second, however effectively we eliminate direct social pressures, it will remain true that people's desires have been formed by them. Men and women have grown up expecting different things of each other. Therefore the system of *indirect* social pressures will tend to perpetuate the previous system of direct ones, because in order to please men women will still have to act as men want them to. It is easy to say in reply to this that if women are no longer dependent on men they simply need not go along with these wishes, but that is too superficial a reply. Whether or not they are actually dependent on men, women are likely to go on wanting them, and if they do not go along with the unreasonable expectations men have inherited from the past they will lose the men to other women who do. To overcome the problem there would have to be an agreement among all women, and that would be quite impracticable; obviously the women who would by nature be rather behind in the race for men would be only too glad to take advantage of some of the front runners' dropping out of the competition, and would have no possible motive for co-operating with them.

Furthermore, the old direct pressures would presumably not only be perpetuated in the indirect pressures on *women*; they would equally be kept going by the indirect pressures of women on men. Women, in their expectation of leadership, independence, strength, chivalry and all the rest in men put men under pressure to keep to these traditional masculine ideals, whether or not the men themselves feel inclined to do so. On both sides the old direct pressures would be continued, through people's expectations, in indirect pressures.

And finally, the *third* influence which tends to fossilize the past is the other which was mentioned earlier in the chapter: people's beliefs about their own and others' natures, and in particular the opinions held by a good many sophisticated sociological and psychological theorists. In judging other people and making decisions for themselves people are bound to go by what they believe to be true, and it is equally reasonable that they should turn to experts: that is what they do when there are problems about the central heating system or getting the roses to grow, and in principle it is quite right that they should have the same reliance on people with greater knowledge when they are judging what is best for people. The trouble is, however, that although things are beginning to improve a little, a great many reputed experts still tend to tell women (who still believe them) that they are made happy and fulfilled by quite other things than are appropriate for men. 'We must start with the realization that, as much as women want to be good scientists or engineers, they want first and foremost to be womanly companions of men and to be mothers',[10] they say, or 'the highest value and the only commitment for women is the fulfilment of their own femininity',[11] and it was ideas like these which, as Betty Friedan said, led women who in theory had every opportunity open to them to neglect or trivialize their studies, cultivate their feminine nature and return in droves to their little houses to fulfil their biological destiny.

Of course there is nothing wrong in principle with psychologists' telling women that they are made satisfied by different things from men: if it is true women should want to know it, whether they are feminists or not. What is wrong at present is that many of the theories almost certainly *result* from preconceived ideas about what it is proper for women to do, rather than providing, as they pretend to, the foundation for them. There are various reasons for fearing this. One obvious one is that by the time the social sciences came along to systematize and explain society, the material they had to work on was already the product of millennia of teaching women to be womanly, and it was bound to be easy to mistake the desires women had learnt to acquire for ones which stemmed from their intrinsic natures. Of course all women would centre their ambitions on marriage and children in a society which allowed no other opportunity to women, but in a situation where everything was entirely taken for granted the real significance of these wishes could easily be overlooked. Another reason for being afraid that psychological theories about women result to a great extent from past prejudice is the striking fact that whenever a woman appeared discontented with her role, that was attributed not to her being *in* the feminine straitjacket, but to her trying to get *out* of it. That shows the depth of the determination to believe that women were intrinsically different from men, and the way it affected apparently reputable and objective investigators.

It is interesting to speculate about precisely why such prejudices existed, and to some extent still do. Much of it must of course be attributable to wishful thinking, and the desire already mentioned of any dominant group to justify its treatment of a subject group by trying to show that the subjects want nothing else. However, it may perhaps also be in part the result of another phenomenon often found when there are two such groups: the dominant group is interested only in the way the lesser group *differs* from itself, and because it is totally absorbed in its own view of things easily comes to presume that the aspects in which it happens to be interested are *all there is* to the members of the other group. Consider, for instance, the way people are terrified that homosexual teachers will seduce children in schools, while having no such fears about heterosexual ones. Because people are interested in the sexual difference they seem to think that homosexuals are *nothing but* their sexual characteristics and therefore sex-crazed. Perhaps the theories about women's main interests being 'to be womanly companions of men and mothers' may stem to a considerable extent from the nature of men's interest in women. Women's sexual and childbearing abilities are only two among *innumerable* abilities which women possess, and it is significant that those two, the only ones women do not share with men and which are therefore of special interest to men, should have been picked out by the social sciences as being *women's* main concern. Anyway, whatever the explanation, the fact remains. The psychological theories which people use in making decisions about the course of their lives do themselves stem from long-established views about what is proper for men and women, and therefore are another force in perpetuating the past.

The situation then is this. The feminist's real cause of complaint in the matter of femininity is that direct social pressures have demanded different things of women and men. Apparently, therefore, these pressures are what ought to be attacked. On the other hand, investigation seems to show that no such attack could possibly be effective enough. The very task of totally eliminating direct pressures looks impossible, and even if that could succeed the evil would still continue, because there are millennia of entrenched effects to contend with as well, and they will not disappear just because the cause does. Indirect pressures and ingrained beliefs will keep the traditions going. And arguments such as these do seem to justify the impulse many feminists give the impression of having: that of wanting to launch a *direct* attack on femininity in all its manifestations, rather than struggle simply with its original causes.

7 · THE DIRECT ATTACK

Making a direct attack on femininity essentially means not stopping until women and men are alike on average in character, occupation and behaviour; indeed, in all matters except the strictly sexual ones. Few feminists, probably, would say that this was what they wanted to achieve; they would be far more likely to say that all they wanted to do was to get rid of the pressures on men and women so that people could be themselves and find their own level. However, although that might perhaps be ideal, the fact is that it is not much help in practice, because of the difficulty (already mentioned) of telling when all separating pressures on men and women have ceased. This is part of a general theoretical problem for philosophy of science. You find out whether two things are alike or different in nature by seeing how they respond to the same influences, but if you are not sure about whether the influences are the same you have to judge *those* by what is happening to the two things in question, and that means making presumptions about their sameness or difference. There is no escaping this problem. This means that in trying to work out whether men and women are under the same or different pressures it is necessary to judge to a large extent by the effects, and therefore it is not surprising if in fact, if not in theory, many feminists do take men's and women's making different choices as in itself evidence of the existence of differentiating pressures. This may indeed be perfectly acceptable methodology, but it must be recognized that the *consequence* is to attack all manifestations of average difference between the sexes, even though the intention was only to remove pressures.

However, any such policy as this is also fraught with difficulty. Just as the other policy, of attacking only the causes, would achieve too little, this would be equally likely to achieve far too much.

The *first* reason for fearing this is obvious, in view of what has been said so far. Although feminists who want to eliminate tendencies to difference in men and women do undoubtedly believe that nature has made men and women alike, at least in all matters of the soul, and that therefore they should be alike, this is a thing about which we really do not know. They may be fundamentally alike, but equally they may not, and any campaign mounted against differences as such *could* have the effect of forcing both sexes into forms as inimical to their happiness as those into which they are moulded by social pressures at present. If men and women do by nature want slightly different things, we shall do no good by making them feel that there is something wrong until they want the same.

Second, even though the wishes and expectations men and women have of each other may be culturally induced and not an inevitable part of their natures, that is not the slightest reason for ignoring them. A liberator must allow people *as they actually are* to make their own choices, because their culturally determined preferences are still theirs.

The *third* problem concerns culture, an immensely complicated and difficult subject which can only be touched on here, but which must not be ignored altogether. For many feminists, part of the direct attack on femininity takes the form of recommending an androgynous culture (not, by the way, 'androgenous', which is the way the word is usually pronounced and which means more or less the opposite of what is intended); one which is shared by women and men instead of differentiating them. However, most people like cultural differences. They do not want to go to India or South America, for instance, and find people dressing and talking in the same way as here, or see the same kind of architecture. Furthermore, it is not just *difference* which is attractive, but its rooting in tradition. Invented ceremonies and customs are never as impressive as traditional ones, and an English family living in a Japanese-style house in London would have nothing like the attractiveness of a Japanese family in the same kind of house in Japan. The whole subject is as obscure as it is fascinating, but the important thing for now is the simple fact that people have a similar kind of enjoyment of traditions associated with sex differentiation, and while feminists must be committed to attacking all cultural distinctions which actually degrade women, the indiscriminate pursuit of an androgynous culture must involve the elimination of innocuous cultural differences as well, and with them the source of a great deal of pleasure to many people.

There is no reason to presume that there are no such innocuous cultural differences. Even though most of feminine culture has been shown to be inherently bad for the equality of women, there is no need to presume that it is true, let alone necessarily true, of all. There is nothing inherently degrading about conventional differences of name, dress, hair styles, or even (to some extent) interests and occupations; no one sees anything to complain about when countries have different national dresses, or tribes are skilled in different crafts, and equally there is nothing inherently evil about men's and women's having such differences of activity and appearance either. Of course things associated with women have traditionally been belittled by association even when they have been inherently equal to things associated with men, and no doubt many androgynously inclined feminists think that a sexually differentiated culture would end by degrading women by that method if by no other. But that, surely, is a thing which feminists of all people should wish to *resist*, rather than avoid. And even if it were impossible to be confident about the success of such resistance, anyone who thinks that it is attractive to keep cultural differences wherever possible must feel that settling for an androgynous culture on the grounds of its avoiding risk is about as commendable a policy as stopping children from climbing trees in case they fall out. The pleasure of climbing trees is worth a good many risks, and so, for most people, must be the pleasure of keeping inherently harmless traditions wherever we can.

Of course no feminist can legitimately want to force women and men into cultural slots of any kind, even minor and equal ones, or say that if something is culturally associated with one sex members of the other must keep away from it. That would directly conflict with what has been said about differential direct pressures. (Perhaps it is worth adding that for the same reason she cannot, either, wish to interfere with people who themselves choose to keep to cultural traditions, even where they are inherently degrading.) However, it is quite compatible with feminism to think it would be pleasant to have, *other things being equal*, a society where men and women tended to choose what was traditionally associated with their sex, and enjoy the differences traditionally associated with the other. It is also compatible with feminism for a woman to choose for herself to keep to what is traditionally feminine to the extent that it does not interfere with more important matters. There need be no feminist objection to such preferences, and this is worth pointing out, because although all feminists should agree that no pressure should be put on other people to force them into or out of cultural slots, many may mistakenly think themselves obliged, against their real inclinations, to avoid everything traditionally womanly.

Of course it *might* be true that everyone would be happier if all sex-based culture disappeared; however it might equally be true that much possible happiness would be lost through its elimination. Any evidence on either side ought to be considered impartially. However, as was argued earlier, debates about political programmes need not confine themselves to discussions of facts and moral principles, and since we need a good deal more evidence to say with any certainty which of the two would make people happier, this is a clear case where it is reasonable to defend preferences. Anyone who finds the idea of an androgynous culture attractive is quite entitled on that ground to look for support from other people to establish one. However, any feminist who finds the idea of eliminating sex-based culture as unattractive as the idea of suppressing national ones is equally entitled to try to work out how much tradition can be kept (perhaps modified) without harm to women. For such a feminist, a direct attack on femininity in all its forms goes too far.

And finally, the *fourth* reason for not trying to solve the problems of femininity by making a direct attack on it in all its forms is that there may be strong *feminist* objections to trying to eliminate all cultural differences between men and women. It is connected with a problem which women share with all other oppressed groups emerging from their down-trodden state; that of how like their former oppressors they want to be. The first impulse is usually to compete with the oppressor on his own ground, but as the movement gathers strength and a sense of its own dignity that desire must come to look less and less acceptable: it is impossible for such a movement to want to go on imitating a group whose prac-tices the very fact of their own oppression forces them to condemn. One possible alternative is to find new ground on which both groups can work together, but for some emerg-ing groups this is not enough. They want to keep at least some of their separateness from the previously dominant group, and demand respect in spite of their difference. Black people do not want to mix in with white ones completely, even in a new grey culture, and women equally may have as little liking for ending their struggle with men in an andro-gynous one. They may be proud of being female, and want what is female to be recognizably different from what is male; they may want to cling determinedly to some existing traditions, and as well as that perhaps resuscitate old ones or even half-invent new ones, in order to keep by their own choice a separate identity for women. That feminists often have some such impulse may be indicated by the fact that for all the ideas of a society which does not differentiate the sexes, there is still much discussion about *women's culture*.

For these four reasons it seems as though any direct attack on all forms of femininity could do considerable harm. It risks unhappiness, coercion, an unattractive uniformity and the loss of opportunity for women to take special pride in being women. The problem of eradicating the evils of culturally imposed femininity therefore needs to be ap-proached with more circumspection.

8 · CONCLUSION

If it is dangerously drastic to mount a direct attack on femininity in all its forms, but inadequate to attack only its causes, what should feminist policy on the subject of femininity be?

The answer seems to be to accept, in the first place, that the business of finding out what women and men are really like, and what kinds of social arrangement would make both happiest, is a slow and unending process. It is best, therefore, not to worry too much about such intractable issues, but to concentrate specifically on what is known beyond question to be bad. One such obviously bad thing is the fact that sex is still commonly taken into account when an action is approved or disapproved, and about which much has already been said. The other extremely important obvious evil is the fact that many of the deeply established conventions which distinguish the sexes do, by their very nature, tend to preserve women's inferior position. It is absolutely essential to identify which conventions come into this particular category, not because any woman should be forced to resist them, but because it is of the utmost importance for everyone to be able to recognize them and make choices on the basis of that understanding. Women who do choose them must at least understand what they are letting themselves in for. Feminists who want to preserve some cultural femininity must be able to make a reliable distinction between sexual traditions which can be allowed to pass gracefully, or even encouraged as part of a pride in being women, and which must be fought tooth and nail. And all feminists who are trying to alter social conventions must be able to justify their policies by explaining precisely where and why the present state of things is inimical to the fair treatment of women, so that they do not lay themselves open to public ridicule by attacking what does no harm, or appears to do no harm.

This is no easy matter. Some areas of danger are clear

enough: all the mores which make it difficult or unacceptable for women to put themselves forward, take the initiative,
prove men in the wrong, make sexual advances, speak
forcefully, rescue men in broken down cars or become more
professionally successful than their husbands and lovers are
obvious feminist targets. Others, however, may present
more problems. Those which undoubtedly have their historical roots in women's oppression may be entirely harmless now, at least in some contexts; others without such
roots may have become dangerous. There are psychological
as well as philosophical questions to be answered before
judgment can be reached in most cases, and the whole area
is one of the most important for feminist study.

The subject is one which will be continued in the next
chapter, in a discussion of the status of women's traditional
work. Meanwhile, however, it is probably worth suggesting
by way of conclusion to this chapter that much of the heat
might go out of the subject of femininity if people would
keep to the subject, and set out to diagnose the real nature
and extent of their worries instead of falling into alarm and
despondency at the very thought that women might become
unfeminine, and looking no further. It is important, before
entering into dispute, to be able to say exactly which characteristics are desirable in women but not men, or the other
way round. What is it that people are afraid of, when they
say they are opposed to feminism because it will result in
women's ceasing to be feminine?

In fact many of the complaints made by anti-feminists
about unfeminine women may not really be about unfemininity at all. There is a popular image of a graceless,
belligerent feminist that is held up as an awful warning to
the rest of womankind in case they are thinking of becoming similarly 'unfeminine'. But – quite apart from any
question of the accuracy of this image – it is not *unfemininity* that is being objected to in this idea of women.
The picture is quite simply *unattractive*, and would still be
unattractive if it depicted men of a similar kind. It is
probably true that it might inspire a little less horror if it

were of men, since several undesirable characteristics seem to be more tolerated in one sex than the other (vanity, silliness and gossiping in women; rudeness, drunkenness and roughness in men), and that is probably why such women are said to be unfeminine. However, *this* kind of unfemininity is not in the least danger of being brought about by any feminist recommendation that the same characteristics should be approved of in both sexes, because the characteristics in question are neither approved nor liked in anybody, male or female.

Forgetting, then, the unpleasant characteristics which are attractive in neither sex, what characteristics are there which are positively liked in women but not men? A little consideration, and comparison of attractive people of each sex, suggests there may be very few. The perpetual fuss about femininity has tended to obscure the fact that to a large extent the same characteristics are *already* admired in both men and women because they are quite simply attractive: independence, strength, gentleness, charm, grace, wit, intelligence, success and the like are admired wherever they occur, and when a woman is described as feminine (which is, by the way, quite rare; far more is said about ones who are thought *un*feminine) the expression usually conveys only general admiration and approval, and the difference between a woman so described and an equally admired man (or an admired woman not described as feminine) would probably reduce to little more than recognizably female dress, and perhaps the graceful acceptance of the occasional holding open of a door. When it really comes to the point, anxieties about special virtues for women, about femininity rather than general unpleasantness referred to misleadingly as unfemininity, may turn out to be in essence little more than a desire that women should go on looking like women. To the extent that that is true it should be made clear. It would narrow the scope of the debate a good deal.

Probably feminists' real complaint should not be that different characteristics are *approved* in men but not women, but rather that a traditional feminine upbringing deprives most women of the opportunity to develop characteristics which, if they had been developed, would have been much admired. Women who have *succeeded* in escaping the feminine bonds have always been thought well of; consider for instance Britain's most successful queens, and such national heroines as Florence Nightingale. There was nothing self-effacing about any of them. Men may have had their own very good reasons for bringing women up to servitude, but the soul of a servant is not an attractive thing, and one of the most infuriating aspects of women's constricted upbringing is that it has made them less attractive, even in the eyes of their constrictors, than they should have been. Man has twisted and pruned woman out of all recognition and *then not liked the results*;[12] 'Her wings are clipped', as Simone de Beauvoir said, 'and it is found deplorable that she cannot fly.'[13] Men do not always know what even they want, and the woman who refuses to be pushed into the cage of traditional femininity will probably turn out to be better liked even by men than if she had allowed herself to be caught. If she is attractive she will probably still be thought of by men and women alike as feminine, at the cost (if it is a cost) of no more than a very few cultural indications of her sex.

6

Woman's Work

I · THE DEVALUATION OF WOMEN

It must be said on behalf of feminists who are inclined to resist any difference in function, convention and expectation between the sexes that they have one very strong argument on their side in men's quite astonishing record of downgrading whatever is associated with women. Margaret Mead[1] commented that in every known society, men's activities were regarded as more important than women's, quite irrespective of what those activities were. 'Men may cook or weave or dress dolls or hunt humming birds, but if such activities are appropriate occupations of men, then the whole society, men and women alike, votes them as important. When the same occupations are performed by women, they are regarded as less important.'

That is very striking, but even without any special knowledge of all known societies we have a pretty good idea of what an uphill struggle we should have even within our own if we tried to establish respect for what has traditionally been associated with women. The average woman is very pleased if she has any understanding of any such male terrain as the engine of a car, but there are still a good many men around whose claim not to know where to find anything in the kitchen is really a boast about their never demeaning themselves with women's work. Women on the tube are happy to be seen reading City newspapers, but no man would dream of knitting in public as some women do. It is quite unthinkable that the general relaxation of conventions of dress which has led to women's wearing trousers might have resulted in men's taking to skirts, for reasons having nothing at all to do with the relative comfort of the two. Girls in schools are doing more science and metal work, but most people are still slightly shocked at the thought that boys might learn to sew. And as Michael Korda in his book on male chauvinism quotes Jules Feiffer as saying, 'Whatever ground woman manages to establish for herself man abandons, denying its importance.'[2] It is not at all difficult to understand the point of view of feminists who see that in any difference there lies potential inequality, and who suspect that wherever there is potential inequality men will contrive to make it actual.

However, not all women are willing to give up the struggle just because they are not very optimistic about the moral improvement of men. There are feminists who think that to abandon feminine things just because men are determined to downgrade them is to give in altogether, and what we should be doing is demanding respect for whatever deserves respect, feminine or not. Hardly surprisingly, this group of feminists is enthusiastically supported by a great many people who want to keep as much as possible of the status quo. Perhaps having realized that there is no point any more in just evading the issue of the relative status of men and women, or trying to make out that the sexes are already alike in dignity, they move to the new position of saying that we certainly *ought* to give a higher value to feminine things, and promise support to the women who try to get it. (Perhaps it is the fact that these non-feminists support the equal-but-different idea which makes some feminists think that they had probably better try to achieve total sexual sameness. If these people want equality in difference, there must be a catch somewhere.)

The argument that we ought to be demanding higher respect for female things appears most frequently in the context of discussions of women's work. It is always being said by people on both sides that it is only because of social values (things which might have been different and could be changed) that women's work is not highly regarded. Margaret Mead, for instance, says[3] 'In our current Western theorizing, it has been too often ignored that envy of the male role can come as much from an undervaluation of the role of the wife and mother as from an overvaluation of the public aspects of achievement that have been reserved for men . . . when the home . . . is undervalued, then . . . women will cease to enjoy being women, and men will neither envy nor value the female role.' Evelyn Home,[4] replying to a man who challenged her to admit that women were inferior to men, said that it wasn't a matter of inferiority or superiority, merely being good at different things, and that men would be nothing like as good at women's special work of bearing and bringing up children. Tessa Blackstone writes[5] 'a redefinition of our values, so that qualities traditionally defined as feminine are raised in status and those traditionally defined as masculine are lowered, would be desirable. . . We need a fundamental revision of social values. The status of traditional feminine jobs, such as nursing or teaching for example, will only rise if society attaches greater importance to nurturing roles generally than it does at present.' And over and over again, especially by everyone who is in favour of keeping women in something like their traditional place, it is deplored that a false set of *values* has sent women scampering away from the home, abandoning the most important work they could possibly do in favour of other things which enjoy quite undeserved prestige, and leaving a generation of bored, undisciplined latch-key children in their wake.

We have, therefore, to work out what attitudes feminists should take to this sort of thing. Should women allow themselves to be persuaded to keep more or less to women's traditional work, and try to get it properly respected? At the very least, should we be trying to demand equal respect for those women who choose to stay at home and those who work outside it? Of course whatever answer we give to questions like these we shall always be left with the problem of whether it is likely that society's values ever will change enough, but before we consider that there are others to be settled. We have first to decide whether the work is of a kind which *ought* to be highly valued, or whether it is *possible* for it to be highly valued. Those are questions which ought to be answered before any practical attempt is made to get people to value women's work more, and in view of all the pressure on women to stay where tradition and (supposedly) nature has put them, women must have a proper grasp of the issues.

2 · PUBLIC AND PRIVATE

The most obvious way to interpret a promise to give higher value to women's areas of work is as a promise to give *higher status* to the people in them, which means more or less to treat them with more deference and consideration. Let us, therefore, consider this implied promise.

In the first place, an undertaking to regard women's traditional work as more valuable than it is now thought to be could not possibly entail giving high status to *everyone* who did it, because status is a relative thing and depends on a comparison of people with each other. Simply being a member of a particular class (in this case the class of people who do women's work) cannot possibly give anyone high status unless the class itself is difficult to enter. Since there is for most women pretty well no difficulty in getting a husband, and none whatever in having children, simply being a wife and mother could not possibly be enough in itself to give anyone high status. There is a (logical) limit to the amount of special respect you can give someone just on the grounds of her being a member of a class of which the dimmest witted and most incompetent woman in existence could equally well be a member. If, therefore, we are trying to increase the value of women's work so that the people who do it can achieve high status, we cannot mean that we want automatic high status for everyone who does women's work. What we must want is for women's work to be regarded as a valuable *sort* of work, so that *excellence* in it earns high status.

Suppose, then, people started to value excellence in women's work more. Could women achieve high status by this means? Of course it depends on what women's special sphere is supposed to be, but it is interesting to note that many professed (male) sympathizers of feminism in the present day, who believe in a male–female division of labour, follow conservatives like Ruskin[6] in saying that this division, in which women are told to seek equality of status, leaves men with the *public* and women with the *private* sphere.

There may well be many ways in which public and private work can be equal; they may require equal skill, for instance, or equal industry, and may have equally important consequences. However as soon as the matter is looked at from the point of view of *status* it is obvious that the two spheres could hardly be further apart. Status is not simply a matter of the position you actually hold on a scale which people think important, but a matter of the position you are *believed* to hold, and the simple fact is that if an area of work is in its essence private, there is a limit to the number of people who can possibly have any idea of where you come on the scale. Status depends to a large extent on scope, and the number of people who recognize your position. If only a few people are aware of the standard of the work you do, and there are no publicly observable criteria for success such as promotion and titles and salary, then from the point of view of most people you are no different from everyone else on the scale. If women's work is private it is necessarily without status, and any promise to give it higher status must be vacuous. The only way status can appear is in publicly observable things, like the quality of husband you have managed to catch.

This fact about the low status of women's work has nothing to do with social values. However correct any society's values, and however well disposed it may be to respect the people who do well in what it values, there is no conceivable way in which people whose work is not known about can be respected. If the promise to value women's work more is interpreted as a promise to give women higher status in their private sphere, that promise is necessarily empty.

It is, incidentally, not only traditionalists with vested interests who fail to see this point. Feminists make the mistake too. For instance, Marge Piercy writes 'Reflecting the values of the larger capitalist society, there is no prestige whatsoever attached to actually working. Workers are invisible. It is writers and talkers and the actors of dramatic roles who are visible and respected.'[7] But how could there be prestige attached simply to working, since *anyone* can work at something? And how can a particular piece of work be respected, if it is invisible? What this passage shows is not, as it tries to, that society has its values wrong in giving too much respect to the frivolous and not enough to the truly worthy, but that we cannot value what we do not know about. That is a simple matter of logic, and nothing to do with capitalist, or any other, values.

3 · DOMESTIC ACHIEVEMENT

However, even though that aspect of things must certainly be important to many women, and they must lament their lack of status, it is not something which actually appears very often in discussions of women's work. Status is a very unfashionable thing to care about, and it seems to be generally presumed that nice people don't. It is not a thing which feminists generally complain about, and if they did they would probably be met with raised eyebrows and remarks to the effect that they would surely not allow themselves to be deterred from doing worthwhile work by the fact that not many people happened to be looking at it.

As it happens status matters a good deal to everyone, even if most people will not admit it. Still, there is no doubt that there are situations in which people should be prepared to do without it, just as there are situations in which we should be prepared to do without any other good thing, and most

of us would say that it was better to do something worthwhile in obscurity than get into the public view by doing
something conspicuous but trivial, and making little use of
our capabilities. And although the status issue is not generally discussed, so that the question of what is worthwhile
is not introduced specifically as an answer to that problem,
it is along such lines as these that apologists for women's
work tend to argue. Housewifery may not be in the public
view, the idea seems to be, but it is an area of the highest
possible achievement nevertheless. If the housewife does
not realize this, and thinks that her life is a failure, that is
only because, like most other people in this society of
mistaken values, she regards as worthwhile only what is
public. What she ought to do is come to a proper understanding of the value of her work, as presumably ought the
people who do come into contact with it.

This is a pattern of complaint about failure and response
about the value of women's work which must be familiar to
nearly everyone, but to illustrate it here is a splendid example from Betty Friedan's *The Feminine Mystique*.[8] This
'prototype of the innumerable paeans to "Occupation:
Housewife" ' comes from Dorothy Thompson, a successful
journalist, in response to a very common occurrence; 'a
woman complaining that when she has to write "Housewife" in the census blank, she gets an inferiority complex'.
She has done nothing of what she planned to do in her
youth, she has wasted her education, and she feels a general
failure.

Then the author of the paean, who somehow never is a housewife,
. . . roars with laughter. The trouble with you, she scolds, is you
don't realize you are expert in a dozen careers, simultaneously.
'You might write: business manager, cook, nurse, chauffeur,
dressmaker, interior decorator, accountant, caterer, teacher, private secretary; . . . you are one of the most successful women I
know.'

As Betty Friedan rightly implies, this sort of thing is the
purest rubbish, so entirely beside the point that it is hard to

know where to begin criticizing it. Its technique consists in *totally ignoring* the real complaint, pretending it is something else, and arguing that that something else is quite unjustified.

What then is the real complaint? Almost certainly part of what underlies it is the issue of status. From the point of view of the census people and everyone else this housewife, with all her education and her special abilities, is no different from millions of other housewives (and nobody would be much impressed if she wrote 'Housewife: i.e. business manager, cook, nurse . . .' since that would not differentiate her from all the others either). Inferiority complexes are usually quite as much about what you think other people think of you as about what you think about yourself. However, perhaps as the housewife herself seems not to realize that her need for status may be part of the trouble, one should not blame Miss Thompson for not taking any notice of it either.

Still, she does no better when it comes to the obvious substance of the complaint. It is, as it is clear to anyone who thinks about the matter for twenty seconds, that the complainer feels that she has abilities which have been neither developed nor used properly, and therefore have in some sense been wasted. But what is the reply to this complaint? It is, more or less, 'Don't be silly; look at all these spendid things you've done', along with a list of things which pretty well no housewife can escape doing, and which has *nothing whatever* to do with the special abilities, whatever they were, the woman thought she was wasting.

In the first place, most of the things on the list do not call for any special skills anyway: what woman of ability could fail to be offended, when complaining that she was not using her abilities, to have it pointed out that she was a successful part-time chauffeur? *Anyone*, just about, could be a chauffeur. In the second place, the duties of a housewife are determined without any reference at all to the capabilities of any particular woman; they have to be done whether she has any aptitude for them or not. It is silly to console someone with being a cook (for all you know a bad one) if she hates cooking but would have been rather good at ballet dancing or car mechanics. And finally, the very fact that so many diverse activities are called for means that there is not much scope even for the woman who has skills which can be used in the domestic field. If she likes cooking or interior design she still cannot become outstandingly successful at either of them because of all the other things which consume her time, and which call either for abilities which she has not or, more commonly, for none at all. And yet she is supposed to feel as satisfied with her accomplishment of such a jumble of mediocre stuff as if she had been an influential interior designer, or a highly skilled couturier, or a racing driver. Some women's abilities may be best used in the home; some women's talents may coincide exactly with what is demanded by each domestic task. It is ridiculous to suggest, however, that there is the faintest likelihood that it will be true for all, or even many.

The woman who feels inferior as a housewife does not need to have it pointed out to her that she is not being idle, which goodness knows she knows only too well. What she wants is to be told how to use the abilities she has, to do something which could not be done by someone capable of less. Otherwise, as she sees quite clearly even though Dorothy Thompson apparently refuses to, those abilities are in some obvious sense being wasted. But Miss Thompson's blindness is impenetrable. She not only refuses to see what is obvious to anyone with half an eye, that neglect or dissipation of skill is waste. She pretends to know that the housewife she is consoling, who cannot escape all these tedious chores, is *expert* in all her 'careers', and pretty well implies that she is entitled to feel immeasurably superior to any woman who is pathetic enough to spend her whole time being a professional interior decorator, and therefore has only one career. That at least is what seems to be conveyed by the crowning absurdity, '*you are one of the most successful women I know*'.

It almost takes the breath away. It is bad enough to imply

that if you use a lot of different skills at different times you must be doing better than someone who specializes in using only one. To presume in addition, with apparently no better evidence than the woman's having to *do* all these things, that she must actually be expert in all of them, is absolutely staggering. And anyway, even if she were, what has that got to do with success, if her ambitions and abilities lie elsewhere? As any intelligent child of five could see, this argument is infinitely adaptable to direct against *any* discontented housewife, to reassure her that far from being a failure, she is one of the most successful people around. Can Miss Thompson really hope to convince any woman that she is a success by producing an argument which would equally well have shown any other housewife that she too was one of the most successful women she knew? What must people like that take women for, in expecting them to be satisfied with such patronizing rubbish?

That was America, in 1949, but it still goes on. There was a BBC radio programme not long ago, one of a series run on the lines of the advice columns in magazines, in which a middle-aged woman of ambitious nature was complaining that she had achieved nothing in her life. The counsellors, instead of giving her some ideas about what she might start to do at her age, and trying to find out what sorts of ambition and ability she had, told her not to be silly: she had been very successful; she had raised a fine son. This would have been bad enough even if it had not been the case, as it happened to be, that she was disappointed in her son.

The counsellors, of course, know nothing whatever about the quality of the son, and so were in effect telling her that she had clearly not wasted her abilities just on the grounds of her having brought a child from infancy to adulthood. But how can it be the slightest consolation to be told, when you had high (or even medium) ambitions in life, that of course you had been a success because you had achieved something achieved by nearly every woman who ever lived? But even if the woman had been delighted with her son, or even if the counsellors had been in a position to tell her that she ought to have been delighted, their reaction would still have been absurd. There is not the slightest reason, other than traditional ideology, to think that the only way to bring up a child properly is to devote to it the entire effort and ability of a highly able mother. However well she had done by her child, of course she had wasted some of her abilities.

Not surprisingly, the counsellors, one of whom was a woman, had had children and done more as well, but they still seemed to expect that their thoughtless reassurances would be useful, and were slightly offended when the woman involved (unlike the usual run of their clients, who tended to say as a matter of course how helpful everything had been) made it pretty clear that the session had not been very useful. It was a pity she had not a more accurate grasp of what was wrong, to tell them.

To be told that you have been successful, when by your own standards, and indeed any decent objective standards, you clearly have not, is patronizing and offensive. It is one indication among thousands that people have lower standards for women, expecting them to be satisfied with less than would satisfy men. It is disguised as an attempt to solve a problem, but only makes it impossible for the real problem to be faced. It is like the problems of ageing. People try to talk about it, and find themselves against a stone wall of polite remarks to the effect that they aren't really old at all. I don't (I think) doubt the good intentions of all these professional reassurers, but it is important for women to make sure that they can see precisely *why* such absurdity is inadequate. If they do not they will only go away from the counsels of the experts thinking themselves a bit neurotic for not being satisfied with what has been so clearly demonstrated to be satisfactory. Men have for centuries been trying to use women's dissatisfaction with their unsatisfactory position as a proof that they will never be satisfied with anything: women must take very good care not to be browbeaten into believing that it is true.

Women's work is specified in area. It therefore makes no

use of any woman's particular abilities, unless by chance they happen to lie where all women are placed. Even where she has abilities appropriate to her situation there are limits to the extent to which they can be used, because of the large amount of other work which has to be done. Women's traditional work allows excellence in nothing except itself as a whole. And even there the ceiling is set too low; domestic work cannot make the best use of the abilities of any highly able woman, and few achievements of any housewife are comparable with what a gifted woman could achieve outside. Many housewives are therefore not using their greatest abilities. They are doing less than they might, and they are therefore wasted.

These inherent restrictions on the achievement of excellence within the home is also relevant to the question of status. It shows that it is not merely the privacy and commonness of women's work which makes it of low status. Even if women by any chance become widely known as housewives, through winning a Housewife of the Year competition or entertaining for a famous husband, there is still a limit to how much they can be valued. Once again, you can be valued only for what people see, and if you achieve less than you might have done people will not know that you have capacities which could have been used for greater things. Most of what any housewife of high calibre is seen to do could equally well have been done by people with lesser abilities: in fact very often people with lesser total abilities make a much better job of looking after a home than women who are highly talented in other directions do. Women's work is of low status not only because of its privacy, but also because of the inherent mediocrity of most of the work.

4 · WORTHWHILE WORK

Still, the discontented woman may be told, that is not the end of the argument. Of course it is a satisfactory thing for any individual to use her abilities to the full, and of course very often it is a good thing for everyone if talented people use their talents. But there are times when it is better that they should not. Sometimes people can do more valuable work by doing something relatively unskilled, but important. If you had a genius for bacteriology it might be better during a time of plague to devote yourself to relatively menial work than to continue the research which might win you a Nobel prize, and it would certainly be better to do routine work in a hospital all the time than work on techniques of germ warfare.

Something of this sort is the basis of one more constant appeal that is made by people who would like to keep women in the home. *You have the care of the next generation in your hands: what could be more important than that?* or *Your life is entirely spent in the service of others: there is nothing more worthwhile.* It is a recurring refrain. Here, for instance, is some more from the same writing of Dorothy Thompson:[9]

All your life you have been giving away your energies, your skills, your talents, your services, for love . . . aren't your children musical because of you, and all those struggling years while your husband was finishing his great work, didn't you keep a charming home on $3,000 a year, and make all your children's clothes and your own, and watch the markets like a hawk for bargains? And in time off, didn't you type and proofread your husband's manuscripts, plan festivals to make up the church deficit, play piano duets with the children to make practising more fun, read their books in high school to follow their study. . .

The woman may not be using her abilities to the full, or getting status as her husband (with his 'great work') and even her children appear to be doing. Nevertheless she is doing much more *worthwhile* things, full of true self-sacrifice (note that she is supposed to be doing everything for love, which implies that there is no reward), sacrifice by implication not only of status, but of the satisfaction of using her abilities to the full.

Or here is a more exalted but equally familiar variation on the same theme, also quoted by Betty Friedan, this time from Adlai Stevenson:[10]

far from the vocation of marriage and motherhood leading you away from the great issues of our day, it brings you back to their very centre and places upon you an infinitely deeper and more intimate responsibility than that borne by the majority of those who hit the headlines and make the news and live in such a turmoil of great issues that they end by being totally unable to distinguish which issues are really great.

Women are bombarded all the time with this sort of thing. As Marion Meade says in her rather unpleasant book *Bitching*, commenting on the lot of the average mother:[11]

It seems like every time she picks up a magazine, she spots a stern reminder from some man who's yet to change a diaper: 'It is a rare and exceptionally gifted woman who does something more important in the outside world than she does during those critical first six years when she is helping to form the personality and character of a child.'

'Rare and exceptionally gifted' is certainly not a description she would ever apply to herself. On the other hand, if the idea were true, then why don't men stay home those first critical six years?

Why indeed. Even if men may believe that women are by nature specially well adapted to the rearing of children, they can hardly argue that evolution has fitted them with any special capacities for dealing with washing machines, and if women are necessary for the skilled part of child rearing perhaps men ought to be clamouring to help with the unskilled ancillary parts of such *important* work. There seems to be no reason why it should be the women who get on with all the obscure but important work, while men are left with all the status-getting and self-fulfilling activity the world has to offer. However, irrespective of what the men may or may not be getting out of it, this argument is bound to give feminists pause. It cannot be denied that it is important to bring children up properly, nor that service to others is a good thing.

Fortunately we do not have to deny either of them to escape this particular trap. The point is this. The valuable work women are supposed to do at home concerns caring for people: nursing, teaching, being available for them and all the rest. It may indeed be true that as a society we undervalue work of this sort, and should regard it more highly, as Tessa Blackstone said in the quotation near the beginning of the chapter. However, even though that is probably true, making the lives of your immediate family better is not a separate species of thing, distinct from the rest of life. If it is valuable, that is only because it is valuable *in general* to make people happy. If you have skills for that sort of thing, why confine your efforts to the service of a small group of people and the odd afternoon in the Oxfam shop? If it is a good thing to make your children musical, it is even better to make *many* children musical; if it is good to cater for your family, it is even more important to run the ministry of agriculture well; if it is important to see that your children get a good education, it is even better to make sure that the whole school system works well. These things are *more valuable*, according to the same principles as make the limited work which women traditionally do valuable at all.

This is not to make the elementary mistake of presuming that someone who can provide well for her family could, by using the same skills, manage food supplies for the whole country: that is not the point. Of course any woman who is good at running her home but would not be very successful at running anything else would do better to stay at home. But still no woman should be persuaded to stay at home, if she is capable of more, on the grounds that that is where the most worthwhile work is to be found quite irrespective of what her abilities are. The most worthwhile work is what does most good to most people, and for most women it will certainly not be found within the confines of their homes.

This conclusion will be disputed immediately. Surely, most people will say, *however* much good a woman can do outside her family, her first duty is still to her children?

After all, she was the one who chose to bring them into the world, and no matter how great a quantity of good she could do to other people elsewhere, those children must still come first. Perhaps that would generally be accepted (though it is by no means a completely uncontroversial matter). Let us agree, therefore, that there can be no justification at all for a woman's neglecting her own children. Does that vitiate the conclusion just reached, that most women should not confine themselves to work in the home, because to do so is to waste their abilities?

At this point there is bound to appear the fierce and familiar controversy about whether children do indeed suffer as a result of their mothers' being occupied with outside work. Defenders of women's right to work tend to say that quite apart from any considerations of what the mother is entitled to, children actually *benefit* from their mother's outside interest. The mother is likely to be less frustrated, and therefore more fun, more broadminded and more interesting than she would be if her children took up all of her time. Also, having less of her own life invested in the children, she is likely to allow them more space to breathe and be independent: it is well known that children who are the be-all and end-all of their mother's existence tend to be smothered by her. Opponents of careers for women, on the other hand, have much to say about children's being and feeling neglected, the harm which arises from a mother's being always tired and bad tempered, and how bad it is for children to come home to empty houses.

Debates of this sort are usually rather futile because they are carried on in such a very general form, when presumably everything depends on particular circumstances. No doubt some children do suffer from the fact that their mothers work; no doubt, equally, many are much better off as a result of it than they would be otherwise. It must depend on the mother, the children, the family and the kind of work. However, it must be accepted that some children *do* probably suffer from neglect by their mothers, and those cases are the interesting ones here. What should a feminist say about them? Perhaps most feminists would agree that the child should come first, and that the mother should sacrifice both her own interests and whatever good she could do elsewhere.

Even if many disagree, however, it does not matter for now, because that is very far from being the end of the argument. For suppose we consider the situation of a mother who does make that decision, and of whose decision most people are likely to approve. Although she may have chosen the best alternative, it is clear that the situation is still not ideal. Her child cannot possibly make full use of all her abilities, and the consequence is that something is still being wasted. It would be much better if some new arrangement could be made which allowed full care of the child *and* full use of the other abilities.

That is the really important feminist point. It is no part of feminism to insist that a woman should work at other things even though her children suffer as a consequence, but it *is* part of feminism to insist that there is something radically wrong with a system which forces so many women to choose between caring properly for their children and using their abilities fully. The feminist who does decide that the children come first, therefore, is nevertheless committed to leaving no stone unturned in a search for a way to rearrange the organization of society so that a woman can do her duty as a mother without neglecting other work she could do for the good of everyone.

It is not in the least obvious how this is to be done, but that is a reason for devoting the full energy and imagination of everyone who has any of either to trying to find a way. It is of the utmost importance that it should be done. That, furthermore, is a proposition which should be supported not only by feminists, but also by all those non-feminists who pontificate on the crucial importance of caring to the fullest extent for the people of the future, and the value of service to others. They should be delighted at the prospect of a reorganization of life and work which would allow women to do more of these good things. If, on the other hand, we find that they are not at all enthusiastic about such rearrangements, and are not willing to try to find them (probably saying that it is impossible for any such solution to be found), we must conclude that they do not regard the work *as such* as valuable, but only when it is directed to the woman's own family. That is to approve of the limitation of good work, and that in turn betrays a preoccupation with women's remaining servants, rather than with any maximizing of what is good.

The original conclusion, therefore, stands. Women's traditional work is, by its very nature, restricted in its scope. (Once again, the essence of femininity is to limit the area in which activity takes place, and the end which it serves.) However, to restrict the scope of good work is to make it impossible to do as much good as might otherwise be done. Therefore the discontent of many women in their homes is not just an unhappy response to society's under-valuing of valuable work, or dissatisfaction because their good work does not give them the personal satisfaction of seeing their abilities used to the full. They are dissatisfied because they *rightly* see that confined work is, other things being equal, less valuable than unconfined work.

This is not to say that no women should be housewives. Some are ideally suited to the work; it does make excellent use of their abilities, and many are probably doing far more valuable work at home than they could do elsewhere, or than their husbands *actually* do. But it is quite wrong to think of it as the most valuable thing which all, or even most, women could do. To hold up home and family as the highest vocation of all is to try to cheat women into doing less than they might, and wasting their abilities.

5 · ON THE GOODNESS OF WOMEN

This is a sort of conclusion which goes severely against the grain of a good many people, and is likely to provoke an indignant response. Surely all the women (and men too, for that matter) who get quietly on with their inconspicuous work are valuable? Surely it is most unfair to make them feel inadequate, and quite wrong to have a system which counts as useless people who do unremarkable or limited work? Surely invisible workers are valuable? There is a strong body of feeling, if not precisely opinion, that the best people of all are the ones who devote themselves inconspicuously and willingly to whatever duty is nearest to hand, without looking further for ways of making an impact on the world.

This is a very tricky area to deal with because many people absolutely refuse to look at it properly, and just assert that of course everyone is equally valuable, and the widow's mite is as important a contribution as that of anyone else. It is easy to understand the impulse behind this attitude, but the sentimental confusions which underlie it are among the worst enemies of the emancipation of women. Under all the assertions of equality the facts of inequality can go unexamined, to the advantage of any group which has the upper hand.

It is necessary to be clear about what is meant when people's value, or worth, is spoken of. Of course everyone is equally valuable in the sense that everyone's feelings should be equally considered. It also makes sense to say that everyone's work is equally valuable in the sense that if you labour to the best of your ability you should be as well paid as everyone else (it is a matter of controversy of course, but it makes sense). It is also reasonable to argue that morally, or in the eyes of heaven, the best people are the ones who make the greatest use of their abilities, whether they are large or small: that is the widow's mite argument. But it is straightforwardly false to say that *contributions* made to society by well-disposed people must all be of the same value. Some contributions are *of course* more valuable than others, and if someone is capable of giving a large contribution, and gives less, something is wasted.

Women have the greatest possible temptation to slip into confusions about the value of the trivial round and common task, because so many of them have spent their lives in confined activities. It is hard, late in life, to face the idea that it might have been better spent in doing something else. However, women above all people are the ones who must resist the idea that the greatest good a woman can do is get on quietly with her limited work, because it is so transparently the result of men's subjugation of women. Why should anyone try to prevent someone's doing as much good as it was in her power to do, except to prevent her getting power in general, keep her in a lesser position and retain exclusive possession of her services?[12] Once the victims have been convinced, however, the oppressors are safe, because if moral goodness consists in inconspicuously getting on with a confined job, you can account for the position of the subject group by attributing it to virtue. Note that Dorothy Thompson said as a matter more or less of course that the woman to whom she was writing was doing all her work *for love*. She may perhaps have been doing it for love, as may any of the millions of women in her position who are said to work for love, but the fact of the matter is that for most women, once they are in the position of housewives, there is no easy escape route, and no way of demanding rewards. Since they are trapped, there is no way of telling whether they are working for love or just because they can't get away, but it is convenient for everyone to imply that it is all a matter of choice and that women make the commendable choice because women are good. 'Women are declared to be better than men,' said Mill, 'an empty compliment which must provoke a bitter smile from every woman of spirit, since there is no other situation in life, in which it is the established order, and quite natural and suitable, that the better should obey the worse.'[13] But we see how it is done. Define goodness as unobtrusive selflessness, and there it is; you are forced to leave activity to the bad. To define goodness in this way is just a device to get the consciences of the oppressed on the side of the oppressor. If women accept it, men have won.

There cannot be a greater goodness, or a greater value of any sort, in any woman's doing less good than she is capable of. A decision to devote oneself to the service of someone else, with no consideration of whether he is worth serving or whether something else is more worth doing, is not the highest goodness but a total abnegation of morality. Germaine Greer was right in saying that women's traditional role forced them into the position of spiritual cripples,[14] since someone who is advised to remain within her sphere without looking for more is being recommended to make no moral judgments. (That, by the way, is one example among many of a feminist pronouncement which sounds preposterous on first reading, but on consideration has much to be said for it.) Goodness cannot consist in the limitation of its activity, or in devotion to what is not worthy of devotion. The only people who would try to argue that it did must have strong vested interests on their side.

Women should of course be willing to make sacrifices when this is the best thing to do. They may willingly sacrifice status if the best work to be done is by its nature hidden or undervalued, and they may sacrifice their personal satisfaction if they can do more by not using their whole abilities than they could by using them to the full in other areas. But still, there are and should be limits to such altruism. It is quite reasonable that it should begin to falter a little when the greater good on whose altar women are asked to lay down these things turns out to be the comfort and status of men.

6 · STATUS AND THE GOOD SOCIETY

It is now time to tidy up some loose ends by returning to the question of status, and modify to some extent an assumption which has been allowed to pass so far; the assumption that the good woman (or, of course, man) is one who is willing to do without status.

There are two elements to status. Roughly, high status

comes of *being thought to hold a high position* on *a scale which is highly regarded.*

It is often implied by people who want women's work to be more valued that its lack of status comes from the absence of the second of these two factors: that the *type* of thing women traditionally do is undervalued. However, whether or not that is true, it makes little difference. No change of *values* could make women's work of high status, because even if their *kind* of work were valued, they could not be seen to hold a high position on that scale. This is because the work is both confined in area and limited in scope, from which it follows both that there are limits to the excellence which can be achieved within that set of values, and that what is achieved is unseen because it is private. (In other words, even if we could make the work of caring for people more valued than it is now, women could still not get much status in their traditional role because in the first place there is a limit to the amount of caring which can be done within the confines of a single family, and in the second place very few people can see how much you do or how well you do it.)

Now a good woman may be prepared to do without status in a good cause. She cannot, however, be prepared to do without status *for these reasons*, because the aspects of her work which make it of low status, its confinement and limited scope, *also* make it less valuable. If she wants to do the most valuable work she can, she must insist on broadening its scope until it allows the full use of her ability, and in doing that she removes the aspects of her work which mean that it is bound to be of low status. Women of high ability cannot accept that they must do work which is *of its nature* of low status (irrespective of what society's values are) because to do that is to accept that they must do work which is by its nature of low value.

Still, it may be said, perhaps they should be prepared to accept low status which stems from the second of the two causes. Surely if the most worthwhile work is undervalued by society it should still be done, and still done well, even though not much status is earned by the people who do it? That is true. However, although women may if necessary have to be prepared to accept low status which has this cause, they should still not be *satisfied* with it. This is not for their own sakes, but because *as long as the people who excel in the most important work are without status, it means that society undervalues their work, and as long as that happens society has the wrong values*. Valuing is not a sort of thing which vaguely goes on at the back of people's minds on Sundays, when they allow their minds to wander to the worthiness of obscure people who do good work. What it *means* for a society to value what is good is for it to reward what is good, and until virtue is rewarded it means that the right things are not valued.

This is perhaps another statement which will be viewed with suspicion. Surely, people will say, virtue should be its own reward? If we reward what is good doesn't that mean that we shall have a society of people who will do good for the sake of reward; of people who only *seem* good, rather than who actually are?

As a matter of fact, whatever muddled ideas people entertain on the subject, it is far from clear that many people have ever really thought that virtue was its own reward. Usually people are exhorted to do without rewards in one place in order to get them somewhere else. Would there be much point in being deliberately self-effacing unless you thought that the last would be first and the meek inherit the earth? Would you try to make sure that your left hand did not see what your right hand did unless you thought God was looking? Perhaps you might, but you are not usually asked to.

However, suppose we agree that the best people are the ones who do good in all circumstances, even when there is no reward whatever, which sounds fair enough. Then certainly, if we had a society which offered no reward for goodness, we could be sure that all the people who appeared to be good really were good. But what about all the others? They would be pursuing the rewards society had to offer, and since goodness was not rewarded, would be doing what was *bad* in the process of getting those rewards. Surely it would be much better to lure the people who wanted rewards into doing good by making sure that it was the good which was rewarded? Although certainly some people would be good only for the sake of the reward, they would, if they had been in a different society, have done *bad* things for the sake of that reward. The simple fact is that although a society which offered no reward for the good might make an excellent obstacle course to test for fitness for heaven, *it would not be a good society*. If we want a good society, we must reward the good.

Furthermore, one reward of virtue (perhaps the only one needed) must be status, because status of its very nature carries influence, and a good society is one where the good people are the influential ones. This is yet another statement many people will immediately resist, because it is widely felt that a good person is one who actually shuns status, and prefers to do whatever is good without anyone's knowing. However, there is no reason at all to accept that. It is only part of the confused idea that to endure suffering and privation is good in itself, and of course it is not. It may be good to endure these things for the sake of a greater good, but there is nothing whatever to be said for putting up with them unnecessarily. If you would have done good anyway, your virtue is not lessened by the appearance of a reward, like public acclaim, which was not the cause of the action in the first place.

However, the case for the good person's not shunning status is even stronger than that. If you are good you must not only realize that there is no need to *shun* status; you must actually *want* it, because it is only when the good are influential that other people become good. It is just not practicable to arrange a state of things in which the good do good without any thought of fame, but we contrive matters so that each good deed is unexpectedly publicized. (This seems to be the sort of ideal most of us have, since we like to know about people who do good, but disapprove if *they* make their good known.) Status and influence must be part at least of the reward of excellence in worthwhile things.

The conclusion then is this. Women cannot be willing to accept a position which by its nature carries no status, because to do so is to accept confined and mediocre work, and therefore to be willing to do less good than they might do. Nor can they be willing to do as much good as possible but remain undervalued by society, because as long as the good is undervalued, society is bad. They may be willing to endure lack of status until society improves, but it cannot be accepted as a permanent feature of women's position.

7 · SEX AND STATUS

Perhaps it should be made clear again what the purpose of the argument in this chapter is.

One thing which was established by the previous two chapters was that feminists must certainly work to make certain that women are no longer pushed by laws, institutions and education systems into areas which are different from men's. There must be no actual and formal restraint on women's or men's activities which is not also shared by the other sex. But achieving that is not the end of the problem, because women still have to make choices about where to go, what is best for themselves and others, which advice to take and which to ignore, and which social pressures to go along with and which to fight. It is dangerous to presume that there must be something wrong until women are making the same choices, and given the same advice, as men, because women and men may be different on average in many ways, and it may be socially valuable to keep to some traditions, and attractive to keep some differences.

These problems may be totally intractable. We may never find the best solution to them. But one thing women can do is assess impartially the value of any path they may be considering. Anything which is not valuable, or does not use their full capacities, is to be rejected outright. There will be no harm in women's tending in separate directions from men's as long as the heights aspired to by the best women are unconfined, so that men would find these parts of women's work genuinely difficult, and not in the way they mean now when they cheerfully say they can't change nappies or manage the washing or boil an egg.

This still leaves the question with which this chapter began, of whether we can really expect activities which are associated with women ever to achieve the status of men's even though they may demonstrably be as important and as demanding. This is probably not answerable, and anyway it is a question for the social sciences, but there are two things which are probably worth mentioning here by way of conclusion.

The first is this. We have been so concerned in recent times about the justification of women's role that we have tended to forget that the underlying problem was, historically, almost certainly that of the *male* role. Margaret Mead was probably right in saying 'The recurrent problem of civilization is to define the male role satisfactorily enough'[15]: the female had a clear role of her own in bearing children, but the male had by nature nothing comparable. If he allowed the female to do everything he did, he might feel superfluous. This may be hard to accept in a highly advanced society where men do all the important things, but it is not difficult to understand in a much more primitive situation, and it is at least possible that something of the same sort may lurk in the depths of many male minds now, as men see women creeping into their firmly established male preserves. *If* that is true, then there does seem to be some hope that men's need to assert their superiority over women may lessen as the importance of women's natural function lessens. Childbearing is much less important than it used to be, partly because increasing the population is the least of our problems at the moment, and partly because now women can choose whether or not to have children that ability has become more obviously one among many, to be used only if the woman wants to use it. Many women from now on may choose not to have children. If men really are at root jealous of women's natural function, which may be true in spite of all indignant denials, the cause of that jealousy is retreating. Perhaps the jealousy itself will retreat with it.

The second point concerns the undeniable fact that men do still, on the whole, resist association with all things recognizably female, because they see them as degrading. However, the analysis of this chapter and the last has shown that although a good deal of the downgrading of women's work is purely arbitrary, this is certainly not true of all, because much of women's work is *inherently* degrading. 'Woman feels inferior', as Simone de Beauvoir said, 'because, in fact, the requirements of femininity *do* belittle her',[16] a matter of which men are as well aware as women are. Since this is so, it is not actually unreasonable that men and outstanding women should leave the fields predominantly occupied by women, because if women's function is *objectively* of low status it is not simply malice or prejudice which makes any area where women are to be found also of low status. Of course people do not want to do work which is customarily done by people whose abilities are thought to be less than most, because their own abilities will be thought less in turn. And what this suggests is that when women are indeed allowed to excel, even if they do it in slightly different areas from men's, there is at least the possibility that things which are associated with women may become as highly regarded as the ones associated with men.

Since it may well be true that women will tend of their own volition to do different things (though of course we do not yet know) it is essential that we should try to make that equal respect come about. As long as we know clearly the difference between what is conventionally and what is objectively of low status or value, there is some chance of achieving it.

7

The Unadorned Feminist

Surprising as it is, after all these years, the commonest public image of a feminist still seems to be of a woman who has disposed of her bra, preferably by burning it in public. This idea is so firmly entrenched in many minds as to be almost equated with feminism at times: a radio interviewer recently asked a woman whether she was going to become-liberated-and-burn-her-bra, and a friend of mine said somewhat coyly of his new daughter-in-law that she was 'rather liberated, and went around without Underwear'. As a matter of fact bras were never burned, as far as I know. But the picketers of the Miss America Pageant in 1968 did provide 'a huge Freedom Trash Can'[1] into which women were invited to throw bras, girdles, curlers, false eyelashes, wigs, and any other such 'woman garbage' they happened to have around the house; and certainly the disappearance of all such fripperies among the ranks of the liberated has become one of the most conspicuous parts of feminism.

As a reaction against the past, and women's having had the importance of their personal beauty forced down their throats for as long as anyone can remember, this is all very easy to understand. Feminism, however, is not supposed to be concerned just with reactions. It is supposed to be providing a blueprint for a better state of things, and there is no doubt at all that many feminists regard the rejection of 'woman garbage' as a *substantial* issue, a thing which feminists ought to be committed to, rather than just a gesture. That actually presents far more problems than may at first appear, and it is important to settle them. Many feminists regard women who persist in clinging to their traditional trappings as traitors to the cause, while on the other hand to many non-feminists this austerity in the movement is one of its most unattractive aspects. Feelings run high on both sides. The purpose of this chapter is to try to sort the issues out.

2 · PRIORITIES

We can start by considering some aspects of the traditions of female adornment which are, to anyone who has any understanding of the matter, *obvious* causes for feminist concern.

The first of these, perhaps the most obvious, is the amount of time, effort and money which women are by convention expected to devote to their appearance, when no comparable demands are made of men. Women's dress, especially when things like hair styling and make-up are taken into consideration, is much more complex than men's; women's fashions change more quickly, and it is far more important for women than for men to have a variety of clothes, and (particularly for special occasions) not to be seen in the same ones too often. All this takes a good deal more effort than most men realize: perhaps they think that because it is all so trivial it can't take much trouble – a mistake men frequently make about all aspects of women's work. Anyway, even reasonably enlightened men are capable of making slightly nasty remarks about women who do not reach the standard, but without any real understanding of how much more is required of women than of men, and how the efforts of women who do conform to the ideal account for a good deal of women's lack of success in other areas. As Simone de Beauvoir said of men's misjudging women in this way, 'It is not a matter of mental weakness, of an inability to concentrate, but rather of division between interests difficult to reconcile.'[2] If women are to succeed in the important things of life, it must be possible for them to be more negligent about dress, if they want to, without sacrificing social presentability in the process. That is most important.

Second, related to this and stemming from it, is the fact that the standards to be reached are impossibly high. This is a problem which has been made much worse by the immaculate images of the mass media, presented after hours of careful staging and with all the techniques of trick photography. In some ways we know that this is all illusion, but it does not prevent the endless struggle to get nearer to the impossible ideal, and the misery (for nearly all women) of never being able to reach it. Standards need to come down.

Third, another phenomenon resulting from mass communications, is that people's tastes have become too standardized; too many kinds of beauty are ignored. What people desire in others is always to some extent determined by what is publicly acceptable; that is inevitable. Where culture is mass produced, however, there is little room for diversity, or groups which have different ideals; everything is squeezed into the same mould. 'Nobody wants a girl whose beauty is imperceptible to all but him . . . the man who likes fat women may feel constrained to enjoy them in secret',[3] as Germaine Greer said. This is equally bad for both men and women. There are bound to be ideals, but while they are too confined far more people than need be are made unhappy; in pleasing the public taste men often cannot please themselves, and women who cannot conform to the demand are made pleasing to nobody. We cannot make everyone equally desirable, but if we can persuade women to put less effort into conforming, more types of beauty may become acceptable.

And finally, for the moment, there are the demands of fashion itself, which have constricted women with corsets, hobbled them with tight skirts and stiletto heels, deformed their feet with pointed shoes, starved them into ill-health and left them unable to run, move, protect themselves or work as long as they dressed as women should. That must all be dealt with as well.

Of course it is being dealt with, largely as a result of feminist effort. In fact many people may think that the battle is won, since women now seem to wear anything they feel like, and in many places (the Civil Service, for instance) it is far more acceptable for women to please themselves in the matter of dress, to be as casual and comfortable and informal as they want, than it is for men. However, as long as it is possible for a man on a formal occasion, wearing his dinner-jacket for the hundredth time, to comment (as one Oxford don did to me) on the 'inelegance' of a woman whose dress he had seen on a previous occasion, there is clearly a good deal that needs doing. It is also a thing which needs concerted feminist effort, since most of us are not up to defying public opinion single-handed. To the extent that this is the motivation behind the rejection of 'woman garbage', it is obviously an important part of feminism.

The problem is, however, that this simply does not account for all that goes on. It is true that there are many feminists who steadfastly refuse to put any effort at all into their appearance, which supports the view that they are determinedly following their own priorities and doing nothing more than that. But that in itself does not account entirely for the deliberately unfeminine style of dress gone in for by nearly all. People have, after all, to choose their clothes whatever they are, and a feminist whose main motivation was to put as little time and money into them as possible should presumably go around in the first and cheapest thing she could find in a jumble sale, even if it happened to be a shapeless turquoise Crimplene dress with a pink cardigan.[4] No feminist would be seen dead in any such thing. Obviously, therefore, the aim is not just to take what is cheapest and easiest, even though considerations of that sort must come into the matter to some extent. Style is important.

This is even clearer in the case of the great majority of feminists who do go to some little trouble to be clean and neat and pleasant. They too tend to go in for the unfeminine feminist uniform, but this has obviously nothing to do with effort. With just as little effort, if they wanted to, they could wear all the time a single comfortable, pretty, simple, easily-washed, drip-dry dress, so avoiding all the problems of fashion, variety, time, money and effort without giving up being pretty and feminine at the same time.

Feminist practice cannot be entirely accounted for, either, by ideas of comfort and practicality. A good many traditional feminine clothes are quite acceptably comfortable, and what counts as practical depends on what you are trying to do. All feminists whose daily life calls for their being prepared to shift a ton of coal at a moment's notice may have to wear the regulation dungarees all the time, but that does not apply to the ones who type or teach or work on production lines, and even the coal-shifters (who have to change their clothes occasionally) have no reason based on time-wasting for not sometimes changing into pretty clothes for a party. The priorities argument simply is not enough to account for all aspects of the adoption of the usual feminist style of dress.

Of course women who dress like this may simply prefer it. They may positively wish to minimize sexual difference in dress, or enjoy being as casual as possible, or find the sort of dress they choose specially comfortable. If they do, of course, there is nothing to be said against it. One legitimate reason for opposing the rigid demands of feminine dress is to allow women to establish their own priorities and do as they please, and if feminists in their dress were doing nothing but pleasing themselves there would be no more to be said. However, that is simply not the case. The fact is that women who dress in a conventionally feminine way, or give the impression of caring about their appearance however little effort it actually takes, are regarded by many feminists as enemies. This attitude has nothing to do with a question of freedom to choose. Anyone who has tried looking feminine in a gathering of extreme feminists knows that the pressures against that sort of appearance are every bit as strong as any pressures about dress in the wider world; in fact at the moment they are probably stronger.

There really is a world of difference between deciding you must reluctantly stop putting much effort into something which has been given too high a priority by tradition, and in treating that thing as something inherently *pernicious*, to be got rid of whether it is any trouble or not. There is obviously more to the feminist rejection of 'woman garbage' than individual decisions about priorities. And as a matter of fact the man in the street, who thinks he knows that feminists burn their bras, also thinks he knows why they do it. It has nothing to do with time or trouble (obviously bras are no trouble); it is, he thinks, all part of a deliberate effort to prevent women's being thought of as *sex objects*.

He does, actually, find this extremely puzzling, since he does not regard braless women as in the least unsexy, but that is what he has been led to believe. Furthermore, frequent comments of feminists seem to bear out his theory. 'It is degrading to make yourself attractive to men', 'Any woman who tries to make herself attractive to men is as good as a prostitute', 'You're a tart, throwing yourself at men . . . a slut', 'To make yourself attractive is to make yourself a male plaything . . . a sexual object', 'Women tart themselves up to get husbands'; and so on.[5] It does seem to be for reasons connected with these ideas that many feminists regard it as essential to look deliberately unconcerned about their appearance and deliberately unfeminine. It is not just a matter of priorities, or freedom for women to do as they like, even though these things undoubtedly come into the matter and perhaps are the only concern of some. There is unquestionably a strong element of resistance to being an 'object of pleasure' for the male. It is this part of the impulse to provide trash cans for feminine fripperies which is the main concern of this chapter.

3 · ON BEING AN OBJECT OF PLEASURE

There is one thing which is perhaps worth clarifying before going any further, even though it involves a slight digression from the main line of the argument. It is that whatever objections may be raised to men's treating women as objects of pleasure, and whatever objects of pleasure are (it is not usually explained), there must be a difference between men's wanting women for that purpose and wanting them *because they give pleasure*. This is because it is supposed to be *bad* to want people as objects of pleasure, but it cannot possibly be bad to want them because they give pleasure: there is no other possible basis for love than what is in some way pleasing to the lover.[6]

Perhaps that sounds too obvious to be worth saying. However, there is a long romantic tradition which holds precisely the opposite, and takes love to be a purely altruistic, unselfish passion, into which the personal gratification of the lover should not enter. The idea reached its apotheosis with Patience,[7] who gave up her childhood sweetheart, Algernon the All Right, because there could be no scope for self-sacrifice in loving someone who was, by his own admission, perfect. She felt bound to choose instead his rival Bunthorne, who would make such an impossibly tiresome husband as to leave the purity of her passion beyond reproach.

Of course that is a perfect *reductio ad absurdum* of the whole idea, since the height of altruism turns out to be so far from the height of love that it has nothing to do with it at all. Still, it is astonishing how pervasive something suspiciously like it seems to be. Usually people do not go so far as to imply that you should actually seek out the unpleasing, but there is a strong suggestion that you should not actually *care* about whether you are pleased or not. It is the basis of the testing game of 'Would you love me if . . . ?' You start by wanting to know whether you would still be loved if you were poor, and then go on to being ugly, or deformed, or crippled (a journalist in a women's magazine once advised a woman to find out whether she truly loved her fiancé by deciding whether she would still want to marry him if he were crippled) and eventually to being stupid, or uneducated, or unpopular, or an alcoholic, or mad (Mr Rochester

told Jane Eyre that he would still have loved her if she had
been mad). Now of course procedures of this sort have some
point: you may well want to find out whether you are loved
for the qualities you think valuable in yourself, or for
qualities which are likely to endure. However, the implication behind it all always seems to be much more than this. It
seems to be that if people really love you for *what you are*,
they shouldn't mind if all these things were different. That
is all very well in the case of wealth (perhaps), but what
about all the others? These are actually your *qualities*. You
cannot reasonably go through a list of all the qualities your
lover loves in you and then say 'you only love me for my x'
as though your real self were something different. People
are their qualities, and it is hardly a proof of not being loved
for yourself that you might not have been loved if you had
been something completely different. People who carry on
in this way always imply that they are afraid that the love
they are offered may be based on too little, but slip into
implying that the best of all love should really be based on
nothing at all.

We love people for qualities they have which are pleasing
to us. People may perhaps *marry* for prudential or altruistic
reasons, and choose their partners for money, solid worth,
dynastic considerations or even devotion to the Revolution,[8] but when there is no more than that there is no love.
How could anything be called love which was not based on
delight? Or even if it were possible, who wants to be loved
like that? We want to be loved because we please our lovers;
nobody wants to be loved in spite of being *un*pleasing.
There is no satisfaction to be found in the idea that your
lover is unselfish enough to be devoted to you out of the
purest altruism, and but for a determination to avoid selfish
pleasure would have chosen someone completely different.

Any woman who wants to be loved (or even liked) by a
man must be willing to be pleasing to him. If a woman is
deliberately unpleasing to men, as some feminists certainly
are, it means that she does not care about what they think of
her. Of course many women now do not care in the least

about men, and that is entirely their own business, but there cannot be any general feminist principle about women's wanting to do without men. It is not intrinsically degrading for women to want men; it has been degrading only because in the past men have not had to bother much about how pleasing they were to women, while women have had to go all out to please men even to survive. In a position of equal dependence and independence between men and women it would not be in the least degrading for either to want, and try to please, the other. And certainly refusing to please men cannot be a *means* to lessening women's dependence on them, because if they can afford to disregard what men think of them it means they are independent already; the most it can be is a gesture of defiance.

4 · SENSUAL PLEASURE

There can be no reasonable feminist principle which says that women ought not to want men, and if women want men they must be willing to be pleasing to them. If, therefore, the rejection of feminine adornment is to be seen as a refusal to please men (which it certainly often is) *and* an integral part of feminism, it must be seen as directed more specifically against particular types of pleasure. It must be directed against men who want women for the wrong reasons. These men are usually said to be the ones who want women as sex objects; the ones who want them for sex and nothing else.

It is probably worthwhile to note in passing a distinction which some feminists draw between women as sex objects (exemplified by the pictures of women in the girlie magazines) and beauty objects (like the ones on the cover of *Vogue*). It is difficult to draw a firm line between the two, since obviously beauty in women is attractive to men even when the beauty is not actually sexy in form, but there is a difference between them. Perhaps the essence of the feminist position can be caught by saying that the protest is against the male's demand that the female should be sensually pleasing to him in all respects, and his (presumed) lack of interest in very much else about her.

Anyway, feminists do complain that men have for far too long wanted women only for these superficial characteristics, and it seems that the feminist refusal to please men sensually may be a way of trying to separate the men who want women for the right reasons from the ones who (as our grandmothers would have said) want only one thing. And certainly it is easy to see why this feeling among women should lead to their determination not to adorn themselves. It is beyond all question true that if you refuse to be sexually pleasing you are not much use as a sex object, and if you are not beautiful you are unlikely to be loved for your beauty. If the aim of the deliberately unadorned feminist is to make sure that men who have the wrong attitude to women have no interest in her, she is likely to succeed.

That, however, does not conclude the matter. Although the method may be a very effective one for getting rid of the tares, it has the rather serious disadvantage of being likely to eliminate most of the wheat in the process as well. Certainly, it will get rid of the men who are interested in women only from the point of view of sensual pleasing, but it is bound to affect at the same time not only them, but also the ones with excellent senses of priority; the ones who value character, intelligence, kindness, sympathy, and all the rest far above mere sensual pleasing, but nevertheless would like that too if they could get it *as well* as all these other things. Caring about such matters is not the same thing as caring exclusively, or even mainly, about them. The best-judging man alive, confronted with two women identical in all matters of the soul but not equal in beauty, could hardly help choosing the beautiful one. Whatever anyone's set of priorities, *the pleasing in all respects must be preferable to the pleasing in only some*, and this means that any feminist who makes herself unattractive must deter not only the men who would have valued her *only* for her less important aspects, but many of the others too. Or if they did still choose her, they

would be less well pleased with her than they would have
been if she had been physically attractive as well. A man
who would not change his woman for any other in the
world might still know that she would please him even more
if she looked like the centre fold from the latest *Playboy*.

If feminists make themselves deliberately unattractive,
they are not only keeping off the men who would value their
more important qualities too little, but are also lessening
their chances of attaching men who care about such things
at all. If they think that is a good thing to do, they must be
prepared to argue that it is positively bad to care about
whether people are sensually pleasing or not; that if you do
not care at all about people's beauty you are morally superior to someone who does. Perhaps some people think
that is true. If so, however, they must also think it morally
bad to care about beauty at all, since beauty is the same sort
of thing whether it is in paintings, sunsets or people, and
*someone who does not care about beauty in people is someone
who simply does not care about beauty*.

Now of course beauty is often of a low priority, and it is
morally good to care relatively little about it when people
are hungry, or unjustly treated, or unhappy in other ways.
Most of us, however, would like people to have beauty as
well as other things, because for most of them it is one of the
delights of life; we complain when the government does not
subsidize the arts, and get angry when people live in ugly
environments. Some people do not care about art and
environmental beauty, it is true, but that just means that
they are aesthetically insensitive. It is not actually wicked to
be aesthetically insensitive, but neither is it a virtue, any
more than being tone deaf, or not feeling the cold, or having
no interest in philosophy or football. People who do care
about it are good when they sacrifice their pleasure in beauty
for something more important, but only then. There is
nothing whatever to be said for the puritanical idea that
self-denial is good in itself. It is good only as a means to an
end.[9]

Much the same goes for the sensual enjoyment of sex. We

may perhaps say that sex is a lower thing than the love of souls, but in order to blame men for caring about it at all in women it is necessary to argue that it is actually a *bad thing, positively* bad, rather than simply something which is less important than other things. But if sensual pleasing is a good thing, why not wear pretty clothes? Why not, in suitable circumstances, dress in ways that are deliberately sexy? To do so is simply to make yourself more pleasing, in more respects, and with very little effort. To refuse to do that may show that you are not interested in men who are interested in sex, but that is a personal preference, and nothing to do with feminist ideals. It can be no part of a serious feminism to argue that there is anything inherently wrong with the sensual enjoyment of sex.

Although it may be morally good to give up sensual pleasure to achieve some other end, there is nothing to be said for giving it up *unless* there is some other end to achieve. Women cannot reasonably regard it as morally reprehensible in men that they should care about what women look like, even though they may reasonably expect them to care more about other things. It is, however, amazing how much general confusion there is about this subject, and how ready the careless sentimental of all types (not only feminist) are to assure everyone that it doesn't matter if you are plain or deformed, because a really nice person won't care. A particularly striking example of this occurred in one of the series of advice-giving broadcasts I was criticizing in the previous chapter. A woman was in extreme distress about relationships with men because she had just had a mastectomy, and the panel of experts, astoundingly, did tell her just that: nice men wouldn't mind. They even went on, in what sounded like a caricature of popular psychology, to assure her that what was really bothering her was her relationship with her mother when she had been a child.

This sort of thing is appalling. There cannot be a man in existence who would not, *other things being equal*, prefer a woman with two breasts to a woman with only one, and niceness has absolutely nothing to do with such preferences.

The attitude of the advisors is one which only drives the unfortunate further into their misfortune, by making it impossible for them to find anyone to take their very real misery seriously.[10] The only person on the panel who gave the woman any useful advice was the one layman, who made suggestions about how she could cope with the situation, minimize shock and embarrassment, and make men comfortable with her. This is just the sort of thing which is needed, and the sort of thing, incidentally, for which the despised women's magazines are invaluable. All the muddled distributors of moral reflections and cold comfort, feminist or otherwise, succeed in doing is to invite bitterness when people realize that according to these impossible standards there are very few 'nice' people around.

It is useless to argue that to foster this kind of attitude discriminates against ugly women. There is no question of fostering, merely of recognizing the inevitable. Of course it is unfair in some sense that some people are born more beautiful than others, just as it is unfair that some are cleverer than others, or have parents who brought them up to be pleasant rather than unpleasant, or are stronger or more agile than other people. Of course we should see what can be done to make things less unjust. However, it is not the solution to cosmic unfairnesses in the distribution of things to try to prove that they do not matter, or that they only seem to matter because of the evils of society. It is not ar evil in society that beauty matters: other things being equal, it is impossible that it should not matter.

Of course other things never *are* equal. In almost any case of ugliness or deformity there are other things which can compensate for all. There are physically unattractive people of such radiance of character that after a very short time their disabilities are forgotten, and to want their company shows no altruism at all in their friends: they are wanted for themselves, as they are. It is said of the eighteenth-century poet laureate, Colly Cibber, who was extremely ugly, that given a ten-minute start he could outdistance any handsome man in the favour of women,[11] and there is no doubt that this sort of thing is already true of some women, too. It is true that until recently the cult of beauty in women has been so strong that ill-favoured women have been too dejected from infancy and too ill-educated to be able to develop compensating personalities, except in the rarest of cases, but while that is a fact which certainly needs feminist attention it suggests that what is needed is more of a change in *women* than in men's attitudes to them. In *It Hurts to be Alive and Obsolete*,[12] for instance, the reader is left with the conviction that it is not the fact that she is 'fat and forty-three' which leaves the writer obsolete, but her self-confessed bitterness.

Still, even though it is true that personality should and often does compensate for defects in appearance, beauty is always going to be important, partly to settle the balance when other things are equal, but more significantly for first impressions. Even Colly Cibber (a man, let it be noted) needed a ten-minute start. People cannot possibly be blamed for making in the first instance towards physically attractive people, because appearance is the most obvious thing about anyone, and it is perfectly reasonable to want to get to know people who are already known to have some things you value: they may turn out to have others as well. Why should there be any virtue in aiming at random, and going for people who have not obviously anything you want, when others clearly have? There are, of course, some people of such outgoing personality that it is more striking than their appearance, and they have the same immediate success as the beautiful ones, but they are rare. Anyway, whichever way it is done, if it is possible to be attractive at first sight, why not be?

The simple fact is that for a woman to make herself physically or sexually unattractive is to deflect all sexual interest: it is to distance alike the good and bad among men; the ones who have sexual interests among others and the ones whose interest in women is all sexual. That, of course, may be what some of the women who do it want. If that is so, however, it must be regarded as a personal inclination of their own; it cannot be seen as a reasonable feminist policy.

Most women want to attract men, and if they do they must (at the very least) not make themselves deliberately unattractive. It is no part of the moral corruption of men that they care about beauty in women, and it is no mark of the highest sexual relationship that it should have no sensual content. For the woman who wants to separate the sheep from the lecherous goats, there is, unfortunately, no alternative to the tedious process of hand sorting. It may be fraught with attendant risks of mistake and calculated deception, but it has to be done; the feminist who tries to make a short cut by her refusal to be beautiful or feminine is left with nothing but the grim satisfaction of finding, after having measured men with an infinite yardstick, that they are all wanting.

5 · PACKAGING

Let us then take it that there is nothing at all to be said for being deliberately unattractive, unless you actually want to keep off everyone who might be interested at all in sensual pleasures, and move on to what is unquestionably another idea at the back of many minds: that it is bad that women should put any *effort* into making themselves attractive to men. As was mentioned before, this is clearly not the whole of the argument against 'woman garbage' because it does not account for deliberate efforts to look unattractive, and choosing one style of appearance rather than another within the constraints of a given amount of effort. Still it certainly is an issue in its own right, and for some feminists perhaps the main one. To dress up, or beautify, or aim to titillate men, is said to amount to *packaging*, which turns women into commodities, and is degrading.

There are a good many aspects to this issue, and it is made very difficult to deal with by the fact that its parts get entangled together and with parts of other separate issues. Still, they must be separated for the purpose of making them clear. A good starting point is the comment of one feminist speaking bitterly during a television broadcast about the effort women were expected to put into their appearance: 'They can't love you as you are, they must love you for what you have become.'

Forgetting the specific issue of beauty for the moment (it will reappear shortly), what about the general idea of being wanted for what you are, rather than what you have become? There are difficulties even about what this means (if it means anything), since what you have become *is* now what you are. However, it sounds as though what is implied is that you ought not to have to make any efforts to change yourself; whatever you are like, people ought to want you that way.

But what is the great advantage in remaining as you are? You might be something quite undesirable. You might be selfish, or careless, or boring, or uneducated, or socially inept, or illiterate, and if you are there seems everything to be said for making a change. Why should anyone be expected to like the original unimproved version? To suppose in some vague way that it must be specially valuable is to allow muddles about the natural to sneak in again. They must be resisted. Whatever is meant by 'what you are' in this context, there is nothing *a priori* to be said in favour of it.

Of course in most matters, like education and manners and morals, people are all in favour of improvement, and this argument would be accepted. For some reason, however, there seems to be an idea that there is something very different about *natural beauty*, and this is a point at which feminists find themselves slipping into the company of surprising allies in the conservative world. Something needs to be said about that in particular, therefore, and the main thing which needs doing is to separate various questions. 'Natural beauty' hides a multitude of confusions, which tend to coalesce into a blur under the general heading.

First, perhaps relatively unimportant in feminism but still worth mentioning, there is the sentimental idea that people are all by nature equally beautiful 'in their own way', and what we should be doing is getting people to recognize that, rather than encouraging everyone to try to conform to current tastes. This one can be dismissed straight away. By any possible standard it is quite straightforwardly *false* that everyone is equally beautiful. It makes no difference to argue that standards change and that there is some standard which could make anyone beautiful: even if that were true (which it almost certainly is not) it is irrelevant. Even if you would have been beautiful according to the taste of five hundred years ago it is not much consolation for being thought ugly now. It is no good to say that we ought to change our standards of beauty to incorporate everyone. No doubt we should aim for greater flexibility, but we cannot alter our standards to the extent of making everyone beautiful without getting rid of ideas of beauty altogether; there can be no standard of beauty if nothing would count as ugly. We cannot recommend that women should do nothing to improve themselves on the grounds that what they should really be doing is trying to make people accept that they are all beautiful just as they are.

The second idea about natural beauty is, roughly, that you can't possibly improve on nature, and therefore should leave well alone. That seems to put an unwarranted amount of faith in nature. Of course people *can* make themselves hideous with too much powder and paint, but that is not the point. That some people fail does not suggest that success is impossible in the nature of things. *Of course* there are things which people can do to make themselves more beautiful and otherwise attractive. It does not matter if beauty is in the eye of the beholder: you can always find out what the beholder likes. You can darken your lashes or pluck your brows or curl your hair, and if those things are thought beautiful, you can in doing them make yourself more beautiful.

And finally (for this purpose) there is the idea shared by feminists[13] and, as I recall, one elderly nonconformist minister, that to attract by artificial beauty is to use false pretences. The idea of this one, presumably, is that a man is cheated if he thinks he has acquired a beautiful woman, and finds too late that when she takes off her false hair and eyelashes and nails, and removes the paint and corsets and padded bra, she is not what she seemed. If that is the idea of false pretences, of course, it does not apply to various beautifying procedures like plastic surgery, careful hair cutting and perming, slimming and the like, since those all have lasting effects. Any objection to that sort of thing must be another confusion about the 'natural' person being the real thing, and the unreal thing being a deception. But what about the less permanent cosmetic devices? Are men entitled to feel cheated by such artificial beauty in women? These days, of course, it hardly applies, since they usually have plenty of time to find out before being inveigled by these illusions into marriage. But anyway, a man who gets a woman who knows how to make herself *look* well, even though nature has made little of her, is obviously better off than a man who gets one who is beautiful neither by nature nor by contrivance; beauty is not a matter of what you *are*, it is a matter of what you *look* like. The idea that beauty is truth, however deeply entrenched in the romantic mind, is just nonsense. And to consider the matter again from the point of view of cheating, it might plausibly be argued that the man who gets a woman with the artistic skill to improve herself is actually doing better than one whose partner is beautiful only by nature: skill in making oneself beautiful has the advantage over natural beauty that it does not turn grey, or wrinkle, or sag, or spread.

Ideas of natural beauty, however they are defined and defended, cannot show that women ought to be satisfied with their looks as they are. We come now, therefore, to another proposition held by many feminists who are opposed to putting effort into appearance; that time spent on looks is time wasted. As one feminist said, 'a woman who spends time on her appearance is one who hasn't anything better to do.'[14] That sounds more reasonable; the argument is that beautifying is bad because it is a waste of time.

However, once the matter has been recast in this form it radically changes its character and, most importantly, ceases to be a feminist question. *The question of how much effort is worth putting into beauty has nothing to do with feminism.* It tends to look like a feminist matter, of course, because it is generally accepted that women make themselves beautiful for men while men go to no such trouble for women, but the idea that this has anything to do with women's not *caring* about beauty in men is a most extraordinary myth. They have not, of course, generally been able to demand it. For one thing, women traditionally had to look for economic security in men (because they could not generally have it in their own right) and that meant that other things had to come before the luxury of choosing a beautiful partner, whereas a man could often indulge himself in this way. For another thing, the general superiority of power of men over women has meant that women have been more anxious to please men than men have been to please women: to capture and keep their men women do all they can in the cause of beauty, while 'Man demands in his arrogance to be loved as he is',[15] as Germaine Greer said. But it is precisely this asymmetry of power which is the feminist question. The *feminist* concern is to make sure that man is in no position to demand more of woman than he is willing to give; the question of how much each ought to demand in general has nothing to do with feminism.

The question of the value of effort put into sensual pleasing returns us to one of the main points of the last section; that beauty was the same sort of thing whether it was in people or anywhere else. If people care about making their rooms pleasant for people to be in, there is nothing at all odd about their caring about whether they themselves are worth looking at. If it is worthwhile to go to the trouble of putting up Christmas decorations, it is equally worthwhile to go to the trouble of making oneself pretty for a party. People disagree about how much effort these things are worth, of course, but that depends on their own personal priorities. In the same way, people differ about how much (purely personal) concern they have in being beautiful, and in how much beauty they want in a partner. Some want a great deal, others do not care so much and would rather have other things. But, once again, there is nothing morally good about being aesthetically insensitive or sensually insensitive in any other way, and women who do care about beauty in men, and men who care about it in women, are not reprehensible.

Feminism is concerned with sexual justice, and not with the ultimate worthwhileness of one kind of preference over another. The fact that some feminists seem to confuse feminism and puritanism, and convey that it is part of the women's movement to see sex and sensual pleasing as a frivolous waste of time, is probably one of the main things which puts people off feminism. Anyone who wants a puritanical movement should call it that, and not cause trouble for feminism by trying to suggest the two are the same.

6 · SEX ON ITS OWN, AND THE OBJECT QUESTION

The argument against insisting that feminists throw away their feminine fripperies has so far taken two stages. First it was argued that there was nothing wrong in men's caring for beauty in women among other things as long as their priorities were right, and therefore there was nothing to be said for feminists' making themselves deliberately unattractive. If they did that, the only people they would attract would be the ones who did not care about beauty, which they might *choose* to do, of course, but not on feminist principles. The second stage was to point out that some people cared a good deal about beauty, a thing which it is possible to do without caring about it to a morally dubious extent, and that it was not unreasonable for a woman who wanted to please an aesthetically sensitive man to put some effort into making herself pleasing in that sort of way. Of course both these things are supposed to apply equally the other way round. Feminists must think it important that women should be in a position to choose sensually pleasing men if they want them.

However, it is now time to go back to the beginning of these arguments, and look at a presumption which has so far been allowed to slip past unchallenged. It is the presumption that although sensual pleasing is bound to have some weight in a sexual relationship, it is still a relatively unimportant thing which should not be the main one in any acceptable relationship. That needs looking into, along with the whole question of relationships confined to an interest in beauty or sex, and the highly charged issues of beauty competitions, pin-up girls, escorts, strippers and prostitutes, by participation in which activities women are so often said to degrade themselves, by becoming objects of pleasure for men.

It must, by the way, be said at the outset that the only interesting questions here are about particulars; a man's attitude to *particular* women, *particular* women's activities, and *particular* relationships. There could be no possible defence of a situation which advocated such activities and relationships for *all* women, and any man who had no interest beyond the sexual in any woman, and chose to ignore everything else about women even though he appreciated the same things in men, would be beneath consideration. That sort of attitude is not under discussion. The issue is of whether we should always object to particular instances of such limited interests and activities, irrespective of the circumstances, and of whether it is a proper concern of feminism to oppose them all.

Looking at the matter very generally to start with, the highly emotive issues of sex and beauty apart, it is quite clear that we do not in general think that there is anything intrinsically wrong with being interested only in certain aspects of people, pleasing people by means of particular skills, entering competitions against other people of similar skill, or earning an income by the use of particular abilities. For instance, suppose a singer heard a splendid pianist at a concert; he might fantasize about giving concerts with her,[16] with no thought about her which went beyond her musical ability. He might try to meet her, in the hope that she would be willing to enter into a limited musical relationship, and she might agree. She might also happily play the piano to please people who were not in the least interested in other aspects of her. She might enter competitions. And certainly she would try to earn her living by playing the piano for the entertainment of people who enjoyed listening to music.

Now all these things are, obviously, in quite close analogy with a good many things about men's and women's relationships. For instance a man might fantasize about sex with a beautiful woman, or might try to meet one he had spotted, with only sex in mind. The woman might go along with it; she might be quite happy to enter into a purely sexual relationship. Women do enter beauty competitions, which are supposed to be run because men enjoy seeing the parade of women. They do earn livings by pleasing men as strippers or prostitutes. If, therefore, there is something bad about the men who want these things and the women who go along with them, why is there not something equally bad about people who are interested in musicians only for their musical ability, and musicians who are happy to go along with that interest, and earn their livings by means of it? Why should it be acceptable to base a relationship on common intellectual interests, but not a common wish for sex? Why should there be prizes for painting pictures, but not faces? Why should it be acceptable to be paid for charming people's ears with beautiful sounds, but not for delighting men's fancies with strip shows and prostitution?

It is said that all these things degrade women, and at present they certainly do. However, there is quite enough degradation in the *surrounding circumstances* to account for women's being degraded, without having to resort to the idea that there is something bad about unsanctioned or commercially motivated sex. Women are degraded by these things because of the public contempt they suffer, because of the fact that many of them have to take these activities up whether they want to or not when there is no other way to make a living, and worst of all because once they have sunk to this level they must suffer endless degradations which result from their weak position. ('When they talk about "niggers" you've just got to go "uh-huh, uh-huh" and agree with them. That's what I really couldn't stand. . . That's why it's selling your soul and not selling a service.'[17]) However, other things, like teaching and manual work, have been made degrading by social attitudes, and in cases like that we have tried to remove the degradation rather than persuade people not to do the work. Why should we not also fight the degradation in the case of prostitution and such things, rather than say that men should not want these things or women provide them?

As usual when there are prejudices to defend, excuses proliferate. Sex is said to be cheapened by money. Why should it be, however? Nursing care is a thing which is often given for love, but we don't think nurses cheapen themselves or the profession when they earn their living by it; we think it an excellent thing that these people should be able to use their skills all the time, and care for more than just their families and friends. What, then, have we got against the prostitute? It is said that people who go in for sex without love are missing a lot. That may be true, but it provides not the slightest argument for never having it without love. You might just as well say that because the pleasantest way to eat was with friends at dinner parties, no one should eat in any other circumstances. It is said that prostitution comes only from bourgeois ideals of marriage, and will go when they do. But that seems purely a matter of faith. In fact it seems in keeping with some feminist ideas to think that when in the liberated future a man wants sex and his woman doesn't, she will pack him off to a prostitute to pay for the pleasure he was hoping to get free from her.

All the analogies drawn in this section, with music, nursing, eating and so on, show that whenever activities disapproved of in sexual contexts are transposed into non-sexual ones they become perfectly acceptable. It seems to be sex alone which has the ability to degrade unless it is purified by the proper sanctions; if no longer of marriage, then at least of love. If we are to accept this rather than resist it, reasons must be brought to show why sex is inherently so different.

It seems impossible to find any acceptable ones. The only explanations of this special attitude to sex which seem to make any sense are historical ones, and they come nowhere near providing any kind of *justification* for them. Historical explanations are far beyond the scope of this discussion, but it seems certain that they must be connected in the first instance with a fear of the magic once associated with sex, and more recently with the tendency of Christianity to see saintliness in mortification of the flesh, and sensuality of all kinds as inherently evil.[18] Few feminists can wish to perpetuate either of those ideas. Furthermore, the feeling that it is virtuous (particularly in women) to confine sex to marriage or some equally committed relationship ought to be regarded with some suspicion by feminists, since that moral demand almost certainly has its roots in the need of men to ensure women's sexual fidelity in order to be sure of identifying their offspring. It was obviously to the advantage of men if women's own consciences could be enlisted to reinforce the social and physical guard already placed on their sexual activities. If this is true, it means that feminists are the very last people who should believe that there is something wrong with sex without the catharsis of love and commitment. Whether or not it is true, however, the fact still remains that anyone who wants to maintain that sexual relationships should be treated as radically different from anything else in life is under an obligation to produce acceptable reasons. It is very hard to see what they could be.

There is also another reason why feminists should not be opposed to people's having purely sexual interests in each other, or making a living by means of the use and enhancement of sexual attributes. Feminists have always objected to the fact that in the past women were allowed to use too few of their abilities, only the ones men chose to be interested in. They now want women to be able to use their abilities to the full. Why should they discriminate against the ones with beauty or talents for pleasing men sexually, and insist that they should do other work they would do less well? Can feminists willingly create a situation where a *new* group of women is left out and has its talents disregarded? It does not sound much in keeping with feminism, and this is reinforced tenfold when we realize that the feminist impulse to bring this about is *a direct result of men's mistreatment of women*. It is only because women who pleased men got more than they should have done in the past that we are so angry about that kind of thing now.

In other words, for feminists to give in to the impulse to persuade women that it is degrading to commercialize sex, or that only wicked men have purely sexual interests in any women, is one of the clearest ways of fulfilling the feminist fear that the oppression of women might be allowed to continue in some disguised form. The attitude to sex of many feminists bears the unquestionable mark of stemming from men's oppression of women.

We should not, therefore, object to women's sexual pleasing of men, not even when they devote all their efforts to it. Once again, the real feminist problem is the unfairness of the present bargaining situation, and the fact that women are in a position to be exploited, and degraded in *that* way. That certainly has to be attacked with full feminist force, and we may even have to have an interim period when all these activities which are *now* degrading are suspended, to allow breathing space to get over the unpleasantness of the past. But no objections we have should be permanent. To slip into that, and go on being outraged by loose or forward women and by prostitutes, is to have swallowed the essence of the male propaganda in its entirety.

7 · CONFRONTATION, AND WOMEN'S CULTURE

The main general conclusion so far is that it is a very serious mistake to confuse feminism with an opposition to beauty and sensuality. Even if there are good arguments against these things, or against giving a high priority to them, they are not feminist arguments. Feminism is concerned only with sexual injustice, and therefore not with these things themselves but only the imbalance of power which allows men to exploit women sexually. The feminist problem is to stop women from being unable to get a fair bargain, or demand from men as much as they give. Therefore it is no part of feminism to insist that women should not make themselves attractive to men; any woman who does that is doing it as a matter of personal preference, and not out of feminist principle.

I want now to return to this last group of women, women who choose for personal reasons not to look attractive to men, and consider its position from the point of view of feminism.

Women may have either of two personal reasons for reacting strongly against the traditional feminine appearance. The first of these stems from not caring at all about dress, or wanting to be comfortable in a particular sort of way, or something else like that. That is not my concern here. The second is more important for feminism. There is no doubt that there are many women who deliberately choose to be unattractive to men because it seems the only way to deflect men's sexual interest.

The reasons for this vary. Some women find it convenient, no doubt, to keep sexual interest to a minimum in their professional lives. Some, presumably, just hate men and want to keep them off. Many others are horrified when they discover the nature of male sexual fantasy and are revolted at the thought that they might ever be the object of it. Others want to escape the nuisance of the wolf-whistle, the leer, and the salacious remark, whose annoyance is infinitely compounded by men's insolent presumption that women are pleased by them. Others want to avoid the danger of rape, or the lesser problem of more honourable pursuers who reproach women with having led men on by their appearance. (It is not only judges in rape cases who say that attractively dressed women ask for all they get; far more reasonable men sometimes imply that if a woman makes herself attractive she is unfair to refuse men's advances.) There is no doubt that one aspect or another of this constant onslaught has driven many women to retreat from conspicuous femininity to avoid the problems of being female.

However, this is not the right way to attack the problem, because it leaves completely untouched the basic trouble, which is that *many men do not treat women properly*. We are probably not entitled to include the fantasies in the bad treatment, since they do not involve actually doing anything to women, but we can certainly object strongly to everything else. A woman should be able to walk along the street without the risk of insolent remarks, attempts to pick her up, or rape. Men should not presume, as many seem to, that now a woman is no longer the property of any individual man she must therefore be the property of all; that if she makes herself attractive she has invited all comers, who are entitled to feel aggrieved if she does not fulfil her universal promise. A woman should be able to make herself attractive to men, so putting herself in a position to have a wide range of them to choose from and increase the chances of finding one who comes up to her requirements, without being open to insulting remarks in the street, and nasty comments about leading on men whose advances she will not accept. Even when she makes herself look not just attractive but actually sexy, thereby expressing an interest in sex, it should not be taken to imply that she is interested in sex with just anyone.

The problem is obviously a difficult one, but what is absolutely clear is that it cannot be solved by women's making themselves unattractive. To do that is to give up in despair. You cannot touch the cause of the leer and the wolf-whistle by making yourself unwhistlable-at, and if you make yourself unattractive because you do not want to lead men on you are conceding by implication all they imply about universal invitations. In fact it is positively bad to protest about the way some men behave to women by putting oneself beyond the reach of what is objectionable, because if some women conspicuously withdraw themselves it probably makes men think all the more that any woman who does not is indeed expressing a general interest in men. Certainly, if all the intelligent and thoughtful women subside into scruffy unfemininity it will confirm men all the more in what they think they know already, that women with intelligence are never worth looking at.

Easy as it is to retreat in a baffled fury from all these intractable problems, and tempting as it is to confront men's complacency with defiance, it does not help because the women who do it cease to be of interest to men. What feminism really needs is exactly the opposite: women who are very desirable to men, but who will have nothing to do with any man who does not treat them properly. If men's behaviour provokes women into trying the other ways, they have pushed them into engineering their own defeat, and have won again.

I suppose that given the current inclinations of many feminists, that and all the other conclusions of this chapter must seem very subversive, and will no doubt be unpopular. However, having gone so far, let me conclude by going still further, and giving yet another defence of women's not abandoning their interest in dress unless their personal inclinations go that way. It is connected with the distinction drawn earlier between sex objects and beauty objects. Women often look beautiful without any question of trying to look sexy, and given that that is so we may ask this question: *why does everyone presume that the beautification of women is all for men?*

Of course some of it is, but there is no need whatever to presume that it all is, let alone that it all must be. Women's dress is by no means all designed to please men. (There was a *Punch* cartoon a few years ago, showing two men looking wistfully at women sweeping past in the long skirts which were then in fashion, and saying 'I like to think that under every maxi there's a mini trying to get out.') It is *quite* possible, as a matter of psychology, for women to wish they were more beautiful without thinking that they would as a result be pursued by a single additional man.

Of course beauty of any sort, and especially beauty in a conventionally feminine (even though non-sexy) mould, will enhance sexual attractiveness. It does not follow from that, however, that these things are inherently sexual. The trouble with these post-Freudian days is that we have got into the habit of presuming that everything which comes by any means into a sexual relationship must itself have something to do with sex. People go around saying that children's attraction to beauty shows their sexual natures, and that if women admire beauty in other women they are either being narcissistic or are lesbians whether they know it or not. There is no reason whatever for falling in with this sort of dogma. It is *not* true that all enjoyment of beauty, even in people, has something to do with sex, and we should be able to insist that women may sometimes make themselves beautiful just because they like everything, including themselves, to be beautiful, or because they have a wish for admiration of all kinds, not just sexual admiration. Even if a woman does not want men, therefore, or for that matter sexual relationships with women, why should she still not be able to make herself beautiful?

If it is true that beauty need not be primarily to do with sex, it provides yet one more reason why feminists should not feel bound to make scarecrows of themselves. And having said so much, let me risk the final horror.

Feminists often express concern about women's culture. Kate Millett, for instance, wrote in the preface to *The Prostitution Papers*, 'I should like to see the new movement give women in the arts a confidence in the value of their own culture,'[19] and the New York Radical Women say in their principles 'We are critical of all past ideology, literature and philosophy, products as they are of male supremacist culture. . . . We take as our source the hitherto unrecognized culture of women.'[20] Very few feminists, however, ever seem to get round to saying what woman's culture is. But surely one of the clearest areas (even though not necessarily the most important) is that of women's dress and personal adornment.

Of course women have had to ornament themselves to attract men, but we have no reason to presume that all women's interest in dress comes from that: it seems far more likely that what happened was that because their interests were so confined this became a special area of interest when all others were closed. The fact that interests and cultures grew under conditions of confinement does not make them less the real culture of that group. We do not want to deny that 'By the waters of Babylon' is part of Hebrew culture just because it was written in captivity. Anyway, if we exclude from women's culture everything they have produced under male dominance we are left with the conclusion that women have no culture. Women's dress was undoubtedly produced largely in response to the *real* interests of women (not the less really theirs because environmental influences helped to form that interest), and for many women at least not something reluctantly adopted as a necessary evil on the way to catching a man.

However, whether or not feminists can be persuaded to adopt that somewhat unlikely proposition, the central point remains. Feminism is a campaign against sexual injustice, and is therefore not, as such, committed one way or the other on the subject of the value of beauty, grace, sensual pleasing and cultural differences. Since these things are for many people among the joys of life, any feminist who seeks massive support for the campaign should make it clear that if she herself espouses austerity and throws away her 'woman garbage' that is nothing more than the use she has personally chosen to make of her new freedom. It is no part of her feminism.

8

Society and the Fertile Woman

I · THE ISSUES

It could be said that in the nature of things, independently of the social institutions of marriages and families and the technological advances which produced contraception, the different reproductive systems of men and women give each sex an advantage over the other. Men have the natural advantage over women of being able to indulge in sex without necessarily finding themselves encumbered with offspring who need caring for as a result. Women, on the other hand, have the natural advantage over men of being able to produce children which are identifiable beyond question as their own, which men, without the voluntary or enforced co-operation of women, cannot.

There may be disagreement about which of the sexes is naturally better off as a result of these differences. However, any debate about the matter would for a long time have been purely academic, because any such state of nature there ever was disappeared earlier than history records, with men's overcoming their natural problem by taking control of women, insisting on their sexual fidelity, and so making it possible to identify their own offspring. Since men were also able to keep their natural advantage of having sex without offspring, as long as they were unscrupulous enough to take advantage of their power over women and then abandon them to the vengeance of the fidelity-ensuring system as soon as they became pregnant, they have for a long time been able to have things either way. Women's demand for safe, effective and readily available birth control can be seen as a demand that women (and good men) should after all this time have the same freedom to combine sex with children or not, as they please.

Perhaps some time in the future, as patriarchal traditions lose their hold, women may choose to forget about monogamy and abandon men to their natural disadvantage of not knowing who their children are, and if that time comes it is not unthinkable that contraception might become a masculist issue. If men found that women were making use of sexual encounters to steal children they then refused to allow men to identify or share, men might want male contraceptives to ensure that they did not impregnate any woman who would not come to reasonable terms in advance. However, that time is not yet, and at the moment women are still contending with their natural disadvantage. That is why birth control, though of interest to nearly everyone, is also one of feminism's overriding concerns.

However, the area is the subject of a great deal of public controversy, which many feminists, with a battle cry of 'Contraception and abortion free and on demand!' do not usually take seriously enough. A very good case can indeed be made out for the whole of what feminists want, but it does have to be made out. It is not so obviously justified as to need no defence.

In particular, several different issues have to be separated. There is not just one general (and easily answerable) question about whether women should have the right to control their own bodies. Contraception and abortion, in the first place, are quite separate issues. Then within each of these subjects there are two entirely different questions to be settled: first, whether the method of birth control in question should be *allowed*, and second, whether it should be state-supplied and *free*. These very different matters tend to be run together when feminists say that birth control should be 'free-and-on-demand' all in one breath, but they must be dealt with separately.

This chapter will, therefore, fall into four main sections, dealing with whether contraception should be allowed, whether it should be free, whether abortion should be allowed, and whether that should be free. The section on the allowability of abortion, not surprisingly, is the longest, and is itself divided into parts.

2 · THE FREEDOM TO USE CONTRACEPTION

The proposition that there should be no law preventing free access to contraceptives is a relatively uncontroversial one in nearly all civilized countries these days. At least, the main opposition to it usually comes from religious groups, and there is no space to discuss their views in a book like this one, because a challenge to their tenets calls for an analysis of the foundations of the religion itself, which has nothing to do with feminism.[1] However, even though the controversy about contraception has now receded a good deal it is still worth discussing the issues, because they do appear from time to time and it is as well to have properly thought-out arguments in readiness for their revival.

Roughly speaking, apart from the objections of religious groups, there seem to be three possible reasons for forbidding or controlling access to contraceptives. One is the fear that readily available birth control will encourage unsanctioned sex; one is the wish of some men to prevent their wives from using contraceptives (there are some who actually succeed); and one is the wish of a state to increase its population. The first two of these do not seem to be worth much discussion, given even the most basic principles about the rights of women. If a woman wants sex that is her own concern, and if it is possible to separate sex and pregnancy she should be allowed to. (It is, incidentally, rather ironic to see some people now wanting to preserve the threat of unwanted pregnancy to make women afraid of indulging in sex, when presumably the original reason for the sanctions on sex was the likelihood of its resulting in pregnancy.) The case of a husband who wants children can be equally briefly dismissed. Any man whose wife wants no more children (or none at all) is no doubt entitled to find another woman to bear his children if he can, but at no point is he entitled to regard his wife as his property, to do as he likes with. The only situation worth discussing in any detail, therefore, is the third: the case of a state which wants to increase its population.

The desire to increase population happens from time to time. Nationalism is a thing which has always encouraged a high birth rate, from Sparta to Nazi Germany and beyond. As Kate Millett said, 'population growth [is closely linked] with the ambitions of a military state; more children must be born to die for the country.'[2] Expanding and developing countries also often want to increase their populations, so that there is more labour at hand for mines, factories and agriculture. Racial minority groups may want to increase their numbers, so that they are not swamped by the majority. And in some places now, a new phenomenon, people are becoming so worried about the future age structure of the population that governments are beginning to think that if they do not encourage the birth of more children there will be no one to look after the present generation when it is old. Countries with such attitudes might perhaps try to prevent contraception, as Nazi Germany did.[3]

We may well object to nationalism, and given the general rate of increase of the world's population we may well object to any encouragement to increase populations at all. However, those issues are not feminist ones. The feminist question is whether, *if* it were legitimate to want to increase a population, it would be acceptable to do so by means of forbidding or limiting contraception. It is not enough to answer, as though it were obvious, that every woman has the right to whatever number of children she wants: that is the question at issue, and if we want to maintain that it ought to be so, arguments must be found.

However, given the conclusions of Chapter 4, this can now be done without difficulty. The argument we need is one of exactly the same form as the one outlined there, where it was concluded that men were not entitled to force women into the home by closing other options to them, because a state should achieve what it wants by giving individuals what they want and not by coercing some of them into what they do not want.

All the same considerations apply here. If a state wants more children what it should do is put its resources into making sure that all the women who want children can have them, because in that way the state gets what it wants by means of making sure that individuals get more of what they want. What it should certainly not do is forbid access to contraception, because that way *the people who get children are not the ones who want them most, but the ones who can least do without sex*. This sort of method of population increase lowers the level of well-being in society, because it forces parenthood on unwilling people, and gives children the severe handicap of being unwanted. It also means that people who are absolutely determined to do without children are therefore forced to do without sex, which does them a great deal of harm and benefits nobody. And furthermore, if state money is going into customs inspectors and police and law courts to control people who do try to get contraceptives, it means that less is available for fertility clinics, childminders and other things which could help women who did want children to bear as many as possible. They too are therefore deprived of possible happiness.

In other words, a state which wants to increase its population has two alternative ways of going about it: it can get what it wants by means of fulfilling the desires of individuals, or by means of frustrating them. To forbid contraception is to take the second of these options, and is therefore quite unacceptable. It may also be added as a corollary that since freedom to control reproduction is to the benefit of all, no child should be able to reach puberty without knowing that contraception is available, and how to get it.

3 · FREE CONTRACEPTIVES

That argument establishes that a state ought to allow free access to contraceptives, but it by no means justifies the feminist demand that contraceptives ought to be state-supplied from easily accessible clinics, and above all that they should be free. Perhaps it seems superfluous to argue that case now that in Britain we actually have a free state-supplied contraceptive service, but there are still people who oppose it, just as there are people who still oppose full sex education in schools, so it is as well to complete the battery of arguments on the feminist side. It is not at all obvious that contraception ought always to be free, especially in any country which did want to increase its population. It is no good just stating that the ability to separate sex and pregnancy is a basic human right, and presuming it is obviously true. It is very easy for people to draw up lists of things they would like and call them rights, but if other people are to be asked to work to supply the money to pay for them, they have to be justified with care.

The fact is that the people who say that they object to paying for other people's pleasures, tiresome as they usually are, have at least a *prima facie* case. For most people, certainly, it is an extremely good thing to be able to separate sex and procreation, because sex is such a good thing and being burdened with unwanted children such a very bad one, but not everyone needs to do it. Some people are not interested in sex, or are homosexual, or are sterile, or want children. Some people want more sex than others. But the way a free service is provided is more or less to collect taxes from *everyone* to provide contraceptives for the benefit only of the people who want them. If we are concerned with freedom, would it not be fairer to leave the people who do not want contraceptives to spend their money on something they themselves would like, rather than make them subsidize the indulgers in non-procreative sex? Should we not reduce taxes, and let people buy their own contraceptives?

That is what an argument about *freedom* would suggest. (It is, of course, true that all kinds of other things are already paid for by all for the benefit of some, but each case of this should be justified; no *general* argument from freedom can provide it.)

Nevertheless it is possible to justify free contraception, not on any general grounds of fundamental rights and freedom, but on specific grounds arising out of times and circumstances.

In the first place, nearly everybody now is worried by the fact that our population is at present too *large*, both in the world as a whole and in our own country. *Obviously* the first thing to do about that is to make sure that, as the slogans say, every child is a wanted child. It is, therefore, well worth our while to make it easy for people to avoid having children, and not to force them to choose between contraceptives and other things like cigarettes or clothes, or food for the other children there are already. When the population needs reducing nobody should have to trust to luck or the safe period and hope for the best. This is one case where we can very easily achieve what is good for everyone by giving individuals more of what they want.

In the second place, however unfashionable it is to say such things, it is a simple fact that there is a pretty high correlation between the groups of people who, for whatever reason, cannot be bothered with contraception, and those most likely to produce children who are going to be very expensive to the state in one way and another. Whatever uncharitable and imperceptive remarks people may make about leaving feckless parents to the consequences of their folly, no one can reasonably blame the children, or think that we ought to allow them to suffer. There are thousands or millions of women who can hardly be persuaded to take care even now that the service is free, and are only too delighted to find obstacles between themselves and the clinic (which is not surprising, given the usual nature of clinics, but that is another matter). If contraceptives had to be paid for there would be no chance of these women's going anywhere near one.

It is beyond question that at present free contraception is one of the best investments of taxpayers' money there is, and people who are obsessed with the idea that they are paying for other people's pleasures should spend more time considering the other things they would have to pay for if they stopped paying for the pleasures. Or rather, they should realize that since people will have their pleasures anyway, paid for or not, what they are really paying for is lessening the bad consequences of those pleasures for *everyone*.

In conclusion, then, feminists have the best possible case for their insistence that contraception should be free and on demand. Its general *availability* is defensible on general moral grounds, and there are overwhelming practical arguments, in the present state of things, for making it free as well.

4 · THE MORAL ISSUE OF PERMITTING ABORTION

Contraception may be a relatively straightforward matter, but the abortion problem is much more complicated. The feminist claim that that too should be free and on demand can probably be justified, but the area is one where feminists often slip up badly by being too cavalier with the opposition. Much is *said* by feminists about 'the unassailable argument, justice for women',[4] but the arguments themselves do not often appear. There is a good deal about how women suffer from not having abortions or from badly performed abortions, but the fact that anti-abortion laws hit women harder than men is not enough to prove that there is anything anti-feminist behind their formulation (as most feminists presume), or even that they do by accident treat women unjustly.

The prohibition of abortion, if it is unjust, is not

obviously so. The innocuous sound of the claim that women want nothing more than the control of their own bodies is misleading. Even if that claim is accepted, any such rights must always be limited by the consequences for other people, and you cannot have the undisputed right to live if the price of your life is someone else's, or the right to be happy at the cost of someone else's misery. Whatever conclusion we come to about the rights and wrongs of abortion, it is quite wrong to ignore the fact that the anti-abortionists have an undoubted *case* when they point out that the mother is not the only person involved in an abortion. There are also the rest of society, the father, and the unborn child to take into consideration. If their claims are to be dismissed, reasons have to be given.

Of course the mother also comes in for the kind solicitude of many anti-abortionists, who would like to protect her from herself, but arguments on that basis can be dismissed out of hand because they are all paternalist. If a woman wants to take the risk of mental or physical damage that is her business, and the only responsibility of other people is to let her know what the risks are. Anyway, even apart from the paternalist aspect, a good deal of what is commonly said is false. For instance, it is said that abortions are illegal because they are dangerous, whereas anyone who took the trouble even to glance at the facts would immediately see that they were dangerous only because they were illegal. We can forget about the mother. The only arguments we need take seriously are the ones about the claims that there are rights of other people which may conflict with her own wishes.

Of these claims which conflict with hers, that of society at large can be dealt with fairly easily, because *as they stand* the arguments in defence of its rights provide no more reason for enforcing the continuation of pregnancy than they do for enforcing its beginning. For instance, some people argue that abortion should be forbidden because it deprives the state of citizens, and in particular that it may deprive it of especially valuable citizens. (Apparently, current principles of therapeutic abortion would have led to the abortion of Beethoven, which is certainly a startling thought.) It is also often argued that it is wrong to abort children when there is a shortage of children for adoption, and childless people desperately want them. However, as these arguments stand, they apply equally against *failing to conceive*. Every unfertilized ovum could have been a child for someone to adopt, and many must have been potential Beethovens. Of course preventing abortion and enforcing conception do not look at all the same, but that is because we think that there are *other* objections to abortion. As long as only the relative rights of the pregnant woman and other members of society are taken into consideration, there is no difference at all between the two cases.

The father's claim must be somewhat stronger, since the child is his as well as the mother's. However, his contribution to its existence is much less than hers: both supply equal amounts of genetic information, but the mother gives in addition all the material substance, and all the labour of carrying and giving birth (at least). Abortion is an all-or-nothing matter, with no possibility of compromise, and therefore if only the parents' wishes are at issue, the mother, with her greater interest, must have the right to decide. If this looks doubtful, and it is felt that there should be no abortion unless both parents agree, that once again shows that other considerations than the parents' wishes are surreptitiously being brought into the argument. There must already be a presumption against abortion, on other grounds. It is, by the way, interesting to note that in the highly controversial case in Britain in 1978 where a man brought a court action to try to prevent his separated wife from having an abortion, all the public discussion of the subject was about the morality of abortion in general. No one concentrated on the specific issue of whether the father should come into the matter *if* abortion in general were acceptable.

We are brought, therefore, to what is beyond any question the centre of all arguments about abortion. They are not really about the safety of the mother or the rights of the father or society; the real question is about the rights of the mother as compared with those of the unborn child. This is the centre of the abortion issue. All the other arguments are brought in only as supplements, and as they all fail they can be disregarded entirely. (It is quite wrong to think that a bad argument may give a *little* support to a conclusion, as some people seem vaguely to think: if the argument does not work, that is that.[5]) But feminists cannot ignore the *prima facie* case that the unborn child has rights. You cannot just assert 'It is clear that the foetus is not a human being, plain and simple. The woman *is* a human being',[6] and think that settles the matter. Yet again, if feminists want abortion at the mother's desire, a case has to be made out, and not just asserted.

If the principles which were formulated in Chapters 3 and 4 of this book are acceptable, there is not much difficulty in doing this, and an argument in defence of abortion might run rather like this. The important things in life are freedom and the prevention of suffering. From the point of view of freedom the mother's claims are unquestionably paramount. She does not wish to have the child, and the child, at that stage in life, cannot reasonably be said to have any wishes at all. From the point of view of the absence of suffering, much the same is true. The mother is likely to suffer, whether or not she has an abortion, as a result of being pregnant against her wishes, but presumably will suffer less as a result of an abortion than she would through bearing and caring for an unwanted child. At any rate, she ought to be allowed to be the final judge of her own degree of suffering. The child, on the other hand, will not suffer at all. Or rather, the foetus *ought* not to suffer at all during abortion, and if it does that is absolutely intolerable and must be stopped. But that apart, there is no doubt that the argument from suffering also supports the mother's right to have an abortion if she wants one.[7]

However, all this argument does is justify abortion according to one set of moral principles, and the trouble is that they are not principles which are acceptable to everyone. Other people may have profoundly different moral intuitions, and those may lead them to oppose abortion. For instance, they may have a view of things which leads them to see human life as valuable to the extent of surpassing nearly all else, with matters such as freedom and prevention of suffering seeming rather unimportant by comparison. Such attitudes are often, though by no means always, religious. They result, when sincere, in a devotion to the preserving of life, and nurturing it with care and respect. It comes not only in objections to abortion. It was apparent, for instance, in a priest who rescued an abandoned pair of Siamese twins, who were separate down to the waist but had only one lower body between them. Many people must find it appalling that this being should have been kept alive, but it is not in the least difficult to understand, and respect, the attitude behind the effort. The same is true of a father I heard of (and, incidentally, one with no religion at all) who devoted his whole life to the care of a son who was so damaged as to be essentially a vegetable. The care produced absolutely no recognizable reward. There are many such people, and there is no trace of anti-feminism in their attitudes, as is particularly evident in these two cases where the responsibilities were taken by men, and it is most unfair of feminists to presume that nothing but woman-hatred could underlie opposition to abortion. Its cause may often be this kind of respect for life. The attitude may not be one which many of us share; we may be able to see no real value in that kind of devotion. But on the other hand it is unquestionably not one which deserves contempt. It often contains a heroism which it is impossible not to respect, even though we may disagree with the end to which it is dedicated.

The feeling of respect for life, furthermore, is probably one with which most feminists (and most people) do sympathize, at least to the extent of regarding the preservation of life as an intrinsically good thing. Most supporters of abortion do not think that it does not matter *at all* if a life stops once it has started. It is just that they think other things more important. To say that something is the least of many evils is not to say that it is unmixedly good, and we may feel regret about the taking of life even though we still think that any woman who wants an abortion should be allowed to have one. It is possible to disagree with the order of priorities of anti-abortionists without regarding their views as stemming from nothing but evil.

So there may be perfectly genuine moral viewpoints which forbid abortion, and feminists *as feminists* cannot quarrel with them because, as has been said before, feminism is *dependent* on moral principles and derives from them: you cannot argue that women are unjustly treated without having principles which are logically prior to your claim, and the debate about those principles is not a feminist one. And it is no doubt obvious that something of an impasse has been reached here, because if two sets of people have radically different moral principles, there is in theory nothing left to discuss. They disagree at the most ultimate level, and there is no common ground on which to base an argument.

But what is to be done about the law in such a case? It is no good saying that people ought all to be allowed to follow their own principles, because that as a matter of fact presupposes *another* moral principle (that people ought all to be allowed to follow their own moral principles in peace), and there is nothing sacrosanct about that one either. Most of us certainly do not accept it. So what is to be done? Are we left with no alternative but to try to force our will on the opposition?

In the last analysis that would probably be true. The question is of whether we have actually got to the last analysis yet.

5 · A FEMINIST CHALLENGE

It is true that if people's fundamental moral principles hold that life is more important than freedom or the absence of suffering, we cannot say that their following them and trying to forbid abortion stems from unjust attitudes to women. *Within those principles* it is not unjust that abortion should be forbidden. However, any anti-abortionists who have been lulled into complacency by that idea should be on their guard again, because *claiming* to be motivated by a set of commendable principles is very different from actually *being* so motivated, and any feminist is still entitled to ask whether people who would have us believe that nothing but the purest principle underlies their anti-abortion stance are really as they seem. People always like to make out that it is principle and not personal feeling which underlies unpopular activities, and feminists have every reason to be suspicious that for all that is said about principles in the context of abortion, what really underlies much of the passionate feeling is not a concern for the rights of the child at all, but a deeply entrenched wish to control and oppress women.

There is no point in just bickering about a matter like this. Feminists who are convinced of the blackness of the male soul will see it as self-evidently true; other people will think it a characteristic manifestation of feminist hysteria.[8] Obviously arguments are needed, and several lines of approach are open to feminists who would like to prove that the apparent principles which people hold against abortion are really rationalizations of something much less respectable. Evidence may be found in psychology, sociology and history, and in present-day horror stories about abortions. In all of these areas we can find evidence to suggest that many people's attitudes to women seeking abortion contain a good deal of hatred and wish for revenge, and that much of the wish to limit abortion stemmed historically from such unexalted things as professional restrictive practices.[9] All of this is extremely interesting and very persuasive. However, in keeping with the line taken by this book, what I want to do is look not at such matters, but at philosophical arguments which lead to rather similar conclusions. A philosophical attack on people's claimed principles can be launched by looking for *inconsistencies* in those principles.

When people claim to be acting from principle what they suggest is that they are being guided by a set of rules which override their own personal preferences when the two conflict. Any genuine set of principles, therefore, must be consistent, because at any point where principles are inconsistent there is no control over what is permissible. This can easily be illustrated. Suppose you claim to be a total pacifist, and also say that all people have the right to protect their property. Now it is obvious that at times these principles may come into conflict. If you find your house being burgled, or your country invaded, you can argue either that you should do nothing to repel the invader, because that would involve violence, or that you should do all you could, because otherwise you would not be protecting your property. At the points where the two principles conflict, therefore, you have really *no principles at all*, because at those points you can do as you like. You can avoid the draft and explain your doing so not by your personal reluctance to fight, but by your pacifist principles; you can attack the burglar and explain it by your principles about the protection of property, without having to say that you were selfishly concerned to protect your own interests in spite of having to damage the burglar in the process.[10] But of course if you can manage to hide from other people the fact that your so-called principles really are in conflict you may often be able to do just what suits you and at the same time use those principles to camouflage your self-interest and convey to others the appearance of moral rectitude.

A feminist, therefore, may reasonably be suspicious that not everyone who talks about the sanctity of foetal life is really motivated by principles which are radically different from hers. She may wonder whether the apparent principles are just being brought in where convenient to give an appearance of respectability to what are really (perhaps unconscious) anti-woman attitudes. And if she can, in fact, prove that her opponents seem to have no consistent principles underlying their practice, she can reasonably argue that they are not motivated by principle at all.

It is true that the feminist who argues in this way produces only a negative argument, a challenge. She does not in the first instance prove that there *can be* no consistent and acceptable set of principles underlying the practice of the opposition, only that she has been unable to find one. Still, that is well worth doing, because it puts the onus on her opponents to produce an acceptable account of what they are recommending. And in the meantime, while she is waiting for their reply, she is entitled to look for other things, like woman-hatred, which might explain what the opposition advocates. And she is entitled to accept these accounts provisionally until it can produce a consistent account of its own.[11]

There are several standpoints from which attacks of this kind might be launched. For instance, a feminist might try to show that the principles which people claimed underlay their objection to abortion were conveniently forgotten when other kinds of killing, as in war or execution, were under consideration. This is the way Simone de Beauvoir[12] argued against the Roman Catholic Church's attitude to abortion: she said that the principles which were supposed to account for forbidding abortion ought in consistency to apply to many cases of these other sorts of killing as well, and of course her argument implied that since the Church seemed quite happy to condone these others its real reasons for objecting to abortion could not be its official ones. Arguments along these lines can certainly be brought against many people now. For instance, even outside the context of religion, someone who believes in (some) war but not abortion has to explain why it is all right to kill the innocent (with a great deal of suffering) in war, but not to give abortions (which cause much less suffering), when in both cases the end in view is the preservation of the quality of life of the survivors. The same sort of problem faces the very many people who are implacably opposed to any abortions, even very early ones, and to any process (like menstrual extraction[13]) which *might* produce abortion, but have no objection to methods of contraception (the coil and in some instances even the pill) which work by preventing the implantation of the fertilized ovum and so amount to the same thing. This is a serious problem for the law, which at present allows the coil, but not menstrual extraction, to be freely available.

However, the subject of consistency in attitudes to killing in general and abortion in particular is an enormous one, and I want to concentrate here on one small area which is of particular interest. It concerns the view that abortion is acceptable in some special cases, but that it is not generally acceptable; a view which is of interest because it is so very commonly held, and is even enshrined in the law of most countries. The arguments to be brought against the consistency of this position will of course leave unscathed the people who are opposed to abortion altogether (which is not to suggest that other arguments of a similar kind might not scathe many of them), but they are important because if they are successful they force people into one extreme position or the other: they show that people must in consistency either object to abortion altogether, or allow it on demand. (Actually they do not entail quite the second extreme, but something so like it as to make little difference in practice. That will be explained soon.) And what they also seem to show is that *where the law allows any abortions at present, it ought in consistency to allow (nearly) all*.

There seem to be three sorts of case in which people who disapprove of abortion in general would accept that it was reasonable to perform abortions, and where the law also finds them acceptable. They are abortion in the case of rape, in the case of a deformed or possibly deformed child, and in the case of damage to the mental or physical health of the mother. In each of these cases arguments will be produced to try to show that the present state of law and public opinion *cannot be accounted for by any considerations based on a concern for the rights of the foetus, but can be accounted for by attitudes to the mother*, which shows that the issues are of genuine feminist concern.[14] They also try to show that *any* acceptable principle which allowed some abortions should also allow nearly all. That is of course, as said earlier, essentially a challenge to people who want to keep something like the present state of things, to produce an acceptable principle which will allow them to do it or to change their attitudes.

6 · ABORTION IN THE CASE OF RAPE

This case is probably the most interesting and the most decisive from the feminist point of view, because there seems to be no possible acceptable reason for allowing abortion to victims of rape while withholding it from other unwilling mothers.

There is of course no difficulty at all in understanding why people think that abortion should be allowed to a rape victim. It certainly does seem most unfair that a woman who has conceived unwillingly, as a result of rape, should be forced to bear her child. That presents no problem, on its own. What is difficult is to reconcile that attitude with maintaining at the same time that other women should not be given abortions if they want them. This can be seen by comparing the cases of a raped and an unraped woman who are seeking abortions, and seeing what the differences in the two cases are.

The first thing which is absolutely clear is that *there is no difference at all in the status of the two unborn children*. This is important, because the usual reason people give for objecting to abortions is something to do with the sanctity of human life, but it is quite clear that if you think abortion is all right in the case of rape you *cannot* think of that foetus as being a full human being, with full human rights. It would be quite unthinkable to take the life of an adult human being to save a different human being from undeserved unhappiness. Imagine, for instance, what would be said if anyone tried to kill someone in order to give vital organs to someone else (perhaps a relative) who had been the innocent victim of a criminal attack. If you really thought that the child of the raped mother was fully human you might do what you could to compensate her in other ways, but would not offer to kill her child. But since the child of the other mother must therefore not be fully human either, you cannot explain reluctance to allow abortion to her by arguments about the sanctity of human life. Since the children are the same, and since neither (apparently) is being counted as of full human status, what is the reason for taking different attitudes to abortion in the two cases?

It is quite obvious that since there is no difference in the children the relevant difference must lie in the mothers, and it is clear what that difference must be. It must be that the raped mother cannot be held responsible for her unwelcome position, whereas the other one can. And this does indeed seem to account for many people's being willing to allow abortion in the case of rape but not abortion in general. We are willing to help people to avoid the consequences of misfortune, but only of misfortune: in general people must be made to bear the consequences of their actions, and this is why women who could have avoided their pregnancies must be made to bring them to term.

The idea that people should have to take the consequences of their actions is fair enough, up to a point. If, for instance, you were careless about your electric wiring, and did nothing about it in spite of constant warnings from other people, you could hardly blame them if they refused to help you when your house burned down. Your family and friends and insurance company would be quite justified in saying that it was all your fault, so you must bear the consequences alone. However, although that is true, it is not a proper analogy with the abortion case. At the moment we are only considering whether unraped women should be *allowed* to have abortions, not whether they should be given *assistance* in getting them. That was one reason for separating so carefully the questions of whether abortion should be allowed and whether it should be state-assisted. The fire analogy suggests that we should perhaps *help* the victims of rape and not others, but it does not show that we should not allow the others to seek their own abortions. The analogy with preventing the others from seeking abortion is not the insurance company's refusing to help with rebuilding a house which had burnt down through your own fault; it is rather as though they said 'It's all your own fault, you must take the consequences, so now we will forcibly prevent your getting a new house even by your own efforts, and make sure you live in a tent for the rest of your life.'

There are in the nature of things no natural, inevitable consequences of most actions. People make mistakes and suffer setbacks as a result, but what happens in the long run depends not only on the nature of the mistake, but also on the action they take to put matters right afterwards. Or rather (and this is the point), the only time when we insist that a particular consequence must follow a particular action, and do not allow people to try to escape the consequence by their own unaided activity, is *when the consequence is intended as a punishment*. Unless we are trying to punish people, we do not actually try to prevent their putting right the bad consequences they have brought on themselves, even though we may refuse to help them.

It looks, then, as though we have here a theory which fits the facts. Since abortions are allowed in the case of rape, the foetus cannot be regarded as a full human being. If, then, pregnancy is forced on other unwilling mothers, it is not because the child is a human being whose life is sacrosanct. Why then are such mothers not automatically allowed to have abortions? One plausible explanation is that the child is being used as an instrument of punishment to the mother, and that talk of the sanctity of life is just being used to disguise that fact.

If that is right, what is the mother being punished for? It cannot be for conceiving, since that is not generally regarded as a crime. The willing mother is not regarded as worthy of punishment, any more than is the unwilling woman who is the victim of rape. It looks as though the only thing which the woman who conceives accidentally has done to differentiate herself from these others is to have indulged willingly in sex without being willing to bear a child. Can that be what is really thought to deserve punishment? Can it be that you are morally all right if you put up with sex if you see it as a means to an acceptable end (having a child) or if it is forced on you against your will, but not if you actually *want* it? It may sound incredible, but there seems to be nothing else which fits the facts. (It is also, incidentally, a theory which would apparently account for a good many of the appalling stories about the practice of abortion.[15] Much of what actually goes on in abortions suggests that if women are to escape the suffering of actually bearing the child, they must be made to suffer in the abortion. It would be very interesting to find out how much correlation there was between people who were generally hostile to sex and those who objected to abortion.)

We seem to have reached the conclusion, therefore, that the readiest explanation of a willingness to allow abortions to rape victims but not otherwise is a wish to punish sex in women who could have prevented their conceptions. This may not be the only explanation which is consistent with the facts, but the onus is now on the many people who will hotly repudiate this account of their motives to provide a more acceptable alternative explanation which also meets the case.

Other explanations, however, are not easy to find. Perhaps someone might try to escape the trap by constructing a theory of a kind which is very popular these days, and say that any child conceived when the mother had the power to prevent its conception must be deemed to have a *contract* with the mother for the support of its life, whereas a raped mother cannot be considered to have entered into any such contract. That certainly is a principle which consistently covers the case, but anyone who tried to say that was really the *reason* for opposing abortion would be hopelessly un-persuasive because of the principle's complete arbitrariness. It would be a transparent rationalization of a position arrived at in some other way. If that were the only thing standing between women and abortion, why have that law of contract rather than another? Why not say that there should be a different one; that a contract should be held to exist only when the mother actually wanted to conceive the child? The child would know nothing about it in either case. If we are to talk about contracts without being open to suspicion of rationalizing some less reputable motive we must be prepared to give some account of why one law of contract is to be preferred to another. It is hard to see what independent arguments could possibly justify the one which is needed here, to uphold abortion only in the case of rape.

Another line of argument could hold that it was unfair to make the issue into one which was so black and white, presuming that if the foetus did not have full human rights it must have none at all. Could we not say that it had *some* rights, and that even though it was not a full human being it must still not be sacrificed wantonly? That certainly sounds a promising line in itself, but we are still left with the problem of explaining why the raped woman merits the sacrifice of the child's life when the unraped woman does not. If we say that the child can be sacrificed for a high degree of suffering (which sounds reasonable), that does not distinguish between the raped and unraped woman, because it alters the criterion for when abortion is allowable. Rape is no longer the criterion; it has changed to one of suffering. Raped women are sufferers among other sufferers. But there is no reason to think that *all* raped women must suffer more than *all* unraped women. It is easy to imagine, for instance, that because the raped woman might be pitied she would be better treated by other people than if she had incurred her pregnancy herself. If we are to keep the distinction between rape and non-rape, how can we then account for allowing the raped woman, but not others, to count as worthy of the sacrifice of the child's life? It looks as though any such justification must depend on ideas of *guilt*, and that brings us once again to the question of what the unraped woman, but not the raped one, is supposed to be guilty of, as well as the separate question of why the 'guilty' ones are less worthy than the others of having their sufferings attended to. This line of argument seems to collapse into something so similar in its consequences to the one which led to the idea that women should be punished for sex that there is effectively no difference between them. (There are some differences, connected with different theories of punishment, but they do not seem relevant here.)

The provisional conclusion, therefore, which must stand until someone finds an acceptable escape from it, is this. Since allowing abortion to rape victims but not to women in general cannot be accounted for by any consideration for the rights of the foetus, because these are the same in both kinds of case, it can be explained only, as far as I can see, by seeing the child as the instrument of punishment for the sexual activity of the mother. It does not follow from that, of course, that everyone who approves of abortion in the case of rape but not otherwise actually has this vindictive attitude, even subconsciously. It is far more likely to result in many cases from muddle; an ingrained idea that abortion is bad, tempered by the charitable idea that it is really not fair to add to the unmerited suffering of a woman who has gone through so much already. There is nothing bad about this impulse, but muddle in matters of principle ought to be eliminated, and that seems to imply that anyone who regards rape as in itself a sufficient condition for abortion at the request of the mother should be willing to allow it in all cases. Conversely, anyone who is not willing to allow abortion on demand should not regard rape as a sufficient condition for allowing abortion. Either way, rape in itself is irrelevant to questions of abortion where the rights of the foetus are at issue; it comes in only with feelings about punishing erring women. It is, therefore, a genuine feminist matter.

7 · ABORTION OF ABNORMAL FOETUSES

We come now to the question of the position of people who are willing to allow the mother of an abnormal or possibly abnormal child to have an abortion at her desire, but not to allow abortion on demand to women in general. Here the arguments which can be brought on the feminist side are less strong. They do not show that there is no principle which *could* account for some such attitude, only that *current practice* does not seem to be supported by any consistent and acceptable principle. Once again it looks as though it is impossible to explain the attitudes people have by reference to the rights of the children, which is the usual ground people give for their objecting to abortion, but that they may be explainable by reference to attitudes to mothers.

Why is the abortion of abnormal foetuses allowed? One possible reason is the suffering of the mother and other members of the family. However, that is not at issue at the moment because that principle might equally well allow the abortion of a perfectly normal child in, say, an overcrowded family, and therefore really comes into the next section, which is about whether abortion should be allowed on the grounds of the mother's health. When people say that abnormal foetuses can be aborted, but that there should not be abortion on demand in general, their position seems to be based on the idea of there being an intrinsic difference between the children in the two cases, rather than anything specifically to do with the mother.

One possible, and likely, reason is perhaps a wish to spare an abnormal child a life of suffering. That does well enough for many kinds of abnormality, but it still does not account for all. One of the commonest grounds for allowing abortion is mongolism, and a mongol child is not by nature unhappy. If it is unhappy it is only because its environment makes it so, and therefore from any argument that mongol children should be aborted on the grounds that they are likely to be unhappy because they are unwanted, it seems to follow that any unwanted child should be aborted because it is unlikely to be happy in its home environment. Since this is not generally accepted we need a different ground for allowing abortion in cases like that. But perhaps it is not too difficult to find. Perhaps the idea is that since the most essential characteristic of human beings is mental ability and level of awareness, anyone who is seriously defective is not really human, and can be sacrificed for that reason. So perhaps we can account for a willingness to abort abnormal foetuses by a combination of two principles: first, that a mentally abnormal one does not count as fully human, and second, that a physically abnormal one is to be spared a life of suffering.

This way of looking at things is not without its problems. One of the most serious is to reconcile this idea with most people's total opposition to infanticide. If a mentally abnormal *foetus* is not fully human and can be sacrificed for that reason, why do the same considerations not apply to a mentally abnormal *infant*? And if the point of abortion in the case of the physically handicapped is to prevent future suffering, why does that not also allow for killing physically handicapped infants? It seems rather hard that you should be eligible to be spared a life of misery if you are lucky enough to be discovered in time, but not if you have the misfortune to have your disabilities undetected until birth. These principles for allowing abortions certainly entail allowing infanticide for the same reasons.

Another problem for anyone who wants to take this line but also forbid abortion in general is to justify abortion of the physically abnormal foetus. If all mentally normal foetuses have a full human right to life, why may foetuses who are only *physically* handicapped be aborted? If they are fully human, surely they ought to be born and then left to decide themselves later whether the quality of their lives was so bad that they would prefer to be without life.

However, leaving aside those tricky problems (which is not to imply that they are unimportant), the most serious difficulty for people who want to uphold present abortion practices is that these allow abortion not only in the case of abnormal foetuses, but also in the case of *possibly* abnormal ones. This is one aspect of present policy which seems absolutely impossible to reconcile with any idea of forbidding abortion in general on the grounds of the rights of the unborn child.

The point is this. In general when people want to forbid abortion they concentrate on the rights of the child, and when they say that it is all right to abort abnormal foetuses they are implying that *because of the difference between these children and normal ones* the whole case is changed; the abnormal foetus is not entitled to the same kind of consideration as the normal one, whose rights are inviolable. But this way of looking at things, even if it had no problems in itself, cannot account for the fact that as things are, many *normal* children are aborted under the policies which prevent abnormal births. A woman is entitled to abortion, for instance, if she develops German measles during the early part of pregnancy. There is a likelihood that the child may be defective in cases of this sort, but it is by no means certain. The situation is even more curious in the case of chromosomally linked diseases like haemophilia. This is a disease which a boy in a carrier family has a fifty-fifty chance of inheriting, while a girl will be either only a carrier or completely free.[16] There are at present no ante-natal means of diagnosing the disease, but it is possible to find out the sex of unborn children, and the procedure at present is to offer carrier women amniocentesis to find out the sex of an unborn child, and abortion if it turns out to be male. This means not only that there is a fifty-fifty chance of aborting a normal child, but also a fifty-fifty chance of allowing an abnormal one (a carrier girl, through whom the misery of the condition will be transmitted) to be born.

The reason why this kind of policy cannot be reconciled with a general prohibition of abortion on the grounds of the inviolable rights of the foetus is that *it does itself* concede that a normal unborn child can be aborted. The case might hold if only children *known* to be abnormal were aborted, but the fact that possibly normal ones can be sacrificed too shows that a normal child is not, in fact, thought automatically to have a full human right to live. If it had such a right there would be no question of killing it. It would be quite out of the question to kill a full human being on the fifty-fifty chance that you might be killing someone else you wanted to kill. (If there are two people in a building, one of whom is a notorious murderer, you do not shoot dead the first one to come out. People do not lose their rights through accidentally being in situations where it is difficult to distinguish them from other people who have not the same rights.) In any such case it would be better to wait until after birth and then kill any child that did turn out to be defective. Even if defective foetuses somehow miraculously acquired full human status at birth in spite of having been without it before, it would still be no worse to kill one then than to abort a normal infant before birth, if that normal child had full human rights all along.

If a normal foetus has rights of its own, those rights surely cannot be rendered null by the fact that we do not *know* whether the foetus in question is of a sort to have those rights or not.[17] Of course we might be excused if we made a mistake, and aborted a normal child we had good reason to think was abnormal, but that does not account for our being willing to sacrifice one which may be abnormal but equally well may be normal. If it may be normal and a normal child has those rights, we must respect them until we find out. And since we do not do this, it must follow that we do *not* regard a normal foetus as fully human, *do* think it can be sacrificed, and therefore are left with the problem of explaining why, in spite of this, we want to prevent the mothers of children who are believed to be normal from seeking abortion.

Obviously it is not going to be an easy matter, and while people who still think that present practice can indeed be explained by reference to the rights of unborn children are working out what principles could justify their position, we are entitled to look for alternative explanations. Once again, we can make sense of everything if we concentrate not on the rights of the child, but on social attitudes to mothers. It can all be explained in terms of two principles. The first is that (however inexplicable it may be) although abortion may sometimes be condoned, infanticide can never be. The second is that a woman who wants a child but by misfortune is carrying (or even may be carrying) one of the wrong sort, which will bring her unhappiness through no fault of her own, is to be pitied and allowed to have an abortion. (As mentioned before, the practice in the case of haemophilia does not stop the transmission of the disease. What it does is give the mother the satisfaction of having a child whose childhood is normal, even though her daughter may have the unhappiness herself of going through amniocentesis and abortions, and may give birth to boys who actually suffer from the disease.) Once again, it looks as though the real purpose behind the practice is to protect 'innocent' women who would suffer if their children were born, while not providing an all-purpose escape route for the 'guilty'; and once again it seems impossible to explain the innocence and guilt except in terms of whether sex was indulged in with the intention of producing children or not. This does seem to account for what actually goes on, and until another more plausible explanation is produced feminists do seem justified in saying that anyone who is willing to allow abortion to a mother with a possibly abnormal child should be willing to allow abortion to any woman at all.

8 · ABORTION FOR THE MOTHER'S HEALTH

Finally there is the matter of abortion on the grounds of danger to the physical or mental health of the mother. People who think this is acceptable presumably take the view that the unborn child has some value, and may not be killed except for very serious reasons. This view certainly goes further towards the feminist position than the other two, because it does by implication concede that the child is expendable for the well-being of the mother, but even so the present state of practice shows a confusion which is unfair to women.

The question is considerably complicated by the complexity of the question of what it is to be in poor health. If the issue really is one of *health* of the mother (that is, trouble inherent to the mother) rather than general distress (that is, trouble which may result from the environment rather than something intrinsic), then the present state of things is certainly a ground for feminist complaint. Since the degree of suffering may be the same in either case, we may wonder why one kind may be prevented by abortion while the other may not, and may think that the readiest explanation is once again in terms of rescuing the innocent (the people who through no fault of their own find their health endangered by pregnancy) while not letting off the improvident, who should have realized that unwanted children would interfere with their lives in one way or another, and therefore should have taken care accordingly.

Still, that may be hair splitting. In practice the whole thing seems to be much vaguer than that, and 'social' arguments are allowed to enter the question (though it is noteworthy that women are referred for decision to *doctors*, who are presumably supposed to be judges of health rather than of happiness). But even so, even bringing the mother's general well-being and that of her family into the question, what are the doctors supposed to be deciding? Presumably whether or not the suffering caused by the child's birth would be great enough to justify an abortion. But why should a doctor decide that? Suppose we agree that it is within the range of medical competence to assess how much suffering a woman will endure as a result of going through with her pregnancy, that still does not account for a doctor's deciding whether she *should* go through with it or not. The question of how much suffering is acceptable as a ground for the sacrifice of the child has *nothing at all to do with a doctor's professional expertise*: it is a matter which a doctor is no more competent to decide than anyone else. If the law really intended that an abortion should be performed on the grounds of a certain level of suffering, but not less, it should stipulate that abortion cases were to be decided by courts, using doctors only as expert witnesses. But nothing like this happens. It is well known that doctors differ radically in the amount of sympathy they have with women seeking abortions, and that the women who eventually get them are not the ones who will suffer most through not having them, but the ones who are lucky enough to have a sympathetic doctor, or who are rich or knowledgeable enough to look around and find one. The real sufferers, as usual, are the least competent and most oppressed.

The conclusion is that as things stand at the moment there is no real concern to estimate the value of the unborn child, or for the degree of suffering which would justify an abortion. All the law does, in effect, is make sure that a woman may not decide for herself whether to have an abortion, and send her to someone else in the position of a suppliant for favours, or even a culprit.[18] It does nothing else. It certainly does not attempt anything in the way of a systematic assessment of the value of unborn children or a safeguarding of their rights, and as the law now stands there is no reason whatever for stopping where we are, and not going forward to a state where all women who want abortions can have them. This would not mean that children were sacrificed any more 'frivolously' than they are at present, given that some doctors allow abortions very freely.

9 · ABORTION ON DEMAND

The essential points in the argument so far about the permissibility of abortion have been these.

First, there can be genuine moral principles, principles by which people may decide to regulate their actions even when it means going against their personal interests, against abortion. A feminist has no right to presume that anyone who opposes her desires on the subject is in any way unprincipled or out to oppress women.

On the other hand, she does not have to accept that people who claim to be motivated by nothing but the purest principle really are, and there are various means by which she can try to show that the opposition's motives are not as noble as they would have us believe. One way of doing this is by looking at the supposed principles, looking at the activities which the person professing to hold them opposes or condones, and seeing whether there are inconsistencies. If the supposed principle which is claimed to be the reason for opposing abortion turns out not to forbid other things which it ought to forbid, we are entitled to conclude that it does not really exist. (If people say that abortion is not to be allowed because there is never any reason for killing the innocent, but do not oppose all wars, we are entitled to infer that they are not really against all killing of the innocent.) Of course people do sometimes have genuine principles which they have not got round to formulating properly, and so we should look to see whether we can find *any* good principles which would account for what is allowed and what is forbidden. If we cannot, we issue a challenge to the other side to say what they are, and meanwhile feel entitled to see whether we can explain what goes on by reasons which have nothing to do with principle.

The arguments of this chapter have been aimed at one particular group of people: those who hold that abortion is morally defensible in some situations but not others. The conclusions have been these. First, that there appears to be *no* acceptable principle which would allow abortion in the case of rape, but not automatically to other women who wanted abortions. Second, that in the case of abortion for abnormal or possibly abnormal infants, and abortion in the case of the endangered health of the mother, current attitudes and practice do not seem to be explicable in terms of any acceptable set of principles; certainly not in any about the value of the life of the unborn child. To the arguments of each of the foregoing sections it should be added that of course anyone who wants to accept *all* the usual reasons for allowing abortion, but still not allow it on demand, has an even greater problem in finding a single principle to cover all three kinds of case than arises for each one separately. In all these cases it does, however, seem possible to explain all that goes on in terms of attitudes to the mother and a wish to punish sex. Apart from that, there seems no other explanation than (perhaps well-intentioned) confusion. People who approve of abortion in the case of rape, therefore, or of the amount of abortion which is allowed by present-day therapeutic practice, seem to have no legitimate reason for opposing abortion on demand.

One question which does arise out of this, however, is whether it follows that an all-or-nothing attitude ought to be taken to abortion, or whether it is possible to find a consistent set of acceptable principles which would allow some abortions but not all. If abortion is allowed at all, must it be allowed on demand?

The question is too large to go into fully here, but something can be said about it. It does seem possible to work out a coherent scheme based on the idea of the value of the unborn child (and, since a properly worked-out system would have to account for more than just principles of abortion, the value of the child when born), and the degree of suffering which would be caused by its being born (or continuing to live). The child's inherent value would determine the level of suffering for which it should, or should not, be sacrificed.

A view like this would make sense, but it could not just be arbitrary, simply asserting out of nowhere that an abortion could be allowed in order to prevent a certain level of suffering of either mother or child, but not otherwise. It would have to be based on some general account of the value of life which applied consistently to all other questions of life and death (including, for instance, such matters as attitudes to war, accident prevention, famine relief, killing of animals and possibly even of plants) as well as to abortion, otherwise abortion 'principles' could be too easily just a matter of whim, and still used as a surreptitious control on women.

I suspect that the only kind of principle which could possibly succeed in allowing some abortions but not all, and which was also consonant with other attitudes to life and death, would be one which took the view that the value of any life was proportional to its degree of complexity and autonomy. This would make the value of the unborn child very slight at conception, but constantly increasing to reach full human rights some time in infancy. As its value increased the reasons for which it could be sacrificed would have to be more serious, and it would not, for instance, be acceptable to have an abortion in advanced pregnancy to avoid some relatively minor inconvenience. As far as I can see, however, any such principle as this would have the effect that no more than the mother's wishes would be needed to justify a *very early* abortion. Since if abortion were readily available all abortions would be early, this sort of principle would in effect allow abortion on demand. I can think of no principle which would allow some abortions but not others and which would not have this consequence.[19]

Whether or not something on these lines is acceptable, however, the important thing is that any view which seeks to prevent (or allow) abortion, either in all cases or only in some, must, if it is to count as a principle, be consistent with other attitudes to life and death.

10 · FREE ABORTION

The question of whether abortion should be free as well as legal is probably not, as a matter of fact, a very important one. It is the illegality of abortion which makes it expensive at present. If women were not prevented by fear and shame from seeking abortions as soon as they became pregnant nearly all abortions would be early, and early abortions are cheap and easy. If private abortionists did not have women at their mercy, and there were a free market, abortion would presumably be very cheap. (The government might intervene to prevent price fixing, perhaps.) If this happened it would probably not make much difference on either side whether the state paid for abortions or whether individuals did themselves. However, the issues of principle are of some importance, and worth discussing.

The arguments for and against free abortion have to be invented to some extent, because on the whole the question of the permissibility of abortion is not separated from the question of who should pay. People who oppose abortion altogether also oppose its being free *a fortiori*, and the ones who think that abortion ought to be on demand also tend to presume as a matter of course that it ought to be free as well. Still, it is not difficult on the whole to guess what form the arguments on the subject of free abortion would generally take. The people in favour of it would talk about people's *needs*. There are many indignant pronouncements from feminists about health and social service workers who forget that their function is to help everyone who is in need. The other side would not deny that women seeking abortion were in need, but would point out that not all needs had the same status. Some needs, like the need for abortion, are self-induced, and people should be held responsible for getting themselves out of trouble they have brought upon themselves.

Suppose for the moment we concede the arguments on the anti free abortion side. Even according to these arguments, some abortions should be free. For instance, as was pointed out earlier, it is at this stage in the argument (rather than when the permissibility of abortion is being discussed) that the issue of sympathy for the victims of rape arises. Since a raped woman is not responsible for her pregnancy, it does not seem fair that she should be expected to pay for an abortion. If we could catch the rapist we should of course hold him responsible, but in general most of us would happily agree that the state should pay. It is one of our strongest conceptions about the function of a welfare state that it should act as an insurance agent, so that those of us who have not been the victims of misfortune as a matter of course help those who have. We might possibly allow considerations such as these to extend to women who have become pregnant as a result of faulty contraceptives, in spite of having taken a good deal of care.

As well as cases like these where free abortion seems acceptable, there may be other cases where the principle that whoever is responsible should pay might itself lead to the conclusion that the state should pay. If, for instance, we agree that it is the moral duty of the state to make sure that no child grows up without knowing how reproduction works and how to get hold of contraceptives, we should also accept the state's responsibility for any pregnancies which arise from ignorance.

Nevertheless, this still leaves large numbers of women who are responsible for their own pregnancies, and if we think that they ought not to have to pay for their own abortions we have to make a case against the position that people should take the consequences of their own actions. It is, by the way, no use retreating into a woolly idea that somehow no one is really responsible in the last analysis for what happens to her: that everyone is the victim of times, places, circumstances, background and social pressures. Even though there may be some sense in which all that is true, it is no use as a premise in an argument for the conclusion that the state ought to take upon itself all responsibility for its citizens' misfortunes. The state is after all composed of individuals, and if individuals cannot be held responsible for what they do, it is hardly reasonable to regard the state as something which can make choices. If we are going to make moral pronouncements about what the state ought to do, we have to allow that people can be held responsible for their activities as well. We must allow in this context that people *are* to a greater or lesser degree responsible for what they do. The question at issue here is the very different one of the extent to which they ought to be *held* responsible for it.

Why do we hold people responsible for their activities?

Why do we say that people must take the consequences of what they do, and get themselves out of trouble they have brought down on themselves? We can suggest two very plausible-sounding reasons. One is that it is unfair to the rest of us, who do take care to avoid trouble, to have to deal with the problems of other people who have been careless. A state which expected everyone to share the consequences of an individual's carelessness would be one which had little concern for individual freedom, because it would be lowering the extent to which what happened to people depended on what they chose to do. When those who take care and those who do not end up in the same situation, there is less that individuals can do about directing the course of their own lives. The other important argument, which is connected with the first, is that what people choose to do is to a great extent determined by the consequences they think will result from their actions. Needs are not things which arise independently of social arrangements; they have a habit of expanding to meet the resources available. If everyone knows that a need will be met by the community as soon as it occurs (the argument goes) no one will bother to avoid getting into difficulty. The result is that the drain on public resources will increase indefinitely, to the detriment of everybody. These two arguments in combination do sound pretty persuasive, and do seem to make a strong case on the anti free abortion side. (At least, they convinced me for some time.)

Now on the basis of all that has been argued so far in this book, it must obviously be said that if the effect of the state's extricating people from the consequences of their own mistakes is to lower the level of freedom available to everyone, it must not do it. If meeting a need increases the level of that need to the disadvantage of everyone, that need should not be met. However, even though that may be true, it is not in itself an argument against *any particular sort* of state help for people in situations of self-inflicted distress, because it is not in the least self-evident that whenever the state comes to the rescue it always has the effect of making people careless about getting into trouble. Sometimes they become careless if they know they will be helped, but not always. Whether or not they do is a matter for empirical investigation in every case. This investigation *must* be made (by experimenting with different sorts of state assistance), because otherwise people are all too likely to invent the consequences to justify what they want to do. People who feel in their bones that women who carelessly get pregnant ought to be punished in some way can very easily justify their feelings (perhaps even to themselves) by saying that free abortions would lead to unfair privations for everyone, so arguing for what they want while keeping their real motives of revenge out of sight. People who concentrate their attention on the 'needs' of women in difficulty may equally well be careless about the consequences for the rest of society, and just presume without evidence that there will be no bad ones. We must find out what really is true.

Probably no one has enough evidence to make any authoritative judgment on this subject, but there are some things which are worth saying.

In the first place, we have no evidence at all to suggest that making abortion easily available would make women careless about unwanted pregnancy. In fact all the evidence we have goes just the other way, and suggests that abortion is such an *inherently* unpleasant business that no woman would willingly choose it, and although its being free might remove one difficulty, it would still never become pleasant enough to be an acceptable alternative to contraception. Until someone can produce some statistics which show that easily available abortion does increase unwanted conception (and even then we should have to be careful that increased statistics showed more than just new cases coming to light) we have no reason whatever to believe it.

The other part of the question, about whether allowing free abortions would significantly lessen any freedom for the rest of us, can be given an answer with a similar degree of certainty. The question is in its essentials like that of providing free contraception. On that subject it has been argued that the public cost of 'not paying for other people's pleasures' would be much greater than that of providing free contraception, because as a matter of fact it seems that many people do not bother with contraception if it is any kind of trouble, and we all have to bear the consequences later on. In the case of abortion we have less such evidence. It seems most unlikely that many women would be deterred by *cost* from having an abortion (especially if ready availability made them cheap) because the situation then is one of acute emergency, calling for quick action. People are very much more willing to find money quickly in that sort of situation than they are to find it to fend off future ills which have not the same reality about them. However, even though that is so, it still seems likely that it would be a good thing to provide free abortions, because if *even a few* women failed to seek abortion because they could not afford it, or tried home abortion, the cost to the state of supporting the unwanted children or repairing the damage to the mother could probably pay for an entire free service. (It has been said that even in America, where of course most people pay privately for medical care, the cost to the state of picking up the pieces after badly performed abortions could alone pay for the whole of a free service.[20]) It does once again seem likely that free abortion might well be a good national investment. If we could show that it was, anyone who *still* wanted to make women pay for their own abortions must have a very deeply ingrained wish to punish women.

Still, this is controversial. If it is right that abortion prices would probably be very low if abortion were legal, it might turn out that no one was put off by having to pay, and then the other side would be right. But if that turned out to be true, the whole issue would be relatively unimportant anyway.

11 · SUMMARY

The conclusion of this chapter as a whole is that the feminist demand for abortion and contraception free and on demand can in its essentials be justified, but that far more argument is needed than usually is given. Contraceptives should, on general moral grounds of individual freedom, be generally available. Abortions *can* be objected to on general moral grounds, but current practice shows that the people who approve of it have no such moral grounds to justify their position, and therefore that they should in consistency allow abortion in general, and without any controversy in the early stages. There are no general moral arguments to show that contraception should always be supplied free by any state, but specific empirical arguments suggest that it is better for everyone that it should be given free, at least for the present. The argument about abortion's being free is much less clear, but there is at least an overwhelming case for trying it, and looking without prejudice at the results. In general the case which has been made out here does in theory fall short of the feminist claim for abortion and contraception free and on demand, but it comes as near to it as makes no practical difference.

The most interesting thing to have emerged, I think, is that some parts of the question of whether abortion should be allowed are indeed feminist questions. If the only issue were the usually discussed one of whether or not the unborn child was human, and whether therefore abortion was a kind of murder, the subject would not be a feminist one at all. Whether something is human or not has nothing to do with feminism. That, however, is not the only issue. Argument shows that current attitudes to abortion must at least to some extent be underlain by vindictive attitudes to sexual activity in women, and supports the empirical evidence that much hostility to abortion is connected with hostility to women. These are matters of the strongest feminist concern.

9

Society and the Mother

I · RADICAL CHANGE

Even when contraception and abortion are as readily available as any feminist could wish, and no child arrives in the world uninvited by its mother, there are for the foreseeable future still going to be children. The time may come when people decide that the human race is not worth continuing, and stop bothering to reproduce, but that time is not yet, and until it comes there will still be the need to care for the children who do arrive. And since at the moment the care of children falls very heavily on women, the feminist concern with women's reproductive function cannot end with making sure that children are born only when their mothers want them.

The whole problem is relatively neglected in public debate, which tends to consist in not much more than demands for twenty-four hour state-supplied crèches from the feminist camp, countered by conservative claims that if mothers were at home with their children as they ought to be we should be rid of most of the problems of modern society. Obviously, however, the subject is one which calls for proper discussion. This chapter tackles some of the central questions, making use of frequently heard feminist ideas as a guide to the essential issues and as a basis for constructing possible arguments, even though the arguments may not actually be ones explicitly used by feminists.

Working on this principle, it seems possible to concentrate the analysis on two central issues. One is about what *arrangements* should be made for child care, how much social reorganization is called for. The other is of who should *pay* for it, state or parents. These are obviously quite separate matters, and although the various opinions people have on the subject of child care range, as one would expect, from conservative to extremely radical, they do so independently on each of these scales. A proposal which is radical in demanding that the state should take the whole financial burden of children may still be, as surprisingly many feminist ones are, quite conservative in leaving many basic social arrangements quite unchanged. And since these two issues are separate ones, it is better to look at each of them separately, rather than considering any particular feminist proposals as wholes.

It is on the subject of arrangements for child care that there seems to be the greatest range of feminist opinion, and the difference between conservative and radical proposals is extreme.

At the conservative end of the scale there is the Wages for Housework campaign which, in its astonishing demand that central government should pay all women (*all* women) for their (presumed) work in the home, is conservative not only in specifically implying that work in the home is women's job, but in the more fundamental sense of wanting to pay people for *work* on the basis of *sex*, which is as extreme a form of sex discrimination as can be imagined. That proposal as it stands must obviously be ruled out on general feminist grounds. However, even a modified version of it, which demanded pay for housework on the basis of work, would still be conservative. Except for making people who worked in the home financially independent, it would leave everything very much as it now is. However, although that is the most conservative of feminist proposals on the subject of child care, others which at first glance seem more radical nevertheless call for surprisingly little social change. For instance, the popular idea of universally available twenty-four hour crèches is an extremely conservative one because it leaves virtually everything as it now is, with the only exception of making it possible for women to leave their children in the care of others while they go off to join the men at work. Much the same is true of schemes of maternity leave. All they do is allow for slightly special treatment of childbearing women, still within the present scheme of things.

However, there are of course far more radical feminist proposals than those. There is, for instance, the popular idea of sharing child care between women and men. Already some women are even insisting on supplementary marriage contracts which specify that the parents shall share equally the work of bringing up the children, and although the details are sometimes almost unbelievably silly (some even list on which days each parent will help with the child's homework and emotional difficulties[1]), the idea is a promising one, and far more radical than the provision of crèches. Some feminists go further than this, at least in their aspirations, hoping that eventually technology will take this male-female sharing of children even to the extent of ending intra-uterine pregnancy. 'The reproduction of the species by one sex for the benefit of both would be replaced by (at least the option of) artificial reproduction: children would be born to both sexes equally, or independently of either, however one chooses to look at it.'[2] And the most radical suggestion of all is of the complete abolition of the family, a proposal which could presumably include anything from simply getting rid of the present nuclear family as the basic unit of society, to an extreme situation where it was ensured that nobody, not even mother and child, had any knowledge of blood relationships at all.

In contrast to this wide variation of feminist views on the subject of social reorganization for the care of children, there seems to be very little difference of opinion on the other subject, of who should take financial responsibility for children. The matter is rather little discussed in feminism, but that in itself is significant because it shows how much is taken for granted. Universally available crèches, for instance, could in theory be paid for either by parents or by state, but most feminists seem to presume without argument that the state should pay for all.

In the discussion of birth control, which also raised the two separate questions of what should happen and who should pay, the question of state subsidies was left until the question of whether birth control was allowable had been settled. Here, for various reasons, it seems better to deal with the questions the other way round, and concentrate first on the issue of who should have financial responsibility for children.

2 · STATE SUPPORT OF CHILDREN

The question of the extent to which the state should pay for the care of children is an exceptionally tricky one to answer, because it is necessary to consider children from two entirely different points of view.

On the one hand, children are of course people, individuals in their own right and as entitled to consideration as anyone else. On the other hand, that is not all they are. *From the point of view of the parents* they are quite different, because children do not just appear out of nowhere; they are born because the parents want them. (This presupposes a proper system of birth control, of course, but that is the situation we must plan for.) And from the point of view of the parents there seems no reason at all for children to be subsidized by the state, because children are not a kind of external drain on the parents' income, but a chosen way of spending it. If we think of children as valued possessions of their parents (which is unquestionably one thing they are) we should not say that it is unfair that four people in one family may live on the same income as two in another: we should say that one couple chooses to spend its income on children, while the other chooses to spend its money on holidays or cars or antique furniture. We should not say that four people are unfairly crowded into the space enjoyed elsewhere by two: we should say that one couple uses its spare rooms to put children in, while the other prefers to keep them for visitors and hobbies.

Of course everything looks very different if the four individuals are considered just as individuals, rather than as two people who chose to bring two other people into existence to keep them company, but nevertheless both ways of looking at the matter are important, and the difficulty of reconciling the two creates problems. People are inclined (not surprisingly) to simplify the extremely complicated issue by considering it more from one point of view than the other, and 'Why should we pay for other people's pleasures?' is the predictable cry of the political right, with the equally predictable response of 'Everybody's needs should be cared for by the community, no matter how those needs arose', from the left.

Feminists are on the whole inclined to the left, which is to some extent at least the explanation of their concern for communal child support. Most would certainly argue that children were far too important to be left to the limited resources of their parents. Many might even be horrified at the idea of considering children as valuable commodities at all. Nevertheless, whether feminists recognize it clearly or not, *it is only when children are regarded in this way that the question of who should support them becomes a feminist one*. The question of how much support the state should give a child in its own right has absolutely nothing to do with justice for women, and the feminist part of the issue concentrates entirely on children as valuable assets. When feminists complain, as they do, that women have for far too long borne the whole burden of reproduction for the benefit of everyone, and that it is now high time that the other beneficiaries of this labour took their fair share of its cost, children are being seen *only* as valuable commodities. There is no escaping this. Therefore, although the fact that children are people in their own right cannot possibly be forgotten, since we are now engaged in a discussion of feminist issues it must be put aside for the moment. For the time being children must be regarded as a commodity which women produce, but which feminists claim is for the advantage of all.

Let us then consider the matter from the point of view of a feminist who thinks that mothers and their children should be entirely supported by public funds, and consider what arguments she might bring in defence of her position. This inevitably calls for a fair amount of speculation and imaginative reconstruction, since the general confusion in the subject makes it very difficult to isolate clear arguments actually put forward by feminists. However, one reasonable way to go about the matter is to start with some claims which look relevant to the issue and which are undoubtedly made by feminists, and see how they fare when put in the form of an argument in favour of state support for women and their children.

One excellent place to start is with the common feminist complaint that women have in their childbearing capacity always been slaves: slaves (depending on the feminist source) to men, the state, capital, or (even more abstractly) the species. Perhaps then what underlies the feminist demand for support for children is the determination that this slavery must now cease, and that men, the state and capital (the species being rather difficult to pin down) must start to pay for the benefits they have so long had for nothing, and come to take for granted. If this is indeed the basis of the feminist demand for state support of mothers and children, how good is it?

The first thing to do is to decide how reasonable it is to say that women are, or have been, slaves to any of these groups. Strictly speaking slavery is enforced, unpaid labour, though by a reasonable extension of the term it can also apply to underpaid work into which some people are coerced by the unfair power of others. Taking a definition along these lines, it is not as unreasonable as it may perhaps sound at first to say that women have been slaves. For instance, it does seem acceptable (if metaphorical) to say that in a state of nature women in their childbearing were slaves to the species, since their biology and their ignorance forced them to reproduce whether they liked it or not. Going beyond the time of a state of nature, since one can hardly register a moral complaint against either nature or the species, it is also quite reasonable to say that women later became the slaves of men for the same purpose. As has been argued elsewhere, men have throughout the whole of history employed all kinds of formal devices to keep women in their power, with the result that even when people did come to understand the processes of reproduction, and women were in a position for the first time to escape their slavery to the species, that very discovery was the cause of their being taken into the power of men. Once again most women were left with no alternative but to spend their lives bearing and nursing the young of the species.

Both these forms of slavery have now virtually gone, but some feminists say that it continues in yet another form. Now it is women's minds which are under alien domination, and, although they seem free, social pressures, the ideology of the family (which many feminists think is itself a capitalist device to ensure a continued supply of workers), heavy advertising campaigns and vast structures of psychological theory still prevent their escaping their reproductive function, and keep them as much enslaved as ever, though the forces which achieve it may be more subtle.

However, if an argument for state support of mothers and children really is founded on arguments about slavery such as these, it is open to very serious objections. In the first place, if the argument is to work at all, it must assert not only that women were slaves in the past, which seems reasonable enough, but also that they still are now, and at that point the argument of the last paragraphs does seem to break loose from its moorings. We cannot seriously argue that all children are produced only because the mothers are socially conditioned to want them. Although no doubt many children are indeed born because of unreasonable pressures on the mothers, so that these mothers may in some sense be counted as slaves, we cannot possibly argue that it is true of all. Many, even most, women actually *want* children, and their having them is in no sense at all the result of slavery. Even if the others should be compensated, the argument from slavery gives no reason whatever for providing most mothers with any state support.

Second, and more importantly, even if most children were now born as a result of some sort of coercion, that would not provide a general argument for state support of children. The proper thing for a slave to do is not demand compensation for her enforced labour, but to insist on freedom. Even if we think that the state should compensate women who have been forced to have children, we must regard that as a temporary measure. In the feminist utopia to which we look forward there will be no slavery, and therefore no need of compensation. (Anyone who thinks that all children are born as a result of coercion must of course think that when that time comes there will be no children at all.) And why, after that, should the state pay anything at all to childbearing women? One of the most striking unreasonablenesses of some parts of feminism is the conjunction of the demand that women should be the sole judges of when and how often they have children with the claim that other people, with presumably no part in the decision, should pay for them.

The point of these arguments is not to show (at least not yet) that there is no feminist case for women's being supported by the state in their childbearing; it is only to show that even if the argument from coercion was legitimate at some times and still is in some places, it will not do as a long-term one. If there is coercion it must be stopped, and if coercion is the argument for state support, once the coercion goes the argument goes too.

However, that argument by no means disposes of the feminist case, and perhaps no feminist would try to use it. There is a much stronger feminist argument to be found in the area, which is rather similar and probably easily confused with the argument from slavery. This other argument does not depend on asserting that women are coerced into childbearing. It concedes that women do in fact want children, but says that *because* they want children, and can be relied on to have them, they are open to exploitation.

Once again it is necessary to do some imaginative construction of a possible line of feminist argument, but most feminists would probably agree that this exploitation came about in two ways. In the first place, other groups (men, state, capital) also want children, but, because they know that women want them, they can leave women to get on with the job of producing them, bearing all the heavy cost of doing so, and then come in and reap the advantages without paying for their fair share. Men, of course, do not take kindly to the idea that women have the main cost of childbearing, and talk with feeling and some justice about slaving at the office to support the wife and kiddies and keep the life insurance and mortgage going. Nevertheless, a man does in general have a family while still leaving the broad outlines of his life unchanged: he would have earned his salary and pushed for promotion even if he had not chosen to spend what he earned on a wife and family. Furthermore, the domestic service he gets from his wife is far greater than he could get by spending the same amount of money on a housekeeper. Usually he does not do at all badly. As long as a woman cannot have her family with as little disruption of what her life would otherwise have been, there is some obvious sense in which the cost of children is much higher to her. And apart from men, capital and the state do get the children without having to pay the women anything at all.

Second, women's having children makes them susceptible to a much more general form of exploitation. Employers, for instance, can make sure that home-based work or work which fits in with school hours is appallingly badly paid, and still be sure that women with children will be there to take it. Husbands can, often without realizing it, take advantage of the fact that a wife with children is in a very weak position, economically and otherwise, and will on the whole be more reluctant to break up the home than he is, and the consequence is that she will put up with more unreasonableness from him than he need from her. Of course not all men and employers do take advantage of these weaknesses, but there is something wrong as long as the opportunity is there.

Perhaps we can forget for now the problem of this second-ary exploitation of women with children, since if other people bore the cost of the children to the same extent as women, women would no longer be in a weak position which left them open to this kind of abuse. We can concen-trate on the central issue: the fact that other people seem to benefit from women's children without having to pay, or pay much, for them. Would an argument based on this kind of consideration be enough to justify the state's bearing the cost of the children? It is certainly a stronger argument than the argument from slavery, but even so it is not good enough.

In the first place, it really is not acceptable for feminists to work on an *ex post facto* presumption that someone else must be benefiting from the children women so kindly provide, and therefore must be in their debt. It is not always obvious that other people are as anxious to have the children as their producers blithely presume. 'If the state wants children', one feminist said, 'it should pay women for looking after them', but she did not even raise the question of whether the state did want children. There are actually very few women whom the public at large views with anxiety lest they should take their graces to the grave and leave the world no copy. The special value of most children is discernible only by their parents, and we need rather more than our own biassed intuitions to prove that other people do in fact find our children of value, and are glad we produced them.

In the second place, even if it were demonstrable that other people did find our children of use to them, it would not follow that they ought to be made to pay for them. What would we think about it if the man along the street, who put a great deal of work into his front garden, set up a barrier on the pavement and started demanding that every-one who walked past should pay for the pleasure he gave them? We always feel outrage at the moral bullying involved when someone provides an unsolicited service and demands payment afterwards, and if women have children anyway to please themselves, why should anyone else have to pay for them afterwards? Something can be useful or enjoyable to people without having a high place on their list of priorities, and if we go round arguing that people should pay for the spin off they happen to get from our pleasures, it means in effect that they get what we choose to give them rather than what they want themselves. Even if this sort of thing came about through a well-intentioned paternalism rather than as an afterthought to self-interest, it would be quite unacceptable. People who accidentally get the benefit of the children women freely have for their own satisfaction are not under the slightest obligation to pay women for them. (This is, incidentally, a most important general point. All kinds of people fall into the trap of producing this kind of bad argument.)

Finally, complete state support for children would be totally unfair to men. Suppose, for instance, that there were free state-run crèches at which women could leave children all day, or any other arrangement which allowed women to have children while imposing no serious financial or other burden on them. The upshot would be that women could, if they wanted to, keep children to themselves and not share them with men, but that men (as well as other women who did not have children) would still have to pay for them through the state system. That seems to be what many feminist demands amount to, but it would put women in a most unfair position of advantage over men.

Anyway, in addition to these three points, there is another argument precisely similar to the one against counting slavery as a justification of state support for women with children. It is that even if we did feel that the state ought to pay women some compensation for the exploitation they do undoubtedly suffer at present, we ought to regard that payment only as a palliative. What we really want is the removal of the cause of the trouble. If women are exploited by other people's sharing in their children without paying for them, or for that matter by being able to exploit them as a result of their having children, we need to change the system so that there can be no exploitation. We need to devise a way of making sure that anyone who does want women's services of childbearing or anything else has to undertake in advance to pay properly for them. What we should not do is allow the exploitation to continue and then demand payment for the damage it does. When people who claim that they are exploited demand compensation rather than the ending of the exploitation, we are justified in wondering whether they are as badly off as they would have us think.

Perhaps, again, no feminist would try to use these arguments from exploitation in support of the demand for state support for childbearing women, but whether or not that is so there is certainly a serious problem for feminists here. It *does* seem as though other people may be benefiting unfairly from the fact that women can be relied on to produce children, and since that is so we ought to consider ways of restructuring social arrangements to make sure that if other people do indeed want children, they must share their cost with women.

3 · THE FAIR SHARING OF COST

What we need, then, are social arrangements which ensure that the people who want children bear the cost of them, to replace the present arrangements under which everyone supposedly benefits from children, but most of the cost (taking 'cost' fairly broadly) seems to fall on women.

The first thing to notice is that if it is indeed true that men, the state and capital do all benefit unfairly from women's work in rearing children, the state and capital do so in a rather different way from individual men. The former two do not benefit from the children until they have grown up and are people in their own right, whereas individual men, on the other hand, have more or less the same interest in

children as individual women have: they want identifiable
offspring with whom to have a special personal relationship.
(I see no reason at all, by the way, to accept what some
feminists hold, that all interest in children comes of a wish
to pass on private property. Even if that was ever true, it
obviously is not now.)

We can also simplify the discussion by forgetting about
capital as a separate entity at this stage. To start with, capital
is not just one big happy family. Its essence is competition,
and there seems no reason to expect one capitalist to pay to
maintain the future workers of another part of industry.
Anyway, whatever is done for and by capital as a whole
must be done by the state, through the mechanisms of social
policy, legislation and taxation. We can ignore capital and
concentrate on the state, presuming that capital's interests
and obligations must be channelled through it. We are left,
therefore, with the state, whose interest in children (if any)
is in them as the adults of the future, and with individual
men, who have the same interest in children as women have.
The problem is of how to make sure that neither of these
two groups is in a position to exploit women.

Let us start with the matter of the state. What arrangements can be made to ensure that the state pays its fair share
of the cost of childbearing, and does not exploit women?
This is a complicated question, but one which can be tackled
quite quickly here because the heavy work has already been
done in Chapter 4, on justice. We saw there precisely the
form exploitation of women by a state which wants children
takes. Women are exploited in their childbearing when they
are coerced into it by the deliberate closing of other options
to them.[3] To end the exploitation, the state must allow
women to compete freely for everything else. When that is
done, the state's exploitation is ended, and if it finds that
enough children are produced in such a fair system, it is
under no obligation to pay women anything more. In fact
the position is stronger than that: *it certainly should not pay
anything more*. State resources should be used as a reward
to induce people to do, for the general good, things they

would not otherwise have chosen to do. It would be an unfair use of public money to pay people additionally for what they had chosen, unconstrained, to do. Of course, if the state did want more children than women chose to produce, it could alter its arrangements and put its resources into making childbearing more attractive, and in that way it would be paying women for producing children. But it is important that it should be done in that way. The way for the state to pay for its future citizens is to do it in advance: to arrange things in such a way that women choose freely to produce all that are required. It is not to decide after the event, as it were, that women deserve to be paid for childbearing.

This is a most important conclusion, because it does clearly define the extent of any state's obligation to pay women for producing children. We are left with no unsatisfactory problems about setting up comparability studies to try to decide how much women's contribution is worth, because the conclusion demands that the only payments to women should be in advance, in the form of inducements.[4] We can tell whether the inducements are great enough by whether enough women decide to have children. As long as there is no coercion, their having them is enough in itself to show that they are being adequately rewarded for it. The only thing the state need do is decide how many children it wants, and provide incentives until people voluntarily produce enough.

We have, therefore, settled the problem we started by considering: that of whether the state should pay for children. The conclusion is that the state is under an obligation to make sure that social structures are just and do not coerce women into having children, but after that is under no obligation to pay anything at all. If it wants children it will arrange to get them: if it does not, women who produce them to please themselves should expect no extra reward. In a situation of justice there is no feminist justification for state care of children; the only possible justifications are temporary ones, demanding compensation for the injustices which we have not yet got rid of.[5]

That in theory solves the problem of the state's contribution to the care of children from the mother's point of view. However, we are still left with the problem of seeing how to arrange things to prevent individual men from taking unfair advantage of women, and making them pay properly for children. (And notice, by the way, that by approaching the question in this way we can avoid all the unseemly wrangles about whether men or women are better off in the present state of things. It is undoubtedly true that at present, because many good men are aware of the structural weakness of women's position, they compensate or even over-compensate by extra considerateness to women. However, if we find a situation of equal institutional strength neither sex will be able to exploit the other. Women will not be at the mercy of bad men, and good men will not be unfairly disadvantaged by their feelings of responsibility to women.)

One way of creating an absolutely fair arrangement between men and women would be this. First, make sure that women are paid as well for work outside the home as men are, so eliminating that advantage which men have, and end all selection discrimination. Second, make sure that there are comprehensive child care facilities – crèches and the like – organized by the state (but at this stage in the argument not paid for by it, unless it turned out to be a good way of encouraging people to have more children). Third, break down the social stigma suffered by fatherless children, and make unconventional groups of people more socially acceptable, thereby giving people the greatest possible freedom to make child care arrangements to suit themselves.

Then the situation would be like this. A woman could, if she wanted, have a child and keep it to herself. It would of course be very expensive and tiring, because she would have to support the child, pay for its day care, and look after it when she was not at work. Still, it is bound to be more expensive to keep a luxury to yourself than to share it with other people. However, she could, if she wanted, agree to share both the costs and the benefits with someone else, perhaps (but not necessarily) a man. They could both work, share the support of the child, and live on an absolutely equal basis, both keeping the possibility of independence with no asymmetry built into the arrangements. Any asymmetry of power would arise out of difference of personality, not of fundamental situation.

This, apart from the business of having to pay for day care, is what many feminist proposals amount to. It does, furthermore, seem perfectly fair to men, women and the state. Women and men could share the children and share the cost if they wanted to. If the state wanted more children it could provide incentives for people to have them and perhaps give the day care free, but unless it wanted more children it should not.

4 · ARRANGEMENTS FOR CHILD CARE

Nevertheless, we are not yet anywhere near the end of the problem. The situation just described may be perfectly fair from the point of view of men, women, and the state, but it has very little else to recommend it, and this brings us to the other main problem in the feminist question of child care: that of the social arrangements which are needed. There seem to be the strongest reasons for being reluctant to regard state crèches as a universal solution to the feminist problems of mothers and children.

In the first place, we really do not know whether such arrangements would be at all good for children. Feminists talk with rapid scorn of 'the myth of maternal deprivation' as though it could not possibly be anything more than another device to oppress women, but for all we know there *may* be some advantage to a child to have its natural mother with it during most of infancy: there is no reason to presume that continuity of such things as smell must be unimportant. Apart from that, there may be disadvantages in bringing up children in groups away from adult life. Some *feminists* think that this goes on far too much already.[6] If it became common practice to leave children in crèches from their earliest infancy the situation would be even worse. This is not, by the way, to say that it certainly must be bad for children to be deprived of their natural mothers or to grow up in special children's groups. It is just that it *may* be, and feminists are no more entitled than the opposition to invent facts to suit their ideology. No feminist programme can start with the *presumption* that children would not suffer from being left in crèches, no matter how well qualified the staff.

Second, it is quite extraordinary that most feminists, in their preoccupation with proving that crèches are all right for children, seem entirely to overlook the feelings of the *mother* about it all. Whatever the child's views on the subject, most mothers do not in the least like the idea of abandoning their children into other people's care. Probably most women would see very little point in having children if they were not closely and personally involved in bringing them up. There is no need to presume that this feeling is entirely culturally induced; it is hard to see how evolution could have produced a female mammal without a strong inbuilt disposition to care for its young. Again we do not know for certain about this, but feminist plans must certainly allow for the possibility, at the very least, that crèches would not suit mothers.

Anyway, even leaving those two highly controversial points open there is one overriding *feminist* objection to adopting the crèche idea as the general solution to the difficulties women have in combining children with a satisfying working life. If we were to adopt it there is no doubt at all that things would be made immeasurably more difficult for any women who did choose to look after their children personally. They would be even more open to exploitation than before, because their position would be worsened by comparison with other women. People presumably would be even less willing than they are now to make concessions

316 · *The Sceptical Feminist*

to their childbearing activities since women in general, with their children in crèches, would need no such concessions. To make crèches the general solution to the problem would severely curtail the choices open to women; a thing which surely no feminist could want. (It is also very easy to imagine that if we did institute round-the-clock child care everywhere, in a few years a new generation of feminists might be rebelling against government policies which 'forced' them to give up their children to the care of strangers, because there was no other way they could arrange to work.)

The crèche proposals, in other words, are *not radical enough*. And as Shulamith Firestone says in the context of the same discussion, even though radical change cannot come all at once, 'radical goals must be kept in sight at all times'.[7] Radical change in the organization of child care, not just sending off the children to state-run crèches, is absolutely essential for feminism.

Since we have very little idea what arrangements will be best in the long run, the important thing now is to insist on *experiment*. Not necessarily sweeping experiments involving the whole of society, but all kinds of small ones, increasing people's options rather than forcing them into new systems, and as many as possible at once so that the successful ones emerge quickly.

At present everything is still very open, but there are some things we could certainly press for straight away. For instance, there certainly needs to be a far greater acceptance of part-time work, with fully proportional pay, proper status, and (since fitness for promotion is hardly ever a function of the number of hours spent on the job) no loss of promotion prospects. This would be a good thing quite apart from specifically feminist considerations, since it would be excellent if people could as a matter of course choose between more money and more free time, but it would obviously be particularly suitable for men and women sharing child care. In addition to this we need more flexible working hours, and all kinds of pre-school facilities for children. There is not the slightest reason to think that part-time nursery schools and play groups do anything but good.

Arrangements of that sort would perhaps be enough to take care of things adequately if women and men decided to share child care on an absolutely equal basis, but on feminist grounds we ought also to make provision for at least the possibility that women might prefer to do most of the child care themselves. If they were really in a strong position to bargain with men about arrangements this need not be a bad thing at all. It is here, for instance, that the idea of wages for housework might come in, but with the wages paid by the husband. Or there could perhaps be arrangements for husbands to pay special dues into a central fund while their wives were away from work having children, to ensure increments, pension rights and the like, so that at the end of the childbearing period the woman was in her own right as well off as the man.

In addition to this, more radical and very important, women should be experimenting with kinds of work which might be made compatible with children. There is much public resistance at the moment to having children underfoot at work, but it is probably important to overcome it. There is no reason why women should not carry tiny children on their backs while doing various kinds of work, and there may be many kinds which are compatible with looking after toddlers as well, who could perhaps be cared for in small crèches close to their mothers. Other kinds of work might be easily compatible with interruptions, resumptions, and changes from part-time to full-time work. Law and medicine come to mind very quickly, but there must be thousands of other possibilities. The real problem at the moment is lack of motivation. Make it essential that these things should come about, and people will devise ways of doing them: if women had been fully involved in work outside the home from the start, as has already been suggested, they would certainly have developed forms of work which were compatible with caring for children. If enough women work now when they have small children, they can still find ways to arrange things.

As well as all this, there are the numberless possibilities of trying to arrange for people to live in groups – perhaps extended families again – and share the care of children. Leaving children with people to whom they are particularly close is very different from putting them in a state-run crèche during the day. Such arrangements would also have the extremely good effect of giving children some form of escape from their natural parents if they did not happen to get on with them very well, and also bring old people more into life than they are at present. Perhaps in the solution of such feminist problems there lies the answer to other social problems as well.

Neither conservatives, who think that women ought to get back into the home and stop making a fuss, nor feminists, who are capable of quite equal dogmatism of other sorts, have the answer yet. It is clear, however, that the feminist campaign should be directed towards radical reorganization of child care, designed to give women as many options as possible, and not drift into an unimaginative and restricting pursuit of the all-embracing state-run crèche, which leaves the fundamentals of the problem untouched.

5 · CHILDREN AS PEOPLE

The argument so far has been this. The central feminist problem about children stems from the idea that the burden of producing children falls heavily on women, but that everyone shares in the benefits. In other words, the problem is one which focuses on the idea of children as valuable commodities. People may exclaim in horror at the idea of regarding children in this way, but there is no escaping the fact that that is one thing they are. People want children; children are not born for their own sakes.

The commonest feminist solution to this part of the problem has been to say that the burden should be taken from women and shifted on to the state, both as the financial provider for the children and as the basic instrument for their care. However, this seems to be wrong for two reasons. First, the main unfairness in women's bearing the burden of child care is not that *the state* takes too little responsibility and gets women's services too cheaply, but that *individual men* do (or at least can). Once the state has eliminated discrimination against women and eliminated some basic unfairnesses in social structures as described in Chapter 4, there is no problem about the state's interest in children: if it wants more it must induce women by rewards to have them; if it does not it need do nothing. What the state *should* do, however, is alter social arrangements so that men and women can arrange to share the care and cost of children, if they want to, on a footing of equality. This could be achieved by having full-time day care for children with both parents sharing the cost. But this is the second point at which the usual feminist suggestion seems to be wrong: it leaves the basic structures of work unchanged, and means that any woman who does want to care personally for her child is in as bad a position as ever, and perhaps far worse. The proposal is not radical enough. It is necessary to try all kinds of radically different arrangements for child care, which may call for fundamental alterations in the whole structure of work.

In a sense that does end the strictly feminist part of the problem of child care. However, the subject is not over yet, because so far we have been considering children only from the point of view of their value to other people, and they must not be forgotten as people in their own right. Regarding them in this way must radically affect what has been said so far about the state's having no obligation to give parents help in the support of their children after those children arrive.

If children are considered only from the point of view of their being assets to parents, it is certainly unfair that anyone else should have to pay for their support, since their arrival was a thing about which no one else had any say. Nevertheless, however much we may argue that parents should not indulge in the luxury of children unless they are willing to pay for them, the simple fact is that children just arrive, often in the families of parents who for one reason or another (whether misfortune or improvidence) have not the means to look after them properly, and children cannot just be sent back like HP furniture.

The most radical and ferocious solution to this problem, no doubt, would be to force some kind of contraceptive implant on all women, and not take it away until they had proved they were in a position to care properly for children. Or if that were technologically impossible, we could take children away from parents as soon as the parents showed signs of not supporting them adequately. However, let us take it for granted that nobody is willing (at least yet) to consider these awful extremes. The children's existence has to be accepted, and so (except in very bad cases) has their staying in the care of their parents. Furthermore, these children have absolutely fundamental rights of their own: they must not be made to suffer for the selfishness or improvidence of their parents. *It is, therefore, the absolute duty of the state to see that their needs are met*. It is also the duty of the state, to reinforce that conclusion, to make sure that a generation of deprived children does not grow up to the detriment of the people of the future.

This seems to have the consequence that however much anyone may dislike the idea of people's indulging in the luxury of children at the expense of everyone else, it is an annoyance which just has to be tolerated. Furthermore, a worse exasperation still seems to be equally inevitable. If adequate care is taken of the children the parents will, through these children, have access to still further benefits. There are some things, like education, medical care and school meals which can be given to the children without the parents' sharing in them, but there are limits: we cannot, for instance, house the children well without doing the same for the parents at the same time. So it looks as though even though children are an asset to their parents, justice to the children means that we have to allow the parents to have that asset at public expense, and to get other benefits through their children as well. And if this is so it seems to mean that all the previous arguments about whether women should be supported in the care of children because of the service they gave to everyone else were effectively beside the point, because if children must be supported in their own right the result is the same. The feminist demand must be apparently met, even though for non-feminist reasons.

However, perhaps the opposition need not give up yet. People who are opposed to much state subsidy of children can in fact argue on quite different grounds (whatever we suspect of their motives) that it is actually wrong of the state to pay much towards the upkeep of children.

It has already been agreed, they may say, that we must be considerate of future generations, and surely one of the worst things we could do to this overcrowded world would be to allow it to become more crowded? It is absolutely essential to stem the rise in population. If we support children, however, we just encourage people to have more, because everyone likes something for nothing and nobody will pass up a luxury which can be got at the state's expense. Things are even worse if we allow the children to be used as a means to other benefits: it is appalling that some people are actually advised to have children to get priority on council housing lists. Therefore even though the present generation of children may suffer through our refusing to give them much help, for the sake of the future their suffering is something we must (reluctantly of course) allow.

There is obviously something in arguments of this sort, and pious indignation about present suffering is not enough to rule them out. (Such indignation, by the way, comes particularly badly from people who are apparently happy to countenance the suffering and death caused by revolutionary violence as a means to future benefits.) However, as they stand the arguments cannot be accepted, because according to the theory of justice outlined in Chapter 4, 'transitional' injustice is not to be tolerated. We have to insist on justice now, even if that means that the future will have a lower total of satisfaction than it otherwise might have had, except when we can be virtually certain that future sufferings will be even greater than those we allow as a means to prevent them. We cannot, therefore, usually even consider allowing the present generation to suffer for the sake of the future.

We must therefore look at the question more carefully. It is a particularly interesting one because of its general form. It takes two important principles, both of which seem absolutely inescapable (the proposition that children must not be allowed to suffer, and the proposition that we must not allow future generations to suffer from overcrowding), but which also seem to be in conflict with each other. Accept one, and you are forced to reject the other. The debate, therefore, tends to take the form of trying to argue that one of the two good things in question is more important than the other and must be held paramount; that the absence of the other must be accepted as a necessary evil.

However, the important thing to recognize about this case and all others like it is that there are two quite distinct problems. One is of trying to make sure that future generations do not suffer the miseries of overpopulation, and the other is of making sure that people now do not suffer unfairly. Now although there are ways of caring for people of the present generation which almost certainly would increase the population for the future by encouraging people to have more children, there is no reason to think that *all* methods of making children now better off will be ones which as a matter of fact encourage parents to have more children. We are so used to thinking about particular kinds of social benefit (family allowances, free school milk, and all the rest) that we tend to forget about the endless possibilities there really are. Even if by the present methods of assisting children we encourage population increase (which is not at all certain), there is not the slightest reason to think this must be true of all possible methods of doing so.

The reason for this is that, perhaps surprisingly, most

people are extremely bad calculators of benefits and losses, and their reluctance to incur expense or eagerness in pursuit of a benefit seems to have almost nothing to do with the amounts of money in question. The psychological impact of a certain amount of money seems to have far more to do with where it occurs than with how great it is. This is noticeable in all kind of areas. For instance, people may think very carefully about the cost of taking public transport somewhere, but not about the often higher price of using the car. Or, as all local shopkeepers know, people who flock to town centres and supermarkets to buy cheap goods never think of taking into account the cost of travelling to get them. Tiny charges put people off all sorts of things, for instance going into museums (so that it turned out to be much better to finance the museums from elsewhere), when no doubt the twenty pence or whatever it was would not have been thought about twice in other contexts, like buying a bar of chocolate. It has already been suggested elsewhere that people are deterred from using contraceptives by their cost, in spite of the fact that the cost of not using them, and having a child, is incomparably higher.

Given these oddities of people's behaviour, what we should do in situations like the one where it is argued that to help children is to risk population increase is this. It is to decide firmly that we will have *both* the good things we want (child benefits and population control) and work on the reasonable presumption that somewhere in the endless possibilities the world contains there is to be found a way of reconciling the two. We remain determined to care for children, but to *find out* (by experiment, not unaided intuition) which methods of doing so lead to population increase and which do not. The results may be surprising. There may be stories of people being advised to have children to get council flats, but there are also stories of people who refuse to take this appalling advice in spite of their serious housing problems. In the same way, no one would ever have imagined that a woman would actually be so delighted with her £25 maternity grant that she would instantly have another child to get another grant, but I have heard of one who did. If that happens even once a year it means we should be putting that money into the funds *at a different point*, where its psychological impact is not so great. We must find out the facts, and anyone who says that child benefits must increase population growth (or for that matter produce any other social evil) *without trying hard to find a way of getting the good without the evil*, must be presumed to be against child benefits for other reasons, and using the supposedly inevitable bad consequences as an excuse to cover other motives.

Furthermore, even if we could demonstrate that there was an inevitable connection between child benefits and over-population, that would still not justify our consigning the present generation of children to deprivation; we should instead try to counteract it by acceptable ways of discouraging population growth. The way to approach this would be by finding out *why people had children*, and then providing other things which they might choose instead. If we found that children were born as a result of ignorance or accident we could provide education and contraceptives; if we found that people were worried about their old age we could make sure that there were proper social provisions for that; if we found they wanted to make an impact on the future, we should try to think of other ways in which that wish could be fulfilled. Perhaps we could also encourage people to have their children late (a thing which is now more reasonable than ever before, since there are pre-natal methods of testing for most of the defects commonly associated with the mother's age), so fitting two and a half generations instead of five into a century, and without depriving anyone of anything except seeing their great-grandchildren.

At any rate, whatever policies we might decide to try, only *overwhelming* proof that looking after children now was bound to cause disaster in the future could justify our abandoning this sort of approach to the problem, and accepting that the evil of child deprivation had to be endured. It is pretty well impossible that there could be such a proof. The state *must* care properly for all children.

6 · THE CONSEQUENCES

So far, then, it has been concluded that the state has no financial responsibility to parents: it owes them nothing for providing its future citizens, though it can, if it wants to, provide inducements in advance to encourage people to have children. Its duty to the parents is limited to *reorganizing* things so that men and women can share the burdens and benefits of child rearing more fairly than is possible at present. It has, however, an absolute duty to see to the welfare of all children, even though there may be no way of preventing parents from benefiting at the same time. We now have to bring the two strands of the argument together, and see what feminists are entitled to demand of the state now that the complicating factor of the child's own rights has been thrown into the question.

This is bound to be a very difficult matter to settle, because whenever any question arises about what the parents are entitled to in their own right there will always be the imponderable issue of how the children will be affected by a decision which goes against the parents. However, even though the practical difficulties may be considerable, some important points of principle are clear. And in particular, there is the converse of the principle that you must always provide support to a child in need even though in doing so you benefit the parents. It is that *unless* withholding support will harm the child, the support should not be given.

Take, for instance, the question of whether there should be paid maternity leave. When a mother leaves work to have a child she is having the child because she wants it; neither the state nor the employer can be presumed to have any interest in the child, and therefore the mother is not, in her own right, entitled to subsidy by either. Therefore any defence of pay during maternity leave would have to be made by reference to the interests of the child, and arguments that the child would suffer without it.

However, it is obviously impossible to produce any general defence of maternity pay along these lines because, however difficult it may be to decide the level of income below which a child suffers, whatever that level is cannot possibly be presumed to occur automatically when a woman stops work. Whether or not it is reached obviously depends on what other income she has. Of course if the level *is* reached then we should insist on payments to the family, but that has nothing to do with *maternity* benefits: such payments would be made, according to this principle, only to make sure that children were not too poor, and they would equally be needed by poor mothers who went on working. Maternity benefits, as such, are tied to the very fact of *having* children. They have therefore nothing to do with the needs of children, but are in effect a reward to parents. Therefore, according to the arguments of this chapter, they can be justified generally only as part of a deliberate state plan to encourage population growth.

The same applies to other child-related benefits. Universally available family allowances are open to the same objections. So, even more decisively, are the demands for free crèches, since a mother who has to pay to leave her child at a crèche *still* earns more than she would have done by staying at home, and if the child did not suffer from poverty through her being at home it would certainly not suffer that way through her working. In all such cases it is irrelevant to point to the sufferings of poor families. The need to relieve such sufferings is absolute, but that has nothing to do with general family allowances and free crèches (even though we might, for convenience, decide that the most convenient way to subsidize poor families' incomes was through such means as those). No benefit which comes automatically with having children, irrespective of whether the children are in need, is justified.

I suppose that to many feminists this must sound like the

ultimate heresy, but there are consolations to be found. The fact is that feminists have mountains to move anyway in trying to persuade everyone that society needs radical reorganization if we are to be fair to childbearing women; there are ranged against us the colossal problems of deeply entrenched customs and institutions and unsuitable buildings, as well as people's conservatism in general and dislike of having small children everywhere in particular. If feminists demand that in addition to being disruptive, inconvenient and unfamiliar the provisions made for women with children should also be free, the unequal struggle is made even more unequal. It is, therefore, just as well that this part of the feminist demand can be dropped without any sacrifice of feminist principle. Perhaps, too, any feminist who has not been persuaded by the foregoing arguments, and still thinks everything ought to be free, should for purely political purposes keep her true intentions dark for a while. The really crucial matter for the liberation of women is to make radical alterations in arrangements for child care, and when those have been achieved there will be time enough to argue about who should pay for them.

IO

The Unpersuaded

I · THE CHASM

The final problem is one which is not really within feminism itself, but is still most important for feminists. It is that for all the strength of the feminist case, feminism is still an unpopular movement.

It is probably also true to say that the problem is one which most feminists do not take seriously enough. It is, after all, only to be expected that feminism will be widely opposed. Whenever there is a movement which is striving for justice, there are inevitably people whose privileges it plans to take away, and it can hardly expect their support. And although many of the present opponents of feminism are people who in fact would *gain* from its success – nearly all women, and all men who find their traditional role uncongenial – it is part of most feminists' theory that such people have been thoroughly brainwashed, and therefore cannot be expected to support feminism any more than can the people whose real interests are in suppressing it. Feminism is bound by its very nature to be unpopular, its supporters seem to think, and therefore there is not much to be done about the matter.

Of course there certainly are people whose hostility to feminism must stem from vested interests, and no doubt (however difficult it is to explain the idea of conditioning) there must be many others who are far too deeply immured in their habits to be capable of understanding other possibilities, no matter how well presented, or how much in their interest. Nevertheless, the idea that all the opponents of feminism must come into one or other of these categories is far too comfortable. Feminists must at least *allow* for the possibility that there are in existence people who, in spite of a vested interest in opposing feminism, would support the cause if they thought it was demanded by justice, but do not think it is. There may also be others who (we think) would have everything to gain from feminism's success, and who are perfectly capable of understanding the issues, but are still opposed to the movement. It is at least possible (and I should think very likely) that there are large numbers of these people, and that they are on the other side because feminists have not presented their case in such a way as to attract them. And if they do exist, their conversion is obviously of political importance.

However, even though it is very easy to say that feminists should take care to present their case more attractively, the fact of the matter is that feminism, by its very nature, is a thing which is extremely difficult to get across. The phenomenon of sexual injustice, of taking it for granted that different kinds of treatment are suitable for men and women as such, is so pervasive, so deeply entrenched and so generally taken for granted that to recognize it for what it is is to have a view of the world which is radically different from that of most people. The feminist sees what is generally invisible, finds significance in what is unremarkable, and questions what is presupposed by other enquiries. And since to the uninitiated this is bound to appear no different from imagining the non-existent, making a fuss about nothing, and gratuitously instigating disturbances in the foundations of society, perhaps it is not surprising that there is still not very much public sympathy with feminism. Without a feminist view of things even the best-founded of feminist pronouncements may appear nonsensical.

The ordinary policeman, for instance, harassing prostitutes with a zeal beyond the call of duty, would be genuinely staggered if anyone suggested to him that his attitudes reflected what is probably the most extreme surviving remnant of women's total subjugation to men: the heavy sanctions against all sexual freedom which were designed to reinforce all the other institutions by which women's sexuality and reproduction was kept firmly under male control. To him it almost certainly seems that it is *respect* for women which leads to his loathing of prostitutes. The ordinary housewife, who thinks as a matter of course that her highest duty lies in devotion to her husband and family, no matter what good she could do by spending less time on them and more on other things, would be quite baffled to hear a feminist say that the morality she was accepting was itself a male device to make women accessories to their enforced servitude to men. If a feminist appeared distressed on hearing a woman of high ability talking with satisfaction of a life spent as her husband's ancillary, most people would think it the height of absurdity. In general, if feminists make their ideas and feelings about such things publicly known, without being able to persuade people to follow sympathetically the line of argument which leads to such apparently preposterous conclusions, of course the people who hear them will be hostile to feminism.

If this hostility is to cease, then, people must presumably be persuaded to look seriously at the whole subject. However, how to achieve this presents considerable problems. There are going to be no miraculous conversions, and relatively few even of the women are going to undergo the traumatic experiences which set some off along the feminist path: finding out the realities of trying to get an abortion, getting into the clutches of a violent husband, or encountering blatant discrimination at work. The experiences which everyone has, and which ought to convert everyone to feminism, are themselves not recognizable as significant by anyone who has not already worked through the whole subject. It seems, therefore, that if people are to be persuaded, the persuading must be done by feminists. But here we seem to encounter a vicious circle, because if feminists are seen as the makers of bizarre and exaggerated pronouncements, stirrers up of trouble and strewers of anarchy, they are bound themselves to be objects of suspicion, and in a weak position when it comes to persuading people to take their arguments seriously.

There is no easy way out of this apparent impasse, but there is one thing which feminists certainly can do to set things going in the right direction. That is to deal immediately with the problems which arise *on their own side* of the chasm created by feminism's inherent radicalism. One of the difficulties about a feminist view of things is that once you are deep into it it is not only a radical transformer of everything, but also extremely compelling, and apt to make you forget what things looked like from the other side. This may be why feminists are generally inclined to attribute all opposition to moral and intellectual shortcomings in their opponents. The feminist who can see the oppression of women in the trivia of everyday life, in much the same way as the religious believer can see the hand of God in what is to the atheist the unremarkable course of nature, may also incline to the common religious view that since the truth is manifest the fallen state of the heathen can be imputed only to Sin, or, in this case, vested interests and conditioning.

However, the feminist way of looking at things is not at all manifest, and feminists must do their opponents the justice of recognizing this. Once we have done it we may be more inclined to try to understand what it is which makes many people of good will resist the movement, and from that work out ways of making them more sympathetic.

The matter is no doubt very complicated, but there do seem to be three particularly striking things which often put people off feminism, and which are worth looking at in some detail. The first is the idea that there is no reasonable feminist case at all. The second is the feeling that the whole thing is very much exaggerated. And the third, which is probably by far the most important (and in whose overcoming we might easily overcome the other two) is that people just do not like what they see of either feminists or their policies; that the image of the movement is very *unattractive*. These three subjects will be discussed in turn.

2 · THE FEMINIST CASE

First there is the matter of the people who cannot see that there is a case for feminism at all; who do not think that women are badly treated by society.

It is, by the way, as said in the preface, very important to separate the question of whether anything is wrong with the situation of women from questions about whether there is any justification for particular ideas of ways to put matters right. Most people, including most feminists, take what conspicuous feminists say about political policy and social theory as integral to the whole cause. However, the question of whether anything is wrong is clearly separable from that of what to do about it if it is, and since it must (as a matter of logic) be easier to persuade someone of the first than of both, even feminists who are passionately committed to their political views should not object to taking the subjects one at a time, and stressing to the uninitiated that there *are* two sets of questions. We must, therefore, start by making sure people understand that when we claim that there is a very strong general case for feminism, we are not (at least yet) saying that men and women are exactly the same, or that they ought to be exactly the same, or that the family ought to be abolished, or that children ought to be left in crèches, or that sex roles are pernicious. Feminists are claiming in the first instance only that women are systematically badly treated by society, and that something ought to be done about it.

Transparent as the case for feminism may seem to all those who are involved in it, however, it is undoubtedly the case that to the average well-educated, well intentioned man (in company, for that matter, with a great many women) it is not in the least clear. What is there to justify the feminist assertion that all men oppress all women, or that this or that is a male plot against the female, or that men are interested in women only as sex objects? He has never plotted with other men against women in his life. He certainly does not regard them as sex objects, since (although his interest in sex is not to be denied, and he sees no reason why it should be) he is as interested in other aspects of women as he is in those same things in men. And as he looks round the women of his acquaintance he seeks in vain for the slightest sign of oppression. They are healthy, prosperous, capable of independence, frequently assertive, denied no educational opportunity, allowed to rise to the heights of success in public and professional life, and if they stay at home and have children that is because they choose to. That choice, furthermore, is one which men have not.

It is true, of course, that the arguer along these lines probably sees nothing of the grossly exploited outworker slaving every hour of the day for a few shillings, or the office cleaner who looks after her children all day and then works half the night as well in a never ending struggle to make ends meet, and it is more or less certain that he has never even heard of some of the horrors to which women are systematically subjected in other parts of the world. These are all things we can bring to his attention. But even if we do, he is likely to be unperturbed. That, he will say, shows only that *some* women are oppressed. It does not show that all are, or that there is any general case for feminism. He may even go on to say that these things, bad as they are, have nothing to do with the oppression of *women* in particular. Many working-class men are also exploited, and all kinds of barbarities go on in foreign parts which are just as bad for the men who get caught up in them as for the women. Oppression is everywhere, and takes many forms. He may perhaps concede that there are one or two aspects of women's lot which could do with general improvement, but they are all, he thinks, rather insignificant. To say that women in general are oppressed is just a silly exaggeration.

It cannot be denied that feminists often exaggerate, or that a mind attuned to oppression will often start seeing it where it is not. However, the exaggeration is nothing like as bad as it looks. Feminism has a better case than at first appears, and to meet the opposition that case has to be made clearly and systematically. Let us consider how such a case might be made out. And for simplicity let us cast it in the classical form of a series of *Replies to Objections*, with the objector (whom we will go on assuming, for no very special reason, to be male) obligingly, if improbably, arranging his objections in such an order as to allow the replies to them to come out as a systematic exposition of a feminist case.

Objection 1 Feminists (says the objector) claim that women are badly treated by society; that women are at a systematic disadvantage to men. But it is absurd to say that women in general are badly treated. Everywhere you look you see women flourishing. Of course some women are badly off, but then so are a lot of men. Why should we do anything to advance the cause of women in general, when so many men are much worse off than many women? That would be quite unfair to men.

Reply It is misleading (says the feminist) to say that feminism is a movement whose aim is to advance the cause of women. That suggests that all it wants to do is give advantages to one group at the expense of another. But feminism is not concerned with *a group of people* it wants to make better off, but with a *type of injustice* it wants to eliminate: the injustice which women suffer as a result of being female. And when we say that women are systematically at a disadvantage to men we are not claiming anything so absurd as that all women live lives of abject misery in the power of men; only that being female usually makes you worse off than a man would have been under the same circumstances. Being at an arbitrary disadvantage through being female is equally unjust whether it means that you have to work all hours of the day and night for a pittance while your husband works a normal day and expects a cooked meal in the evening, or whether it means that you can't quite make it to being Lady Chief Justice because the job is unfairly given to a man. The type of injustice is the same in both cases, even though the second woman is probably much better off than the husband of the first. It is this *kind* of injustice to which feminists are opposed.

Objection 2 (In which the testosterone contingent, and others of similar persuasions, make their appearance.) It may be that a woman has to work twice as hard as a man to get to the top of any profession, and that in any situation a woman is likely to be worse off than a corresponding man. That, however, is only because men are more dominant than women, and generally superior. Anyway, even if women were intrinsically equal to men, they would still be handicapped by having children. Women's inequality is a natural phenomenon. If we arranged things so that as many women as men succeeded in life it would be rather like trying to arrange the Olympic Games so that people in wheelchairs had as good a chance of succeeding as the best athletes. It could be done; we could make men and women equally successful at everything, but only at the cost of artificially holding men back and pushing women forward, and a general lowering of standards from which everyone would suffer. Women should accept their natural limitations.

Reply Our complaint is not *simply* that women do not succeed as often as men, or that they have to work twice as hard to do as well. Perhaps women are not as competent at many things as men are; perhaps they are held back by hormones and a tendency to hysteria or whatever (though we think it most unlikely); certainly children have always got in the way of women's doing other things, and still do (though that seems rather a reason for trying to arrange things so that women can care for children and still make their full contribution to society than for giving up women's case in despair). However, our complaint has nothing to do with the natural problems from which women suffer. It is that things are made systematically harder for women than for *men in the same position and with identical abilities*. Women are discriminated against. And, incidentally, the very fact that men have for so long made it difficult or impossible for women to do certain kinds of work and reach certain elevated positions shows that really they do *not* believe in women's natural incompetence. If women had been by nature unable to do all these things, there would have been no need for special devices to keep them out.

Objection 3 But men don't make it harder for women to succeed. Employers are always doing what they can to advance women; husbands put up with amazing inconvenience to help their wives' careers. The complaint is quite unfounded.

Reply We have certainly no wish to deny that such good and generous men exist, though we feel entitled to be sceptical about whether there are all that many of them. But our main reply is John Stuart Mill's:[1]

Whether the institution to be defended is slavery, political absolutism, or the absolutism of the head of a family, we are always expected to judge of it from its best instances. . . . Who doubts that there may be great goodness, and great happiness, and great affection, under the absolute government of a good man? Meanwhile, laws and institutions require to be adapted, not to good men, but to bad.

Good men will, of course, treat women properly under any circumstances, but as long as social institutions give men an advantage over women, which bad men can use if they want to, feminists have cause for complaint. We should not be at the mercy of men. It is the social institutions of which we complain primarily, rather than about the behaviour of individual men, much as that may sometimes leave to be desired. (This is, incidentally, a thing some feminists seem inclined to forget. Some seem to be led into implausible exaggeration of men's behaviour by a feeling that the feminist case rests more heavily on arguments that men *individually* treat women badly than it does. Whatever individual men do, we have legitimate cause for complaint in the fact that social institutions distinguish men from women as such, quite irrespective of their other abilities and characteristics, and make everything harder for women.)

Objection 4 But whatever may have been true about

social institutions in the past, there are none now which distinguish between men and women. Women can do anything now, and so for that matter can men. There is nothing to stop women from being prime ministers or judges, if that is what they want to be, or, for that matter, men from being nurses or househusbands. If they do not do these things, it is not because there are any *institutions* stopping them.

Reply In complaining about institutions we are not referring only to highly formalized things such as laws, systems of social security, sex-selection policies for education and professions, and the like. Even in those cases, of course, there is still much blatant discrimination left. But we are meaning to include among institutions far less formal ones than these, and take into account such things·as deeply entrenched conventions and habits; there are still countless ways in which the two sexes are differentiated. Different things are still commonly thought proper for men and women as such. In order to get public approval, there are many contexts in which the sexes have to behave differently.

Objection 5 Even if we allow this rather stretched use of the word 'institution', the feminist point is still not made, because those discriminatory institutions do not stop anyone doing anything. Women can do anything they want now (family if they want, career if they want) and have, therefore, nothing to complain about.

Reply We are not claiming that social institutions generally make things *impossible* for one sex which are possible for the other. The statement 'women can do anything now' is misleading. The real question we have to consider is not whether women *can do* certain things, but how difficult it is for them. If social institutions of any degree of formality or informality make it harder for one sex than for the other, there is institutional discrimination. If a woman has to work harder than a man of equal ability to advance as far, or if she has to sacrifice more (a family, public approval and so on) to do it, there is institutional discrimination. The same, of course, is true if a man cannot stay at home and look after children without braving slightly sneering comments from the neighbours. You would have to be amazingly adept in the skills of stout denial to deny that many things are made harder for one sex than for the other.

Objection 6   Even if it is true that the social environment systematically differentiates between women and men, that is still not enough to prove that women are the ones who come off worse. The two sexes probably do as well as each other out of any differences there are. It is hard to say. Perhaps men do worse. Women actually have far more choice than men in many ways: they can either make themselves independent or stay at home protected by a man, as they please. The second option is virtually closed to most men, and anyway they could not take it without being exposed to public contempt. Whatever advantages men have, women have others.

Reply   Of course we agree that there are some drawbacks to the male role and some advantages to the female one, at least for some men and some women. Nevertheless, you cannot seriously maintain that the two are equal, or that men's is worse. If you consider the past there is no doubt at all that the whole structure of society was designed *to keep women entirely in the power of men*. Of course things are now much changed, but we have still by no means escaped the past. Our modern customs and ways of thinking are not completely emancipated from it. This shows most clearly in the matter of status (and status is power, even though not absolute power). Taking the lead, one of the strongest status indicators of all, nearly always falls by convention to men. The man gives orders, drives the car, makes the advances in courtship. In couples where these roles are reversed there is a tendency for social disapproval or mockery; the man is henpecked, the woman wears the trousers. In courtship, a woman who does what men are expected to do is forward, or desperate, or a slut. The present institutions bring about nothing like equality in difference, and since they give most power to men it must be said that, in spite of the odd drawback, men have the advantage.

Objection 7   All that has been shown is that the male role carries with it more power and status, but why do you say that is an advantage? To the extent that men's power is actual it just brings the weight of responsibility, which women have not. In fact very often what happens is that men are so aware of their responsibilities that they lean over backwards, and allow selfish women to trample all over them. To the extent, on the other hand, that men's higher status is nothing more than a social expectation that men should not be outdistanced or led by women it is a nuisance to have to live up to it, especially now that women are not held down in the way they used to be. In fact the male role has nothing to recommend it at all, and it is time we had Men's Liberation.

Reply By all means start your Men's Lib; we quite agree that being male is not all a bed of roses. However, don't make the mistake of thinking that your movement would be in opposition to ours, because the drawbacks you have mentioned are not arguments *against* feminism, but *for* it. Get rid of the differential social expectations of which feminists complain, and men can, if they want, have all the advantages women have. Status, responsibility and dependence will be determined by the natures and inclinations of individuals, not by sex. Men who think the male role a heavy burden should be rushing to embrace feminism. Since, however, we seem in no danger of being submerged in seas of recruits, and since the average complainer about male responsibility would not change places with his wife or secretary for anything, we are entitled to suspect that the male role is not as burdensome as some men would have us think, and that men on the whole are inclined to keep their privileges while complaining about them.

Of course, neither objections nor replies end here, but enough has been said to show the line a general defence of feminism might take. Presumably some feminists would want to argue in a different kind of way. However, all should be prepared to make some such defence of their position, to persuade the well-intentioned critic that what they have to say is worth looking into.

3 · THE PRIMARY STRUGGLE

It is, of course, by no means certain that the opposition will accept all this, because proof is not the same as persuasion and the power of stout denial is infinite, but let us optimistically presume that everything so far has been conceded. We can now go on to another objection that is very commonly levelled at feminists: that they *exaggerate* everything so much that it is impossible to be as sympathetic to their case as it would be if more moderate claims were made. Feminists may have some sort of case, but it is a relatively trivial one and far too much fuss is made about it.

The accusation of triviality takes two forms, one particular and one general. The particular one is about feminists' making too much of small details: the supposedly neutral use of 'he' in the language; the fact that children's books tend to depict women in aprons; women's being expected to cater for the office party, and so on. In all such cases there is no substitute for detailed argument to show that the level of fuss is not unreasonable; an argument usually taking two stages, the first to prove that the phenomenon in question really is sexist, and the second to show that it has significantly bad consequences for women. Often such arguments can be produced. In other cases feminists may have to change their minds about the seriousness of the matter in hand.

However, there is clearly no scope for general argument on such subjects here, so we should move on to consider the common accusation of the triviality of feminism as a whole. '*How*,' we are asked, '*can you talk about the comparatively insignificant oppression of women, when set beside the issues of racism and imperialism?*'[2]

Robin Morgan, who quotes this attack in the introduction

to *Sisterhood is Powerful*, follows it immediately with a determined feminist defence.

This is a male-supremacist question. Not only because of its arrogance, but because of its ignorance. First it dares to weigh and compute human suffering. . . Second, the question fails to even minimally grasp the profoundly radical analysis beginning to emerge from revolutionary feminism: that capitalism, imperialism, and racism are *symptoms* of male supremacy – sexism.

She also adds that half of the oppressed people of the world are women, and that we have to fight 'for these sisters to *survive*' before there is any chance of being able to talk to them as oppressed women, and concludes, 'More and more, I begin to think of a worldwide Women's Revolution as the only hope for life on this planet.'

In sentiments of this sort she is joined by countless other feminists. For instance, there is the Redstockings Manifesto once again:[3] 'Male supremacy is the oldest, most basic form of domination. All other forms of exploitation and oppression (racism, capitalism, imperialism etc.) are extensions of male supremacy.' There is also Shulamith Firestone, who says that radical feminism 'sees the feminist issue not only as women's first priority, but as central to any larger revolutionary analysis'.[4] She quotes as well an earlier feminist, Angelina Grimke:[5] 'The slave may be freed and woman be where she is, but women cannot be freed and the slave remain where he is.' And there is Elizabeth Gould Davis, who thinks that 'restoring women to their age-old leadership in government while men confine themselves to their gadgetry and games . . . may constitute the last hope for mankind'.[6] For all of these writers the main contention against the sceptical anti-feminist is the same: *feminism is the primary struggle*. This is the contention we now have to assess.

We had better start by distinguishing two issues which might arise under the primary struggle heading. There seems little doubt that most of the feminists who make the claim think that *as a matter of fact* if women's wrongs were put right everything else would go right too, and that justifies their giving first priority to women's issues. Mixed in with this, however, there seem to be hints of a different idea, that feminism is *morally* the most important issue, and sexual oppression the worst type of oppression. That question had better be discussed first.

The question is obviously an important one. In spite of Robin Morgan's strictures on the arrogance of 'daring' to assess degrees of suffering, it is surely morally outrageous that anyone should *fail* to do so. Some forms of suffering and oppression are much worse than others, and (other things being equal) we should obviously concentrate on the worst sorts first. Is women's oppression the worst kind of oppression?

It is often said, apparently in defence of some such position as this, that women are the poorest of the poor and the most oppressed of the oppressed, and that wherever there is a badly treated man, there is a woman attached to him who suffers even more. Perhaps that is true; it seems quite likely. However, if it is intended as an argument for the moral primacy of feminism it seems to rest on some confusion between feminism as a movement *to improve the position of women* (to benefit a particular group of people) and as a movement *to eliminate sex-based injustice*, and it works in neither case. If the worst off people in the world are women that is an excellent reason for attending to their sufferings as the highest priority, but no reason at all for generally advancing women. If, on the other hand, feminism is, as we are taking it to be, an attack on sex-based injustice, the fact that the worst off people in the world are women is no defence at all of the priority of feminism, because their position might be much worse in virtue of the kind of suffering they endured *in common with their men* than in virtue of what they were subjected to because of their sex. Their being the worst off people does not make the primary issues feminist ones. In fact Robin Morgan's argument that we have to fight for the very survival of many women before we can begin to discuss the problems they suffer as women (which may look like a defence of the importance of feminism), is actually an argument *against* putting feminism first. Their being in danger of not surviving is not primarily, if at all, the result of their being women.

To argue that sexism was morally the most important issue it would be necessary to show that if all sex-based injustices were immediately eliminated, that in itself, irrespective of any additional benefits which might follow from it, would immediately remove all the worst problems of the world. Could that possibly be true? It seems unlikely. Certainly some of the things which women suffer as women are appalling, but they seem no worse than other kinds of institutionalized slavery which still exist, or brutal dictatorships (of left or right), or the exploitation of abjectly poor countries by rich ones. The elimination of any of these kinds of injustice might bring about a greater good than righting the wrongs of women. However, even if that is not true, even if the worst injustices suffered by women are the worst there are, it does not follow that feminism *as a whole* should be of the highest moral priority. Feminist issues are not, as some feminists seem to suggest, an all-or-nothing matter. Some of the injustices suffered by women as women are much worse than others, and even if it were our first moral duty to eliminate the worst of them, nothing would follow about the others. Certainly in the West, where women may suffer injustice but their treatment is not *atrocious*, feminist issues could not possibly be said to have the highest priority. There seems little doubt, for instance, that we should eliminate a worse evil than sexism if we could instantly get rid of all child-deprivation. More controversially, I think that the same is true of people's appalling treatment of animals, which is a particularly serious matter because human chauvinism is such a respectable position to hold that most people do not even *pretend* to care about it. There seems little doubt that in the West, and probably in the world in general, sexism in any form is not the most important moral issue.

Perhaps, however, no feminist would claim that it was,

once the argument was cast in that form. Let us, therefore, consider what is undoubtedly at the centre of the primary struggle argument: the idea that if feminist issues could be settled, that would as a matter of fact put the world to rights, and it is that which justifies giving the highest priority to feminism.

This is a matter which it is important to establish properly, if we are to act on it. If feminist issues are not of the greatest *moral* urgency, we need *very good practical* arguments to persuade us to put them first. It is no good saying as a defence of the position that people who do not see things this way have 'failed to grasp' the radical analysis of the new feminism. They may have grasped it perfectly well but disagree with it nevertheless, and although assertion is common in this area, argument tends to be rather thin.

Usually the idea that if women's problems were put right all other injustices would disappear seems to be based on historical theories about women's oppression being the earliest form of oppression: the first enslavement of people by other people, out of which all other forms of oppression rose. However, there are two problems about this. The first is that the historical theory is itself a *highly* controversial one, which some feminists seem to want to accept on very little better evidence than its fitting the prevailing ideology. (One feminist in a university discussion group was asked what her evidence was for saying that women were the first slaves, and said she didn't know, but there must be some.') But even more important than that, even if we could prove that women were the first slaves, and even if we could prove in addition the very different proposition that there was a causal connection between women's enslavement and subsequent sorts of oppression, it still would not follow that putting things right for women would put everything else right. There would be no reason whatever to presume that there was *still* a causal connection between women's position and other kinds of injustice. The others show every sign of being firmly enough established to go on existing in their own right. You might as well try to argue that if you repatriated all the French people in this country we should all start speaking Anglo-Saxon again.

Another recurrent idea seems to be that in a society of sexual justice, women, who are naturally better fitted to be rulers than men, would take over all government while men occupied themselves with harmless amusements, and we should all be better off as a result of that.[8] However, although I am as ready as the next feminist to think that we might do a great deal better if all important matters were left in the hands of women, if arguments of that sort are to be used in defence of giving high priority to feminist issues we need harder evidence to support them than our own flattering intuitions. Such evidence is conspicuously lacking. Even if we could prove that matriarchies did once exist, for instance, and even if we could show that they had been ideal societies, that would not be enough to show that women would be the best rulers now that everything was so radically different.

It seems, therefore, that any claim that feminism ought to be regarded as everyone's first priority fails for lack of evidence, and that at least until more is forthcoming that claim ought to be dropped. That does not, however, concede total victory to the opposition. Even if feminism is not the most important issue there is, that does not provide the slightest reason for saying that it should be ignored until after The Revolution, or whatever other great cause is said to take priority. We are not limited to doing one thing at a time, and anyway the most serious issues are very often the ones which, for one reason or another, we are not in a position to do very much about. If feminist problems are to hand, we do better to tackle them immediately than sit still and fret about not knowing how to put the world economic system to rights. No man is entitled to use his dedication to some great cause as an excuse for not doing all he can to deal with injustice to women whenever it comes his way, which, it may be added, is most of the time.

Feminists, in other words, do not need the primary struggle argument to attack any man who agrees that it is unfair that women should wash his socks, but thinks that the unfairness is so insignificant that we had better not bother to do anything about it until we have finished abolishing capitalism. You can work to abolish capitalism, if that is what you want to do, while sharing sock-washing and speech-making fairly between men and women. That sort of line is the best one for feminists who want to say that the fight against sex-based injustice must be fought immediately. There is no need to fall into implausible exaggeration, which only weakens the case.

4 · ATTRACTIVENESS

Finally, we come to the aspect of feminism which probably produces the strongest resistance of all to feminism: the fact that most people think of the movement as an inherently *unattractive* one. They dislike what they see of both feminists and feminist policies, and the result is not only a disinclination to join with feminists, but even a resistance to listening to what they have to say.

This is a very serious matter for the feminist who wants to win converts, because most people's sympathies are far more dictated by their feelings than by anything else, and if those feelings are against feminism it is unlikely that any amount of argument will be effective. This is not even quite so unreasonable as it may appear. The importance of attractiveness is not just a psychological one, because there are all kinds of situations in which reason is simply incapable of determining which political line is the best to take. No matter how carefully we research into the social sciences and use the results as the basis of social planning, the extent of our ignorance and the enormous numbers of variables involved mean that we can never even approach certainty that our policies will have the effects we hope for. This means that very often the most *rational* thing to do is join forces with sensible, reasonable, attractive people, who look as though they are heading for a kind of world which would be worth living in. Even if people were more rational than they are, therefore, attractiveness would still be important, and feminists could not afford to be unconcerned about the unattractive image of feminism.

It is no accident that feminism is so generally disliked, since like other movements of its kind it contains a high potential for unattractiveness in its very nature. However, once the problem is taken seriously it should at least be possible to see where the difficulties lie, and so take the first step towards eliminating them. I want to concentrate, in conclusion, on three particular problems which feminism seems to have in this area.

The first of these is that the movement suffers from a natural hazard of all reforming movements, of being identified in the public eye with their conspicuous extremes. This is pretty well inevitable, since a woman who is not a conspicuous feminist is not likely to be thought of as a feminist at all by most people, but it is unfortunate that there is nothing which earns conspicuousness so quickly as doing or saying things that people dislike or disapprove of. The result is that the feminists who are most strident, bitter and generally unprepossessing (and such feminists certainly do exist) are taken to be typical of all, even though they are certainly not. Furthermore, this trouble is compounded by the fact that many other women, whose general opinions should certainly count as feminist, are reluctant to associate themselves with such unattractiveness, and fall into prefacing their feminist opinions with 'I'm not a feminist, but . . .' It all strengthens the general conviction that no attractive woman is a feminist.

No doubt part of the solution to this problem is to try to persuade these other feminists to agree that that is what they are. However, a more fundamental way of looking at the problem is to move a step further back, and ask why it is that *individual* feminists are so often unattractive (at least to the outsider). The image of the movement comes from the individuals in it; if large numbers of them are unattractive, the movement as a whole is bound to be so too, and it seems that the nature of feminism raises problems about attractiveness for individual feminists quite as much as it does for the movement as a whole. Those are the most important ones to try to resolve.

The first of these is particularly tricky to deal with. It is the inherent difficulty of being attractive while rebelling against a situation which is rigged from the start to your disadvantage. As Germaine Greer said, 'Because they have the upper hand, men usually conduct themselves with more grace than women do upon the battleground.'⁹ Grace is attractive, and men can carry on smoothly in their positions of advantage, using patronizing tones of voice with women or taking their services for granted often without even realizing it, admired by all, while looking with disdain at the women who do summon up the moral courage to challenge the status quo, and who became, in the unequal struggle, strident, nagging, troublesome, humourless, bitter, and generally disliked. It is most unfair, but it is a fact. It is also one which few people understand. Most people tend to think in a vague sort of way that feminists ought to be much *nicer* about their campaign if they are going to go in for it at all, without there being much comprehension of how very difficult it is to do anything about the status quo from within its conventions. Society tends to take an unreasonably dim view of makers of fusses and upsetters of apple carts. Feminists who do get trapped into ungracious behaviour can, with a great deal of justice, argue that the women who manage to remain 'nice' are nearly always giving in, and putting up with what ought to be resisted. This is quite true. Many strong, feminist women allow themselves to slip into collaboration with the opposition rather than appear in so unpleasant a light.

This is a serious matter, and not only because of public relations. For women themselves there is nothing so wearing and draining as fighting an endless battle of nagging and backbiting, whose main result is to make them seem as unpleasant to themselves as they do to everyone else, however well they may understand the situation they are in. I suspect that finding a way to escape this trap may be one of the most important issues for present day feminism. Perhaps part of the solution, at least as a temporary measure, may just be to keep off that particular battleground altogether, by keeping out of the way of men who are likely to push women into such a position, and at all costs avoiding getting into their power as wives, mistresses or employees. Meanwhile, in the long term, feminists should probably be going in for an intensive study of social psychology, with a view to applying their discoveries to situations such as these. It must be possible, if we are determined enough and take the question seriously, to find techniques of one-up-woman-ship; ways of taking the opposition by surprise, and emerging triumphant from the tricky corners without any sacrifice of grace or humour. That, however, is a different subject, and yet another which is far beyond the scope of this book.

The final attractiveness problem inherent to feminism, on the other hand, is something which it is appropriate to discuss, or at least speculate about, here. This problem is that it is extremely difficult to be a feminist of any sort, even a relatively inconspicuous one, without doing and recommending things which people will certainly dislike and disapprove of. Feminism is in its nature radical, bound to pursue policies which are at the very least unfamiliar, and since people's wishes have been formed in a background of tradition, feminism cannot help opposing many of those wishes.

This is indeed what happens, and most people see the feminist movement as opposed to the very substance of their dreams. The traditional ideas of romance, which depend on keeping men and women in their relative positions of power and dependence, still preoccupy at least nine-tenths of the population. Most women still dream about beauty, dress, weddings, dashing lovers, domesticity and babies; most men still aspire to success with beautiful women, relationships in which they are dominant, and a home where their slippers are warmed and their wishes given priority over everything else. There may not be much hope, for most people, of fulfilling these wishes in their entirety, but if feminists seem (as they do) to want to eliminate nearly all of these things – beauty, sex conventions, families and all – for most people that simply means the removal of everything in life which is worth living for. Feminists are bound not to be liked if their feelings and aspirations seem so totally alien to those of most people.

Furthermore, feminists may well feel that this particular problem of attractiveness is one they can do nothing at all about. It is absolutely essential to take a radical approach to feminism, because if the old troubles are not removed by their roots they will only go on sprouting to plague us for ever. If feminists alter their policies just to make themselves more attractive to the unconverted they might as well give up the struggle altogether; and therefore, it seems, unpopularity must just be accepted as a fact of revolutionary life.

To a large extent there is no doubt that it must. There is no point whatever in modifying radical policies in an attempt to please the public, even those parts of it which are not so self-interested or so deeply conservative that they will automatically resist substantial change of any kind. However, what might nevertheless be possible is for feminists to make themselves and their policies more attractive without any sacrifice of radicalism at all. It is necessary to enter an extended speculation at this point, but I suspect that feminists may be putting off more people than they need, and (which is why the subject is an appropriate one to go into here) that their doing so may stem from a particular kind of confusion.

The first part of the speculation is that the deepest root of many people's opposition to feminism may not be simply self-interest or conservatism, and not even their failing to understand that it is necessary to sacrifice some things they value in order to achieve others which are more important. It may rather be their thinking of feminists as people whose ideas about what kinds of thing are enjoyable or worth having are radically different from their own. If this is true, it would certainly account for a good deal of resistance to the movement. However badly you may think you are treated under the present system, there is not the slightest point in supporting a movement which offers you fair shares but appears to offer them in a kind of world it would be a misery to live in, devoid of all the things which made life worth living. It would be better to go on having unfair shares in the world as it was. And you could be the most passionate devotee of justice in the world, and still not think there was much to be said for joining forces with a group of people whose commitment to justice seemed to consist in planning to deal out scrupulously fair shares of what nobody wanted.

I suppose many feminists might well say that they really had different kinds of preference from people in general, and would put this down to their having abandoned all the likes and dislikes which had been inculcated by a corrupt patriarchal society. However, to continue the speculation, I suspect that feminist preferences may often seem radically different from other people's, and indeed may even become radically different, as a result of the blurring of an important distinction. It is one which has already been referred to in the section on feminist dress: the difference between something which must be got rid of because it is bad in itself, and something which must go because, in spite of being inherently good or harmless, it is getting in the way of more important things.

There are certainly bound to be a great many things which people in general find attractive and desirable, but which feminists must insist on getting rid of. However, there is a world of psychological difference between being told by a revolutionary movement that some of the things you value must *unfortunately* go because the cost of keeping them is too high, and having it implied that these things have no redeeming features whatever, are valued at all only because people have been conditioned into approving of them by a society which has nothing to recommend it, and must be got rid of at the first opportunity quite irrespective of any further harm they might cause. The first kind of revolutionary looks like a fundamentally congenial kind of person who is trying to be realistic about possibilities; the second looks like an incomprehensible alien from another world. And if feminists are not fully alive to the distinction between what is bad in itself and what is bad in its consequences, and slip into thinking of everything as *simply* good or bad – to be recommended or not recommended – it is not surprising if they often appear, quite unnecessarily, in the second light.

As Simone de Beauvoir said, 'One can appreciate the beauty of flowers, the charm of women, and appreciate them at their true value; if these treasures cost blood or misery they must be sacrificed.'[10] There is no need for feminists to say or think that there is nothing good about many of the things other people value; only that they cost more than they are worth. The sacrifice can be recognized as a sacrifice without any risk to feminist policies, or any attenuation of feminist energies in pursuit of them. We can, for instance, accept that the killing of an unborn child is an intrinsically bad thing, but still be totally committed to the campaign for abortion on demand because we think other things are more important than saving foetal life. We can agree that life will in some sense be poorer for women's spending less effort on beauty than they used to, while still insisting that they should be using their energies on more important things than their appearance. Slightly differently, we can accept that there is something very attractive indeed about the traditional ideal of the family, with the cheerful wife making a haven of home for her husband and children, but still resist it to the last as a general ideal, because most women cannot fit themselves into the picture without far too great a sacrifice of their inclinations and abilities. There is absolutely no need for any feminist to imply (as some seem to) that unborn children do not matter in the least, that beauty is totally worthless, or that the ideal of the family is pernicious from beginning to end.

It may well be the appearance of their having such uncongenial feelings, rather than the policies themselves, which make feminists seem so alien to many people. If this is so, it means that feminists could take the first step towards making the movement less unattractive to outsiders simply by showing themselves more aware of the good *aspects* of the traditional view of things, at the same time as insisting that many must go because they cannot be kept without injustice to women. However, to continue the speculation, a more careful distinction between what is bad in itself and what is bad only in its consequences might have even further reaching results. Feminist policies might actually be *made* more attractive to other people (and, for that matter, to many feminists themselves) without any sacrifice of feminist principle. Once feminists allow themselves to admit that some of the things they want to abandon may not be *intrinsically* bad, they may be able to devise ways of keeping some of them after all.

Various examples of this have already been suggested. We can keep some beauty of dress, once it has been accepted that it is not the beauty which is objectionable but the disproportionate fuss and inconvenience which have traditionally gone with it, and which can be attacked independently. We may find we can keep some cultural sex differences, once it is realized that it is only the ones which are degrading to women which are actually harmful. And though perhaps at present we have no better idea than crèches as the solution to the problem of the working mother, if we accept that crèches are not ideal, rather than feeling obliged to argue that mothers want to be with their children only because they have been conditioned into it, there may come a time when we can think of something better. With a more careful separation of the elements and aspects of good and bad, both in what feminists want to achieve and in what they are trying to replace, radical feminist policies could be far less austere than they are at present. Much of the present unattractiveness is quite unnecessary.

And this is an excellent point on which to end, not only because it is important in itself, but also because this *un-necessary* unattractiveness of feminism brings the argument back to where it started, at the very beginning of the book, with feminism's tendency to undermine its own intentions through leaping too hastily to conclusions.

This can be seen by reference to the ideal of radicalism. Feminists are anxious that their policies should be radical, because they are afraid that if they attack only the symptoms of the traditional oppression of women, leaving its roots untouched, the trouble will keep on reviving, perhaps in new and unfamiliar forms. That, as far as it goes, must be right. The difficulty, however, comes in deciding what policies really *are* radical: which ones will *really* eliminate all traces of the traditional oppression. If too hasty judgments are made, policies may be formulated which look radical to the superficial glance, but which really perpetuate the trouble because they are too simple a reaction against the past. The consequences will then be exactly what was feared in the first place: feminist policies will be insufficiently radical to prevent the evils of the past from appearing in a new form. And, to continue the speculation of the previous paragraphs, it does seem likely that some feminists' failure to distinguish carefully enough between the good and bad *aspects* of the patriarchal traditions which are obviously bad *overall*, and in particular to be too quick to see everything about entrenched tradition as dangerous to women, may have exactly that effect.

Consider how some radical feminist thinking seems to go. (If this is a caricature, it is a recognizable one.) Feminists recognize that many things about tradition are oppressive to women: families, the association of women with children, sex roles, femininity, beauty demands and innumerable others. Even the very existence of the sex distinction itself is seen by some feminists as oppressive. Therefore, the radical impulse seems to be, *get rid of all these things entirely*. And it is easy to see the point. If families are eliminated, families will no longer oppress women; if we end women's special connection with children, children will no longer come between women and whatever else they want to do; if people can be persuaded by some means to stop caring about

beauty, beauty demands will stop diverting women's attention from matters of much greater moment. And if we find
that by the progress of medical science we can end the sex
distinction altogether, then it will follow as the night the day
that we shall be able to stop sex distinctions from causing
any trouble whatsoever.

However, tautologously true as all that may be, if such
policies are supposed to be *radical* in taking away all traces
of women's domination by men, undoing the evil of the past
by pulling it up by the roots, they fail completely. This is
because they do leave a residue of evil, much of which is
probably unnecessary, and which can also be traced to the
direct influence of the past.

The potential for harm of such sweeping policies must be
obvious. Although the total removal of the situation which
allows the existence of some evil would certainly eliminate
the evil *in that particular form*, it might easily cause new and
different toubles. People no longer encumbered by families
might find themselves instead discontented and rootless;
mothers freed from the demands of their children might find
a new frustration as large as the new freedom; women whose
faces had been their fortunes might find themselves left
without any fortune at all; and the loss of pleasure in sexual
difference might seem to everyone a very high price to pay
even for the total elimination of all possibility of sexism. It
is true that some such drawbacks might be inevitable, losses
to be accepted for the sake of great gains. However, it is
equally true that many might not be, and perhaps might well
be avoided altogether by a less direct rejection of the past.
And if unnecessary problems did arise through feminists'
feeling impelled to reject the whole of some patriarchal
structure or attitude, problems which could have been
avoided altogether if the reaction had been less direct, it
would mean that tradition *was* still being allowed to cause
trouble, in however unexpected a form.

Radical feminism cannot go in for a simple rejection of
everything which happens to have male fingerprints on it,
because to do that is to accept part of the legacy of patriarchy,

by conceding that the traditional packages must be left intact, to be accepted or rejected as wholes. It is to *accept* that if certain things exist at all, they must take the form they have always taken: one oppressive to women. But that is not in the least radical. What is necessary is to insist on *splitting up the packages*, looking at the good and bad aspects of tradition and keeping what is good wherever we can. That is the radical thing to do, even though it may produce policies which look reformist to the casual glance.

Unless feminists do this, they once again fall into the trap of setting out on a path which leads away from the goal they themselves want to achieve. The radical impulse to rout patriarchy turns unnoticed into a perverse device for perpetuating its influence. Whenever, in their determination to escape the evils of the past, feminists react too hastily and discard too much, and in doing so make their plans for a feminist future less good for everyone than need have been the case, they are allowing the shadow of the past to stay and dim the future. Patriarchal man has a kind of success, since even though he may not see much to please him in what is to be brought about, he can at least take a grim satisfaction in seeing the effects of his social arrangements linger on to the detriment of women. But matters may be even worse. If by the same haste feminists make their policies look so bleak and unattractive that even women themselves prefer the present state of masculist injustice to the drab and severe alternative which feminists seem to be offering, patriarchy's triumph is complete. Feminism concedes a major victory with scarcely a struggle, and by its own policies contrives its own defeat.

If all this is right, and a too-hasty reaction against the legacy of the past is indeed alienating many of feminism's natural supporters, it constitutes the final argument against the largest group of people who claim to have little time for reason and argument in political matters: the ones whose perpetual refrain is that reason is useless because *people are not rational*, and will never be persuaded by reason out of their prejudice or self-interest. Of course this group must be right in its basic claim. Few people, even among the most committed supporters of rationality, would want to argue that the suffragettes would have done better to have maintained a sweet reasonableness than they did by chaining themselves to railings or leaping under horses. However, this undoubted fact gives no ground whatever to the anti-rationalist argument, because the first political purpose of care in reasoning, in feminism as in any other movement, is *not* the conversion of outsiders by rational persuasion. It is making sure that feminists themselves do not inadvertently set out on courses which will undermine their own intentions, by formulating policies which actually work against their own goal of eliminating injustice or by embarking on political strategies which will turn out to have played into the hands of the enemy.

If reason is bound to be generally ineffective as a means of confounding the politics of the opposition, then certainly the main practical tools of feminists must be non-rational persuasion and hard political manoeuvering. However, the last thing which follows from this is that reason is not worth bothering about. What follows is that the greatest possible care must be taken not to make the uphill grind even worse than it need be, through the careless presentation of a feminist image and feminist policies which drive the movement's natural supporters back into the traditional camp. If a more careful formulation of radical feminist policies will lead not only to a better plan for the future, but also to a kind of radical feminism which is attractive and understandable to the people who are at present its opponents, then no feminists – least of all the ones who feel that reason has no place in political achievement – can afford to be careless in argument. The very impossibility of reaching most of the unpersuaded by the force of reason becomes the final demonstration of the indispensability of care in argument amongst feminists themselves.

Traditional Spheres
and Traditionalist Logic[1]

I

The fundamental conviction uniting the opponents of feminism has always been that women and men should occupy separate spheres. There have been many variations on this theme: opinions have differed to some extent about what is proper to each sphere, about how much neutral space there should be belonging to neither, and about the extent to which trespassing in the other sex's sphere should be tolerated. Still, through all the variations of detail the ground has remained constant. All traditionalists hold that women and men should have different functions in society, and that each sex should avoid the character and activity that is the proper preserve of the other.

Almost as constant has been the kind of argument produced in defence of this separation. It is appropriate for the sexes to act and be treated in these different ways, it is said, for the simple and obvious reason that they *are different*. In the words of one eloquent defender of the traditional spheres, 'Each has what the other has not; each completes the other. They are in nothing alike, and the happiness and perfection of both depends on each asking and receiving what the other only can give.'[2] Present-day traditionalists may have fallen off somewhat in extremity of view as well as in style of expression, but their position remains in essence the same. It is still widely regarded as obvious that since the sexes are different, any well-judging society must have different expectations of them and treat them in different ways. Of course it must: all moral behaviour, and for that matter rational behaviour of any kind, depends on the recognition of differences. No one thinks it appropriate to treat the sick in the same way as the well, or the strong as the weak, or the old as the young; and in the same way it would be ridiculous and wrong for the sexes to be treated as though they were the same.

This way of putting the matter makes it sound like a liberal and sensitive arrangement for the good of all. But in spite of the attempts of some traditionalists to assure women that difference does not imply inequality,[3] or even (let them warm to their task a little) that women's position is really one of particular value and privilege, to the feminist it seems that no amount of subtle redescription can turn subjection into power, or make positive virtues of the weakness and inadequacy supposed to suit woman to her lowly position. Through all the euphemism there still comes the view of Aristotle, who attempted no such tactful suggestion of equality in difference when he said that a female was female in virtue of a certain *lack* of qualities, and Thomas Aquinas, who thought a female was a defective male.

It is not surprising, then, that feminists who want to resist conclusions about the subordination of women usually start by attacking the claims about female inferiority traditionally invoked in their support; and there have been two main ways of doing this. The original one was straightforwardly to deny the alleged differences between the sexes: female inadequacies that had any existence at all outside the self-serving male imagination were attributed to men's own manipulation of women. The other, more recent, has been to accept that there are indeed differences, but to claim that mistaken patriarchal values have given unmerited status to masculine pursuits and abilities, and correspondingly denigrated those of women.

Now there is of course nothing wrong in principle with investigating either of these possibilities. Far too many myths about the natures of the sexes have been around for far too long, and no doubt a good many traditional values need rethinking as well. There is, however, one serious drawback to these lines of attack. Because they depend on denying the premisses of the traditional argument in order to reach a non-traditional conclusion, they both by implication accept its logical structure, and in doing so unintentionally assist a series of sleights of hand by which the traditionalist has managed to keep the real problem of the spheres from being seen at all.[4]

For the time being, therefore, it may be interesting to forget all debates about patriarchal values and the natures of the sexes – even conceding, for the sake of argument, the most outrageous claims on these subjects that any traditionalist may care to make – and concentrate instead on the remarkable piece of reasoning by which the positions of women and men have for so long been justified.

2

Traditional arguments for the separate spheres go along lines like this:

Premiss 1: General principle specifying how people should act/be treated.
Premiss 2: Empirical claim that women and men differ in the relevant respect.

Conclusion: Women and men should, in this respect, act/be treated differently.

If the argument ever gets beyong the stage of vague generalizations, different spheres-defenders may well fill in the details differently, depending on what they think the positions of men and women should be. But, typically, you might get this sort of thing:

The strong should protect the weak.
Men are strong, women are weak.

Men should protect women.

I shall return later to the substance of this familiar fantasy, but for the moment all that is at issue is its form. Weakness and protection are to be understood as place-holders for whatever qualities and activities may be appealed to in any standard traditionalist argument.

Now the first thing to notice here is that if this argument is to work as a justification of the separate spheres as we have known them, it needs to be expanded. To recommend the traditional arrangements is not just to say that men and women ought to do different things, because the sphere separation has been a matter of differential *treatment* of the sexes, in laws, institutions and conventions. If the traditional spheres are to be justified, so must be this differential treatment. The argument therefore needs to go something like this:

> The strong should be expected/required/put under pressure to protect the weak.
> Men are strong, women are weak.
>
> Men should be expected/required/put under pressure to protect women.

The pressures involved in imposing different aspects of the spheres traditionally cover a wide range, from outright prevention of alternatives to mild disapproval of aberrations, but since the issues are the same for all I shall move indifferently between them.

Still, this clarification may not seem to make much difference. The claim is now that if you agree that if it is right for the strong to be under pressure to protect the weak, and that men are stronger than women, you cannot consistently deny that men should be under pressure to protect women. The logic still seems compelling, which is probably why most feminists who want to resist the conclusions of such arguments feel bound to resist one or both of the premisses. Nevertheless, there lurk in this innocent-looking pattern of argument two significant ambiguities, from which it derives all its plausibility.

Consider first the second premiss. This is essential to the

argument, because the claimed sexual difference is being offered as the justification of the different treatment recommended in the conclusion. But care needs to be taken with propositions asserting differences between groups in this way, because, quite irrespective of any questions about their truth, there are all kinds of different ways in which they may with linguistic propriety be intended and interpreted. 'Men are stronger than women' may mean 'all men are stronger than all women'; but it may equally mean such lesser things as 'the average man is stronger than the average woman', 'most men are stronger than most women' or 'the strongest women are less strong than the strongest men'. There is also a corresponding range of possible interpretations of the conclusion. If the argument is to be valid, therefore, the conclusion must take a form appropriate to the second premiss. If the second premiss is understood as a claim about most women and most men, it can support a conclusion only about how most men should be expected to treat most women; conversely, if the conclusion is understood as applying to all men and all women, it needs for its support a second premiss asserting a universal difference between men and women.

This is important, because the traditional spheres theorist is not someone who believes that if we all went around putting pressure on the strong to protect the weak, it would, incidentally, turn out in consequence that more men found themselves under pressure to protect women than the other way round. The traditional view of the separate spheres is that *all* men should be expected to behave in particular ways and *all* women in others, and that means that what needs to be defended is a universal interpretation of the conclusion. But in that case you need a universal interpretation of the second premiss; and here lies the problem. Even the most dyed in the grain of male supremacists, and even with women's educational disadvantages to assist his prejudices, could hardly claim that all men were stronger (or whatever) than all women. The premiss derives any plausibility it has from its weaker, average interpretations. But an average interpretation of the second premiss does not support the conclusion that there should be a universal differentiation; and, worse than that, actually makes the conclusion *inconsistent* with the general principle invoked to justify it. If all men should be under pressure to protect all women, and men are stronger than women only on average, it follows that puny little men should be expected to go around protecting hefty Amazonian women. And whether or not that can be justified (perhaps it can), it is not even compatible with the principle that the strong should protect the weak, let alone a consequence of it.

That is the first problem; but it still does not conclude the matter, because even within the specification of universality there is another problem about the interpretation of the conclusion. Suppose, however implausibly, some hard-bitten traditionalist really did insist on accepting a universal interpretation of the second premiss. That would raise problems of a different sort, but it would avoid the objection just outlined: a claim that all men are stronger than all women does indeed seem to support the conclusion that all men should be expected to protect all women. But another distinction needs to be made. It is one thing to say that there should be pressure on the strong to protect the weak, and in doing so predict that this will, as it happens, result in its being appropriate that any given man should find himself under pressure to protect women. It is quite another to defend, as the traditionalist must, laws, institutions and conventions which specify the differential treatment of men and women *as such*. If the argument is to defend the separate spheres of tradition it needs to support what might be called the strong, or prescriptive, version of the universal conclusion, and not just the weak, or predictive, one.

Perhaps this seems to present no trouble. If it is acceptable to have rules about the protection of the weak by the strong, and if all men are stronger than all women, it may seem to follow without difficulty that there should be rules about the protection of women by men. But once again things are more complicated than at first they appear, as becomes apparent if we start with the question of whether these rules about men and women are supposed to be in addition to, or instead of, general rules about the strong and the weak.

Obviously the principle that the strong should protect the weak cannot justify the existence of rules about men and women *rather than* about the strong and the weak, since it provides no reason for saying that what matters between the sexes should not matter equally within them. But neither, on the other hand, can it justify adding a rule about men and women to an existing rule about the strong and the weak in general, since (*ex hypothesi*, given the second premiss) all men would already be required by its provisions to protect women. You cannot justify the addition of a new rule to an existing one by invoking a principle whose requirements are already entirely met by the first. Quite the contrary: if the new, sex-specific rule achieves anything that the existing, general one does not, that can only be because it is *not* the case that all women are weaker than all men, and that the general rule, left to itself, would bring about the protecting of some men by some women. The sex-specific rule achieves nothing *unless* it overrides the general one, in which case (once again) it not only fails to follow from the principle supporting the general rule, but actually conflicts with it.

The most familiar line of argument in defence of the sexes' spheres, in other words, takes all its plausibility from systematic fudging. General claims about differences between women and men mask the distinction between their universal and average interpretations; claims about what ought to happen blur the difference between predictive and prescriptive forms of the universal conclusion. The argument is valid with the universal form of the premiss and the predictive form of the conclusion, but only then. The weak, average version of the second premiss cannot support either universal version of the conclusion, and even the universal premiss cannot support the strong, prescriptive conclusion. And yet the premiss is plausible only if understood in the weak version, and the conclusion needed by the traditionalist is the prescriptive one. The argument entirely depends for its plausibility on a double fallacy of equivocation, which, when exposed, shows that the required conclusion actually contradicts the general principle invoked in its support. Confusion could hardly be worse confounded.

If arguments of this kind, so widely taken to justify the separation of sexes into their traditional spheres, exemplify the logic which men have counted as their special preserve, it is perhaps not surprising if some feminists have decided that men are welcome to it.

3

What this analysis implies is that there are really two quite distinct separate spheres issues.

First there is the question of what might be called weak, or naturally occurring, spheres. If men and women do differ on average in various ways they will tend to make different choices against a background of the same opportunities and to be treated differently as a result of the impartial application of general principles, and there arises the question of the extent to which this separation will happen. This is an *empirical* question, and it can have no general answer because that will depend not only on the nature and extent of tendencies to difference between the sexes, but also on the nature of background values and opportunities. Against some backgrounds there might well be more natural sphere separation than against others.

Then, quite differently, there is the question of what might be called strong, or imposed sphere separation, which is a matter of differential treatment of the sexes as such. The question here is the *moral* one of whether such differentiation can be justified; and once again it is not to be presumed that there is a general answer. It may well depend on what kind of differentiation is at issue; some kinds may be justifiable and others not.[5]

Traditionalist arguments of the kind I have been considering depend on blurring the distinction between the two kinds of sphere. The trick is to pretend that what needs

justifying is the naturally occurring sort, and to do this by
making claims about sexual differences which, if true,
would support the conclusion that it was appropriate that
men and women should tend to do different things and find
themselves being treated in different ways. But this shows
fiendish cunning (or rather would, if there were any reason
to think it arose from design rather than confusion) since it
distracts attention from the massive apparatus of law and
convention designed to keep the sexes in their spheres
irrespective of whether it suits them or not, which is what
really needs justification, and which – since the sex-specific
rules would have no purpose if the sphere separation would
come about naturally through the impartial application of
general ones – the traditional argument actually under-
mines.

The issue of natural spheres will be returned to later. For
now the problem is the differential treatment of the sexes
recommended by all red-blooded traditionalists, and whose
justification has run into difficulty.

Now the corkscrew logic of the most familiar line of
argument obviously does not show that strong sphere separation cannot be justified at all. Other arguments might
succeed where that one failed, and determined traditionalists will, as Mill pointed out, soon be back 'throwing up
fresh intrenchments of argument to repair any breach made
in the old . . .'[6] But as we prepare to meet such new
attempts, we should start by being clear about what exactly
is being defended, since whether a conclusion follows from
a particular set of premisses is likely to depend critically on
what that conclusion is. We need an account of what kind of
differential treatment is being recommended for the sexes.

This is not a straightforward matter. There are variations
in traditionalist opinion, and each variation must be assessed
on its own merits; tradition need not stand or fall as a whole.
Nevertheless, there are distinct family resemblances between most established views about the position of women,
and even moderate, recent versions show distinct traces of
their rigid ancestry. An analysis of the original separate

spheres in our own tradition will at least illustrate the kinds of difficulty attempts at justification are likely to encounter, and suggest useful lines of feminist attack.

Consider then, the situation as it was not so long ago in the Christian West, and still is in many parts of the world. There were two broad aspects to the differentiation of the spheres. First, there was the exclusion of women from male territory: from most education, from the professions, from most respectable or remunerative employment, and from participation in the making of law. And second, there was a clear asymmetrical definition of relationships between women and men, subjecting women to powerful constraints of many kinds, and in particular defining the relationship between women and their husbands in such a way as to give virtually complete power to men. Female unchastity and infidelity provoked ferocious social sanctions; a woman's property was her husband's, so that even if she lived separately from him, and even as a result of his fault, anything she earned was his; her children also remained his, to the extent that he could prevent her from seeing them.

When the matter is put like this, any pretence of equality between the spheres appears in its full absurdity. No doubt many women have been happy in their situation; no doubt many of them would not have changed places with their menfolk. Nevertheless, the differential treatment that brought about the traditional separate spheres was of a kind to exclude women from virtually all power and independence, and place them systematically in the power and service of men.

4

How, then, could traditionalists set about justifying arrangements of this kind?

The most familiar line of argument for keeping women away from men's territory depends on the claim that women cannot do whatever it is, or cannot do it as well as men, or will never rise to the sublime heights of male achievement.

Most such claims are manifestly false, as feminists quickly produce evidence to show. But all arguments of that form anyway fall straight into the logical confusions already outlined. If women cannot do whatever it is, or fewer women than men can do it, then the selection procedures already needed for the exclusion of substandard men will automatically keep them out. Conversely, if special prohibitions against women achieve anything that such normal selection procedures do not achieve, that can only be to keep out the women who would, by those standards, have got in; and whose exclusion, therefore, can hardly be justified by the claim that the standards are not being met. Either way the logic is hopeless.

And the familiar efficiency argument, which always seems to be wheeled in as first reserve when the original one collapses, is nearly as bad. The claim that you have to keep all women out of something because *most* of them cannot do whatever it is, and would put much too much of a strain on the selection processes if they tried, may sound more promising at first. But it depends on empirical premises of stunning absurdity: on the idea that it is not only so well known and obviously true that women are not up to the task that there is no point in even letting them try, but also that women themselves are so widely unaware of this self-evident fact that they will clog up the system by applying in droves. And, quite apart from its dependence on this modest invention, the argument still does not work because it gives no reason for rejecting any women who are so obviously exceptions to the (supposed) generality of their sex that there can be no sensible reason at all for not considering them, or those who of their own initiative produce evidence that they are suitable. Justifying the exclusion of women from men's sphere is a trickier matter than the complacent traditionalist suspects.

The usual arguments in defence of traditional arrangements for the personal relationships of the sexes fail in just the same way. The simplest of these are to the effect that these arrangements come about because of the natural differences between the sexes: men ought to dominate because they are naturally dominant and generally superior; women should be dependent because they are pretty helpless on their own and naturally inclined to a life of submission to superior beings whose strength is needed for their own protection. But quite apart from anything one might say about the premises of arguments like this, the logical problem arises again. If the arrangement would come about as a result of individual choice, that cannot justify the existence of rules and pressures which, according to the argument, would have nothing to do. You cannot, for instance, sneer at a henpecked man on the grounds that a man ought to be head of his household *and* claim that the justification of men's being heads of households is their natural dominance; if they were all dominant there would be nothing to sneer at, and, conversely, if there is something to sneer at, at least some men are by the criterion of dominance unsuited to their position. All such simple arguments, at least in their familiar forms, are non-starters.

And if we move beyond these first attempts to more ingenious arguments about women's need of men, things get even worse. The weak need the protection of the strong, it is often said; or childbearing women (and we are reminded that until recently most women were pregnant or nursing most of the time) need men to look after them and their children and get the food. But these arguments not only run into the already discussed difficulties of trying to deduce conclusions about men and women from premises about such qualities as strength and weakness; they also manage to get into new and impressive tangles of their own.

Consider, for instance, what you would do if you were really setting out in an unprejudiced way to arrange for the protection of the weak. You would probably start by trying to make the weak stronger, or by giving them extra powers to defend themselves. You might also try to lessen the power of the strong, or impose restrictions to prevent their getting out of hand. The very last thing you would do is systematically deprive the weak of all other options in order to force them into dependency on the very people from whom they might be presumed most to need protection, and then provide social and legal powers to make the strong stronger still, as has been the case with women and men. The idea that the weak can be protected by being abandoned to the power of the strong involves as remarkable a piece of twisted reasoning as can ever have been devised.

Much the same goes for arguments about the needs of childbearing women. If you were really concerned about the well-being of women and children, and also thought that women needed men to help them, you would hardly think of rules making it difficult for women to escape from men since, according to your hypothesis, women would be anxious to hold on to them anyway. What you would need would be rules to keep *men* in order. You might reasonably insist on the chaperoning of men, to make sure they did not go around idly begetting children without committing themselves to their support, and on men's being subject to social ostracism if they were found to have eluded this vigilance and *fallen*. And given that your concern was for the protection of women and children, you would also want to make sure that they were left as well off as possible whenever men did try to evade their responsibilities, perhaps by making it harder for men to divorce women than the other way round, or putting a straying man's possessions into the control of the deserted woman. You would also be anxious to see that women were sufficiently well-educated and employable to fend for themselves if all else failed. Nothing could be further from this than the traditional arrangements, which not only allowed men to scatter their maker's image through the land without suffering much in the way of social consequences, but also systematically deprived women of any adequate means of supporting themselves independently of men, and made matters even worse by heaping ferocious social penalties on unsupported women and unauthorized children. Once again, feminists need hardly bother to dispute traditional premises while traditionalist logic is in such a ramshackle state.

And if it is said that this is all irrelevant to modern traditionalists, who recommend nothing like these dark institutions and only want to encourage a society of feminine women and manly men – well, let them try to find a coherent justification of whatever it is they do want to defend. The fact that something is not as bad as it once was is not a reason for thinking that justification is no longer needed, and there is not the slightest reason for thinking it easier to find a coherent positive justification for what is moderate than for what is extreme. Anyone who doubts it should try. Perhaps success is possible, but in the light of what has traditionally passed for justification, we can reasonably say that we will believe it when we see it.

5

In the meantime, while we are waiting for the appearance of plausible arguments to traditionalist conclusions, we can consider another aspect of this matter.

Sometimes when people produce confused arguments they are simply making mistakes about difficult issues. Often, however, political and moral arguments are so egregiously dreadful that no one starting from the premises could conceivably have reached the conclusion through unprejudiced mistake; and when this happens, it is obvious (if not to the perpetrators themselves) what must be going on. People want a particular conclusion, and they want to justify it in terms of publicly acceptable moral principles; but since their real reasons for wanting the conclusion have nothing to do with those principles, it becomes necessary to botch a connection by inventing convenient facts, or by standing logic on its head, or both. And when the analysis of arguments shows this to have happened, it naturally raises the question of what is really going on. Or at least (since people often cling to traditions just from habit of mind) of why it all got going in the first place.

As it stands, that question is an empirical one, for historians and psychologists, and perhaps evolutionary biologists, rather than philosophers. Nevertheless, it is one to which logic is relevant. People do not make ridiculous mistakes of logic, or invent facts, when they are seriously trying to work out what to do, and seeing what kind of argument could actually support the required conclusion might provide at least the basis of an interesting hypothesis about motivations. It would, anyway, increase the pressure on defenders of the spheres, since if some proposed and intrinsically sound line of justification were not to their liking, it would be injudicious to leave it alone in the field.

Let us then, partly (but only partly) for feminist amusement, consider what kind of plausible and coherent line of argument might support the conclusion that there should be the traditional separate spheres. And since the logic of the traditional defences is so *utterly* perverse – with most of the arguments not merely failing to support their conclusions, but actually contradicting them – radical measures suggest themselves. Rather like the Fairy Queen in *Iolanthe*, who sorted out an otherwise intractable tangle of problems by the simple expedient of inserting the word 'not' into an inconvenient item of fairy law, we might see whether we could get the logic into a better state just by reversing the traditional premisses.

Consider first the arrangements for marriage. The conclusion that has to be supported is that there should be rules of the traditional asymmetrical kind governing the relationship of the sexes. Now it is commonly said by men that women want men: that they want to be attached and subordinate, that they like being domestic and dominated, that love is their whole existence, and all the rest. But this myth makes no sense at all of the situation. If women wanted these arrangements, and in particular wanted them more than men did, what was supposed to be the point of an all-pervading set of rules and conventions to force women into their dependent situation? As Mill pointed out:

The general opinion of men is supposed to be that the natural vocation of a woman is that of a wife and mother. I say, is supposed to be, because judging from acts, from the whole of the present constitution of society, one might infer that their opinion was the direct contrary. They might be supposed to think that the alleged natural vocation of women was of all things the most repugnant to their nature, insomuch that if they are free to do anything else . . . there will not be enough of them who will be willing to accept the condition said to be natural to them.[7]

Once again, there is no point in a rule unless it brings about what would otherwise not happen. If women really wanted to attach themselves to men in the traditional way, the asymmetrical rules forcing women into the power of men would have no point at all. They would have a point, on the other hand, if the situation were the opposite of what patriarchal tradition made out, and it was men who wanted these arrangements while women did not.

That avoids one striking problem of the traditional account, by making sense of the *direction* of asymmetry in the arrangements. But although it supports the aspect of sphere separation that involves pressures, and asymmetrical ones at that, it does not yet begin to give an account of why sex, rather than some other characteristic, should have formed the basis of the separation, let alone of why women's sphere should have its particular, highly distinctive form. A coherent justification of the spheres needs to take acount of both these matters.

Tradition, which made out that women wanted men more than men wanted women, tended to explain this by making men out to be strong, brave, adventurous, creative, inclined to genius and all the rest, while women were passive, nondescript, and generally incapable of coping on their own. That is obviously no use as part of an argument to the conclusion that women must be prevented from escaping from men. To make it work we must obviously substitute a premiss to the effect that women have something highly desirable that men want. Should we therefore simply reverse tradition here too, and say that it is really men who have all the negative qualities, and women all the good and desirable ones?

That may be tempting to feminists for various reasons,

but it will not do. Quite apart from any questions about empirical plausibility (and feminists must not copy their opponents' bad habits of inventing convenient facts) this would still leave untouched one of the fundamental problems about most traditional arguments: their attempt to reach conclusions about differential treatment of the sexes on the basis of premises that make reference only to non-sexual characteristics. If we are to find any justification for differential treatment of the sexes as such, we must get away from all the incidental and derivative characteristics which may (or may not) tend to be associated with one sex more than the other, and turn our attention to what *really* differentiates them; focus on what each really has that the other has not, and makes women as such different from men as such.

This is not too difficult. Leaving aside such modern discoveries as hormones and chromosomes, since they could not have been involved in the setting up of traditional arrangements, there seem to be only three differences of any importance.

One of these is the difference of function in conception: sperm and ovum are different. In this difference, however, it is hard to see any grounds for one sex's wanting to bind the other to it more strongly than the other was willing to be bound, since the difference is reciprocal. Each sex is so far necessary to the other, and there is to this extent (for once) genuine equality in their difference. There is no basis for asymmetrical rules to be founds here.

Another difference arises in (hetero)sexual relationships as ends in themselves. Once again, the sexes' functions are reciprocal: to the extent that either sex is necessary, they both are. But here, perhaps, potential for asymmetry may begin to set in. It might be speculated that men's sexual needs were in general greater than women's, and if so, that women might have to be constrained to cooperate in order for men to be satisfied. Fortunately, however, we need not try to settle that matter. Even though that might explain sexually asymmetrical rules of some kind, it could not begin to account for the form of sexual laws and conventions that we are considering. Traditional rules, in their demands for monogamy and chastity, were designed to *limit* women's sexual activity, rather than to coerce them into sex whether they liked it or not.

That leaves what is undoubtedly the most significant universal difference between the sexes. *Only the female can actually produce offspring*; and this is an ability corresponding to which the male has nothing at all.[8]

It is worth commenting at this point on the remarkable fact that even at this advanced point of the feminist era large numbers of people will, when asked about differences between the sexes, embark on a list of (supposed) differences that characterize women almost entirely in terms of inferiority to men. Everything possible is wrong with this. Most of these claims are anyway highly disputable, showing conspicuous signs of having been invented for the purpose of demonstrating the natural appropriateness of the traditional spheres; and anyway, even if they were not, they all still concern characteristics which differentiate the sexes only on average, or, sometimes, which are possessed to a higher degree by the occasional man than by any woman. It is one of the most pernicious consequences of shoddy traditionalist argument that it has become common to think of average differences of characteristics and abilities between the sexes as what actually differentiates them. As a matter of logic, questions about the average differences between two groups cannot even be raised until they have been distinguished as groups on other grounds; and obviously the essential differences between men and women must be *sexual* ones.

When the question is not about the derivative, average differences between the sexes, but about what makes them male and female – what puts all men on one side of the divide and all women on the other – the difference obviously has nothing to do with strength or genius or enterprise or sensitivity or patience or anything of the kind, but with reproductive capacity. And in this the sexes have generally reciprocal abilities, with the striking exception that *women* can do something that *men* cannot. In a situation of equality women can go off and produce children without men's having any control over the matter (at least, men could prevent it only by total cooperation in a boycott of sex, and a tiny number of weak or unreliable men could sabotage the whole thing); men cannot produce children without women – as, it should be said, present-day men are increasingly becoming aware. The principal difference between the sexes, in other words, seems to be women's having an ability that men have not, and (to reverse along with other aspects of tradition the Aristotelian contribution to the subjugation of women) it would be closer to the truth to say that *men* were *men* in virtue of a lack of qualities, rather than that women were women on that account.

That certainly looks promising as the beginning of a justification for rules tying women to men rather than the other way round. If one group has some ability another lacks, there is a prima facie reason for its being wanted by that other group. And in fact it is more than promising, because this way of looking at things exactly fits the form the control of women has traditionally taken. The detailed arrangements are just what would be produced by a desire of men to take over women's natural advantage, ensuring as far as possible that all children born became the recognizable offspring (originally property) of some man. Women are by nature able to ensure that they have offspring and to identify them as their own. Men can do neither, as long as women are on the loose, but the traditional arrangements made it virtually impossible for women to make any kind of way in the world without attaching themselves to a man, and the sanctions against unchastity and infidelity made sure that most children were born to recognized fathers. The importance of this to men also shows in the traditional ownership of children by fathers (only recently changed in the West, and still prevalent in other traditions such as Islam), and is suggested by the still almost-universal stamping of children with the father's name, to make a definitive announcement of what has always been – in spite of all the constraints – inherently uncertain.

With all these radical reversals of the empirical parts of the traditional argument, the logic ceases to be absurd. Women are to be coerced because they cannot be relied on to cooperate willingly, and what they are to be coerced into is a pattern of life and behaviour making it impossible, without enormous cost, for them to use their distinctive ability except when some man can identify the offspring as his own. The arrangement effectively makes women's extra natural ability effectively men's own. All the argument lacks now, to complete the conclusion about the separate spheres, is a value premiss to support the conclusion that this *ought* to happen.

Tradition is apt to invoke benefits for women here or, failing that, some general social good. The first is pretty implausible, since women apparently need to be coerced into the arrangement,[9] and the second looks like one of those claims about the good of society that starts by discounting the interests of half its members, as in the case of the arguments about women taking men's jobs. But, once again, things start to look plausible if we reverse these traditional claims to altruism, and put in their place a simple premiss to the effect that what matters is men's getting what they want. Then the argument becomes straightforward. The conclusion about the separate spheres follows without difficulty.

So there is the required value premiss. And there, mainly by means of reversing all the components of the traditional defence of the separate spheres, we find the basis of a logically sound and empirically plausible argument to the conclusion that women should be in their traditional sphere. It just has the slight drawback that its value premiss is not one to which many traditionalists are going to want to (be seen to) appeal, since it is not well adapted to the purpose of persuading a subject group of the natural inevitability of its position, or of appealing to disinterested pursuers of justice. No doubt that is why this line of justification is not often offered in public.[10]

While pursuing this engaging line of enquiry, perhaps we might also add by way of coda a parallel speculation about the exclusion of women from men's terrain. In our own tradition this has often worked as part of the same enterprise: if women were excluded from everything else they were forced into dependence on men. But that does not work in contexts (much of the world) where women do most of the productive work; nor does it work as a justification for excluding women from particular areas of work in societies where they can support themselves by other means, or of making admission more difficult by setting higher standards or other obstacles. But once again we can try the Fairy Queen technique. The argument that special rules are needed to exclude women, because women cannot do whatever it is, does not work, as we have already seen; and, once again, since the division is made on grounds of sex, any justification would need to refer to sexual differentiation and probably to women's extra ability. To fill in the reason here we could speculate, in line with some observations of anthropologists, that since women could do everything men could do *and* something else, it was necessary, if men were not to feel completely useless, for them to keep something to themselves and pretend women could not do it. That is less neat than the arguments about putting women into the power of men; but once again it is a reasonable working hypothesis which serves adequately as the basis of a challenge. Any traditionalist who is unwilling to accept this account of policies that exclude women is at liberty to offer other justifications.[11]

This is not to say that it is necessarily impossible to produce a logically sound, empirically plausible and morally acceptable defence of the traditional arrangements or their modified descendants: perhaps sufficiently ingenious searching could produce more acceptable justifications. It seems rather unlikely, however. Here we are, after all, expected to swallow arguments in defence of tradition which depend on our accepting that rules are necessary to bring about what would have happened anyway, that rules whose only effect is to prevent people's acting in ways suitable to their natures can be justified by principles about suitability, that the weak can be protected by being abandoned to the control of the strong, and that child-bearing women can be protected by rules and conventions that make them helpless without the protection of a man. We are also expected to overlook woman's rather striking extra ability, and see her whole essence as a series of inadequacies and absences, while at the same time transforming men's inability to bear children into a special aptitude for everything else. If such contortions form the basis of the best set of arguments in defence of the traditional spheres that can be produced for public consumption, it may reasonably be inferred that ones that are morally, empirically and logically reasonable cannot lie immediately to hand. And until they can be found, we are entitled to conclude that the traditional arrangements have no other justification than the arbitrary advantaging of men.

6

There is, however, one other possible line of defence remaining to the unrepentant moderate traditionalist. He can simply drop the traditional, imposed spheres, and avoid all the logical problems by reverting, instead, to the defence of naturally occurring ones, and in doing so turn the argument about imposed differential treatment back on feminists themselves.

And, indeed – though he may not express it in quite this way, because he has probably not disentangled the two kinds of sphere – he is in effect already doing so. Of course women should not be subjected to arbitrarily disadvantageous treatment (this neo-traditionalist will say); of course feminists were right to oppose it all. But now, in enlightened parts of the world, there is no such differential treatment left to oppose. Women now have all the freedoms men have, and the fact that they still tend to lead lives different from men's, and to be treated differently, comes only of natural differences which result in their being differently affected by the same circumstances. And furthermore (the argument goes on), there would be even more differentiation than now appears if we could have perfectly natural sphere separation; but this is now prevented by feminists themselves, who, in their anxiety to repudiate the traditional spheres, are exerting on the sexes differential pressures of their own. The sexes are being pushed by feminism, against their nature, towards each other's spheres. Women overloaded with work outside the home on top of their duties to their children and really longing for the active protection of a man, and men bullied into feeling guilty if they cannot adapt to equality and domesticity, are evidence of this. Feminism is now the problem, and when we remove these new feminist pressures on women and men we shall find that the sexes tend of their own accord to the separate spheres that nature always intended.

The most likely feminist response to this kind of argument is simple denial, which is right as long as we are careful about which aspects of it to deny. It cannot reasonably be denied, for instance, that women and men may well, left to themselves and without direct differential treatment, tend towards differences of some sort, even if perhaps too fuzzy round the edges to qualify as spheres. The mere existence of present-day differences cannot in themselves prove that the old differentiating pressures still exist. It may also be true that feminists do sometimes leap too hastily to conclusions about the real natures of the sexes and what situations they ought to occupy, and in their eagerness to break down the original spheres may subject them to new differentiating pressures of their own. But even if both those are true, there still remains the new traditionalist's main claim: that there is no longer any sphere imposition from his own side,[12] and that we should therefore accept as naturally occurring all the differentiation that does exist, and more, if we allow for feminist counterpressures.

The claim that the differentiating pressures that produced the traditional spheres have now gone is an empirical one, and there is a limit to what can be said about it here. But the short answer is that it is simply false.

In the first place, it must not be forgotten that there are vast parts of the world where the position of women is atrocious in law, convention and practice. And Western liberals are not entitled to say that this leaves their own feminist credentials unaffected. There were, for instance, sanctions against South Africa under apartheid; if there are no such sanctions against countries whose women still have the legal status of possessions, and can within law and convention be treated with abominable cruelty by husbands and fathers, that in itself suggests that the subjection of women is still regarded in the supposedly enlightened world as a minor matter, rather than the major human rights issue it actually is.[13]

But quite apart from that, this enlightened world has still a good deal to do within its own borders. Sphere separation of the strong kind exists whenever there is differential treatment of the sexes as such, and an enormous amount of this still goes on. And while it is not to be presumed that any such differentiation must be unjustified, much of it is still of recognizably traditional form, and is likely to be as difficult to justify as the rest of tradition.

First, there are still some laws and formal institutions that make distinctions of a broadly traditional sort along the lines of sex. Some tax and nationality laws and many social security policies are of this kind, and once again the fact that there are fewer of them than formerly does not provide a shred of justification for the ones that still exist. These also shade into semi-official practices which continue the traditions: reluctance to intervene in domestic violence, notorious judicial attitudes to rape, and so on.

Second, many social conventions and expectations are still expressed in terms of explicit sexual differentiation. Men who say they don't like pushy women, teachers who ask for strong boys to move the furniture and boys who say that girls shouldn't be doing science, are all making sexual differentiations in their treatment of the sexes, and mostly of the traditional kind.

Then, as well as all this, there is all the differential treatment that is denied or even unrecognized by its perpetrators. This is inherently difficult to prove, since when two people are treated differently it may be because of any of the differences between them, and when a man is treated differently from a woman this may not be because of their sex. Statistics cannot show, either, that sex is the real differentiator, because if men and women tend to differ in non-sexual respects that will in itself lead to a tendency to differential treatment on other grounds (which is, of course, what the natural spheres theorist is claiming). Nevertheless, systematic experiment can prove that, in spite of all the protests, it is still going on.

For instance, in one experiment groups of young mothers were watched on different occasions as they played with toddlers: first with one in blue dungarees, called Adam, and then with one in a pink frilly dress, called Beth. Adam and Beth were treated and described differently; they were the same child.[14] In another experiment groups of women undergraduates were given articles to read, three by women and three by men, and dealing with fields generally thought of as masculine, feminine and neutral. For half of these groups the articles written by men were attributed to women, and vice versa. 'A general bias against women was found regardless of the field, and even in traditional feminine fields an article was considered more valuable and its author more competent when that author was a man. The bias was strongest in the case of "masculine" fields with a female author.'[15] In both these cases the subjects of the experiment would certainly have claimed to be responding only to what was immediately before them; in both the structure of the experiment shows that they would have been mistaken.

There is also one other significant way in which differential treatment still comes about. Since any half-competent oppressor will try to disguise the bonds that keep a subordinate group in place by claiming that the arrangements are the result of nature rather than contrivance, the idea that women are naturally suited to their subordinate sphere has become one of the most entrenched parts of tradition, remarkably resistant to change (as other research shows) even in the face of overwhelming evidence. This means that even when sex as such is not the ground of differentiation there may still be sex differentiation in practice because of mistaken beliefs about the correlation of sex with non-sexual characteristics, which beliefs are themselves a legacy of the traditional spheres. The spheres linger on in that form too.

These are not minor matters. In addition to all we know about these things, there is a mass of psychological evidence to show that expectation affects not only the assessment of individuals and their performance, but also the performance itself. If a teacher is told that some randomly selected children are high-flyers, that group will do better than it otherwise would have done. (I gather the same is true even when experimenters are told they are dealing with high-flying rats.) If it is generally believed that women are naturally suited to their traditional place, that is enough in itself to account for their having been unable to escape it.

So the reply to the new traditionalist must be, quite simply, that he is wrong. The old differentiating pressures have not gone; the differentiation that remains is not all of the natural kind, and much of it is traditional in form. And if he wants to keep to the principles he now claims to hold, his course is clear. He must join feminists in their determination to root out the remains of tradition, since it stands in the way of his own stated principles.

He will join the movement, if he does, at a difficult time. At least when women were kept in their place by law no one could deny that this was the case, and it was obvious how to change it. But now that we need sophisticated research and experiment to uncover much of the differentiation, everything is much more difficult: it is harder to persuade the unsympathetic that the problem even exists, and nobody knows how to make the changes that are needed. Still, if he really means what he says he should be committed in principle to doing whatever can be done; indeed, he should actually be delighted at the prospect, since until the differentiating pressures have gone he will not be in a position to prove his claims about the naturally occurring spheres.

It would be pleasing to think of the old enemies of feminism in the way these arguments seem to leave them, with strong traditionalists baffled into retreat as they try to construct a coherent justification of the unjustifiable, and neo-traditionalists newly enlisted under feminist colours. Since it is not unheard of for people to persist in irrational and indefensible positions, however, perhaps that may be too much to hope. And in that case feminists must take satisfaction instead in the recognition that as long as this fails to happen, and their opponents persist in either form of tradition without justifications of a quite new kind, traditionalists have themselves been forced into the dependence on unsupported intuition so long said to indicate the inferiority of women, and conceded to feminists the fields of principle and logic.

The Great Gulf
of Feminism

1 · INTRODUCTION

The claim of this paper is that there are going on under the name of feminism two radically unconnected kinds of idea and activity, whose distinctness seems not to be generally recognized, and whose conflation presents a considerable danger to the movement.

On the face of it, the distinction in question sounds so far from unrecognized as hardly to merit comment at all. It is most simply characterized as the difference between the pursuit of sexual equality against the background of prevailing ideals and standards and the challenging of those ideals and standards themselves; and that, as it stands, is probably the most familiar basis of all for classifying the range of opinion in a notoriously diverse movement. According to this view of things, feminism started with the aim of achieving for women the rights and opportunities already available to men; but then, while some feminists continued to think that nothing more was needed, others began to argue that since all the background institutions and norms had themselves been established during millennia of male supremacy they must themselves be permeated by maleness, and that there was a limit to the value of what could be achieved by women's seeking only (as Germaine Greer said) 'equality of opportunity within the status quo; free admission to the world of the ulcer and the coronary'.[1] And so the traditional feminism of equal rights and equal opportunities – often referred to, disparagingly by the unsympathetic, as *liberal* feminism – became regarded by feminists who wanted to go on to the second stage as tinkering with the surface of the problem, and offering women only the illusion of liberation in a world created by men in their own image. The new feminism was seen, by contrast, as *radical*, going beyond the old demands for equal rights by calling into question all patriarchal values.

There is a sense in which the gulf that is the subject of this paper is appropriately understood as dividing the pursuit of equality for women within the status quo from feminist challenges to the status quo itself. Everything depends, however, on how the two sides are interpreted. The analytical structure I want to propose here, and which I think is essential for the proper analysis of feminist issues, starts by sounding familiar enough, but may be unexpected in detail and in its implications.

What I want to argue is this.

First, although the original kind of feminism – the sort whose preoccupation is the equal treatment of the sexes, and which I shall for convenience call traditional or *egalitarian* feminism – has, indeed, been in some recognizable sense liberal, to think of it as essentially liberal is to mistake accident for essence. The traditional, equalizing feminism is best understood as having nothing to do with liberalism.

Second, this kind of feminism has in itself, when taken seriously enough, great radical potential: quite enough to cope with Germaine Greer's concerns, and others of a similar kind. The relatively cautious aims of the early feminists were far more limited than was justified by the principles on which their equalizing arguments implicitly depended, and feminists can push far into the terrain that would normally be thought radical while still pursuing nothing more than equality within the status quo, even where that status quo is broadly liberal.

Third, it is of course possible to become more radical still by going further and rejecting the status quo against which the equalizing is supposed to happen. At this stage, however, the change is not a matter of degree, but of kind.

What is going on here is not a radical extension of egalitarian feminism, pursued by feminists who want a thoroughgoing solution to the problems of patriarchy rather than cosmetic touchings up, but something totally unrelated to it. If particular proposals made at this level are feminist at all, they are so in a quite different sense, *unconnected* with the first. This strand of feminism lies on the other side of the gulf.

And, finally, it is not just that the two sides are unconnected. The unconnectedness might not matter if the two aspects were recognized as distinct; but if they are not (and evidence of their conflation is everywhere), the consequences may be serious. If the second kind is mistakenly thought of as a radical extension of the first, there is a danger that, far from purging feminism of all patriarchal taint, it may have effects that are seriously conservative, tending to entrench significant aspects of the traditional subjection of women, and to undermine what are, by any feminist standards, essential aims of the movement.

The rest of the paper is in four parts. The first argues that the traditional, egalitarian feminism is best understood as having nothing to do with liberalism, and, liberal or not, as having great radical potential in its own right. The second discusses the other kind of feminist activity, for convenience of contrast (but tentatively) referred to as *radical* feminism, and explains why the two are unconnected. The third shows how problems may result from their confusion, and suggests how they may be avoided. The final section is about the implications of these arguments for feminism as a movement.

2 · EGALITARIAN FEMINISM

2.1 · *Feminism and Liberalism*

When feminism as we know it began to develop as a significant movement in the mid nineteenth century, there was a massive structure of laws, institutions and conventions rigidly defining the positions of the sexes, to the conspicuous disadvantage of women. Women were excluded from most areas of education and from most kinds of work that might offer respectability or independence. This left them with hardly any respectable alternatives to marriage, and in marriage they were subject to constraints that systematically placed them in the power of their husbands. And since they had no voice in the making of laws, there was very little they could do about it.

The first aim of feminism therefore was, and still is in many parts of the world, to remove all the laws that imposed specific disadvantages on women, and to that extent bring about equal treatment of the sexes. The next, by a natural extension, was to attack the informal devices – typically discrimination in education and work – which worked as the continuation of law by other means.

Now it is easy to see why the pursuit of this kind of equality attracted the label of liberal feminism. Feminists were demanding for women the rights and opportunities that were increasingly being accepted as the entitlements of men, and which are now thought of as characteristic of liberalism. By the time the scattered protests about the traditional position of women had swelled to a volume that could not be ignored, it was widely accepted that people should not be confined to the positions into which they were born, and that both individuals and society benefited when everyone was free to rise as far as their merits would allow. People, or at least men, were encouraged to fix their eyes on 'removable inequalities': on the example of self-made men, and the vistas of success (supposedly) opening on the road of hard work, sobriety and thrift. And although defenders of the traditional position of women did their best – as defenders of tradition typically do – to justify their convictions in terms of these prevailing principles, it was increasingly clear to all impartial investigators that this simply could not be done. The various devices that kept women in their traditional place were not a *consequence* of liberal principles; they were independent of and even incompatible with them, and gave arbitrary advantages to men at the expense of women. The first aim of feminism was to remove these arbitrary advantages, and in that respect bring about equality in the treatment of the sexes.

Feminists who pursued this line were, therefore, liberal feminists, in the sense that the removal of the anomalous restrictions on women would have the effect of bringing women under the same liberal principles as directed the lives of men. And, as it happened, most of them were probably positively in favour of the prevailing ideals. But when the matter is put in this way it can be seen that the feminist pursuit of equality was quite distinct, in principle, from anything to do with liberalism. Liberalism is a particular political theory, in competition with feudalism, socialism, fascism and all the rest. But any such set of ideals can have superimposed on it, and at odds with it, restrictions that arbitrarily disadvantage one group; and the feminist pursuit of equality, whose aim was the removal of the superimposed restrictions that confined women to their sphere, would have been exactly the same kind of thing if it had occurred against any other background and had aimed at the impartial treatment of women and men by any other set of standards. The moral underpinnings of the campaign for women's equality can be specified without any mention of liberal principles. An objection to arbitrary disadvantage appeals not to any positive principle about how people should be treated and society organized, but only to the minimal, negative idea that the interests of one group's members should not be regarded as intrinsically more important than those of any other's.[2]

A traditional liberal feminist, in other words, should not be thought of as someone whose primary purpose is to get the principles of liberalism properly implemented, and who thinks that if that is done everything will be as it ought to be for women and everyone else. That conflates two quite distinct aims. Rather, she should be thought of as committed to identifying and eliminating the preconceptions about women which potentially interfere with the proper implementation of *any* general principles, and which cumulatively, if not necessarily individually, amount to an arbitrary disadvantaging of women. How different this is from a positive desire to implement liberalism can be seen from the fact that if such a feminist is working against a non-liberal background she will not, *qua* egalitarian feminist, make any attempt to bring liberal principles into being; all she will do is try to bring about the impartial application of whatever principles do prevail. Conversely, if she is working against a background of liberalism she will not, again *qua* egalitarian feminist, be concerned with failures of liberalism in other areas, or with the working out of other kinds of anomaly within liberalism itself.

To put the matter in a helpfully familiar if not entirely accurate way, the traditional feminist campaign can be seen not as anything specifically to do with liberalism, but as against *double standards*.[3] A complaint that standards are double – not impartially applied to both sides – is quite distinct from a complaint that any particular standard is in itself wrong. A campaign to change background political values is quite different from a campaign to get women and men treated according to the same set of values, whatever those are, and it is this that traditional, egalitarian feminism[4] is essentially about.

2.2 · *Radical Equalizing*

When the original kind of feminism is seen in this way, as a movement to dislodge the preconceptions about the position of women that prevent the proper implementation of any general ideals and principles, it is clear that it does not, so far, make any positive recommendations at all about how women should be treated or how society should be organized. The demand for equality, in the sense of the ending of arbitrary privilege, so far entails nothing at all about the ways in which either sex should be treated. Specific political arguments so far take only an *ad hominem* form, directed to anyone who accepts the minimal principle that one group's interests should not be arbitrarily preferred to another's, and whose ideas about the position of women are incompatible with the principles that are appealed to in other contexts. '*Since* these are your principles,' the feminist argument goes, '*this* is what your treatment of women ought to be.' The specific political recommendations of traditional liberal feminists are the consequence of this kind of equalizing against a liberal background.

It may be objected, therefore, that although this way of looking at things does in some technical sense break the connection of traditional feminism with liberalism, it does so only at an absurdly high price, and in a spurious way. If liberal feminism as it is usually understood is regarded by radical feminists as unsatisfactory because it leaves too much of the traditional background intact, the kind of neutral egalitarian feminism described here must seem feebler still because it leaves in place *any* background, even ones that are much less satisfactory than liberalism. And anyway (the objection may continue), there is no point in making this subtle distinction between mere equalizing against a liberal background and positively accepting that background. Egalitarian feminism may be so neutral as to entail nothing positive about the treatment of women, but there is no real difference between a positive endorsement of whatever background is in place and a mere failure to produce a positive alternative. Even if traditional feminists have not actively been pursuing the ideals of liberalism they might just as well have been, since all the policies they have pressed for amount to getting women properly treated by liberal standards. If they do not propose some other standard, therefore, an impartially applied liberalism is just what their efforts will achieve.

Now it is true that if you are seeking equality against a particular background without challenging it you are effectively accepting it. It is also true that it would be more radical to try to change the background as well, since a movement that sets out to make only one kind of change is less radical than one whose aim is to make that and another.[5] The next stage will be to consider the kind of feminism that aims at making both kinds of change. Before that, however, it is worth recognizing how startlingly radical egalitarian feminism can potentially be, even while remaining constrained by broadly liberal ideas.

Suppose, then, we decided to leave our ordinary, prevailing, vaguely liberal and rationalist background intact, and to do nothing but concentrate within that framework on getting rid of the anomalies resulting from preconceptions about the nature and situation of women. What kinds of thing should we need to do? An adequate account of the possibilities here would need a book in itself, but some indication needs to be given for contrast with the second part of this paper. Consider, then, as a relatively simple illustration, the familiar issue of employment, and the liberal principle that any job should go to the person best able to do it.

Here the first aims of egalitarian feminism are familiar and relatively straightforward. It is easy to show that all the traditional arguments for keeping women out of men's territory simply fail in their own terms.[6] The first task, therefore, is to remove the restrictions against women, and allow them to compete on the same terms as men.

But complications quickly set in. If the idea is to make sure any job is done by the most suitable person, it is not enough to remove the formal restrictions; you also need to make sure that informal discrimination in the selection process is not producing the same effect in other ways. That prompts tighter rules to control informal discrimination; but when feminist research suggests, as it quickly does, that there are systematic failures of impartiality of which their perpetrators (and presumably also observers) are quite unaware,[7] it becomes clear that even the most stringent rules are not enough. Research is needed, first into the extent of the unconscious bias that still exists, then into the kinds of mechanism by which it might be counteracted and (a different kind of enquiry) into the moral acceptability and political practicality of whatever strategies look as though they might have some chance of working. And then, eventually, there comes the political task of trying to implement whatever policy is decided on.

This work alone is enough to keep seventy feminists with seventy mops sweeping for seventy years. But even this only scratches the surface, because since working practices developed at a time when women were excluded, there arises the obvious possibility that even with perfectly impartial selection the present arrangements might not be the best ones to achieve what they are supposed to be aiming at (such as productivity in business, to keep the illustration as simple as possible). They are conspicuously ill-adapted for combining with the care of children; they may also, for all we know, be unsuited to women in other ways as well. Perhaps women may tend to produce better results – even given the present aims of employers – by rather different methods from men, which have been systematically overlooked. If so, and if a radical reorganization of work that made things better for women could also produce better results for employers, such a reorganization would itself be justified by the aims of egalitarian feminism, because failure to make the change would amount to benefiting men in a way that ran counter to the principle of getting the work done as well as possible.[8] Once again research and experiment are needed, followed by the moral and political assessment of options for change. But potentially (everything depending on what is turned up by the analysis) egalitarian feminism could provide a justification for change in almost everything we think about the organization and conduct of work, still without going one whit beyond the liberal idea of getting things done as well as possible for the good of all, or the liberal feminist idea that this is certainly failing to happen, to the cost of all and the arbitrary advantage of men.

This is only the roughest of sketches, and of only one small area of feminist concern, but it does suggest something of the radical potential of a thoroughgoing egalitarian feminism against a liberal background. It also shows, incidentally, the need for care in any feminist debate about the need for changes in values and standards, and the adequacy of pursuing equality within the status quo. Although at one level all that has been described goes on within the status quo (a broad liberalism), it also allows for very many changes to social arrangements, values and standards, at what might be called more superficial levels. If it turned out that women tended to achieve better results in work by different methods from men, and those methods had previously been disregarded or denigrated, that would justify changes in the criteria used to assess promising candidates and approaches to problems; if it turned out that under-valued female skills (perhaps in personal relationships, to take a typical feminist example) produced unexpectedly good results of a straightforwardly productive kind, this line of argument would justify their becoming valued. And if such arguments could justify a radical reorganization of working practices, there is a sense in which they would have justified sweeping changes in the status quo. But still in all these cases the argument for change at the relatively superficial levels would itself appeal to deeper values and standards. The claim at each stage would be that beliefs and habits of mind either about the nature and position of women, or which arose during the time of their exclusion, were incomptible with the values and standards appealed to at a deeper level, and worked to the arbitrary disadvantage of women.

Arguments of this kind, potentially defending changes of a far-reaching sort, apply in all other areas of social and intellectual concern. Work may be the most obvious example, but similar problems arise for education and participation in public life. There is also the whole issue of arrangements for relationships between the sexes and the rearing of children, where it takes very little argument to show that the traditional arrangements will not do – they gave arbitrary advantage to men by any standards – but where, even within liberalism, it is not in the least clear what should be put in their place. Then, going beyond questions of political values, there is the wider question of beliefs about the nature and position of women. Once the traditional position of women has been recognized for what it is, it becomes clear that a great many received beliefs must be questioned, since tradition has always tried to hide the devices that keep subordinate groups in their place by fostering the idea that their natures would keep them there anyway. This means that a radical rethinking is needed of large tracts of history and the social sciences, and even, to some extent, biology. And in other parts of academic investigation, special consideration needs to be given to whether the actual or potential contributions of women may have been systematically disregarded for reasons incompatible, at a deep level, with prevailing standards of judgement and rationality. This is still all justified by the feminist pursuit of equal treatment, whose radical potential is again considerable.

How much would be changed by a feminist movement that actually succeeded in achieving equality within any status quo – something we are not in sight of yet – would presumably depend on the status quo at issue; what has been said assumes some kind of liberalism and other familiar standards. But since the traditional separation of the sexes has been so pervasive as to have influenced just about every aspect of life, it seems likely that the attempt to do nothing more than eliminate the traces of arbitrary male privilege will leave hardly any part of life and thought untouched. The feminism that seeks equality within the status quo, properly understood, is as radical as any movement there has ever been.

3 · RADICAL FEMINISM

3.1 · *The Distinction*

Nevertheless, however radical the effects of traditional egalitarian feminism, the fact remains that it will still, *ex hypothesi*, leave the status quo at the deepest level intact, and that any policies that result will still be determined by these deep principles. And if those principles themselves are wrong, feminists may well say, the pursuit of equality for women within them will be useless or worse. What is the point of arguing for equality within liberalism, if you think liberalism itself is wrong? What is the point of showing the implications for attitudes to women of prevailing ideals of scientific enquiry or aesthetic judgement or rationality, if you think they are themselves misguided? The only result will be that everyone is treated wrongly. And so feminists who disapprove of prevailing values at the most fundamental level move to ground more radical still, on which there begin to appear feminist theories about the background itself – feminist ethics, political theory, philosophy, epistemology, science, and all the rest – whose concern is to go beyond the exposure of woman-related anomalies within the present scheme of things and tackle the foundations.

How much of this goes on in feminism it is difficult to say, partly because claims about the need to change values and standards are often ambiguous between levels, and much of what sounds at first like this radical[9] kind of feminism may really be only the egalitarian sort. Many feminist proposals that are sweepingly disruptive of the present state of things may turn out, on the classification proposed here, to be of the traditional, equalizing kind, and justifiable in terms of quite familiar values and standards when these are taken seriously enough.

However, since I am here concerned only to distinguish between different aspects of feminism, and not to make empirical claims about how much of either there is, this does not matter. For the purpose of explaining this classification it is enough to take as illustrations a few cases that seem to be clearly on one side or the other. The following, taken pretty well at random from feminist literature spanning the last fifteen years, seem to represent strong currents of opinion, but nothing here depends on how strong they actually are.

Perhaps the most striking place to start is right at the roots, with logic. Traditional feminist argument makes a good deal of use of perfectly ordinary logic, which differs not at all from the kind (usually) recognized by the opposition. So, for instance, when James Fitzjames Stephen[10] says of his attempted proof that men should be heads of households that it is as clear as a proposition in Euclid, the egalitarian feminist criticism would be not that he was using the wrong kind of logic, but that he simply got the argument wrong. The idea that people who are committed to particular standards of reasoning can nevertheless make mistakes (and motivated mistakes) is a perfectly good part of our intellectual tradition. But some feminists have challenged logic altogether. Dale Spender, for instance, says, 'Women in the movement are increasingly capable of coping with the illogicality of traditional logic and with the ostensible irrationality of holding contrary beliefs to be "true".'[11]

Then there is the area of moral and political theory. The contrast here is illustrated by Alison Jaggar, writing about feminist criticisms of Rawls:

[Okin] has also attacked Rawls's assumption that the parties in the original position will be heads of households, correctly noting that this precludes them from considering the justice of household arrangements. Benhabib has argued that those who reason behind Rawls's veil of ignorance are so ignorant of their own circumstances that they have lost the specific identities characteristic of human agents . . .[12]

This is a good illustration of the divide. It is one thing to argue that Rawls, having put his people behind their veil of ignorance, has drawn the wrong conclusions about the arrangements they would choose. That is a feminist criticism of the egalitarian kind, because the claim is that he could not have come to this conslusion, even given his general premisses, if he had not been overlooking the interests of women. It is quite another to argue that Rawls's whole approach is misguided anyway,[13] which is what Benhabib is claiming when she proposes instead a 'communicative ethic of need interpretations', which '[acknowledges] the differences of concrete others in ways compatible with the contextualist concerns that Gilligan attributes to women who utilize the ethic of care'.[14] This second criticism is of the radical feminist type, as is, for instance, Sara Ruddick's claim, also referred to by Jaggar, that 'a moral standpoint that is distinctively feminist . . . can be found in maternal thinking'.[15]

Then there is the whole area of science. Once again, egalitarian feminism can launch any number of attacks on long-established claims about the nature of the world in general and women in particular. This is the kind of thing Mill did, for instance, in refuting his opponents' claims to know the natures of the sexes by simply pointing out that since women and men had been in systematically different environments since the beginning of history (as everyone knew), no observed differences between them could be confidently attributed to nature.[16] This involved no new theory of knowledge: it was a straightforward consequence of recognized views about scientific method, as caught by his own, eminently sensible, canons of inductive logic. Or, to take at random a more recent case, the introduction to the recent edition of *The Sexual Life of Savages* claims that Malinowski made various mistakes in his interpretation of the Trobrianders' family relationships because of assumptions he had made about the unimportance of women's possessions.[17]

Contrast this with (again more or less at random) Linda Alcoff's and Vrinda Dalmiya's claims[18] that 'traditional epistemology has reduced much of women's knowledge to the status of "old wives" tales', and their conclusion that 'the key factor is traditional epistemology's focus on propositional knowledge' – 'knowing that', as opposed to 'knowing how'. Egalitarian feminism has itself, by appealing to familiar standards of scientific procedure, the potential to argue that particular kinds of knowledge, or claims to knowledge, have been systematically disregarded because of their association with women. This new suggestion is, however, quite different. It is that a particular set of standards for distinguishing knowledge from lesser things is mistaken, and that goes beyond the claim that attitudes to women are unjustified in the terms of the people who profess those attitudes.

Alcoff and Potter also say, while claiming that there is a great diversity of approaches to epistemology within feminism, that 'for feminists, the purpose of epistemology is not only to satisfy intellectual curiosity, but also to contribute to an emancipatory goal: the expansion of democracy in the production of knowledge.'[19] Here, once again, we have the new, radical feminism.

3.2 · Why Feminist?

Now there is much that could be said about feminist theories of these kinds; indefinitely much, in fact, since there are indefinitely many theories in the air. It is therefore important to make clear at the outset that my concern here is a very limited one.

I shall *not* be concerned here either with the (empirical) question of whether prevailing theories are what their feminist opponents say they are, or with that of whether the proposed feminist alternatives are as different as their proponents claim. So I shall not, for instance, be considering whether standard epistemology really cannot cope with 'knowing how', or whether the ethics of care are really so different in principle from anything in Rawls, or how standard Rawls's views are. Nor shall I discuss the merits or demerits of any of these radical feminist theories, which is partly why a very small number of illustrations is adequate for my purposes. Whatever the suspicious reader may think can be inferred from the text about my opinions in these matters, my concern here is not with whether they should be regarded as good or bad, but only with the limited and quite different problem of *where they fit into feminism*. And the immediate problem is of why any of these approaches should be counted as feminist at all.

There is nothing specifically feminist about the areas of enquiry themselves. Enquiries into the problems of ethics, political theory, scientific method, epistemology and even logic go on all the time, and are standard philosophical activities; the search for general criteria to distinguish right from wrong, truth from falsity, or reason from unreason, are interesting in themselves, and to be pursued by anyone who thinks the answers matter. It is sometimes said that they are of feminist concern because women are members of all unjustly treated and misrepresented groups,[20] and therefore have an interest in all questions of justice. But even though this is no doubt true, that makes these matters the concern of feminism only in the way that they are equally the concern of the homeless, or child labourers, or indeed anybody with the potential for suffering injustice. If feminists want women properly treated and thought about (as of course they do) they must want proper attitudes in place to ensure that this happens, but so must everyone who wants anyone properly treated. There is nothing specifically feminist here.

But anyway, it is not just that the *areas of enquiry* are claimed as being of legitimate concern to feminists. If feminists, *qua* feminist, are challenging *particular* positive views about all these matters, the idea must be that there is something unfeminist about the ones they are challenging and something correspondingly feminist about the alternatives being offered. What is it about these proposed answers, then, that is supposed to make them feminist? Or at least, why are certain *kinds* of answer – allowing for controversy within a type – counted as feminist? What is the basis, for instance, of Alcoff's and Potter's claim that feminist epistemology is about the democratization of knowledge? Or of Ruddick's that maternal thinking can provide the basis of a specifically feminist approach to ethics?

There seem to be two main possibilities here, which need to be distinguished and considered separately even if some theories are counted as feminist for both reasons. One is that something may be feminist in virtue of being essentially female in origin; the other is that it may be feminist in virtue of having a feminist justification.

3.3 · *Women's Values*

The first possibility is quite familiar, and clear from some of the examples above. Many of these ideas seem to be regarded as feminist because they are thought of as typical of women, or perhaps of feminist women.

The idea that women have special approaches and special ways of doing things is a recurring theme in feminism. It shows above in Dale Spender's claim[21] about feminists' having discovered that contrary propositions can be true (or rather 'true'), and in Gilligan's and Ruddick's ideas about women's approaches to moral thinking. But it comes up everywhere, and it raises the obvious possibility that some ideas are claimed as feminist because their recommenders think of them as characteristically female.

Is it then appropriate to count particular ideas about ethics, politics, science and the like as feminist just in virtue of their being essentially female? Sometimes feminists say, or imply, not. Alcoff and Potter, for instance, say that they are describing particular epistemological theories as feminist only because it happens to be among feminists that they can typically be found; others, such as Jaggar,[22] say definitely that feminist ethics is not a matter of substituting female for male values. On the other hand, the very fact that this distinction needs to be pointed out and rejected suggests that the usage has to some extent become entrenched.

However, there is no need for my purposes to go into this question – an empirical one about word use – since all that matters for my purposes here is to say something about the consequences *if* the word is used in this way. The most important point is that if this is a possible meaning of 'feminist', it must be recognized as entirely different from the previous one.

The essence of the original, egalitarian feminism, as described here, is the identification and elimination of entrenched ideas about the position and nature of women which have the effect of overriding more general ideas about ethics and rationality, to the arbitrary advantage of men.

This has nothing whatever to do with women's ways of doing or thinking about things. All it needs for its basis is the idea that there is something inherently unjust about arbitrary disadvantaging, where that means, quite specifically, disadvantageous treatment that cannot be justified in terms of whatever general principles the recommender of the treatment accepts in other contexts, and must therefore be seen as benefiting the members of one group at the expense of the other as an end in itself. This kind of feminism can in principle be as effectively pursued by men as by women. Men, though they may not always reliably do so, are capable of identifying the fallacious arguments by which the anomalous treatment of women has traditionally been defended, and exposing the invention of convenient facts. They are also capable of doing the research necessary to find out whether subliminal devaluation of women's abilities is still going on, and whether women tend to use different means from men to pursue the same ends, and whether women and men work better in different kinds of environment. There is also no reason in principle why they should not be as thoroughly involved as women in the politics of bringing about change; indeed, women were so shackled in the early days that political progress had to depend to a large extent on the good will of men. None of this depends on what it feels like to be a woman, or even to be unjustly treated. And, of course, the converse applies; women are quite capable of overlooking or disregarding all these things.

If the word 'feminist' is used to describe certain ideas and attitudes in virtue of their being regarded as distinctively female in kind, therefore, it must be recognized that the word is being used in a quite different sense from the one already identified, according to which a feminist is someone who is trying to eliminate the arbitrary advantages of men.

3.4 · Feminist Justifications

Suppose, then, if only for the sake of argument, that at least some ideas really are feminist in this second sense of being strongly connected with women. Even if that is true, nothing yet follows about whether there is anything to be said in their favour. The claim that some ideas or approaches are distinctively female is, as it stands, technically compatible with the proposition that they are nonsense; and if that were the case, the claim that they were women's would be no more than a restatement of the old familiar conclusion that women (or feminist women) were simply *bad* at all the subjects in question. Taken as they stand, the claim that women in the movement have been making all these discoveries about logic might imply no more than that women could not do logic; the claimed discovery of women's different style of moral reasoning might be – as was indeed asserted until feminists started digging their heels in – proof that women were not fully fledged moral beings; their wanting to have all kinds of previously scorned ideas counted as knowledge might be just one more piece of evidence that women could not distinguish evidence from gossip or science from superstition. In the absence of any reason to abandon existing standards of rationality and ethics, therefore, the implication of some of these claims about women's approaches would just have to be that women were irrational, bad at science, morally confused and all the other things men had been saying for a long time.

A book on feminist ethical theory, or philosophy, or science, or epistemology, is, however, clearly not intended as a compendium of the continuing irrationalities of women, nor even as a neutral statement of facts about them. In being described by feminists as feminist, these ideas and attitudes are obviously being *recommended*; and that raises the next question. If they are being recommended, on what basis is this? Is it supposed to be *on feminist grounds*? Whether or not they are feminist in the sense of being female, can any of the radical feminist ideas be counted as such in virtue of being justifiable by feminist argument: arguments about proper attitudes to women? If so, this would give a different possible reason for counting particular ground-level views, and all their positive higher-level implications, as feminist.

This also seems a familiar feminist idea. Moral, political, epistemological and other ideas are frequently described by feminists as male or patriarchal, apparently with the implication that there is something about them that feminists can, as feminists, legitimately object to. Alison Jaggar,[23] for instance, specifically says that 'feminist approaches to ethics are distinguished by their explicit commitment to rethinking ethics with a view to correcting whatever forms of male bias it may contain.' Statements of this kind make it sound as though some theories are being counted as feminist because they are required for the achievement of proper attitudes to the ideas and interests of women.

Intuitively, this sounds quite promising. All the background ideas that are the object of radical feminist attack made their appearance at a time when men were running everything. If, therefore, women have, even on average, different interests from men's, or different preferences, or different ways of thinking about and doing things, these are more than likely to have been squeezed to the side; and, on the face of it, it seems only right that this state of things should be changed.

However, even though it sounds plausible enough at this level of vagueness, feminists know – or should know – all about the dangers of keeping ideas and arguments in a state of blur, since that is just how the devices by which women were kept in their place managed to remain invisible for so long.[24] Close attention to the details of what was (and is) going on was necessary to expose them, and the same kind of care is needed here too.

If men and women really are systematically different in various ways, it is indeed likely that the background ideas and values of any society will have a considerable influence on how relatively well the sexes do, even without any arbitrary favouring of either (where 'arbitrary', as before, refers specifically to advantages that cannot be justified in terms of general background principles, whatever those are). If men and women have different interests, as their difference of function in the production of children alone makes likely, some kinds of social arrangement are likely to be better for one than the other. If they tend to be good at different things, which sex fares better will depend to some extent on what kinds of thing are valued; if they have different ways of looking at the world or doing things, which is most comfortable will depend partly on the kinds of idea that prevail. The sexes may well have different vested interests in what kinds of values and standards are socially entrenched, and this may make it seem as though the elimination of bias towards the male in prevalent standards is as much a matter of feminist concern as is arbitrary preference of the male within a set of standards.

But this raises the question of what kind of movement feminism is supposed to be; and by this I intend not a sociological question about what the attitudes of women who think of themselves as part of the movement actually are, but rather a question for any individual feminist, about what she thinks of herself and what she is doing.

Now feminism could just be regarded as a self-interested movement: a conspiracy of women to get things more to their personal liking, and planning to push men out of power just because that would be better for women. But if feminism is thought of like that it is of no moral and little intellectual interest, and certainly not entitled to support from people in general. Few, if any, feminists seem to have that view of things. Pursuers of feminist ethics are not moral cynics concerned only with the practical problem of devising the ethical standards that will be best for women, while hoodwinking other people into thinking that there is some more objective reason for following them. The idea of feminist scholarship is not just to invent and entrench whatever standards of knowledge and skill will result in the greatest respect for women. Obviously the idea is that the recommended changes *ought* to happen. Their advocates are motivated by ideas about rightness, justice and the best way of doing things, and think that changes in fundamental

values and standards are necessary for the proper treatment
of women and, for that matter, of everybody and everything
else as well.

If feminism is thought of in this way, however, there is an
immediate logical problem about the idea that radical feminist theories – particular theories of ethics, rationality and all
the rest, which, unlike egalitarian feminism, have positive
implications for the ways we ought to do things – might be
feminist in virtue of having a feminist justification. To give a
feminist justification of some conclusion is presumably to
show that it is required by proper attitudes to women. But
in order to reach such a conclusion you need to appeal to
some criterion that specifies what proper attitudes would
be; and that in turn means that at the most fundamental
levels feminist justifications are impossible. Basic ideas
about values, standards, principles, about both ethics and
rationality, must be in place for a morally motivated feminism to get off the ground at all. You cannot, without flagrant
question begging or a retreat into the politics of self-
interest, to do it the other way round, and say that because
some set of ideas has particular results for women, it must be
wrong.[25]

This is a quite general point. What it implies is that any
argument to positive conclusions about the way women or
anybody should be thought of or treated will turn out, when
pressed, to depend on premisses more fundamental than
feminism.

Suppose, for instance, you have some theory of ethics
you want to criticize *on feminist grounds*. How might you
do it? For the traditional, egalitarian feminist there is in
principle no problem: you try to show that your opponents'
moral view of things is internally wrong, and contains an
unresolved, arbitrary preference for men. This is Okin's
criticism of Rawls. But now suppose you take the idea that
feminism should be attacking the foundations, and move to
the idea that Rawls's whole approach is misguided anyway,
perhaps proposing, like Benhabib, to substitute for it some
version of the ethics of care. (And also supposing that you

can show that the care ethics claims really are different from anything in traditional ethics, which Okin, for one, doubts.[26]) How might your argument go?

That would depend on the precise nature of the theory you were defending. It would make a difference, for instance, whether you were presenting the care ethic as a rival to the other, aimed at supplanting it, or whether perhaps you thought the two should be given equal weight. (This indicates another kind of complexity in ground-level feminist theory.) But suppose for the moment you wanted the care ethic to be given equal weight. How could you justify that? Perhaps by appealing to some relativist idea that people were all entitled to their own moral view, or that different groups' approaches should be treated with equal respect? But in that case such a principle is needed for the feminist conclusion that the two approaches should be given equal weight. That principle must therefore be morally *more fundamental* than the feminist claim about giving equal weight to the ethics of care; and it is *itself* not justifiable by feminist arguments, because the feminist arguments depend on it. (And if a feminist justification of it were to be attempted the same problem would arise.) The feminist conclusion that the ethics of care should be given equal weight would therefore work *only* for someone who was already convinced, on non-feminist grounds, about the fundamental relativist principle. Anyone who rejected that, and as a result the inference to the conclusion about the ethics of care, would therefore be rejecting the conclusion on grounds that had nothing to do with feminism. So any disagreement about whether the ethics of care should be accepted is, ultimately, not a disagreement about attitudes to women, but about the principles that determine attitudes to anything.

That is a hypothetical line of argument (though not, I think, an implausible one), but the principle applies generally. The same problem arises, for instance, with Alison Jaggar's idea that feminism is concerned with the removal of male bias from ethics. There is no difficulty about this as long as we are in the territory of traditional egalitarian feminism: a male bias – an arbitrary preference of men – in many received, higher-level moral standards (of female chastity, for instance) can be exposed by appeal to more fundamental standards. But this is no longer possible when the fundamental standards themselves are at issue. Perhaps it may be claimed that there is bias whenever men's moral values are given more weight than women's. But to regard this as objectionable is to depend implicitly on some further principle such as that everyone's, or all groups', values should be equally regarded, which is itself being treated as a moral principle more fundamental than either men's or women's, and must itself be decided independently of feminist considerations.[27]

The same goes for feminist epistemology. What might be offered in the way of a feminist justification of new approaches to epistemology? The egalitarian feminist can easily argue that many beliefs about women are unjustified by the standards of the people who hold them, or that women's claims to knowledge have been unjustifiably overlooked. But things are very different if it is thought that there are feminist grounds for complaint apart from these, and an attempt is made to produce a feminist argument for different epistemological standards. Suppose, for instance, it is argued that women have kinds of knowledge that are systematically ignored because they are not recognizable by the standards of prevailing epistemology, and that new standards are necessary in order for women's knowledge to be recognized as such. That may look like a feminist argument for a new epistemology, but in fact it presupposes what it is meant to be proving. Unless an epistemology according to which women's knowledge claims are genuine is already assumed, there is no basis for the claim that women have knowledge that present standards ignore. The epistemology is needed to support the first premiss of the argument, and therefore cannot be reached by means of it.

In other words, anyone who wants to provide a feminist justification of some ground level theory is confronted with a dilemma. If the conclusion can be defended by means of an argument about how women should be treated or regarded, that argument must appeal to deeper principles about how people should be treated. The conclusion therefore cannot be a fundamental principle, and the argument in its defence works only *ad hominem* against anyone who already accepts the ground level principles in question. Conversely if it is a ground level principle, it cannot be given a feminist justification that does not either beg the question or make feminism a matter of simple self-interest. There can be no feminist justification of fundamental principles.[28]

There is really nothing mysterious about this. The point is just that if a movement such as feminism is to be based on principle – if it is to be anything more than a group of people bent on getting their own way – it must have the principles in order to get going at all. To the extent that any feminist can make any positive recommendations at all about what should happen (including, incidentally, the positive recommendation of staying within the liberal/rationalist status quo) she must be doing so on grounds that are not themselves feminist;[29] to the extent that she cannot find these, she must be in doubt about the course of feminism. If these ground-level theories of radical feminism are themselves feminist, therefore, they are not so in virtue of having a feminist justification.

4 · THE GULF AND ITS CONSEQUENCES

4.1 · *The Gulf*

That argument has been rather long and involved, and the reason for its having been presented at all may perhaps by now have slipped out of sight. It may help to recapitulate.

The original problem was to establish what might be meant by describing as feminist particular theories about fundamental questions of ethics and rationality, and there seemed to be two possibilities. The first was that they were characteristically female in origin; the second was that they had a feminist justification. What the foregoing arguments have tried to show, however, is that the second of these must be ruled out on logical grounds. If feminism is a morally and rationally motivated movement, it needs principles of ethics and rationality in order to get going at all, and therefore cannot itself provide a justification for such principles. If the positive theories counted as feminist are justified at all, their justification must be general rather than feminist. That means that if they are feminist at all it must be for some quite different reason, and the only candidate seems to be their being in some way characteristically female in origin or nature.

To what extent this argument works as a criticism of current radical feminist theory is difficult to say. It is difficult to say, anyway, how much of feminist theory is radical (in the sense specified earlier) and how much egalitarian, and it is equally difficult to say how many feminists would claim that their radical theories had a feminist justification and how many would be happy to accept the analysis given here. It is often impossible to map on to a new framework what has been said against the background of a quite different one. What has been concluded here is, however, in line with what often seems to be intended by radical feminists. I doubt whether many defenders of care ethics, for instance, would argue that it should be recommended either because women were entitled to have their perspectives respected (irrespective of what those were) or because that would make things better for women; the impression given is that this way of looking at things is regarded as simply *better* than the kinds of ethics regarded as patriarchal.

However, this is not intended as an account of what any feminist would say, but of what the analysis compels. Radical feminist theories cannot have a feminist justification, and therefore the only sense in which they can be feminist seems to be something on the lines of their being characteristic of women.

And here, at last, appears the gulf that is the subject of this paper. Egalitarian feminism, as identified here, is a movement to end the arbitrarily disadvantageous treatment of women against whatever background it occurs. It therefore has a feminist justification, but has nothing to do with women's special approaches to anything: men can in theory be just as good egalitarian feminists as can women. The radical feminism that aims to change the background standards themselves, on the other hand, cannot claim that its positive theories, whatever they are, are feminist in virtue of having a feminist justification. If, therefore, they are feminist at all, it seems that they must be so for the quite different reason that they represent women's ways of doing things.

Put simply but usefully, traditional egalitarian feminism is a movement to achieve what is right *for* women,[30] though its activities need not be carried out *by* them. The feminist aims of the new feminism, in contrast, are not specifically *for* women, but are ones typically pursued *by* them.

The contrast drawn here is not just a linguistic trick or an insignificant curiosity. What the arguments imply is that these two aspects of feminism are not merely different, but *quite unconnected*, and therefore that a commitment to egalitarian feminism in itself implies *nothing whatever* about what positive theories should be accepted about wider questions of ethics and rationality. Particular conclusions at this fundamental level are not radical extensions of egalitarian feminism, and must be defended quite independently. That means that an egalitarian feminist may, *without any jeopardizing of her[31] principles*, completely reject what is said to be – and may even *be* – feminist in the second sense, of being characteristic of women. It is clearly possible in principle to object to the arbitrary disadvantage of women without thinking that the underlying principles we should adopt are ones that happen to be generally accepted by women – if indeed there are any.

It is therefore a mistake to think that women who hold positive epistemological and moral and political views opposed to those claimed as feminist by the new, radical feminism are manifesting the way oppression has got into their souls. If these ideas are patriarchal at all (a highly contentious matter in itself, let it be stressed), they are so only in a sense of patriarchy corresponding to the second kind of feminism: of being characteristic of men rather than women. There is therefore no feminist reason for rejecting them. There is a gulf between two quite different kinds of patriarchy, just as there is between the corresponding kinds of feminism.

4.2 · *The Problems*

So far the claim is just of disconnection between the kind of feminism that demands equality within the status quo, in the specific way explained, and the kind that challenges the status quo as well by offering specifically feminist theories about wider problems of ethics and rationality. But if the two really are so distinct, it may seem hardly worth making a fuss about them. What positive harm can result from their going around under the same umbrella? Everyone knows that feminism is a broad movement; why should it matter if quite distinct elements are embraced by it?

To this the answer is that it would not matter at all if they were reliably recognizable as distinct. Unsurprisingly, however, they are not. The distinction between challenging unequal treatment against a particular background and making positive recommendations about what the background should be is often difficult to see at all, no doubt partly because it is usually hidden in practical politics. As the earlier discussion of traditional, liberal feminism showed, its supporters' political aims would have been exactly the same whether they thought of themselves as pursuing equality for women, or liberalism, or both. If in addition to this the aims on both sides of the divide are indifferently given the label 'feminist' – or one of the correlatives 'male', 'patriarchal', and (a recent charmer) 'phallocentric' – the distinction becomes virtually invisible.

This is not a matter of purely academic interest; it is

potentially dangerous for feminism. If the distinction is not recognized, the radical kind of feminism, far from offering a full-blooded extension of the egalitarian kind, may actually work to undermine it.

I say 'potentially' and 'may' because the purpose of this essay is to recommend an analytic framework without which, I think, the issues cannot be properly understood, and not to give an account of what is going on in practice. What follows should therefore be understood as being about dangers, rather than actual damage. I think, however, that no one sympathetic to the line of argument so far will have any difficulty in recognizing exemplifications of all these possibilities.

The most fundamental danger is that of destroying the foundations which were essential for the launching of egalitarian feminism in the first place. To take the most extreme case here, any feminist who wants to undermine logic, and thinks that (so-called) male ideals of consistency are to be shunned by the enlightened, immediately loses the possibility of sustaining any of the egalitarian feminist *ad hominem* arguments, because they all depend on showing that the traditional position of women cannot be justified in terms of prevailing principles. If inconsistency does not matter, it does not matter that the arguments used for having kept women out of male preserves are incompatible with the criteria used for the selection of men within them, or that the traditional position of women in marriage is incompatible with the principles usually invoked to justify it. Unless inconsistencies of this sort are objectionable there is no such thing as arbitrary disadvantage, and traditional feminists have nothing to complain about. Egalitarian feminism cannot even begin.[32]

Similar problems arise if feminists start adopting, for instance, radically relativistic epistemologies. Most traditional ideas about epistemology allow for distinguishing between claims to knowledge and actual knowledge. They allow, for instance, for our coming to recognize that people may not know what they claim to know, and for our saying instead that what they believed turned out not to be true. This is what feminists of the traditional kind have frequently, and with excellent (standard) reasons, said about many of the patriarchal ideas that have been perpetrated about the nature and place of women. If feminists start to think instead of 'knowledges',[33] in which that distinction is lost, then all the patriarchal nonsense becomes just one knowledge among others. This is a serious matter. An egalitarian feminist, knowing how much of the equalizing work remains to be done, will think it alarming if feminism manoeuvres itself into a position from which it becomes impossible to say that traditional views about women and matters connected with them are quite simply *false*.

Those are particular problems arising from particular kinds of feminist theory, but there are more general ones that arise from counting as feminist any kind of attack on fundamental values and principles. The most important of these is the danger that any feminist emphasis on the need for change at that level may undermine the traditional project of achieving equal treatment, by concealing the extent to which arbitrary disadvantaging is still going on. Claims that the proper treatment of women demands new sets of standards rather implies that what is wrong has been caused by the prevalence of the old ones, and that can only distract attention from the fact that those others were never properly applied to women in the first place.

So, for instance, if feminists say 'male rationality, after all, has been supplying reasons – for centuries – for the oppression of women; why emulate it?'[34], the implication is that prevailing standards of rationality have been a significant cause of women's oppression. Anyone who has (necessarily on non-feminist grounds) reached the conclusion that there is nothing wrong with traditional standards of rationality, might therefore be pardoned for concluding that since other (mistaken) standards were needed to show that women had been oppressed, they were not really oppressed at all. But traditional rationality has not justified the oppression of women. Men have *claimed* that it has, but that is a quite different matter, and it is not difficult to show that most of the arguments that have been doing the rounds for centuries are full of kindergarten mistakes in logic.[35] If instead of exposing these feminists demand new standards of rationality and logic, and make claims about feminist work that is 'quite logical, rational, and true in terms of quite *different criteria*, perspectives, and values than those dominant now'[36] they might just as well wrap them up in pretty paper and send them off to patriarchal man as a birthday present.

Similarly, producing new epistemologies to back up claims that women's knowledge has often been disregarded, or new theories of ethics to show that women's moral reasoning is (at least) as good as men's, makes it easier to overlook the fact that women were not, in the past, failing by traditional, male, standards; they were failing because their way was beset with obstacles that men had put there. If feminists demand new criteria for the recognition and pursuit of knowledge and justice, and imply that this is necessary for a proper view of women, that makes it easier for men to think they were right all along about women's failing by the traditional ones.

Related to this, there is also a danger that this kind of emphasis will tend to confirm conservative views about the nature of women and their differences from men. Defenders of the traditional position of the sexes have always had to claim that women were different from men in most respects in order to account for their occupying such a different position in life; as has already been commented, the most effective way to cover up the devices by which a subject group is kept in its position is to invent characteristics which would result in its being there anyway. To the egalitarian feminist, therefore, it must be a matter of alarm if a strand of feminism seems to claim that women are particularly good at just the kind of thing men have always been delighted to agree that they are good at: new and original forms of logic, a preference for intuition over evidence, and moral attitudes tied to the immediate and personal.

Claiming new values and standards as feminist also lets

men get away with the idea that all the traditional ones are intrinsically theirs, and that women's are different. When the egalitarian feminist sees that men have got somewhere first and have taken the trouble to keep women out, her immediate presumption is that they have found something worth having, and want to keep it to themselves. To retreat into saying that if men have something there must be something wrong with it is to undermine the position of the egalitarian feminist by colluding in men's sequestration of their ill-gotten gains.

Then, finally, there are all the political problems that are bound to arise when distinct issues are regarded as linked. People starting with views about ethics and epistemology that are opposed to the kinds claimed as feminist, and finding themselves in consequence accused of patriarchal attitudes (if male) or having let patriarchy into their souls (if female), may well conclude that since feminism demands the abandonment of these views, feminism must be nonsense. If the gulf is invisible, they will be unaware that there is another kind of feminism, entirely compatible with their views, and will not look far enough into the matter to have any chance of discovering how deeply ingrained and extensive the remaining problems are.

A converse problem arises from the other direction. Women who start by thinking of themselves as feminists may easily take it for granted that all the radical feminist theory must be part of that commitment, especially if it is presented as such by women's studies departments and feminist literature. They may as a result accept ideas which they would have rejected if they had recognized them as distinct and assessed them separately.

Between these, there is also an unhappy group that (rightly) starts from each end independently, and ends with a common disease of our times: the severe cognitive dissonance that comes from feeling it their moral duty to believe what they really find incredible, and to respect what in any other context they would think worthless.[37] They know that feminism is well founded, and as a result give institutional and political support to what they think of as feminism, but which is incompatible with everything else they believe. This may be better for feminism than outright rejection, but it is hardly ideal. When there is tension like this, something, some time, is bound to snap.

5 · THE SOLUTION

5.1 · *Why Egalitarian Feminism is Necessary*

There is one obvious reply to all this that might be made by radical feminists. It does not matter if egalitarian feminism is undermined in this way, because unless the radical ideas are in place egalitarian feminism is useless, and once they are there it is no longer needed.

It is all very well (this argument might go) to claim that trying to change the background and pursuing equality within it are two different things; perhaps they are. But even if this is right, the point is still purely academic. Whatever the theoretical separation of the two elements – even if we agree that the equalizing project is feminist but an attempt to change fundamental values is not – you cannot in practice pursue the first without committing yourself one way or another about the second. It is frequently possible to think separately about things that cannot be separated in practice. You can decide separately what landscape to paint and what medium to paint it in, but you still have to settle for one medium or another, and, whether you give it any thought or not, the one you choose will influence the finished picture. Even if feminism is seen in essentially neutral terms, there-fore, committed only to ending the arbitrary disadvantage of women against whatever background it occurs, in prac-tice all feminists are going to have to decide what policies to pursue. So even if they should not, *qua* feminists, be trying to decide between various theories of ethics, epistemology and the like, nevertheless whenever egalitarian feminists set about their work they will in doing so either have to go against the prevailing values and standards or, by default, endorse them. There is no neutral course.

Furthermore (the argument may continue), if feminists want to put things right for women, there really is no point in going for equality within the status quo. If the status quo at the most fundamental level is wrong, that will only mean that women are treated and assessed in the wrong way, along with everyone else. All feminists should therefore be seeking out the wrongs of present society at the deepest level and trying to put those right, because to do anything else is to acquiesce in them.

And if that is done (the argument may conclude) there is no need to think any further about the old, equality-within-the-status-quo kind of feminism, because if you get the right fundamental values implemented, everything will be all right. Radical feminism supersedes egalitarian feminism, and so may undermine it with impunity.

If this sounds plausible, consider an analogy. Suppose you lived in a country whose laws you regarded as unjust, and which also had a corrupt judiciary. You would want reforms of both, but you would still see them as distinct problems. It would in principle be possible to tackle either on its own, while leaving the other uninfluenced; there would be no reason, a priori, to think that getting rid of one set of problems would bring about any improvement at all in the other. It might, by accident: one set of improvements might be brought about by means that, as it happened, influenced the other too; but there would be no necessary connection, and you would still have to recognize the two problems as distinct in order even to assess how much progress was being made on each front.

Now you might just decide that until the laws themselves changed it would be better not to do anything about the judiciary. The immediate effect of success would be the efficient implementing of the unjust laws, and it might be better, all things considered, to leave things as they were until the laws could be changed as well. That would depend on the circumstances. But on the other hand it would be clear that a successful campaign for a change in the laws could not be a *substitute* for reform of the judicial process, because that would leave the corruption in place, and prevent the proper implementation of the just laws themselves; you would still need a separate programme of judicial reform. And, conversely, *unless* there was positive reason to prefer an unjust to a just implementation of the present bad laws, you might as well start your reform of the judiciary straight away, on the grounds that it would have to be done some time, and – other things equal – the sooner the better.

The point about egalitarian feminism is similar. Of course if you end the arbitrary disadvantages from which women suffer, they will then be treated impartially by prevailing background standards. If you do not like this background, you will not like what results. On the other hand, the unequal treatment is a distinct problem, and one that must be tackled if whatever principles you do favour are to have any chance of being properly implemented when you succeed in persuading people to adopt them.

Perhaps this seems unlikely. Perhaps it seems that a sweeping change of background principles and ideals would automatically bring with it the ending of the anomalous treatment of women. If so, however, it is once again instructive to look back to the early stages of feminism, because one of the most striking things about the situation in the nineteenth century – to us, now – is how *invisible* the anomalies were. Mill showed in great detail how all the arguments for women's traditional position failed, and yet people were still convinced that there must be a justification *because their beliefs about the nature and position of women had a strong, independent existence*. This was why they would go on, as Mill pointed out, 'throwing up fresh intrenchments of argument to repair any breach made in the old.'[38] Like most of us most of the time, they put all their efforts into trying to fit the elements of a familiar but incoherent system together, rather than trying to expose the inconsistencies and deciding which bits had to go.[39] And where this kind of thing is going on, you would not expect a change of background principles

– say, from liberalism to socialism – in itself to get rid of the tendency to treat women anomalously, any more than you would expect the passing of new general laws in itself to eliminate judicial corruption.

This was the point of the claim, at the beginning of this essay, that arbitrarily disadvantageous treatment of women might exist against any background. Having a set of attitudes to women that prevents the proper implementation of whatever background principles you have is a quite distinct fault from having the wrong set of principles, and there is no reason to think that the correcting of either need have any effect on the other. And this is not just a theoretical possibility. One of the remarkable things about the traditional position of women has been its ability to withstand sweeping political change of other kinds. It survived the transition from feudalism to liberalism and to communism virtually intact; it survived the great declarations of the rights of man in the American and French revolutions. At each stage the traditional position of women became newly rationalized in terms of the prevailing principles, because it was independently accepted. Unless the habits of mind whose existence is independent of the background values are clearly recognized for what they are, they will remain invisible; and this is why the traditional, egalitarian feminism cannot be dropped from the agenda.

5.2 · *The Nature of Feminism*

The situation then is this. There is no connection whatever between egalitarian feminism and radical feminism, where those are understood as defined here. Inevitably, however, since the same term is applied to both, they will be seen as connected, and if this happens, egalitarian feminism is likely to be seriously undermined in several ways. But egalitarian feminism is essential; radical feminism, even if its ideas are justified, cannot supersede it. This seems to suggest one obvious conclusion. Egalitarian feminism should be regarded as the whole of feminism, and the recommendation of particular positive theories and values not as part of feminism, but as an entirely separate issue. The gulf should be seen not as running through the middle of feminism, but as marking its boundary.

How outrageous this suggestion will seem I have no idea. It certainly has the consequence that a good deal that now goes on under the name of feminism should be thought of as separate, but on the other hand if the foregoing arguments are right, the case for keeping it within the boundaries should seem rather weak. The idea of counting as part of feminism something that has *no connection whatever* with egalitarian feminism, and *no feminist justification*, sounds highly counterintuitive, and my own suspicion is that most of the impulse to use the term in radical contexts comes from a mistaken belief that these connections and justifications do exist. There is also the problem that if 'feminist' can legitimately imply nothing more than having special connections of some sort with women, there is a serious question about what, if anything, really is in this sense feminist. There are disputes about whether many so-called feminist approaches are really different from aspects of quite standard thinking (knowing how in epistemology, caring in ethics), or whether they do have any special connection with women. All this strengthens the case for the conclusion that the search for positive theories of ethics and rationality should not be counted as part of feminism, or particular conclusions as themselves feminist.

Suppose, then, that this were conceded, and egalitarian feminism accepted as the whole of feminism. Feminist politics would then be seen as limited to the removal of the obstacles in the way of equal treatment, and not, as feminist, concerned with the question of what the background should be against which that equality was to be brought about. The area encompassed by feminist scholarship, though still vast (egalitarian feminism still has a great deal to do) would contract, so that (for instance) there was no more feminist philosophy, but only the application of philosophy to the study of feminist issues; no more feminist science or history or social science, where those are understood as positive theories about how those subjects should proceed, but only the raising of feminist issues within them. What would be lost by taking this view of things?

It seems to me that nothing of any significance would go, but that a good deal would be gained; far more, in fact, than the mere removal of the dangers outlined earlier.

Most importantly, this way of looking at things does not exclude from the movement anyone who would previously have been included. This is one way in which the analysis I have been recommending differs from the more familiar liberal/radical picture described at the beginning of this essay. According to that way of looking at things, you are either the kind of feminist who wants equality within the status quo or the kind that does not, and if you are the first you cannot be the second. But this analysis is different, because the gulf is not between *feminists*; it is between different kinds of feminist idea and argument. All feminists are on this analysis egalitarian feminists, so the splitting off from feminism of certain ideas currently counted as feminist involves no separation of people. Quite the opposite, in fact, because women who reach (*ex hypothesi* on non-feminist grounds) conclusions about ethics and epistemology unlike the ones now claimed as feminist can no longer be regarded as corrupted by patriarchal preconceptions and therefore as less than fully feminist.

This does not in the least imply that feminists, male or female, should stop investigating these issues. They can investigate and reach conclusions about them just as much as before, just as everyone has always been able to, even if not *as* feminists. Furthermore, a good deal of the investigation may still be feminist, even if the issues and conclusions themselves are not. An egalitarian feminist can look at even the most fundamental ideas to see whether woman-connected anomalies may be creeping unobserved into particular formulations of them, or to see whether good ideas and approaches may have been overlooked because they are characteristically female. The only difference is that positive conclusions about which should be accepted, as opposed to negative ones about particular shortcomings, no longer count as feminist.

Furthermore, all these enquiries can go forward with the great advantage of being disentangled from spurious association with egalitarian feminism, which can too easily give by association an undeserved strength to any theory described as feminist. If that connection is broken, impartial assessment is much more likely. And at the same time, egalitarian feminist analyses can go on just as they always did, with a good deal more force and clarity for having shaken off any confused connection with the other issues.

This way of thinking about things does not even make matters more difficult for feminists who believe that women's ways of doing things are on the whole better than men's, and that the world would be a much better place if they prevailed – which I imagine most feminists believe to some extent, whether or not it is part of their official doctrine. It just calls for a redescription of what is going on. It means that the values supporting this conclusion should not be called feminist (because they are not justified by feminist argument), and that the attempt to get them recognized and established is not itself a feminist campaign. On the other hand the campaign to get such values accepted may involve egalitarian feminism, to make sure they are not rejected because of their association with women. And anyone who pursues ideals that are in fact strongly associated with women's approaches and abilities has an additional reason for the pursuit of egalitarian feminist ends, since it will be essential on these grounds alone, and quite independently of anything to do with justice for women, to make sure that women are playing their full part in influencing the course of events.

Nothing is lost entirely by this approach, therefore, and very little is lost even to feminism. And in the meantime, on the positive side, this contraction in the scope of feminism potentially strengthens it considerably as a movement.

Although individuals who are feminists may oppose each other about these other, non-feminist matters, they can still see themselves as united in their feminist aim of trying to remove the beliefs about women and their place that have developed a life of their own, and interfere with the impartial implementation of any standards or values. This means that while some feminists may be hoping for the overthrow of liberalism, they can at the same time happily support liberal feminists in getting liberalism properly applied to women, because *the means of doing so* is the disruption of the traditional ideas about women, which would, if unchecked, go on to disrupt socialism, or for that matter fascism, as well.

And, furthermore, this does also allow for there being such a thing as a feminist who has not reached conclusions about these wider issues at all, and remains agnostic about them. Indeed, I should like to think, given the extreme intractability of moral and political theory and the foundations of epistemology, that there were rather a lot of them; not many people are in a position to have reached firm, reasoned views about such difficult matters. The great advantage of traditional, egalitarian feminism is that although there is an immense amount of it still to be done – in the way of analysis, research and implementation – its moral basis is very simple: nothing more than the idea that there is something wrong with a simple preferring of male over female interests as an end in itself. It means that feminist aims of this kind can be confidently pursued while we are still puzzling about more difficult matters.

This way of thinking about feminism also increases its political power. Because the moral basis of egalitarian feminism is so simple, its aims are less likely to be disputed than are more fully blown political theories. Not many people are going to argue for the arbitrary advantage of men; as, indeed, is shown by the enormous trouble taken to rationalize the position of women, by people who want to maintain it, in terms of more acceptable principles. If the essence of feminism is limited to its egalitarian form no one has any excuse for opposing its principles; and once those are recognized, it becomes relatively straightforward to show how much remains to be done, and to expose the slippery arguments of people who do not want to do it. And even people who are willing to express unconcern about justice for women will find it difficult to defend the continuing existence of *any* kinds of belief and prejudice whose effect is to override whatever values they do profess.[40]

Regarding the egalitarian part as the whole of feminism is politically powerful in another way as well, in making it clear why there is a continuing need for the movement, and why it cannot be subsumed under any other campaign. In particular, it focusses feminism in a way that deflects the persistent attacks of the People people, who keep (rhetorically) wanting to know why we should have a women's movement, rather than a people's movement that would be concerned with everybody. If the nature of egalitarian feminism is properly understood, it is clear that feminism is necessary not because women are of special importance, nor even because you have to start somewhere and this is as good a place as any, but simply because there is a *distinct kind* of injustice suffered by women, which cannot be analysed in terms of any other.[41] General questions of justice, which are relevant to everybody, are not feminist; the problems about the arbitrary treatment of women, however, are separate, and justice will never be achieved until they are recognized and solved on their own.

There is only one thing that is really lost in all this, and that is the idea that the scope of feminism is the putting right of everything. To feminists who see feminism as the essence of their political identity, therefore, and not just one element of it, I suppose this proposed change must seem enormous, and not just one of detail. If so, this is obviously a serious matter. No one bound up with feminism as a name and an ideal, with all its emotional implications, is likely to change happily to the idea that feminism is just one cause among many, let alone whose importance among those many is as open to debate as any other matter of political priorities.

This does matter, very much, because feelings and attachments always do matter.[42] Nevertheless, it must be admitted that this is just what this argument has been about. My own perception is that the view of feminism presented here makes very little difference to its substance, and that most radical feminist ideas could, with virtually no loss, be translated into these terms. On the other hand, the implications for large parts of feminist literature, and for the feel of the movement and the emotions behind it, may be considerable.

My hope must be that, if all these arguments are right, the recognition of how much feminism has to gain through this different perception of what it is may itself change those feelings.

Notes

Introduction to the First Edition
1 Perhaps it should be noted at this point that towards the end of writing this book, as a result of discussions with my City University class, I had to go through the whole manuscript removing supposedly neutral uses of 'he' and 'man' from the text. I used to think feminists were making a fuss about nothing on this subject, but they are not. It seems to be clearly demonstrable that: (a) (a philosophical point) the use of 'man', 'he' and the like are not sexually neutral at all (see Janice Moulton, 'The Myth of the Neutral Man' in *Feminism and Philosophy*, eds Vetterling-Braggin, Elliston and English); and (b) (a psychological point) the common use of these male words does influence people's unconscious attitudes to women. (I am grateful to Tany Alexander for providing me with evidence on this subject.) It is extremely difficult to make the necessary paraphrases without spoiling style. I think I agree that we should get used to using 'they' as a singular word (Jane Austen does it, so it must be stylistically all right), but I have yet to steel myself to it.

Chapter 1   The Fruits of Unreason
1 Reprinted in *Sisterhood is Powerful*, ed. Morgan, p. 583. Only brief references to sources will be made in the footnotes: full details of the books referred to will be found in the bibliography.
2 Ibid., p. 601.
3 This is meant as a logical, rather than chronological account. In practice women may well be concerned about justice for women before they ever get round to thinking about justice in general. As a matter of logic, however, concern for justice for

a particular group must derive from general principles of justice.

4 Of course you might, en route, decide that your original principles of justice were mistaken, and have to change them. But then the oppression of women would have to be re-established according to these new principles: still the advantage of women could not be taken as the criterion for justice.

5 There is nothing wrong with putting forward theories which go beyond the evidence; it is absolutely essential that one should. Furthermore, it is a commonly held view in modern philosophy of science that science cannot progress except by presuming theories to be true and seeing what the consequences of making that presumption are. Feminists are quite entitled to see how far they can get by using particular theories about women. But although it is reasonable to try to explain away evidence which conflicts with the theory, it is not generally reasonable to ignore it altogether.

6 I owe this example to Professor J. N. W. Watkins, who drew my attention to his review in *The Times Literary Supplement*, 4 February 1977, of *The Radicalization of Science*, eds Hilary and Steven Rose. The suggestion about rejecting cloning comes from an article in that book by Hilary Rose and Jalna Hammer.

7 It is just as well that the search for the truly female and the determination to eradicate the male has to be given up for these reasons, because feminists can tie themselves in knots while trying to work out which is which. By the time it has been established that most of the ways in which women think and act are the result of male influence, and feminists have alarmed themselves with the recognition that even their evolution must have been seriously affected by men's choice of mates, it begins to look as though the only way to eliminate all traces of the male is to annihilate all women as well.

8 In *Sisterhood is Powerful*, ed. Morgan, p. 379.

9 Greer, *The Female Eunuch*, pp. 108–9.

10 Rowbotham, *Woman's Consciousness, Man's World*, p. 16.

11 In *Sisterhood is Powerful*, ed. Morgan, p. 379.

12 Rowbotham, *Women, Resistance and Revolution*, p. 12.

13 Quoted in Elizabeth Gould Davis, *The First Sex*, p. 315.

14 Beauvoir, *The Second Sex*, p. 201.

15 Greer, *The Female Eunuch*, p. 109.
16 Ibid.
17 *Sisterhood is Powerful*, ed. Morgan, p. xx.
18 From Rowbotham, *Woman's Consciousness, Man's World*, p. 16.
19 In *Sisterhood is Powerful*, ed. Morgan, p. 584.
20 Beauvoir, *The Second Sex*, p. 344.
21 *The Rights and Wrongs of Women*, eds Mitchell and Oakley, p. 11.
22 Beauvoir, *The Second Sex*, pp. 347–8.

Chapter 2 The Proper Place of Nature

1 Beauvoir, *The Second Sex*, p. 109.
2 Ibid., p. 333.
3 See above, p. 34.
4 See Alice Rossi, *The Feminist Papers*, p. 293.
5 See Steven Goldberg, *Male Dominance: The Inevitability of Patriarchy*. I am grateful to Bernadette Hill for bringing this subject to my attention.
6 Mill, 'The Subjection of Women', p. 203 of *The Feminist Papers*, ed. Rossi.
7 Millett, *Sexual Politics*, p. 133.
8 Mill, 'The Subjection of Women', p. 200.
9 Mill, 'On Nature', p. 371 of *The Essential Works of John Stuart Mill*, ed. Lerner.
10 Mitchell, *Woman's Estate*, p. 58.
11 Firestone, *The Dialectic of Sex*, p. 10.
12 Greer, *The Female Eunuch*, p. 29.
13 Mill, 'The Subjection of Women', p. 203.
14 Hume, *A Treatise of Human Nature*, pp. 473–6; Mill, 'On Nature'; one of his 'Three Essays on Religion', in *The Essential Works of John Stuart Mill*, ed. Lerner, pp. 367 ff.; Moore, *Principia Ethica*, pp. 41 ff.
15 Mill, 'On Nature', p. 370.
16 Ibid., p. 376.
17 Ibid., p. 377.

18 Ibid., p. 381.

19 Hume, *A Treatise of Human Nature*, p. 475.

20 Passmore, 'Attitudes to Nature', pp. 251 ff. in *Nature and Conduct*, ed. Peters.

21 Ibid., p. 252.

22 Popper, *The Open Society and its Enemies*, vol. 1, p. 60.

23 Friedan, *The Feminine Mystique*, p. 77.

24 Mill, 'On Nature', p. 378.

25 It may seem from this that we can justify keeping to the natural where the natural is the normal, because that at least is thought to be safe. Mill said that at one time each innovation 'was doubtless made with fear and trembling until experience had shown that it could be ventured on without drawing down the vengeance of the gods' (ibid., p. 377), and although we may not literally think that now, we still are wary of the 'unnaturalness' of putting women on the pill, or seeding rain clouds, or testing nuclear weapons, because we are unsure about the long-term consequences. This shows, however, only that we are right to be *wary* of the unnatural in this sense; it does not show that it is necessarily bad. If it were, we could never be justified in experimenting with any innovations.

26 As a matter of interest, try applying this analysis to the propaganda about natural foods and natural medicines.

27 Again, see how this analysis works on the subject of natural childbirth.

28 Austin, *Sense and Sensibilia*, Chapter 7.

29 Hall, 'Excluders', from *Analysis*, 20 (1959), reprinted in *Philosophy and Ordinary Language*, ed. Caton.

30 Millett, *Sexual Politics*, p. 132.

31 Mill, 'On Nature', p. 378.

Chapter 3   Enquiries for Liberators

 1 The words will be treated as synonymous throughout.

 2 James Thurber, 'The Bears and the Monkeys' in *Further Fables for Our Time*.

 3 Berlin, 'Two Concepts of Liberty' in Berlin, *Four Essays on Liberty*, p. 125.

 4 Almost invariably other people, rather than things, because

complaints about limitations on freedom are the subject of moral indignation, and blame is a thing which can be levelled only at morally responsible beings. That is why we complain about lack of freedom, but not generally about lack of power. As Rousseau said, 'The nature of things does not madden us; only ill-will does' (quoted ibid., p. 123).

5 Ibid., p. 122.

6 Decter, *The New Chastity*, p. 51.

7 Rowbotham, *Woman's Consciousness, Man's World*, pp. 75–6.

8 Mill, 'On Liberty', in *The Essential Works of John Stuart Mill*, ed. Lerner, p. 263.

9 'No More Miss America!' in *Sisterhood is Powerful*, ed. Morgan, p. 584.

10 Quoted Firestone, *The Dialectic of Sex*, p. 20.

11 More accurately, of course, *more* or *less* conditioned, and in certain ways rather than just in general. Throughout arguments of this sort it must not be forgotten that freedom is a matter of degree.

12 Greer, *The Female Eunuch*, p. 309.

13 One situation in which disagreement would arise would be, for instance, on the subject of whether it would be worthwhile to bring new people into the world or not. Someone who wanted freedom and the absence of suffering would say that it was worthwhile to bring new people into the world only because they were wanted by people who already existed. Someone who wanted to maximize happiness would say that it was worthwhile to bring new people into the world, as long as they would be happy, without depending on the wishes of people already in existence. See, e.g., Glover, *Causing Death and Saving Lives*, p. 69.

Chapter 4   Sexual Justice

1 Strictly speaking, it is the question of *distributive* justice, as opposed to *retributive* justice, which is concerned with desert, reward and punishment. I think that questions of retributive justice actually reduce to questions of distributive justice, but that is controversial and fortunately not relevant here. 'Justice' and 'fairness' will be treated as synonymous throughout.

2 This does not mean that to act with substantial justice is to act

all the time according to the laws you think there ought to be. Allowance has to be made for the fact that people take into consideration the laws as they are, even though they may be unjust.

3 Rawls, *A Theory of Justice*, p. 60 *et passim*.

4 For instance, Rawls's criterion applies to the distribution of what he calls primary social goods, rather than to well-being. Also he does not make it clear whether he would allow inequalities *only if they increased the well-being of the worst off* or whether he would allow them *as long as they did not harm the worst off*. I suspect he inclines to the first of these two. The principles of justice suggested here, however, entail the second, since there is no justification for making one group less well off than it might be unless doing that would actually increase the well-being of a group which was worse off.

5 Rawls, *A Theory of Justice*, p. 99. I think this account of things is actually wrong: according to the difference principle the relative positions of men and women cannot be determined by looking at the positions only of the groups of men and women. The position of the worst off group of all (which might be, say, low-paid manual workers) is the criterion. It is *possible* that making women's average position *worse* in comparison with men's average position could increase the well-being of the worst off group of all, and so achieve greater social justice. However, I shall have to ignore this for the purpose of simplicity in the discussion.

6 See Rowbotham, *Woman's Consciousness, Man's World*, p. 95 for an account of one incident concerning women and buses.

7 Mill, 'The Subjection of Women' in *The Feminist Papers* ed. Rossi, pp. 214 ff. *et passim*.

8 Ibid., pp. 205–6.

9 This point needs one qualification. The point is that no society can ever, in justice, have a policy of irrelevantly leaving out any group from the competition for desirable places in society: to do so is tantamount to *declaring* that the social structures are unjust. However, an individual who thinks that the structures of society are unfair to one sex or the other may decide to go against the rules; that is, may decide to practise (say) some surreptitious reverse discrimination. That may be all right, in the way that overt reverse discrimination may be all right (see

the next section). What is not all right is to build selection discrimination into any rules, or to practise it surreptitiously if you think the rules are just.

10 Rawls, *A Theory of Justice*, p. 60 *et passim*.

11 Defined as the things people may reasonably be presumed to want whatever else they want. Rawls, *A Theory of Justice*, pp. 62, 92 *et passim*.

12 One way of looking at this, for people who are familiar with Rawls, is to bear in mind that the people in the initial assembly would be ignorant of *when* they would be born, as well as everything else.

13 The only justification for making the worst off now worse off would be to prevent future generations being worse off still.

14 Nozick, *Anarchy, State and Utopia*, pp. 169–72.

15 In a lecture to the Minority Rights Group, London, 1977.

Chapter 5   The Feminist and the Feminine

1 From Elinor Rice Hays, *Morning Star, A Biography of Lucy Stone*, New York 1969, p. 83. Quoted Friedan, *The Feminine Mystique*, p. 79.

2 See, e.g., Shulamith Firestone, *The Dialectic of Sex*, p. 11.

3 Millett, *Sexual Politics*, p. 132.

4 Simons, *Sex and Superstition*, p. 30.

5 Millett, *Sexual Politics*, p. 133.

6 Marks, 'Femininity in the Classroom', in *The Rights and Wrongs of Women*, eds Mitchell and Oakley, p. 183.

7 Paternity was a late human discovery. See, e.g., Gould Davis, *The First Sex*, p. 87.

8 See, e.g., Mead, *Male and Female*, p. 157.

9 See Gould Davis, *The First Sex*, p. 37, Mead, *Male and Female*, p. 81 and *passim*; see index under 'initiation ceremonies'.

10 Bruno Bettelheim, 'The Commitment Required of a Woman Entering a Scientific Profession in Present Day American Society'. Quoted Weisstein in ' "Kinde, Kuche, Kirche" as Scientific Law: Psychology Constructs the Female' in *Sisterhood is Powerful*, ed. Morgan, p. 229.

11 Friedan, *The Feminine Mystique*, p. 38.

12 This happens even within traditional ideas of femininity. There

was once a very sad letter from a woman to an advice columnist, saying that she had always dressed as her husband said she should, and gone without make up because he did not like it, and now her glamorous, painted cousin had appeared on the scene he was discontented with her dowdiness. Men who think they are in favour of natural beauty and disapprove strongly of paint in their wives and daughters nevertheless do usually admire impressive women whose beauty is far from natural.

13 Beauvoir, *The Second Sex*, p. 336.

Chapter 6 Woman's Work

1 Mead, *Male and Female*, p. 157.

2 Korda, *Male Chauvinism*, p. 122.

3 Mead, *Male and Female*, p. 102.

4 In *Woman*, but too long ago for me to be able to track down which issue.

5 Blackstone, 'The Education of Girls Today', in *The Rights and Wrongs of Women*, eds Mitchell and Oakley, p. 201.

6 See Millett, *Sexual Politics*, p. 146.

7 Piercy, 'The Grand Coolie Damn', in *Sisterhood is Powerful*, ed. Morgan, p. 476.

8 Friedan, *The Feminine Mystique*, pp. 36–7.

9 Ibid., p. 37.

10 Ibid., p. 54.

11 Meade, *Bitching*, p. 152.

12 The same line of argument has of course been used to keep many oppressed groups, and not just women, in their subservient position. No ruling class likes presumption in its servants, and any attempt to go beyond the confines of prescribed duty (even to do what is good) is morally objectionable.

13 Mill, 'The Subjection of Women'. Quoted in 'Verbal Karate', in *Sisterhood is Powerful*, ed. Morgan, p. 632.

14 Greer, *The Female Eunuch*, p. 115.

15 Mead, *Male and Female*, p. 158.

16 Beauvoir, *The Second Sex*, p. 147.

Chapter 7 The Unadorned Feminist

1 'No More Miss America!' in *Sisterhood is Powerful*, ed. Morgan, p. 585.

2 Beauvoir, *The Second Sex*, p. 109.

3 Greer, *The Female Eunuch*, p. 59.

4 I owe the essence of this illustration to Bernadette Hill.

5 These are all quotations from feminists, collected by Carol Lee.

6 The arguments to come in this section apply only to situations in which the beloved is chosen. They do not apply to love between relations, or to long-entrenched love between people whose qualities have changed to some extent since the relationship was formed.

7 In *Patience*, the Gilbert and Sullivan opera.

8 See Charlotte Bonny Cohen, ' "Chung-kuo Fu Nu" Women of China', in *Sisterhood is Powerful*, ed. Morgan, p. 461 *et passim*.

9 Incidentally, the idea that self-denial is good in itself is probably as good an example as one could find of a *conditioned response*. People learn to give things up as a means to an end, but get so used to the idea that giving things up is virtuous that they begin to feel they ought to do it anyway, and have guilt feelings about enjoying themselves.

10 There are various horror stories of unsympathetic surgeons dismissing such worries as 'just vanity'.

11 I owe this piece of information to Ted Honderich.

12 Zoe Moss, 'It Hurts to be Alive and Obsolete: The Ageing Woman', in *Sisterhood is Powerful*, ed. Morgan, p. 188.

13 Another of the feminist comments collected by Carol Lee (see n. 5) was 'A woman who dresses up to get a man is using false pretences.'

14 This was also recorded by Carol Lee.

15 Greer, *The Female Eunuch*, p. 261.

16 They are implied to be of opposite sex only because of the analogy to be drawn with sexual relationships, and for no other reason.

17 Millett, *The Prostitution Papers*, p. 36.

18 A fascinating account of Christian asceticism, particularly as it related to women, is to be found in Marina Warner's *Alone of*

All Her Sex: The Myth and the Cult of the Virgin Mary. See, for instance, Chapters 4 and 5.

19 Millet, *The Prostitution Papers*, p. 21.

20 In *Sisterhood is Powerful*, ed. Morgan, p. 584. ·

Chapter 8 Society and the Fertile Woman

1 If, for instance, someone says that abortion is out of the question because the Bible says so, the first question to be asked is why one should take any notice of the Bible. That is obviously not a question to be tackled in a book on feminism. Since I can see no good reason to accept any claims of people to have direct knowledge of the will of God, any such arguments must be left out of the discussion.

2 Millett, *Sexual Politics*, p. 224.

3 Ibid., pp. 226–7.

4 Lucinda Cisler, 'Unfinished Business: Birth Control and Women's Liberation', in *Sisterhood is Powerful*, ed. Morgan, p. 319. In spite of this small criticism, this is a very good and important factual study of birth control.

5 There is a difference between *arguments* and *evidence*. Of course small pieces of evidence, none very significant on its own, can accumulate to support an impressive conclusion. A collection of bad arguments to a particular conclusion, however, are as useless cumulatively as they are individually.

6 Betsy Stone, 'Women and Political Power', in *Feminism and Socialism*, ed. Jenness, p. 35.

7 This is of course a very sketchy justification. One reason for not giving it more fully, apart from considerations of space, is that there is a very good defence of abortion, along similar lines, in Jonathan Glover's *Causing Death and Saving Lives*, an easily available and very readable book.

8 For the record, this is what I thought before looking into the matter more carefully.

9 See Mary Gordon, 'The Predicament', in the *New York Review of Books*, 20 July 1978, and the two books reviewed there: Linda Bird Francke, *The Ambivalence of Abortion* (Random House) and James C. Mohr, *Abortion in America: The Origins and Evolution of National Policy* (Oxford University Press).

10 This is *not* to say that it is impossible to find a consistent set of

principles which would dictate that you should attack burglars and avoid the draft. It is only being argued that these principles *as they stand* are inconsistent, and do not dictate which action should be taken.

11 Of course even if someone had a consistent set of principles, that would not prove that the *motives* behind any actions were what they appeared to be. You may be able to find a consistent set of good principles to hide very bad motives. However, that is not a thing which can be proved by arguments about consistency.

12 Beauvoir, *The Second Sex*, p. 222. This chapter is very good generally on the subject of abortion.

13 This is a technique for evacuating the lining and contents of the uterus by gentle suction. It can be used just to get periods over quickly, but will produce abortion for up to about eighteen days after a missed period. I am grateful to Betzy Dinesen for most of my information on this subject.

14 Most arguments about abortion concern such matters as whether the unborn child is a person, and whether abortion is therefore murder. Questions like these have nothing to do with justice for women, and are therefore not feminist questions.

15 Simone de Beauvoir (*The Second Sex*, p. 226) comments on the deliberate withholding of anaesthetics during abortions, for which there could be no other reason than a wish to punish. This may no longer be official policy, but it still seems to happen. One of the contributors to Marion Meade's *Bitching* (p. 96) describes an abortion where she was told, with no reason given, that she could not have an anaesthetic, and then told when she was screaming with pain 'You're getting just what you deserve' and 'Remember this next time you fuck.'

16 Haemophilia is connected with the X chromosome, and the disease exists when the individual has no unaffected X chromosome. Since a male has only one X chromosome, if that is affected he has haemophilia. The female, however, has two, and if only one of them is affected she will not have the disease, though she will be a carrier unless both are clear. It is almost impossible for both the female's X chromosomes to be affected.

17 This argument would probably be rejected by people who accept what is known as the doctrine of Double Effect. An

account of this, and objections to it, can be found in Jonathan Glover, *Causing Death and Saving Lives*.

18 This all reinforces the empirical evidence to suggest that much of the present restriction on abortion has its real origins in the wish of the medical profession to have as much power as possible in its hands.

19 The acceptability of such a view can best be estimated by looking at some of its consequences for abortion and infanticide. These things seem to follow:

1 Infanticide of normal infants is not acceptable; the mother's main suffering has passed after the time of birth, and if she does not want the child it should be adopted.

2 A mentally subnormal child is (on the autonomy and complexity view) consistently less valuable than a normal one of the same age, and therefore can be sacrificed later to prevent a comparable degree of suffering. Given that a mentally abnormal person may cause suffering to others, as well as being of lesser intrinsic value than normal people, this could allow for infanticide in cases of mental abnormality.

3 A physically, but not mentally, deformed child would have the same intrinsic value as a normal one, but could be sacrificed at a later stage because the potential suffering its life would be likely to cause would be greater; suffering to the child as well as others.

The principles underlying this, by the way, are unaffected by arguments that the degree of suffering and so on has been miscalculated here. If, for instance, someone argues that mentally abnormal children do not cause suffering, then that alters the practical judgment about the circumstances in which it should be sacrificed, but not the principles (of value and suffering) which underlie that judgment.

20 Lucinda Cisler, 'Unfinished Business: Birth Control and Women's Liberation', in *Sisterhood is Powerful*, ed. Morgan, p. 292.

Chapter 9   Society and the Mother
1 See Decter, *The New Chastity*, p. 159.
2 Firestone, *The Dialectic of Sex*, p. 12.
3 There are various possible forms of option-closing. Chapter 4 mentioned the excluding of women from work they would

otherwise choose to do; Chapter 8 mentioned withholding birth control to close the sex-with-no-children option. Deliberate option closing is defined by its having social cost, as explained in Chapter 4.

4 In theory arguments of this sort should settle all pay comparability problems. *In a state of justice* market forces could be left to settle everything: people would not do unpleasant jobs unless they were properly paid, and if people flocked to other jobs it would prove they were rewarding in themselves and did not need high pay. At present, of course, people can get attractive jobs, sit on them, and pretend that they are so unpleasant, demanding or whatever that they deserve higher pay.

5 Into this category, too, might come a general argument for state support of poor families who could not afford children, on the grounds that everyone ought to be able to have something so important, and poverty should not be allowed to stop them. But in a socially just society, where money was properly distributed, this would not apply. People should be able to choose what to spend their money on, and the state should not decide which desires are 'important' and to be subsidized.

6 See, for example, Firestone, *The Dialectic of Sex*, Chapter 4.

7 Ibid., p. 233.

Chapter 10   The Unpersuaded

1 Mill, 'The Subjection of Women', in *The Feminist Papers*, ed. Rossi, p. 209.

2 Morgan, *Sisterhood is Powerful*, p. xxxix.

3 Ibid., p. 599.

4 Firestone, *The Dialectic of Sex*, p. 42.

5 Ibid., p. 119.

6 Gould Davis, *The First Sex*, p. 336.

7 I am grateful to Peter Alexander for this story, and for other valuable accounts of feminism in practice.

8 See, e.g., Gould Davis, *The First Sex*, p. 336.

9 Greer, *The Female Eunuch*, p. 283.

10 Beauvoir, *The Second Sex*, p. 462.

Appendix 1   Traditional Spheres and Traditionalist Logic

1 This essay is a considerably revised version of 'Separate
   Spheres', which appeared in *Applied Ethics*, ed. Singer, and
   which itself made use of material that appeared, *passim*, in *The
   Sceptical Feminist*. This version was written for *Empirical
   Logic and Public Debate: Essays in Honour of Else M. Barth*,
   eds Krabbe, Dalitz and Smit, pp. 319-38.

2 John Ruskin, *Sesame and Lilies*, 'Of Queen's Gardens' (1865).

3 This has lately (1993) been in evidence in the debate about
   women priests in the Anglican church.

4 This point is discussed in the following article, p. 414f.

5 This last point is important, and inadequately stressed in the
   text. The analysis presented in this paper tries to show that it is
   difficult, and probably impossible, to provide a coherent
   defence of the kind of differential treatment of the sexes (strong
   sphere separation) that has been found in most societies – what
   I am calling here the *traditional* spheres. What is *not* claimed is
   that *any* differential treatment of the sexes as such (any strong
   sphere separation) must be wrong. That is claimed in Chapter
   5, where it is argued that all direct differential pressures must
   be wrong, but I now think it is a mistake.

   This essay draws a contrast between weak, or naturally
   occurring, spheres, and strong, or imposed, spheres, and in
   places gives the impression that the weak variety have been
   shown to be acceptable in principle and the strong unacceptable. That is not the case. I am meaning to claim only that
   strong spheres *of the traditional form* seem impossible to
   justify. That leaves open the question of whether other kinds
   of direct differential treatment of the sexes as such might be
   morally acceptable, but leaves plenty for feminists to be getting
   on with anyway.

6 Mill, *The Subjection of Women*, p. 2. Several of the arguments
   in this paper are to be found, in rather different forms, in Mill's
   essay.

7 Ibid., p. 49.

8 It may be objected that this is not true, and that there is
   reciprocity in difference here too, since men have the natural
   advantage of being able to engender children without being
   landed with pregnancy, nursing and child care. This is quite
   true, and it is arguable that this is a very considerable advantage
   (see for instance Dawkins, *The Selfish Gene*, OUP, Oxford,

1976, Chapter 9). However, it is not relevant in this context because the question is not about which sex it is preferable to be, but about attributes either sex might have that the other could actually want. Women might want men for strength or intelligence, if men had those to a greater degree than women, because people close to the possessors of such attributes can benefit from them; but women cannot attach themselves to men in the hope of sharing their ability to spread their genes with impunity. There can surely be no real doubt that, historically, overwhelmingly the most important difference between the sexes was that women could produce children and men could not.

9 As with the efficiency argument discussed earlier, you would need premises to the effect that (a) it was established beyond reasonable doubt that this was better for women but that (b) women were so universally misguided that, in spite of its having been established beyond doubt, they could not recognize the fact. And if you were using this in support of the conclusion, you would need positive evidence for its being true, not just the logical possibility that it might be.

10 Hume does give essentially this argument for 'the modesty and chastity which belong to the fair sex' (*Treatise of Human Nature*, p. 570); but supports it with the value claim that it is not right to expect a man to support children that are not his. That sounds as though it derives from perfectly familiar ideas about justice, rather than the simple advantage of men, but there are problems about it. One is that there is much more to the sphere separation than just this identification. If nothing more than this were at issue it would not matter if women chose to go and have children on their own, but this was made difficult both negatively (depriving them of most other means of life) and positively (severe social penalties if they lived independently of men without forgoing the having of children). The arrangements amount to a male *taking over* of women's special ability. Furthermore, even if Hume's argument did completely account for them, it is difficult to see why the same principles of justice should not equally demand that men should support any children they fathered, and result in the kinds of arrangement described at the end of section 4, above.

11 I am not, by the way, denying that there might be something to be said for men's having some territory of their own, and for

something like this reason; I am increasingly under the impression that this matter of men's feeling redundant might be extremely serious. What is out of the question, however, is that they should keep anything resembling their *traditional* territory. See note 5, above.

12 It should be emphasized that none of these arguments is meant to imply that the continued existence of the imposed spheres is a simple result of male power over women. They are perpetuated by deeply entrenched conventions and beliefs, which are followed and held to a large extent by women as well as men. To understand the traditional subjection of women in this way is to recognize that there is no need to claim that individual men treat individual women badly.

13 See e.g., *Amnesty*, 59, Jan./Feb. 1993, Amnesty International British Section, London.

14 A. Lake (1975), 'Are We Born into Our Sex Roles or Programmed into Them?', *Woman's Day*, January 1975, pp. 24–5, quoted in Oakley, *Subject Women*, p. 96.

15 P. Goldberg (1968), 'Are Women Prejudiced Against Women?' *Transaction*, 5, no. 5, pp. 28–30, quoted in Oakley, *Subject Women*, p. 126.

Appendix 2 The Great Gulf of Feminism

1 Greer, *The Female Eunuch*, p. 296.

2 It may be argued that this is itself a specifically liberal principle, and if so I have no interest in disputing the matter. It is still quite distinct from the rest of liberalism, and can be held by someone who rejects the rest.

3 This is potentially misleading, because 'double standards' can mean different things. Here I mean specifically what has just been described: differential treatment that is anomalous in the sense of not being justifiable in terms of general principles otherwise prevalent.

4 I shall be using the term 'egalitarian feminism' technically, to refer only to the position described here, and not to imply any other kinds of egalitarianism. An egalitarian feminist is not, as such, committed either way on how much equality there should be in society in general, or even about how equal the sexes should actually be.

5 At least, it is more radical in the literal sense of going for two lots of problems at the roots. It does not follow that the results

must be more radical in the inaccurate, colloquial sense of causing more visible disruption. The combination of the two might in principle produce less disruption than either alone, depending on what they each involved.

6 This topic is discussed *supra*, pp. 136 ff., and in the previous article, *passim*.

7 See previous article, p. 382.

8 This slightly extends the original claim that the business of egalitarian feminism is to dislodge the preconceptions about women and their place that worked to the arbitrary advantage of men. Preconceptions about other things – such as working practices – that have the same effect also need to be dislodged.

9 I shall use the term 'radical' for the kind of feminism that wants to change the status quo at the foundations rather than just seeking equality within it, though not entirely happily because quite a lot of the policies commonly thought of as radical come into my egalitarian category. The familiar terms do not map properly on to the classification being argued for here; if they did, there would be no need for a different classification.

10 Stephen, *Liberty, Equality, Fraternity*, p. 196.

11 Spender, *Man Made Language*, p. 103.

12 Jaggar, Alison, 'Feminist Ethics: Some Issues for the Nineties', *Journal of Social Philosophy*, 20–21, 1989, pp. 91–107.

13 There is a sense in which this illustration makes the point particularly well, because Rawls's theory is a very specific one, and there is no need for the purposes of this argument to claim that it is the most generally accepted theory. Okin's point does not depend on any claim about how representative Rawls is of prevailing views. The point is that the original, egalitarian kind of feminist criticism is that some policy shows a preference of men that is arbitrary in the sense of not being justifiable in terms of any general principles otherwise used by *whoever is recommending the policy*, and the new kind is about criticizing the general principles appealed to. It does not matter how prevalent the views in question are; the distinction is between two kinds of criticism that may be made of *anyone's* position.

14 Jaggar, *Journal of Social Philosophy*, 20–21, p. 104.

15 Ibid., p. 104.

16 Mill, *The Subjection of Women*, p. 38 and *passim*.

17 Malinowski, *The Sexual Life of Savages in North-Western Melanesia*.

18 *Feminist Epistemologies*, eds Alcoff and Potter, p. 11.

19 Ibid., p. 13.

20 e.g. in *Feminist Epistemologies*, eds Alcoff and Potter, p. 4.

21 *Supra*, footnote 11.

22 *Feminist Epistemologies*, eds Alcoff and Potter, p. 91.

23 Ibid., p. 91.

24 See previous article, pp. 360–65, ff.

25 This needs clarification. I am not claiming that ethical theories are arrived at in empty space and then applied to the real world; moral reasoning typically proceeds by looking at the implications of candidate theories, and regarding intuitively unacceptable implications as prima facie reasons for rejecting the theory. Any assessment of normative ethical theories must, therefore, involve looking at their implications for women; and any discounting of bad implications because they were only women's would be a serious subject of *egalitarian* feminist concern. But that only means counting the effects for women in the same way as any other effects are counted. It cannot mean that because some result is bad for women, or less good for women than men, the theory must be wrong; all ethical theories have worse implications for some people than others, and to accept an ethical theory on the grounds that it is best for you is simply to abandon ethics and go for self interest – which, as I have said, is not for many feminists the idea underlying feminism.

26 Okin, *Justice, Gender and the Family*, p. 15.

27 This allows for the sake of argument that ideas of this kind can even be made coherent.

28 It may well be asked where these fundamental theories are supposed to come from, and what sort of justification can be given for them. This is a question that usually arises at this point in the argument, and seems to be (in practice) redolent with the threat of radical scepticism. Fortunately, however, it is not a challenge that needs to be met here. All I am claiming is that whatever the answer is, it lies beyond feminism; and that conclusion is not affected by the threat that there may be no answers at all. In fact the immediate problem of finding such justifications lies not with the critic who is claiming that they cannot themselves be feminist, but with any feminist who wants to make positive claims about the way things ought to

be. Anything that is said about misguided attitudes to women must presuppose that answers have been found to these fundamental questions, otherwise there can be no criterion for recognizing what is misguided. If we have no general standards for what counts as knowledge, we cannot claim that women's knowledge has been systematically underestimated. The radical sceptic can make no positive claims about feminism at all.

29 Note that this is equally true about the minimal principle that men's interests should not be given more weight than women's as an end in itelf, which I have offered as the effective basis for egalitarian feminism. That has no feminist justification either. Anyone who rejected it would be immune to even the simplest arguments about the injustice of women's position – and, probably, to most kinds of moral argument. What makes that principle different from others, however, is that – mainly because it is so minimal, and in itself implies nothing positive about what values, standards and social arrangements there should be – it is effectively uncontroversial. People who defend the traditional position of women go to great lengths to avoid seeming to appeal to the idea that men's interests should be given preference over women's, and this is why arguments that appeal only to that ideal have such power. As soon as you get into more substantive theories, that do have on their own specific implications for policies and actions, there is inevitably more scope for controversy.

30 *Ex hypothesi* not *just* for women. Since the traditional inequality of women overrides *any* positive principles, anyone who wants any positive principles at all implemented should support egalitarian feminism. But the means of implementing the principles properly is to put things right for women, which is why the matter is a feminist one.

31 'Her' is of course technically inappropriate in most of this essay, since feminists can on this analysis be of either sex, and it would probably have been more striking to put 'his'. However I shall merely note (once again) this unsolved problem, and not try to do anything further here.

32 Neither, for that matter, can any other kind of principle-based feminism, or any kind of intellectual argument. Whatever feminists may claim about this, they cannot keep to it, for reasons described in the original first chapter of this book. This

is just a mistake, probably caused by mistakes about male
rationality.

33 See e.g. Elizabeth Grosz, 'Bodies and Knowledges: Feminism
and the Crisis of Reason', in *Feminist Epistemologies*, eds
Alcoff and Potter, pp. 187 ff.

34 Elisabeth Young-Bruehl, 'The Education of Women as Philosophers', in *Reconstructing the Academy*, eds. Minnich, O'Barr
and Rosenfeld, p. 13.

35 See previous article.

36 Grosz, 'Bodies and Knowledges: Feminism and the Crisis of
Reason', in *Feminist Epistemologies*, eds Alcoff and Potter, p.
209. The paragraph from which this is taken is worth quoting
in full. It refers to the work of another feminist, Luce Irigaray:

> Irigaray's work thus remains indifferent to such traditional values
> as 'truth' and 'falsity' (where these are conceived as correspondence
> between propositions and reality), Aristotelian logic (the logic of
> the syllogism), and accounts of reason based upon them. This does
> not mean her work could be described as 'irrational', 'illogical', or
> 'false'. On the contrary, her work is quite logical, rational, and true
> in terms of quite *different criteria*, perspectives, and values than
> those dominant now. She both combats and constructs, strate-
> gically questioning phallocentric knowledges without trying to
> replace them with more inclusive or more neutral truths. Instead,
> she attempts to reveal a *politics* of truth, logic and reason.

37 It will perhaps be apparent that the arguments of this paper do
not apply only to feminism. The same problems arise in the
context of race and class.

38 Mill, *The Subjection of Women*, p. 2.

39 Chapter 1, p. 49.

40 This is a point I was groping after in this book, in the argument
that women got an unfairly small share or an unfairly small
whole (p. 143). That is indeed (as the chapter argues) what
happens if you have discrimination in work against a background of liberalism. But that is just a specific case; the point is
in fact general. *Whatever* principles you think ought to be
implemented, having them overridden by anomalous treatment of women means that they will themselves be less well
fulfilled and that women will be arbitrarily worse off. Disadvantaging women in this way has a *cost* in terms of *whatever*
else is supposed to be being achieved, as well as being wrong in
itself.

41 Women can, of course, suffer – both as individuals and as women – other kinds of injustice as well; they may suffer from the prevalence of general unjust principles as well as, or instead of, failures of impartiality. But in *that* case there is no need for a separate feminist campaign; the injustices to women are part of more general injustices. I think this differentiation is extremely important for the sorting out of feminist theory; its implications are considerable, and have not even been hinted at in this article.

42 For a related discussion see p. 51.

Bibliography

The bibliography lists only books referred to in the text.

Alcoff, Linda and Potter, Elizabeth (eds) *Feminist Epistemologies* (Routledge, New York) 1993.

Austin, J. L., *Sense and Sensibilia* (OUP, Oxford) 1964.

Beauvoir, Simone de, *The Second Sex*, trans. H. M. Parshley (NEL, London) 1960.

Berlin, Isaiah, *Four Essays on Liberty* (OUP, Oxford) 1969.

Caton, Charles E. (ed.), *Philosophy and Ordinary Language* (University of Illinois Press, Urbana) 1963.

Decter, Midge, *The New Chastity and Other Arguments Against Women's Liberation* (Wildwood House, London), 1973.

Firestone, Shulamith, *The Dialectic of Sex* (Jonathan Cape, London) 1971.

Friedan, Betty, *The Feminine Mystique* (Penguin, Harmondsworth) 1965.

Glover, Jonathan, *Causing Death and Saving Lives* (Penguin, Harmondsworth) 1977.

Goldberg, Steven, *Male Dominance: The Inevitability of Patriarchy* (Abacus, London) 1979.

Gould Davis, Elizabeth, *The First Sex* (Penguin, Harmondsworth) 1975.

Greer, Germaine, *The Female Eunuch* (Paladin, St Albans) 1971.

Hume, David, *A Treatise of Human Nature*, ed. L. A. Selby-Bigge (OUP, Oxford) 1897.

Jenness, Linda (ed.), *Feminism and Socialism* (Pathfinder Press, New York) 1973.

Korda, Michael, *Male Chauvinism* (Coronet Books, London) 1974.

Krabbe, Erik C. W., Dalitz, Renée José, Smit, Pier A. (eds), *Empirical Logic and Public Debate: Essays in Honour of Else M. Barth* (Rodopi, Amsterdam and Atlanta GA) 1993.

Lerner, Max (ed.), *The Essential Works of John Stuart Mill* (New York) 1961.

Malinowski, Bronislaw, *The Sexual Life of Savages in North-Western Melanesia* (Beacon Press, Boston) 1987.

Mead, Margaret, *Male and Female* (Penguin, Harmondsworth) 1962.

Meade, Marion, *Bitching* (Garnstone Press, London) 1973.

Mill, John Stuart, *The Subjection of Women* (Virago, London) 1983.

Millett, Kate, *Sexual Politics* (Avon Books, New York) 1971.

Millett, Kate, *The Prostitution Papers* (Paladin, St Albans) 1975.

Minnich, Elizabeth et al., *Reconstructing the Academy* (University of Chicago Press, Chicago) 1988.

Mitchell, Juliet, *Woman's Estate* (Penguin, Harmondsworth) 1971.

Mitchell, Juliet and Oakley, Ann (eds), *The Rights and Wrongs of Women* (Penguin, Harmondsworth) 1976.

Moore, G. E., *Principia Ethica* (CUP, Cambridge) 1962.

Morgan, Robin (ed.), *Sisterhood is Powerful* (Vintage Books, New York) 1970.

Nozick, Robert, *Anarchy, State and Utopia* (Blackwell, Oxford) 1978.

Oakley, Ann, *Subject Women* (Martin Robertson, Oxford) 1981.

Okin, Susan Moller, *Justice, Gender and the Family* (Basic Books, New York) 1989.

Popper, Karl, *The Open Society and its Enemies* (Routledge, London) 1962.

Rawls, John, *A Theory of Justice* (OUP, Oxford) 1972.

Rossi, Alice (ed.), *The Feminist Papers* (Bantam, New York) 1974.

Rowbotham, Sheila, *Woman's Consciousness, Man's World* (Penguin, Harmondsworth) 1973.

Rowbotham, Sheila, *Women, Resistance and Revolution* (Penguin, Harmondsworth) 1974.

Simons, G. L., *Sex and Superstition* (Abelard-Schuman, London) 1973.

Singer, Peter (ed.), *Applied Ethics* (OUP, Oxford) 1982.

Spender, Dale, *Man Made Language* (RKP, London) 1980.

Stephen, James Fitzjames, *Liberty, Equality, Fraternity* (University of Chicago Press, Chicago) 1991.

Thurber, James, *Further Fables for Our Time* (Penguin, Harmondsworth), 1960.

Vetterling-Braggin, Mary, Elliston, Frederick A., and English, Jane (eds) *Feminism and Philosophy* (Littlefield, Adams & Co., Totowa) 1977.

Warner, Marina, *Alone of All Her Sex: The Myth and the Cult of the Virgin Mary* (Picador, London) 1976.

Index

Discover more about our forthcoming books through Penguin's FREE newspaper...

Penguin
Quarterly

It's packed with:

- exciting features
- author interviews
- previews & reviews
- books from your favourite films & TV series
- exclusive competitions & much, much more...

Write off for your free copy today to:
Dept JC
Penguin Books Ltd
FREEPOST
West Drayton
Middlesex
UB7 0BR
NO STAMP REQUIRED

READ MORE IN PENGUIN

In every corner of the world, on every subject under the sun, Penguin represents quality and variety – the very best in publishing today.

For complete information about books available from Penguin – including Puffins, Penguin Classics and Arkana – and how to order them, write to us at the appropriate address below. Please note that for copyright reasons the selection of books varies from country to country.

In the United Kingdom: Please write to *Dept. JC, Penguin Books Ltd, FREEPOST, West Drayton, Middlesex UB7 OBR*

If you have any difficulty in obtaining a title, please send your order with the correct money, plus ten per cent for postage and packaging, to *PO Box No. 11, West Drayton, Middlesex UB7 OBR*

In the United States: Please write to *Penguin USA Inc., 375 Hudson Street, New York, NY 10014*

In Canada: Please write to *Penguin Books Canada Ltd, 10 Alcorn Avenue, Suite 300, Toronto, Ontario M4V 3B2*

In Australia: Please write to *Penguin Books Australia Ltd, 487 Maroondah Highway, Ringwood, Victoria 3134*

In New Zealand: Please write to *Penguin Books (NZ) Ltd,182–190 Wairau Road, Private Bag, Takapuna, Auckland 9*

In India: Please write to *Penguin Books India Pvt Ltd, 706 Eros Apartments, 56 Nehru Place, New Delhi 110 019*

In the Netherlands: Please write to *Penguin Books Netherlands B.V., Keizersgracht 231 NL–1016 DV Amsterdam*

In Germany: Please write to *Penguin Books Deutschland GmbH, Friedrichstrasse 10–12, W–6000 Frankfurt/Main 1*

In Spain: Please write to *Penguin Books S. A., C. San Bernardo 117–6° E–28015 Madrid*

In Italy: Please write to *Penguin Italia s.r.l., Via Felice Casati 20, I–20124 Milano*

In France: Please write to *Penguin France S. A., 17 rue Lejeune, F–31000 Toulouse*

In Japan: Please write to *Penguin Books Japan, Ishikiribashi Building, 2–5–4, Suido, Bunkyo-ku, Tokyo 112*

In Greece: Please write to *Penguin Hellas Ltd, Dimocritou 3, GR–106 71 Athens*

In South Africa: Please write to *Longman Penguin Southern Africa (Pty) Ltd, Private Bag X08, Bertsham 2013*

READ MORE IN PENGUIN

A CHOICE OF NON-FICTION

The Time Out Film Guide   Edited by Tom Milne

The definitive, up-to-the minute directory of over 9,500 films – world cinema from classics and silent epics to reissues and the latest releases – assessed by two decades of *Time Out* reviewers. 'In my opinion the best and most comprehensive' – Barry Norman

The Remarkable Expedition   Olivia Manning

The events of an extraordinary attempt in 1887 to rescue Emin Pasha, Governor of Equatoria, are recounted here by the author of *The Balkan Trilogy* and *The Levant Trilogy* and vividly reveal unprecedented heights of magnificent folly in the perennial human search for glorious conquest.

Berlin: Coming in From the Cold   Ken Smith

'He covers everything from the fate of the ferocious-looking dogs that formerly helped to guard East Germany's borders to the vast Orwellian apparatus that maintained security in the now-defunct German Democratic Republic ... a pithy style and an eye for the telling detail' – *Independent*

Cider with Rosie/As I Walked Out one Midsummer Morning
Laurie Lee

Now together in one volume, Laurie Lee's two classic autobiographical works, *Cider with Rosie* and *As I Walked Out One Midsummer Morning*. Together they illustrate Laurie Lee's superb descriptive powers as he conveys the poignancy of a boy's transformation into adulthood.

In the Land of Oz   Howard Jacobson

'A wildly funny account of his travels; abounding in sharp characterization, crunching dialogue and self-parody, it actually is a book which makes you laugh out loud on almost every page ... sharp, skilful and brilliantly funny' – *Literary Review*

READ MORE IN PENGUIN

A CHOICE OF NON-FICTION

Bernard Shaw Michael Holroyd
Volume 2 1898–1918 The Pursuit of Power

'A man whose art rested so much upon the exercise of intelligence could not have chosen a more intelligent biographer ... The pursuit of Bernard Shaw has grown, and turned into a pursuit of the whole twentieth century' – Peter Ackroyd in *The Times*

Shots from the Hip Charles Shaar Murray

His classic encapsulation of the moment when rock stars turned junkies as the sixties died; his dissection of rock 'n' roll violence as citizens assaulted the Sex Pistols; superstar encounters from the decline of Paul McCartney to Mick Jagger's request that the author should leave – Charles Shaar Murray's *Shots From the Hip* is also rock history in the making.

Managing on the Edge Richard Pascale

The co-author of the bestselling *The Art of Japanese Management* has once again turned conventional thinking upside down. Conflict and contention in organizations are not just unavoidable – they are positively to be welcomed. The successes and failures of large corporations can help us understand the need to maintain a creative tension between fitting companies together and splitting them apart.

Just Looking John Updike

'Mr Updike can be a very good art critic, and some of these essays are marvellous examples of critical explanation ... a deep understanding of the art emerges ... His reviews of some recent and widely attended shows ... quite surpass the modest disclaimer of the title' – *The New York Times Book Review*

Shelley: The Pursuit Richard Holmes

'Surely the best biography of Shelley ever written ... He makes Shelley's character entirely convincing by showing us the poet at every stage of his development acting upon, and reacting to, people and events' – Stephen Spender

READ MORE IN PENGUIN

A CHOICE OF NON-FICTION

Riding the Iron Rooster Paul Theroux

Travels in old and new China with the author of *The Great Railway Bazaar*. 'Mr Theroux cannot write badly ... he is endlessly curious about places and people ... and in the course of a year there was almost no train in the whole vast Chinese rail network in which he did not travel' – Ludovic Kennedy

Ninety-two Days Evelyn Waugh

In this fascinating chronicle of a South American journey, Waugh describes the isolated cattle country of Guiana, sparsely populated by an odd collection of visionaries, rogues and ranchers, and records the nightmarish experiences travelling on foot, by horse and by boat through the jungle in Brazil.

The Life of Graham Greene Norman Sherry
Volume One 1904–1939

'Probably the best biography ever of a living author' – Philip French in the *Listener*. Graham Greene has always maintained a discreet distance from his reading public. This volume reconstructs his first thirty-five years to create one of the most revealing literary biographies of the decade.

The Day Gone By Richard Adams

In this enchanting memoir the bestselling author of *Watership Down* tells his life story from his idyllic 1920s childhood spent in Newbury, Berkshire, through public school, Oxford and service in World War Two to his return home and his courtship of the girl he was to marry.

A Turn in the South V. S. Naipaul

'A supremely interesting, even poetic glimpse of a part of America foreigners either neglect or patronize' – *Guardian*. 'An extraordinary panorama' – *Daily Telegraph*. 'A fine book by a fine man, and one to be read with great enjoyment: a book of style, sagacity and wit' – *Sunday Times*